# How Novelty and Narratives Drive the Stock Market

"Animal spirits" is a term that describes the instincts and emotions driving human behaviour in economic settings. In recent years, this concept has been discussed in relation to the emerging field of narrative economics. When unscheduled events hit the stock market, from corporate scandals and technological breakthroughs to recessions and pandemics, relationships driving returns change in unforeseeable ways. To deal with uncertainty, investors engage in narratives which simplify the complexity of real-time, non-routine change. This book assesses the Novelty-Narrative Hypothesis for the U.S. stock market by conducting a comprehensive investigation of unscheduled events using big data textual analysis of financial news. This important contribution to the field of narrative economics finds that major macro events and associated narratives spill over into the churning stream of corporate novelty and sub-narratives, spawning different forms of unforeseeable stock market instability.

NICHOLAS MANGEE is Associate Professor of Finance at Georgia Southern University and Research Associate for the Institute of New Economic Thinking program on Knightian Uncertainty Economics.

STUDIES IN NEW ECONOMIC THINKING

The 2008 financial crisis pointed to problems in economic theory that require more than just big data to solve. INET's series in New Economic Thinking exists to ensure that innovative work that advances economics and better integrates it with other social sciences and the study of history and institutions can reach a broad audience in a timely way.

**Recently published:**

*Macroeconomic Inequality from Reagan to Trump: Market Power, Wage Repression, Asset Price Inflation, and Industrial Decline* by Lance Taylor

**Titles forthcoming in the series:**

*Never Together: The Economic History of a Segregated America* by Peter Temin

*Money and Empire: Charles P. Kindleberger and the Dollar System* by Perry Mehrling

# How Novelty and Narratives Drive the Stock Market

## Black Swans, Animal Spirits, and Scapegoats

NICHOLAS MANGEE
Georgia Southern University

CAMBRIDGE
UNIVERSITY PRESS

# CAMBRIDGE
## UNIVERSITY PRESS

University Printing House, Cambridge CB2 8BS, United Kingdom

One Liberty Plaza, 20th Floor, New York, NY 10006, USA

477 Williamstown Road, Port Melbourne, VIC 3207, Australia

314–321, 3rd Floor, Plot 3, Splendor Forum, Jasola District Centre,
New Delhi – 110025, India

103 Penang Road, #05–06/07, Visioncrest Commercial, Singapore 238467

Cambridge University Press is part of the University of Cambridge.

It furthers the University's mission by disseminating knowledge in the pursuit of
education, learning, and research at the highest international levels of excellence.

www.cambridge.org
Information on this title: www.cambridge.org/9781108838450
DOI: 10.1017/9781108974899

First published 2021

Printed in the United Kingdom by TJ Books Limited, Padstow Cornwall

*A catalogue record for this publication is available from the British Library.*

*Library of Congress Cataloging-in-Publication Data*
Names: Mangee, Nicholas, 1983- author.
Title: How novelty and narratives drive the stock market : black swans,
    animal spirits, and scapegoats / Nicholas Mangee, Georgia Southern University.
Description: 1 Edition. | New York, NY : Cambridge University Press, 2021. |
    Series: Studies in new economic thinking | Includes bibliographical
    references and index.
Identifiers: LCCN 2021024837 (print) | LCCN 2021024838 (ebook) |
    ISBN 9781108838450 (hardback) | ISBN 9781108971409 (paperback) |
    ISBN 9781108974899 (epub)
Subjects: LCSH: Investments–Psychological aspects. | Stock
    exchanges–Psychological aspects. | BISAC: BUSINESS & ECONOMICS /
    Finance / General
Classification: LCC HG4515.15 .M363 2021 (print) | LCC HG4515.15 (ebook)
    | DDC 332.6019–dc23
LC record available at https://lccn.loc.gov/2021024837
LC ebook record available at https://lccn.loc.gov/2021024838

ISBN 978-1-108-83845-0 Hardback

*To Daniel and Ruth*

# Contents

# Figures

# Tables

# Preface

When historically unique events hit the stock market – from corporate scandals and technological breakthroughs to recessions and pandemics – underlying relationships driving outcomes change at times and in ways that would be difficult to foresee. Investors cope with imperfect knowledge about new market dynamics by relying on threads of popular stories, or narratives, that help them deal with now greater uncertainty and model ambiguity. This idea, which serves as the central theme of this book, can be traced back to the works of Knight (1921), Keynes (1936), Hayek (1945, 1978), and Popper (1946, 1957) suggesting an inherently unstable relationship between novel events, emotion, and asset-price fluctuations. Great early thinkers of financial market behavior espoused the precariousness of knowability *ex ante*, the powerful impacts of the improbable, the objective openness of the future, and, thus, the need for narratives to help make sense of it all. This is the essence of the Novelty–Narrative Hypothesis (NNH) under financial market instability.

Even in the absence of major historical macro events sending shockwaves through markets, there are diverse streams of somewhat novel corporate-related micro events flowing at all points in time. That all nonrepetitive, or unscheduled, events have the potential to destabilize the processes driving returns and volatility implies a continuous and interdependent relationship between narrative dynamics and stock market uncertainty. The first half of 2020 illuminated on a grand scale these tenets of modern-day capital markets.

No investor in 2019 could have anticipated the arrival nor full impact of the COVID-19 pandemic, the onset and depths of the Great Lockdown Recession, nor the crash of global oil markets, all unfolding within a matter of weeks during the first quarter of 2020. The events were too unique for their likelihood to have been assessed with an objective probability distribution *ex ante* and historical data provided little guidance for quantitative assessments of future returns. Combinations of macro and micro novelty rendered probabilistic forecasts insufficient. The Western world was on lockdown. Stock price volatility skyrocketed, causing circuit-breaker rules to halt trading on market exchanges. Facing imperfect knowledge, investors, policy-makers, and the public alike all relied on a confluence of personal priors, incomplete information, judgment, and sentiment – a collective brew of narrative dynamics – to deal with the sheer opacity and true uncertainty of the future.

At the macro level, new stock price relationships involved stories about Depression-era unemployment, the oil dispute between Saudi Arabia and Russia, the shuttering of small-business America, the untested capacity of the United States healthcare system, social and economic distancing, and the adequacy of government and central bank responses. Concurrently, micro-level stories were about firm bankruptcy, management shake-ups, loan programs and credit extension packages, employee layoffs, and supply chain disruptions. For some firms, the narratives involved entire redirections of resources under the Defense Production Act. Cascades of unanticipated macro events transformed the continuous ripples of smaller-scale change into raging flood waters of instability, altering stock return relationships at both the firm and aggregate level. The higher orders of structural change and uncertainty unfolding in Q1 2020 impaired market participants' ability to quantitatively forecast which possible future states describing returns would prevail. Confronted with great model ambiguity, narrative dynamics became a natural part of the forecasting landscape. However, even in the absence of crisis, recognizing that financial market relationships inherently undergo unforeseeable change implies an outsized role for narrative dynamics as a rational part of forecasting future returns.

However, mainstream researchers in economics and finance have rarely incorporated narrative dynamics into their investigations of stock market fluctuations. Nobel Laureate Robert Shiller in his

2017 presidential address to the American Economic Association argued that, "The field of economics should be expanded to include serious quantitative study of changing popular narratives." (p. 967). Indeed, the literature has given insufficient attention to relevant information contained in the inertia, emotion, and uniqueness of story threads coursing through financial markets day-to-day. This book responds to Shiller's call by offering the first comprehensive empirical application of narrative analysis to the US stock market based on nonrepetitive events, unforeseeable change, and macro versus micro Knightian uncertainty (hereafter KU). The extensive findings from assessing NNH may further our understanding of the "wild gyrations" observed in the US stock market and shed light on several long-standing anomalies such as the excess volatility puzzle first documented by Shiller (1981).[1] Moreover, the book may help to inform researchers, practitioners, and policy-makers alike about which modeling approaches are best suited to handle the ubiquity of nonrepetitive events and the unforeseeable change they trigger in stock market relationships.

Motivation and subtitle for this book stem from four areas of contemporary research in economics and finance whose overlap has provided much insight for the overarching thesis. Granted their differences, the approaches sketched herein all suggest that the time-series dynamics of nonrepetitive events and associated popular narratives may contribute useful information for understanding the inherent instability of stock market relationships.

First, the Black Swan theory of Taleb (2007) rests on the human folly in focusing on observations of the past when forecasting a future that our "fragility of knowledge" prohibits any basis for quantitatively understanding *a priori*. Black Swan theory treats the disproportionate impacts of highly improbable events – think financial crises, global

---

[1] Akerlof and Shiller (2009)'s book *Animal Spirits* opens its chapter on the behavior of asset prices by stating, "No one has ever made rational sense of the wild gyrations in financial prices, such as stock prices. These fluctuations are as old as the financial markets themselves." (ch. 11, p. 131).

pandemics, terrorist attacks, and technological breakthroughs – as "equal to uncertainty" and the preeminent source of change in market outcomes. Taleb (2007) consistently promotes the importance of what we do not know and forcefully relegates the scientific community's traditional focus on the repeated and routinely observed.[2] Historically novel events are more sensational, more difficult to interpret, and, therefore, more likely to contribute to the dynamism of narrative stories through time. Importantly, this book extends the Black Swan view to include those stock market events, such as industrial accidents, CEO turnover, and labor strikes, that are not as historically dramatic as, say, the Great Depression or the global financial crisis, but nevertheless are nonrepetitive in nature, and, thus, to some extent unique. Call them "Grey Swan" events.

Second, the recent work of Shiller (2017, 2019, 2020) represents the first attempts to advance the foundational importance of narrative dynamics for explaining aggregate economic behavior. Shiller's research asserts that changing, or mutating, narratives are the most influential story threads in the economy, spreading from person to person with contagious forces akin to an infectious disease and intimately connected to dramatic economic events in US history. His work on narratives has shown how, through basic analysis of news-media content and word counts from Google Ngrams, popular interest about secular stagnation, the Laffer curve, Bitcoin, housing bubbles, and so on, can feedback into major episodes such as the business cycle expansion of the 2010s, the Great Depression, and the global financial crisis. Narrative effects occur as public interest (and presumed economic and financial behaviors) display a regularity of dramatic growth in impact during the high-frequency transmission stage that eventually plateaus into a narrative-saturation phase accompanying a

[2] Taleb (2007) refers to the reliance on Gaussian principles of repeated observations assumed identically and independently distributed as converging in expected value to their supposed true objective probability, that is, the frequentist approach in classical probability theory, as the "Great Intellectual Fraud" when applied to the social sciences. (p. xxiv).
Mean-variance finance models, for instance, are rooted in the frequentist approach.

decline in public interest. Shiller's work throughout the years relating news-media effects, popular stories, and investor confidence to stock market behavior has motivated throngs of studies and has opened the door for alternative research projects, such as this book. However, as will be extensively discussed in forthcoming chapters, this book's methodological and empirical approaches, and, importantly, epistemological framing of the importance of narrative dynamics for understanding market behavior, are quite dissimilar to Shiller's.

The third source of inspiration comes from the Animal Spirit theory on shifts in requisite emotion necessary for assessing future states of financial market outcomes under uncertainty. By "animal spirits" I am not referring to extraneous psychological maladies whose impact on behavior dissipates over time (Howitt and McAfee, 1992) earmarked by bouts of investor "insanity" (Lewis, 2009). Nor am I referring to the feedback effects between sentiment and asset-price demand that cause speculative bubbles and excess volatility due to "irrational exuberance" (Shiller, 2000). Rather, I am referring to the endogenous, innate sentiment states continuously assisting investors in interpreting the expected impacts of news on future returns when facing uncertainty (Frydman and Goldberg, 2011; Frydman et al., forthcoming; Keynes, 1936).

Uncertainty gives rise to an insufficient basis for assessing tomorrow's outcomes with objectively known probabilities, implying the need for "affective influences" over beliefs and "endogenizing animal spirits" (DiMaggio, 2002). In researching this book, I was pleased, but not surprised, to see how much of the overarching story of changing narratives and requisite sentiment underpinning business decisions is woven into extant literature from sociology and cognitive psychology. Narratives are inherently part of the sociological, psychological, and, in fact, rational aspects of forward-looking human behavior, and, therefore, need to be more wholly considered in the fields of economics and finance.

The fourth source of motivation for writing this book is derived from accounts that emphasize the importance of unforeseeable change in asset markets. These include scapegoat models (Bacchetta and van Wincoop, 2004, 2006, 2009, 2013), research on imperfect knowledge (Frydman and Goldberg, 2007, 2011, 2013), and, in particular, the recent modeling structures based on KU Economics and ambiguity (Frydman et al., 2015; Frydman et al., 2017, 2019). Though they differ in a number of important respects, each of the three bodies of work places temporal instability in the relationships driving stock, and other asset, market returns at the core of their accounts. Scapegoat models, for instance, produce instability in financial market processes as investor attention shifts across a time-varying set of fundamental factors, whose recent headline movements match that of the asset price, when forecasting future returns. Because they do not fully predetermine which information investors deem relevant or in which ways they may matter for expected returns, these approaches allow for fundamental factors beyond conventional data to drive outcomes in partly open ways. Therefore, they also imply that unanticipated shifts in forecasting strategies may be influenced by behavioral considerations that afford sentiment an important role assisting individuals' diverse interpretations of news' impacts.

In synthesizing insights from these four broad approaches to modeling stock market outcomes, this book is equally aimed at academics and financial market practitioners alike. And, if I have done my job, it will be accessible to anyone with a cursory interest in nonmechanical relationships driving the stock market. There will be just as much descriptive and qualitative analysis as there will be more formal empirics. One chapter discusses Kuhnian paradigm shifts, another presents wordclouds of KU events, another tracks spillover effects from twenty years' worth of daily macro and micro unscheduled events, another presents trading strategies based on indices of corporate novelty, while another compares periods of narrative intensity to formal structural change in fundamentals-based stock market relations. Hopefully, the reader will find that this book accomplishes three things.

First, the importance of novelty and narratives for stock market instability under radical uncertainty will be supported by exploring insights of the great early thinkers, emphasizing Knight, but also ushering in Keynes, Hayek, and Popper. This stage of the analysis will be accompanied by recent evidentiary support on the power of stories from neuroscience, anthropology, and sociology with a particular focus on the developments of narrative psychology. Standard approaches toward uncertainty in economics and finance assume that market participants have a model in mind that, barring random exogenous shocks, offers a fairly good representation of reality. Other disciplines' findings hold clues suggesting that there is no such determinate model under true uncertainty. Rather, if a Kuhnian paradigm shift is underway, the scientific community of researchers will eventually advocate for theoretical modeling structures and statistical toolkits that *allow for* the unstable, yet ongoing, dance between novelty, narratives, and uncertainty in the stock market.

Second, the book will offer a big data textual analysis of KU events, novelty, and popular narratives contained in *Dow Jones, The Wall Street Journal, Barron's, MarketWatch,* and *Bloomberg News* stock market reports. Advances in big data analytics have catapulted the field of semantics forward through advanced algorithms and machine learning that enhance semantic search, linguistic meaning, and narrative context. This book presents novel indices based on macro and micro KU that hone in on the widespread influence of all nonrepetitive events reported as driving stock market behavior across massive volumes of daily news reports from 2000 through 2020. Large-scale novel events such as recessions and financial crises are major drivers of instability. However, the vast majority of stock market novelty, and thus unforeseeable change, stems from the minutiae of nonroutine corporate events churning at the micro level. Of course, macro and micro uncertainty events are closely related as instability originating with the former spills over onto that of the latter.

This book is the first of its kind to develop indices tracking the universe of such destabilizing forces through financial news analytics.

The indices track KU event novelty, relevance, sentiment, inertia, and compositional variation (diversity) based on the highly sophisticated *RavenPack* news analytics platform covering second-by-second details of US stock market events. Categories of the most popular KU events are presented and their importance tracked through time with easy-to-interpret illustrations. Time-series properties of particular KU groups are then compared to major historical events including the COVID-19 crisis, the global financial crisis, the US debt sequestration, the US Tax Cuts and Jobs Act, and the US–China trade war, but also to a wide array of company-level and industry trends.

Third, the book will present empirical analyses and case studies documenting how the KU indices relate to statistical instability observed in relationships driving stock returns, volatility, trading volume, and equity fund flows. Periods associated with the highest KU narrative intensity – think interactions of unscheduled events with the most extreme sentiment, novelty, relevance, and inertia – will help to inform the formal structural change analysis. Do the narrative intensity periods align with identified breakpoints in posited stock market relationships? Case studies are woven throughout, offering a comparative historical backdrop of novel events occurring at the macro and micro level likely to have unhinged investor forecasts, and thus market prices, away from previous relationships. The results suggest that novelty is more the rule than the exception for understanding nonmechanical stock market behavior and that textual analysis is keenly suited to allow for the unforeseeable change and KU such events engender in driving outcomes.

Time-varying narratives contained in financial news allow researchers to detect and expose the relevance of social, economic, institutional, political, international, and technological events within the context and zeitgeist of different subperiods of US stock market activity. In early research, I read and scored 4,206 stock market summary wrap reports from *Bloomberg News*. In doing so, I quickly realized that I was witnessing structural change in stock price relationships unfold right before my eyes. The novel events and associated narratives that investors deemed relevant changed in dramatic and difficult to anticipate ways over time, yet shared features with time-series properties of stock market price fluctuations. One chapter in this book will conduct a narratological analysis of the scapegoat hypothesis based on this manually scored *Bloomberg News* data.

Most of my research agenda has utilized textual analysis of narrative accounts as a window into the equity marketplace, as a kaleidoscope of testimony from professional participants whose trading decisions and behind-the-scenes views ultimately determine prices. The ubiquity of nonrepetitive events implies processes driving stock market outcomes are far too complex and interconnected to forecast outcomes based on probabilistic rules *ex ante*. In this spirit, all observers of financial markets face ambiguity. Novelty and imperfect knowledge precipitate the need for narratives when the environments' parameters have shifted in unforeseen ways.

What better medium for capturing the importance of nonrepetitive events for narrative dynamics and market instability under uncertainty than financial reports from the largest news analytics outlets? I hope this book makes a compelling case. News analytics in finance, and narrative economics more broadly, are growing research areas. As Taleb (2007) remarks, "You need a story to displace a story ... stories are far more potent than ideas; they are also easier to remember ... Ideas come and go, stories stay" (p. xxxi).

# Acknowledgments

In my third year in the PhD program at the University of New Hampshire, I followed a suggestion to read and score stock market news reports to assess the competing implications across classical, behavioral, and imperfect knowledge-based asset-pricing models. Soon thereafter, Roman Frydman, Michael Goldberg (my advisor), and I ventured to *Bloomberg* headquarters to share our research ideas with its news team. Who knew where that trip would lead my research? I am very grateful to Roman, Michael, and *Bloomberg News'* Nick Baker for that opportunity.

This book is a culmination of my entire research agenda since that has been greatly influenced by my work with Roman and Michael. Our countless conversations and research interactions over the years that have shaped many ideas about unforeseeable change in financial markets have found their way into the book. Their early work on Imperfect Knowledge Economics illuminated the importance of unanticipated shifts in asset market relationships by tracing numerous puzzles to both traditional and behavioral approaches' reliance on probabilistic representations of change. Moreover, I have been privileged to witness first-hand the unfolding of macro-finance models based on Knightian Uncertainty Economics through Roman's work with colleagues at the University of Copenhagen. I thank them both for sharing their knowledge and insights with me.

I am thankful for the years of research support from Armstrong State University. I am grateful for the support of Rob Johnson, the summer research grants from the Institute of New Economic Thinking (INET), and the editorial wherewithal of Tom Ferguson. INET has given me numerous opportunities to interact with prominent researchers on an international stage in dynamic symposium settings. I have certainly benefited from this exposure. I am grateful for

Cambridge University Press' interest in my book and the editorial aptitude of Philip Good. I appreciate the thorough copyediting of Sarah Pfeifer Vandekerckhove. I am grateful to the participants at the University of New Hampshire's Graduate Economics Seminar where I presented findings from this book. I want to thank the following mentors: Linda Bleicken, Brian Chezum, Bob Durocher, Bruce Elmslie, Peter FitzRandolph, and Yassaman Saadatmand. I acknowledge a one-semester sabbatical from Georgia Southern University and I thank my colleagues and department chair Joe Ruhland for supporting my research endeavors.

I am forever grateful for my mom and all she has done for me as a person over the years. I thought about my dad often as I wrote the book. I am deeply thankful for my wife Ruth's steadfast love and support. Finally, I am most thankful for the blessing of our new baby boy Daniel who made any challenges in writing the book appear so small.

# PART I  Novelty, Narratives, and Instability

# I    Stock Market Novelty and Narrative Finance

Where there is novelty, there is instability. Where there is instability there is uncertainty. Where there is uncertainty there are narratives – narratives are the currency of uncertainty. As the first two decades of the twenty-first century have made palpably clear, novel events such as 9/11, the subprime mortgage crisis, the fiscal cliff, the US–China trade war, Brexit, the US corporate tax overhaul of 2017, the COVID-19 pandemic, and the oil market crash of 2020, can lead to dramatic change in the relationships driving stock market returns. The timing and magnitude of instability from such large-scale "macro uncertainty" events are impossible to foresee *ex ante* and can be difficult to comprehend, even in hindsight. For each nonrepetitive event, investors were forced to abandon precise quantitative prediction and grapple with ambiguity about which forecasting model to place the greatest confidence in as visibility of the future was dim at best.

As evidence presented here shows, narratives about the economy, war, natural disasters, monetary and fiscal policy, social constructs, institutions, culture, political elections and so on, naturally and necessarily became part of investors' information sets during unprecedented times. This book advances a view that nonrepetitive events cause instability and Knightian uncertainty (KU) in stock market relationships, forcing narrative based emotions and cold calculation to be inextricably intertwined under the Novelty–Narrative Hypothesis (NNH).

The novelty of the COVID-19 pandemic and ensuing events of Q1 2020 unleashed into circulation stories that served as necessary simplifications for an unprecedented situation whose complexity was unfolding in unforeseeable ways in real time. Famous economist

Frank Knight would have remarked that shutting down the Western world produced true, or Knightian, uncertainty in the stock market because the likelihood of its occurrence, and possible future states of the world, could not have been "reduced to an objective, quantitatively determined probability" (Knight, 1921, pp. 231–232). Even those wishing to liken the crisis to the swine flu or the Spanish flu were left searching for the right narrative for comparison as, unlike other pandemics, COVID-19 brought economic and social interactions to an unprecedented standstill. The US was under a state of emergency, individuals were under stay-at-home orders, nonessential businesses shuttered: Economic and social distancing became the new reality overnight. Not only would the crisis impact stock prices as investors weighed the business and household costs with, among other factors, the stimulus and recovery measures instituted at the Federal Government and Central Bank levels, but it would also have greater implications for the economy as a whole. How long would it take for businesses and various industry sectors to recover? Would the conduct of business activity ever be the same?

From February to March 2020, when COVID-19 became more than a seemingly isolated virus thousands of miles away, US stock market participants revised their forecasting strategies in dramatic, unforeseeable ways. After reaching record highs on February 19, the *Standard and Poor's 500 Index* (SP500) lost over one-third of its total value by March 23, wiping out the entire gains of 2019 and bringing an end to the decade-long bull market. On March 16 alone the SP500 lost 12.7 percent – the third-largest daily loss in over 100 years–triggering a Level 1 circuit breaker to halt all trading just minutes into the morning session. The COVID-19 impact on the broader economy was just as striking.

International supply chains seized up. Food distribution channels became severely kinked. Global oil demand plummeted. Consumers abandoned small-business commerce especially in the service sector. Initial jobless claims spiked from 282,000 in mid-March to 3 million the following week to over 6.5 million by March 28 to another

6.5 million by April 9. That is, over 16.8 million newly unemployed filed for insurance claims in just three weeks. Total private sector jobs declined by 701,000 in March – the first nonfarm payroll reduction in over nine years. The Federal Reserve Bank slashed its overnight borrowing rate by over 100 basis points in just three weeks while the US Federal Government's $2 trillion stimulus measure stood as the largest in our nation's history.[1]

The future was bleak. Macro uncertainty was high and the trickle down into micro-level (firm and household) uncertainty was more of a flood rush. Many voices warned of deep recessions across the Western world, a possible reduction in Q2 US GDP by 30 percent, unemployment rates eclipsing 25 percent, and a 10 percent haircut to corporate profits.[2] As of this writing, the Bureau of Economic Analysis advance estimate for Q1 Real Gross Domestic Product reported the economy shrank by an annualized 4.8 percent.

No one could have foreseen the coronavirus pandemic or the full extent of its impact on communities and markets, households and firms, domestic and abroad. COVID-19 wasn't even part of investor discourse through the end of 2019.[3] Yet, in a matter of weeks the inherent instability of stock markets was exposed on a grand scale as macro and micro uncertainty fused and the importance of narrative dynamics was brought to center stage. Stories surrounding COVID-19 and the Great Lockdown Recession were fueled by a combination of historic reversals in economic and financial trends, reliance on

---

[1] Daily SP500 data is based on closing prices and is collected from www.yahoo.com/finance. Initial jobless claims data is collected from the Bureau of Labor Statistics. Small-business and nonfarm payroll jobs data is collected from the ADP National Employment Report. Fed Funds data is collected from the Federal Reserve Economic Database (FRED).

[2] Consider the *Bloomberg News* stock market wrap report from February 25, 2020 that states, "The market is pricing in a significant slowdown in GDP and a 10% impact on earnings," according to Zhiwei Ren, portfolio manager at Penn Mutual Asset Management. Consider further the *Bloomberg News* wrap report from March 23, 2020 that reads, "Morgan Stanley warned the epidemic could cause U.S. GDP to shrink a record 30% in the second quarter. Federal Reserve Bank of St. Louis President James Bullard said the country's jobless rate may hit 30%."

[3] The coronavirus was first mentioned in *Bloomberg News* end-of-the-day US stock market wrap reports on January 22, 2020.

personal priors and judgment, and diffusion of extreme levels of emotion, panic, and anxiety – a potent combination for narrative propagation in financial markets. As news of an impending recession hit the shores of US stock markets like a tsunami, communication threads ensnaring COVID-19 were nothing short of ominous and exhausted media space daily.[4] It is no wonder the transmission of stories about major economic and financial events through society has been likened to the contagion and spread of infectious diseases (Shiller, 2017, 2019, 2020).

The COVID-19 story threads were expansive in their scope. Will a recession in the US occur and, if so, how deep will it be and for how long will it last? How much damage will be done to the labor market and how might the US handle tens of millions recently unemployed? How many jobs will be permanently lost? Will the small-business loan program work? In which industries will bankruptcies and unemployment be most concentrated? How will the bounds of our gigeconomy be tested as individuals pivot toward ever-more remote forms of commerce and employment? How will the capacity and quality of the US healthcare system be tested?

How will distribution hubs become reenvisioned across developed versus emerging markets? Will airlines receive a Federal Government bailout and what will the transportation industry look like in three months or three years hence? How will the OPEC oil dispute between Saudi Arabia and Russia impact supply-side factors important for stock market returns? Will financial markets shrug off the crisis and instead focus only on stimulus measures over the medium run? What new ideas, companies, social norms, healthcare, and government policies will emerge after the crisis has abated? Will COVID-19 become seasonal? What would a second wave look like?

---

[4] For example, as of March 12, 2020, *The Wall Street Journal* Economic Forecasting Survey found that, of the economists surveyed, the average expected probability for a recession occurring within the subsequent twelve months was 48.8 percent (https://economicgreenfield.blogspot.com/2020/03/the-march-2020-wall-street-journal.html).

How will economic and diplomatic relations with the eastern Asiatic world be affected?

Investor interpretations of each query for forecasting returns live well beyond the bounds of conventional data releases. Rather, the ways in which participants think about the answers are enveloped in an interconnected web of narrative structure that they are exposed to and participate in on a daily basis. There are plotlines involving prominent entities (protagonists in the form of government officials, central bankers, politicians, CEOs, countries, corporations, news organizations, social movements, and institutions) interacting each with particular sets of objectives (quests and goals) whose likelihood of coming to fruition is so highly dependent on myriad other factors and entity-decisions (interdependence on ally or opposition) that quantitative rule-based assessments of possible future states becomes inadmissible (indeterminacy of relationships driving outcomes).

It is the case that such plotlines are predominantly characterized by events that are nonrepetitive, or unscheduled, and, therefore, to some extent, historically unique. Yet, corporations must make million- and billion-dollar decisions today about which assets to invest in, which production processes to research and develop, which forms of human capital to employ, which funding sources to open up to and so on. The contingent nature of cash flow prospects into the dimly lit forecasting horizon necessitates narrative thought on behalf of any profit-seeking investor facing imperfect knowledge and inherent ambiguity about how the actual returns process will unfold. Yet, stock market instability and the KU it engenders are not just the consequence of major large-scale systemic events.

Novel events occur at the macro level, but also, and much more frequently, at the company, or micro, level – think bankruptcies, IPOs, debt restructuring, credit ratings, labor layoffs, product recalls, new R&D, management shake-ups, share buybacks and so on. Novel corporate events even reflect the relatively inconspicuous, sometimes mundane, sources of KU in the stock market, such as firm revisions to earnings guidance, changes to analyst ratings, rejections of acquisition bids, merger delays, facility closures, the setting of price targets, changes to executive salaries and so on. Indeed, there is a wide spectrum of Grey Swan events relevant for the stock market. Large-scale shifts in the process driving stock returns coupled with, and often amplifying, smaller-scale shifts imply that different types of change in market relationships are constantly unfolding each and every day. Foreseeing the timing and magnitude of instability in all of its diversity and complexity *ex ante* is beyond human capacity.

When nonrepetitive events hit the stock market, investor reasoning bends toward storytelling as a useful form of survival tactic, defense mechanism, or cognitive satisficing tool when previous relations driving returns have come unhinged in unforeseen ways. This implies that capital market forecasting models must reflect the roles of soft information that trigger cognitive functions such as resemblance that inform story structure and contextual meaning. Thinking about future developments impacting returns within a narrative framework is necessary under uncertainty and model ambiguity but also desirable to the mind. Story structure helps shape incomplete information and emotion into cognitive guideposts and anchors when novel events offer little basis for using past data in forecasting. Fortunately, advances in machine learning of unstructured text have provided major news analytics firms the processing tools necessary to track the universe of nonrepetitive macro and micro events and associated narrative considerations for the stock market.

Did you know that over two-thirds of the events explicitly identified in *Dow Jones* news reports as important for influencing US corporate prospects and share prices are considered unscheduled? Or that over four-fifths of macro events for the US are considered unscheduled? Or that there are over 1,300 different categories of unscheduled macro and micro events that might shake investors from their existing forecasting strategies in unanticipated ways? Or that the prevalence of micro uncertainty events dwarf macro uncertainty events in the stock market? But that the latter cause spillover effects onto the former when combined with narrative components of senti-ment, novelty, relevance, and inertia? These key findings (presented in Chapters 5 and 8) suggests that stock markets are inherently unstable, true uncertainty is predominant, novelty is a ubiquitous feature of unforeseeable change in asset-price relations, and narrative dynamics are important linkages in this framework.

These are the pillars of NNH advanced herein. Simply put, this book is about the intimate connection between nonrepetitive events, narrative dynamics, and structural change in the US stock market through the philosophical lens of KU and the methodological lens of big data textual analysis of financial news reports. The objective is to inform observers of financial market outcomes on the ubiquity of historically unique events, on the narrative reasoning surrounding them, on the unforeseeable change and uncertainty they engender, on the empirical tools that reveal their importance, and on the modeling approaches best suited to deal with such instability.

The story about stories is that humans have a propensity to tell them, to tell them in internally consistent ways over a period of time, in ways that rationalize the arrival of new information with their prior qualitative beliefs about how the world works. Narratives are about informational meaning and humans are undoubtedly meaning-makers. Narratives reflect culture, societal norms, and popular zeit-geist. They also captivate imagination, influence thought processes, and drive decision-making behavior in reflexive ways. Cognitive dissonance and cognitive consistency imply that the narratives people tell take on a qualitative, or directional, shape over time conveying a perceived "positive" versus "negative," or "bullish" versus "bearish," overall impact in the aggregate.[5] Humans tell stories because stories themselves are alive and cognition demands it of us in a world where

---

[5] When individuals subconsciously suppress information that conflicts with their prior beliefs about a particular situation this is known as cognitive dissonance. The elevation of other information that does align with their priors is cognitive consistency. See Schlicht (1983) for an application to utility theory and welfare economics and Hosseini (1997) for applications challenging neoclassical rationality under uncertainty.

relational parameters often change in unique ways. Narratives seep into our consciousness. Some narratives are more flexible and can be contorted as time passes. Other narratives become increasingly cemented into our reasoning as we age. Of course, there is no objective way to think today about how we will think tomorrow about the future. Narratives hold the temporal clues.

Yet, studies connecting novel events and associated narrative dynamics are oddly absent from the vast majority of contemporary economics and finance research. Nobel Laureate Robert Shiller's recent work (Shiller, 2017, 2019, 2020) has opened the door for the importance of narrative dynamics in explaining aggregate market outcomes. Shiller assumes that public interest as measured by tracking Google Ngram and ProQuest searches of terms such as "secular stagnation," "stock market crash," "Bitcoin," "profiteer," "housing bubble," and "Laffer curve" is a proxy for narrative dynamics. Shiller connects the frequency of references to these terms, or percentages of articles containing them, to major events such as recessions, economic booms, and financial crises. His analysis likens the contagion effects of narratives to the transmission of disease from person to person by applying the word-counts and reference frequencies to the Kermack–McKendrick SIR infectious disease model. Under this account, the rate of narrative spread (infection rate) is equal to the contagion rate $c$ times the product of those susceptible $S$ times the number infected $I$ all minus the product of the recovery rate $r$ times the number of people sharing the narrative (i.e. infected) yielding the differential equation,[6]

$$\frac{dI}{dt} = cSI - rI \tag{1.1}$$

During a "narrative epidemic," the public's interest will follow a sort of bell-shaped curve skewed to the right. The model assumes to be independent of other outside ideas – essentially dismissing

[6] This is the baseline SIR model where contagion and recovery rates are assumed constant over time. See Kermack and McKendrick (1927) and Shiller (2017) for more details on the SIR model.

the diversity and interrelational nature of forecasting under market instability and uncertainty. To be sure, Shiller's contributions in this area have advanced the view that "changing" narratives underpin their longevity and potency for impacting major economic events. And, like this book, Shiller connects story threads to factors reflecting culture, society, politics, and the zeitgeist of the times. However, in stark contrast to the chapters that follow, his work treats narrative dynamics as largely exogenous to the marketplace, germinating in the mind of one or just a few individuals. Additionally, Shiller frames the importance of stories for market outcomes as being amplified due to various mental and personality "disorders" and "conspiracy" thinking. By contrast, NNH implies that narrative dynamics are naturally at play in markets as investors interpret nonrepetitive events' impacts on future returns as part of rational forecasting under unforeseeable change and the uncertainty it engenders.

Most of Shiller's empirical analysis is based upon bag-of-word references tracking mentions from the internet database of books and articles. This book, too, presents several findings supporting NNH based on Google Trends searches and bag-of-word approaches. Shiller relates narrative dynamics (i.e. force, transmission, and duration) to whether the story thread is "punchy," popular, or simple to understand. For Shiller, narratives cause major aggregate events such as economic recessions and depressions through feedback effects that do not necessarily reflect the underlying market conditions. This book, on the other hand, presents findings where the nonrepetitive events catalyze narrative dynamics that are shown to reflect univariate properties of the raw underlying data (Chapter 11 in particular). But, when narrative proxies do depart from the underlying data, which can be the case, this book shows that it is a consequence of the story thread tracking either the intensity and importance of the data or a time-varying set of fundamental factors (Chapters 2, 7, and 11).

Of course, Shiller's earlier work on stock market "bubbles" and excess volatility popularized models of feedback effects between media-driven stories and asset demand that become increasingly disconnected from fundamentals over time through investors' "irrational exuberance" (Shiller, 2000). By contrast, this book conducts in-depth empirical analyses relying on the dynamics of actual narrative components such as relevance, novelty, emotion, and inertia explicitly connected to *contextualized* stories about market fundamentals and other relevant events reported by major financial news firms as driving corporate prospects and stock price fluctuations day-to-day. The granular detail of textual news analytics applied to each one of the millions of narrative accounts is striking and enables a wide range of formal empirical assessments of NNH for the stock market.

Though Shiller's recent research has attempted to change the status quo, much work remains, especially on the analytical front. Based on the percentage of JSTOR articles that include the term "narrative," economics and finance are by far the lowest in rank when compared to other social sciences (Shiller, 2017). In Aliber and Kindleberger's classic book *Manias, Panics and Crashes: A History of Financial Crises* (Aliber and Kindleberger, 2017), there is not a single mention of the term "narrative." This introductory chapter advances a view of narrative economics and finance as applied to novelty-driven stock market instability, setting the analytical stage for the rest of the book and NNH. Historical context for narrative dynamics when market environments change in unforeseeable ways is sketched from a social science viewpoint. Importance of the nonrepetitive nature of unscheduled events for propagating narratives will be underscored. In doing so, benefits from applying narrative analysis to financial news reports are emphasized with a foreshadowing of the main descriptive and empirical findings presented in subsequent chapters.

## I.2  THE NOVELTY–NARRATIVE HYPOTHESIS

In his presidential address to the American Economic Association, Shiller (2017, p. 967) defines narrative economics as, "the study of the spread and dynamics of popular narratives, the stories, particularly those of human interest and emotion, and how these change through time, to understand economic fluctuations." The term "narrative" for this book means a thematic string of stories that portray a consistent and simplified, yet subtly changing, view of a larger, more complex relational structure. The term "subnarrative" means a thematic string of more granular, or individualized, stories that contribute to the qualitative, yet subtly changing, inertia of a larger story thread, or narrative. Both narratives and subnarratives are part novelty, part emotion, part relevance, and part inertia. Much more on this in subsequent chapters.

Nowhere are notions of swirling narratives and contagious stories more commonplace than in the stock market. In July 2019, the US stock market extended an historic ten-year bull market run with the SP500 eclipsing 3,000 for the first time on July 10. With equity markets and the economy barreling along – nonfarm jobs just exceeded expectations by adding 224,000 jobs and government officials continued to tout the market's prosperous rise – it seems strange that a shift in underlying narratives may have been unfolding over the preceding twelve months. A Google Trends search for "recession" for the five-year period July 2014 through July 2019 is plotted in Figure 1.1.[7]

The plot shows an upward trend in internet search interest for the word "recession" particularly evident from January 2018 through July 2019. The peak search interest occurred in December of 2018 with another evident spike in March 2019. A quick textual analysis from the December 4 *Bloomberg News* stock market wrap report reveals the subnarratives that contributed, in part, to the upward trending "recession" interest observed in Figure 1.1. The report reads,

U.S. stocks plunged, with the Dow Jones Industrial Average tumbling almost 800 points, as a litany of concerns wiped out the rally in risk assets. Trade-sensitive shares sank as angst mounted that the U.S. and China made no meaningful progress on the trade front this weekend.

[7] For all Google Trends searches presented in this book, the vertical axis values, as per Google's explanation, "represent search interest relative to the highest point on the chart for the given region and sample period. A value of 100 is the peak popularity for the term. A value of 50 means that the term is half as popular. A score of 0 means there was not enough data for this term."

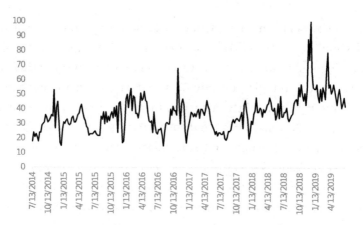

FIGURE 1.1 The figure plots the US Google Trends searches for "recession" during the five-year period July 2014 through July 2019. The vertical axis measures search interest.

Financial shares got hammered as the yield curve continued to flatten, with the latest nudge from a hawkish comment by a Federal Reserve official ... Adding to the risk aversion was news that U.K. Prime Minister Theresa May's push to avoid a so-called "hard Brexit" may be at risk. "Today's move feels like the market is a scorned lover. It had believed, for whatever reason, that progress was being made at the G-20 and that turns out to be murky – it feels lied to," said Michael Antonelli, a managing director at Robert W Baird & Co. "Then a pile of negative Brexit news, Williams starts to ramp up hawkish talk, then we have our yield curve acting like it got run over and boom, we puke."

(*Bloomberg News, December 4, 2018*)[8]

The excerpt suggests that trade-sensitive and financial shares contributed most to the market's drop, but largely in the absence of conventional economic data releases or firm earnings announcements.[9] What toppled the market was that "angst mounted" over little progress in the US–China trade dispute, Theresa May's efforts for a smooth Brexit "may be at risk," and that Fed official Williams'

[8] John Williams is the president of the Federal Reserve Bank of New York and vice-chairman of the Federal Open Market Committee (FOMC).

[9] The US Department of the Treasury reports daily Treasury yield curve rates at its online resource center.

hawkish "comments" were a "nudge" toward an inverted yield curve, a historic harbinger for an upcoming recession. These are the "litany of concerns" each emanating from a somewhat historically novel event; in this case, a wobbling trade negotiation and comments from a foreign prime minister and the vice-chairman of the FOMC. Stories have inertia, due in part to the reinforcing prods of such novel events, and it is likely that versions of these subnarratives were also underpinning a larger economic narrative connected to the March spike in "recession" search interest.

To be sure, whatever hard data is released by the Bureau of Economic Analysis, the Bureau of Labor Statistics, and other government entities will also become part of the larger recession narrative, either reinforcing it or dampening it depending on its directional consistency with KU events' interpreted impacts on outcomes. And, one cannot ignore the potential reflexivity of how market participants' beliefs about the future, which drive their decisions today, help to shape the realized outcomes, and narratives, of tomorrow.[10] The higher order uncertainty effects from the interactions of macro and micro KU events will be discussed in Chapter 8.

Fast forwarding the five-year period by just eight months to include the COVID-19 crisis gives us a sample from April 2015 through March 2020 and an updated plot of Google Trends searches for "recession." The results of Figure 1.2 are striking. The landscape of public interest in "recession" changes dramatically once the COVID-19 crisis is introduced. Now, there are illustrative differences in recession queries clearly concentrated in the spikes during August 2019 and March 2020 with the global max occurring at the latter date. One quick look at the *Bloomberg News* wrap report for the stock market reveals the underlying fears of a COVID-19-induced economic recession during peak search interest on March 16.

---

[10] For a treatment of this type of reflexivity in financial markets see, for example, Soros (1987).

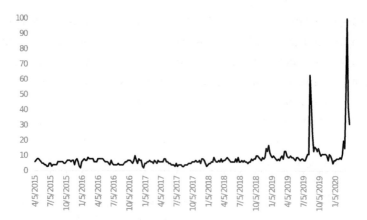

FIGURE 1.2 The figure plots the US Google Trends searches for "recession" during the five-year period April 2015 through March 2020. The vertical axis measures search interest.

The stomach-turning ride on global financial markets took a dramatic turn Monday, with U.S. stocks plunging the most since 1987 after President Donald Trump warned the economic disruption from the virus could last into summer. The S&P 500 sank 12%, extending losses as Trump said the economy could fall into a recession. Equities opened sharply lower after central bank stimulus around the world failed to mollify investors worried about the damage the coronavirus is inflicting on economies. The negative superlatives for American stocks are piling up. The S&P wiped out its gain in 2019 and is now down almost 30% from its all-time high. The Dow Jones Industrial Average lost almost 13%, falling 3,000 points to close at a two-year low. The Russell 2000 had its worst day on record, losing more than 14%. "This is different. The thing that is scarier about it is you've never been in a scenario where you shut down the entire economy," said Steve Chiavarone, a portfolio manager with Federated Investors. "You get a sense in your stomach that we don't know how to price this and that markets could fall more." While the Fed cut rates toward zero and stepped up bond buying, investors continued to clamor for a massive spending package to offset the pain from closures of schools, restaurants, cinemas, and sporting events. Companies around the world have scaled back activity to accommodate government demands to limit social interaction.

*(Bloomberg News, March 16, 2020)*

This particular news excerpt is likely to be read over and over again for years to come as it details a monumental day in US stock market history. First, the market tanked after President Trump announced that the "economic disruption from the coronavirus could last into the summer." This is an example of a somewhat novel event, the presidential announcement, communicating the interpretations of an even more novel, and unforeseeable, event, COVID-19, forecasting yet another nonrepetitive event, a depressed economy lasting months if not longer. Second, the stock market plunge itself is a novel event standing as the third-largest daily loss in over 100 years of recorded data.

Third, the report shows that stories are part KU events and part emotion by suggesting that "negative superlatives for American stocks are piling up" and that narratives surrounding the Central Bank stimulus attempts "failed to mollify investors worried" about the economic fallout from the virus. It then states that, by contrast, "investors clamored for a massive spending package" from the US Federal Government. It is interesting that the market clawed back some of the losses on sequential trading days March 23 through March 27 as details of the $2 trillion US stimulus were becoming clearer and the bill was signed into law – the uncertainty was being reduced, albeit marginally. The Central Bank and US Government measures had different narratives associated with them – the former had a more bearish connotation for investors while the latter more bullish. Whatever their actual efficacy on local, regional, and national economies, investors attached different story threads to each policy prescription.

Fourth, the report speaks to the more nuanced factors at play in the economy, namely the broad closures of "schools, restaurants, cinemas, and sporting events" and the business pullback from "government demands to limit social interaction." Finally, the report itself speaks to the KU surrounding the collective events and time period, suggesting that "This is different ... scarier [since] you have never been in [such] a scenario." And, that consequentially the market "does not know how to price this." This was indeed an unprecedented period in the US, and around the world. And, the textual content of the stock market report was able to shed light on the novelty of events and their associated narratives and subnarratives influencing the dynamic and unforeseeable change in processes driving returns.

Salience theory suggests investors pay attention to asset-price payoffs that are most different (Bordalo et al., 2013). Narratology as applied to financial markets would suggest that investors pay attention first to the events that are most different (novel) and then, second, to a subset of those KU events whose associated subnarratives are qualitatively most consistent with overarching narratives and expected returns. If a novel event's interpreted impact on returns can be contorted (some requiring more than others) to align with an investor's priors, training, judgment, beliefs, or intuition, it may become one additional string of a larger narrative thread. For example, concurrent subnarrative news about a merger, a pharmaceutical trial, a political election, and a firm's debt restructuring could inform a larger narrative about economic activity and bullish or bearish future returns. The qualitative consistency matters for narratological dynamics. When novel events unfold, selective similarity and cognitive satisficing are fuel for particular subnarratives to become amplified and part of larger narrative inertia over time. Indeed, results of these processes are evident in many of the financial news excerpts provided in this book.

Of course, there are myriad narratives, many conflicting, being spread among different social, economic, cultural, and political communities of people across different regions of the US at any given point in time. Nevertheless, how narratives emerge, interact, and change is not wellunderstood by economics and finance researchers. The underlying relationships are too complex to truly comprehend, especially within models that predetermine how change unfolds over time. As Shiller (2017) recognized, "the relation between narratives and economic outcomes is likely to be time-varying" (p. 997), that narratives are "major vectors of rapid change in culture, in zeitgeist, and in economic behavior" (p. 972), and that it is, in part, the "change in narratives [which are important for] understanding fluctuations"

(p. 967). One cannot discuss novelty and narratives without placing change, specifically unforeseeable change, in stock market relationships at the core of the analysis.

As will be seen from narrative evidence presented in Chapters 4 through 12, subsets of unscheduled corporate events that underpin investor beliefs about future stock returns undergo significant shifts in their importance during different subperiods of time such as those characterized by excess volatility. As markets have experienced with the Lehman Brothers bankruptcy, the subprime mortgage meltdown and ensuing global financial crisis, and now with the COVID-19 pandemic, price collapses are bellwethers for extended periods of financial calamity. Though no one knows how long they will last, dramatic reversals from asset-price peaks triggered by large-scale macro events are typically marked by waves of ensuing novel events and instability at the micro level. For the subprime mortgage crisis, the novelty of frozen commercial paper markets and excessive financial sector leverage led to highly irregular variation in investor beliefs through distorted assessments of "quantifiable risk" (Gennaioli and Shleifer, 2018).

The narrative connection between novel events, market instability, and uncertainty can be seen in the December 4, 2018 *Bloomberg News* stock market wrap report. Perhaps researchers and market professionals could assess with an objective probability distribution the possible outcomes and measurable odds therein for future interest rate decisions at FOMC meetings. This is largely a risk assessment since Fed Funds rate decisions are repetitively drawn observations based on routine calendar releases. However, the array of potential future outcomes from talks between presidents Xi and Trump or from a no-deal Brexit are much less susceptible to the frequency-based statistics of standard deviation and expected value. Interestingly, the March 16, 2020 *Bloomberg News* wrap excerpt contained virtually no scheduled factors, such as quarterly earnings announcements, whose impacts on possible future states could reasonably have been assessed with quantitative probability measures. Again, the nonrepetitive nature of KU events gives little basis for objective, probability-based forecasts *ex ante* and promotes the importance of narrative dynamics for thinking about the future. This situation is emblematic of what Frank Knight would consider true uncertainty.

In his 1921 book, *Risk, Uncertainty and Profit*, Frank Knight underscores the fact that "business decisions deal with situations which are far too unique … for any sort of statistical tabulation to have any value for guidance. The conception of an objective measurable probability … is simply inapplicable" (p. 231). Knight recognized that "unanticipated, dynamic changes" in relations driving future business conditions stem from nonrepetitive events. These are the key factors underpinning "real change," the impacts of which are genuinely unknowable to any individual *ex ante*.[11] Indeed, as Chapter 2 in this book shows, there is much empirical evidence of many different forms of structural change found in stock return relationships that would be difficult to fully anticipate in a probabilistic sense.

Knight was well aware of classical economics' insistence that, "We must first discuss one change at a time assuming the others suspended … This is the way our minds work" (1921, pp. 16–17). However, the ability to statically "deal with a complex situation as a whole … rarely ever happens" (p. 17) in capitalistic markets. But it is not change as such that is the focus under true uncertainty. Knight makes the compelling connection that "Profits are … the result exclusively of dynamic change" and quickly identifies "the fundamental question of the difference between a change that is foreseen a reasonable time in advance and one that is unforeseen" (p. 35). As he put it, "if all changes were to take place in accordance with invariable and universally known laws, [so that] they could be

---

[11] Keynes also shared Knight's view that we "cannot depend on strict mathematical expectation, since the basis for making such calculations does not exist" (Keynes, 1936, pp. 162–163). See Sakai (2018) for illuminating comparisons of Knight versus Keynes concerning their respective treatments of risk, ambiguity, and uncertainty.

foreseen for an indefinite period in advance of their occurrence ... profit or loss would not arise" (p. 198).

This book builds on Knight's astute observation that it is "unanticipated change" underpinning returns from business decisions by focusing on unscheduled macro and corporate micro events all too often overlooked by researchers, but the primary source of financial market instability. Much previous literature has assumed changing relationships in stock, and other asset, markets can be modeled in a determinate fashion *ex ante* with a stochastic process, such as a Markov switching rule. This is a fundamental departure from Knight's assertion "that change in reality does not usually just happen, but is largely itself the result of human activity" (p. 36). In his Nobel lecture, Hansen (2013, p. 399) echoes Knight's emphasis on the folly of representing participants' understanding over time with determinate accounts by arguing that rational expectations models "miss something essential: [Knightian] uncertainty [arising from] ambiguity about which is the correct model" of the process driving aggregate outcomes.

Of course, some novel events cause changes in business contexts whose impacts on return relationships are more acute, such as labor strikes, data breaches, bankruptcies, CEO turnover, product recalls, and industrial accidents, while changes from other events unfold only gradually over time, such as technological advancements, financial leverage, mergers and acquisitions, and capital investment projects. Whether sharp and transitory or gradual and persistent, novelty's impacts on the stock market stem from "our ignorance of the future" (Knight, 1921, p. 198). After all, "It is a world of change in which we live, and a world of uncertainty. We live only by knowing something about the future; while the problems of life, or of conduct at least, arise from the fact that we know so little. This is as true of business as of other spheres of activity" (p. 199).

How novelty drives structural change in the stock market and leads to popular stories is a central question of this book and the basis for NNH. The dynamics between novelty, instability, uncertainty,

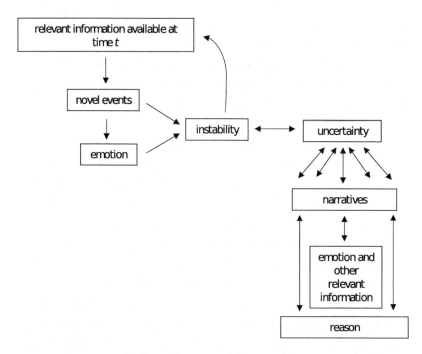

FIGURE 1.3 The figure plots a rough framework for sequential and interactive relationships between novel events, instability, uncertainty, narratives, and emotion in asset markets.

narratives, and emotion can be simplified in Figure 1.3 as a diagrammatic treatment of NNH for asset markets.

Several relational conclusions can be drawn based on Figure 1.3. First, novel events are part of the available and relevant information set at time $t$. Novelty creates emotion that together interact to cause instability in the relationships driving market outcomes. Instability, in turn, becomes part of the information set. Second, instability causes increased degrees of uncertainty in the marketplace that can feed back into the degree of instability present at any given point in time. Third, in the face of uncertainty, narratives emerge that contain emotion and other relevant information – say, macroeconomic or financial data also unfolding at time $t$. Narrative threads interact with each other and with participants' interpretations of information that may feed back into market uncertainty. Fourth, the narratives then lead to a reasoning or rationality for thinking about the most appropriate forecasting strategy describing the processes driving future outcomes. The reasoning then undergoes feedback with narratives as one shapes the other and vice versa. Figure 1.3 is a dramatic simplification of the asset-market dynamics at play, but serves as a rough template for how novelty, instability, uncertainty, and narratives may all be related under NNH.

Chapter 2 presents the overarching idea of NNH and the empirical instability in relationships driving stock-price fluctuations and volatility. A cursory literature review of structural change in the US equity market will be presented and a case will be made for inherent model ambiguity and the rational need for investor sentiment and narrative interactions under uncertainty. Attention is paid to the different forms of transitory versus more persistent change in stock market relationships and the event categories likely underpinning them.

## 1.3    NARRATIVE DYNAMICS AND EMOTION: EVIDENCE FROM OTHER DISCIPLINES

Imaginations may swirl and dramatic experiences may be recalled as the mind enters "narrative mode" (Bruner, 1986). Which forecasting strategy should one place the greatest confidence in for thinking about the future returns process today? Given the complexity of financial market interactions day-to-day, no one, let alone an economist or hedge fund manager, knows the answer in any definitive sense. This is one reason why the returns from speculation – "knowing better than the market what the future may bring forth" (Keynes, 1936, p. 170) – are so high. Individuals have an internal desire, especially when facing uncertainty, to form opinions based on their own stories, experiences, perceptions, and beliefs, about a particular situation. With "our ignorance of the future, incomplete knowledge, and imperfect inference, it becomes impossible to classify instances objectively, and any changes brought about in the conditions surrounding the formation of an opinion are nearly sure to affect the intrinsic value of the opinion itself" (Knight, 1921, p. 259).

Investor judgment requires narratives and emotions because it is the collection of experiences and stories that stick to our memories the most, prompting salient feeling, and that come to the forefront of our reasoning when making decisions about complex interdependent scenarios. For instance, Frydman et al. (forthcoming) find that stock market participants' optimism or pessimism about the future affects how they interpret today's news about dividends and interest rates when forecasting stock returns. The authors find, however, that this effect is highly irregular, both in timing and in magnitude.[12] Knight states that,

> the 'degree' of certainty or of confidence felt in the conclusion after it is reached cannot be ignored, for it is of the greatest practical significance. The action which follows upon an opinion depends as much upon the amount of confidence (i.e. sentiment) in that opinion as it does upon the favorableness of the opinion itself. The ultimate logic, or psychology, of these deliberations is obscure, a part of the scientifically unfathomable mystery of life and mind.
>
> *(1921, pp. 226–227)*

This book offers an expansive treatment of the role of sentiment for NNH by assessing the emotional context surrounding nonrepetitive events' interpreted impacts on future stock returns with an event sentiment score (ESS). Stories are inherently emotional and popular stories elicit the most visceral of feelings and emotion. Following Knight (1921), Keynes (1936) and the recent theoretical advancements of Frydman et al. (2019) and Frydman and Goldberg (2015), this book argues for a fundamentals-based role for psychology in driving aggregate outcomes in financial markets.[13] Consistent with Hansen's previously mentioned insight, novel events introduce ambiguity onto participants' forecasts concerning which model is most useful for

---

[12] Additionally, the authors provide evidence that sentiment's role in interpreting fundamental news also holds for *ex post* stock returns.

[13] Frydman et al. (2019) introduce theory dubbed the Knightian Uncertainty Hypothesis wherein the authors develop a way to recognize both risk and KU when confronted with time-series data on aggregate outcomes in macroeconomics and finance.

thinking about the future. There are tons of financial models potentially appropriate for understanding firm cash flow prospects and future returns at any given point in time – who can say with any confidence that a particular one is the right one for *a priori* thought when parameters shift in unforeseeable ways? Sentiment, as a critical component of narrative dynamics, helps to flesh out which model and forecasting strategy investors might place the greatest confidence in "calculating where they can, but often falling back for their motive on whim or sentiment or chance." (Keynes, 1936, p. 163)

That unforeseeable structural change necessitates narrative-based emotion is supported by well-developed research areas such as neuroscience, cognitive psychology, and sociology. Endogenous emotions are found to be connected to memory formation, individual identity, dramatic recall, imagination, and even physiological stimuli. Indeed, much of the evidence suggests that researchers in economics and finance have largely ignored the inherent interaction between emotions and cold calculation in explaining individual behavior in real-world situations commonly fraught with uncertainty.[14]

In fact, scientists in these fields have argued that the bulk of experimental evidence supporting a sentiment-based view of decision-making is entirely in line with rational behavior as defined by other social sciences at large. Commenting on the status of rational choice theory in economics, Verweij et al. (2015, p. 3), for instance, state, "In neglecting the role of emotions, rational choice theory is out-of-step with present-day neuroscience – a point that has been made by a variety of brain researchers." Unfortunately, it has been longstanding practice in economics and finance to associate the effects of sentiment with forecasting errors, random perturbations, bouts of irrational behavior and other factors represented as being orthogonal to fundamental considerations and reasoning at large.[15]

---

[14] For previous studies in cognitive psychology and neuroscience advancing past the duality of behavioral-emotion or calculated-cognition for successful decision-making, see Damasio (1994), Koenigs et al. (2007), and Krajbich et al. (2009).

[15] Even when the two categories of emotions and strict calculation are intentionally separated by researchers – as in the conventional dual-systems approach developed in

This may be one explanation for the lack of narratological studies in economics and finance. Beyond arguing for a mere synthesis between the two realms, this book argues that emotions and calculation share interrelational space underpinning rational forecasting behavior as implied by NNH.

Findings from disciplines outside of economics and finance support various links in the NNH apparatus. Chapter 3 briefly surveys the relevant evidence from the fields of neuroscience, psychology, anthropology, and sociology as they pertain to the dynamics of NNH. The evidence focuses on the role of affective states and emotions driving expectations when confronted with historically unique events. The findings referenced are from both experimental and natural settings. The chapter discusses the "narrative mode" framework of Bruner (1986) exploring the unsystematic part of the mind used to "imagine" possible states of the world. The famous cognitive psychologist elevated the idea that story-based thinking through linguistics and narratives brings meaning to novel experiences that inform day-to-day decision-making, especially when the surrounding environment is undergoing change. Additionally, views of "endogenous animal spirits," (DiMaggio, 2002) "emotional embeddedness" (Bandelj, 2009), and "creative action theory" (Joas, 1996; Whitford, 2002) as they may be applied to structural change and uncertainty in stock markets will be discussed.

## 1.4  TEXTUAL ANALYSIS, FINANCIAL NEWS, AND NARRATIVES

Volumes of textual analysis studies have investigated unstructured data from financial news reports, finance message boards, and corporate disclosures for their informational content in explaining stock market outcomes. Yet, research on KU through narrative

neuroscience and psychology - the results suggest a very strong, if not disproportionate, role for emotionally intensive considerations to explain outcomes (Albrecht et al., 2010; McClure et al., 2007).

news analytics is virtually absent in the contemporary finance literature.[16] Evidence of narrative dynamics in this book is based on millions of daily stock market news stories over the last two decades of data. The stock market stories are keenly able to detect the corporate, economic, cultural, social, institutional, and political trends affecting stock market behavior within the contextual zeitgeist of the times. The book presents the only comprehensive big data analysis of nonrepetitive events and associated narrative elements of emotion, relevance, novelty, and inertia applied to structural change in aggregate and firm-level stock market relationships.

Das (2014) and Loughran and McDonald (2016) offer excellent surveys of textual analysis in finance. Financial news analytics are able to deal with unforeseeable change in asset-price relations, to allow for fundamentals-based sentiment, and to track the rich and nuanced information, both quantitative and qualitative, that investors follow on a daily basis.[17] Chapter 4 discusses the benefits of financial news analytics for exploring NNH under KU as applied to the stock market. One section emphasizes the ability of textual data analytics to allow for the timing and magnitude of structural change to unfold in highly irregular and unforeseeable ways. Another area discusses its ability to gauge the relative and contingent importance of both macro and micro KU events for returns.

This book's analytical assessment of NNH is based on the universe of financial news from *Dow Jones & Company*, which includes *The Wall Street Journal*, *Barron's*, and *MarketWatch*, and

---

[16] The study by Friberg and Seiler (2017) is an exception. The authors use textual analysis of SEC filings to categorize firms and industries based on KU and ambiguity finding that those with higher values, as measured through bag-of-word term searches related to "uncertainty," are generally riskier, carry more liquidity, and seek greater hedging through the use of derivatives. See also Baker et al. (2016).

[17] This book focuses on aggregate and firm-level stock market behavior using narrative analysis of financial news reports. As such, the present analysis indirectly reflects information contained in corporate disclosures, 10-k reports, or firm-issued risk-prospecti. For financial risk studies focused on these sources of textual analysis, see, for instance, Bao and Datta (2014), Campbell et al. (2014), Loughran and McDonald (2016) and references therein.

the daily stock market wrap reports from *Bloomberg L.P.* These international firms are leaders of the financial news analytics industries. With over 25,000 employees combined worldwide, these firms have a global presence for high quality, reputable news analytics. Their news feeds are often found scrolling across screens at traders' desks. Models of risk management, asset allocation, return prediction, and portfolio choice have seen improvement when news analytics output and proprietary data from these firms are quickly incorporated. Of course, the famous *Bloomberg* terminals offer software, data, and news analytics used by the largest financial institutions, research organizations, and top business schools around the world. And data from *Dow Jones Newsfeeds* has been used in the most widely cited and seminal papers using textual analytics to investigate stock market behavior (e.g. Tetlock, 2007).

One section of Chapter 4, using an automated text mining program, presents narrative word clouds from *Bloomberg News* stock market wrap reports based on a lexicon dictionary of KU entities and events for the last twenty-eight years. The word clouds track the importance of the Mexican peso crisis, NAFTA, Clinton's presidency, the Russian debt crisis, to the battery of mergers in the late 1990s, to the global financial crisis, debt sequestration, and US fiscal cliff, to the Tax Cut and Jobs Act of 2017, to President Trump's trade war with China, to Brexit, and to the COVID-19 crisis. The word clouds illustrative variation of KU terms reported as driving daily stock prices is indicative of instability triggered by the novel events that are likely to have fueled investor narratives during different subperiods. Frequency histograms show that numerous KU entities and/or events are mentioned over 250 times in a given year's worth of daily wrap reports. The R code used to generate the word clouds and histograms is provided in Appendix A and can be used for applying the KU event lexicon dictionary to any financial text.

Alternatively, more formal time-series evidence on novel events and narrative dynamics for the US stock market presented in Chapters 5 through 12 is based largely on unscheduled events identified by the *RavenPack* news analytics platform over the period January 2000 through March 2020. *RavenPack* is a unique source of explanatory and predictive analytics derived from *Dow Jones Newsfeed*, *Wall Street Journal*, *Barron's*, and *MarketWatch* articles published over the last two decades. The product dataset is rich with structured information including over 2,000 identifiable stock market event classifications, the majority (over two-thirds) of which are somewhat novel, or unscheduled, in nature. The primary *RavenPack* data source is based on millions of corporate-specific events identified from the equity news outlets as impacting firm investment prospects and/or share prices. The secondary dataset from the same news sources is based on macro US events such as Federal Reserve Bank activity, armed conflicts, trade agreements, fiscal policy changes, natural disasters, congressional hearings, and so on, and is used for the narrative-subnarrative investigation conducted in Chapter 8. Important for NNH, both datasets are sorted to include only those identified novel events that are classified as "unscheduled."

*RavenPack* automatically tracks and monitors relevant information on tens of thousands of companies, government organizations, influential people, key geographical locations, and all major currencies and traded commodities as they are related to outcomes observed in US equity markets. Among the many benefits for this book, *RavenPack* produces sentiment, novelty, relevance, and inertia scores (and twenty-eight other metrics all described in Appendix C) of event classification data all in a matter of milliseconds of news' release. Output from the identified nonrepetitive events are used to produce KU indices that are interacted throughout the empirical chapters to generate proxy narratives at both the micro and macro levels.

Methodologically, the platform detects narrative dynamics by incorporating both algorithmic and human-expertise approaches to textual classification and data generation. Hybrid approaches such as *RavenPack*'s to textual analysis are found to be the most promising for capturing intended context and relational meaning in big data environments. *RavenPack* quantifies positive and negative perceptions on facts and opinions reported in the financial news and understands the magnitude of event extremities. The platform continuously analyzes relevant information from all major financial newswires and other trustworthy sources, producing real-time news analytics with the ability to identify relevant "news" from "no news," important determinations shown to influence stock market behavior (Boudoukh et al., 2013; Chan, 2003). These features and more of the *RavenPack* analytical platform allow for identification of unscheduled events and the initial classification into narrative components in a consistent, transparent, and tractable way making it an excellent candidate for assessing the implications of NNH from textual news accounts.

## 1.5   THE KU INDICES

Chapter 5 introduces the KU data classification hierarchy structure. The 51 KU groups into which the 1,395 unscheduled event categories are classified are discussed in detail. A KU event record – containing the thirty-two output fields from *Ravenpack* – is offered as an example of an unscheduled event's scoring. Appendix D provides a glossary of every disaggregated unscheduled event category whether classified at the micro or macro level. Chapter 5 presents the baseline micro KU index generated from monthly count data for unscheduled corporate event categories tracked by the *RavenPack* platform along with an examination of its basic time-series properties. Variation in the micro KU index is compared to major episodes in US history.

Chapter 6 conducts a deeper analysis of the unscheduled corporate events by generating indices based on event relevance, novelty, inertia, and sentiment. Periods of "highest" narrative intensity are identified by combining the most relevant corporate KU events with those with the most extreme sentiment (optimism or pessimism) and highest degree of novelty. These are the periods against which the formal structural change analysis of stock market outcomes in Chapter 10 will be compared.

The KU sentiment measure based on *RavenPack* analytics is derived from three proprietary methodologies for identifying emotion that emphasize context and meaning: traditional, expert consensus, and market response. Event sentiment scores are based on a hybrid approach combining algorithmic processing powers with financial expert understanding of stock market context. The algorithms reach far beyond strict bag-of-words dictionary-based approaches to textual analysis while the manual component involves hundreds of financial market professionals trained on tens of thousands of financial news articles.[18]

Because story sampling is based on a limited data range, there always exists the possibility that new economic terminology, trends, types of reporting, or market forces may emerge after the sample period. Indeed, the meaning of narratives, and context within which they are understood, change over time, as do a nation's institutions, social values, and politics. In order to account for these temporal changes, all *RavenPack* classifiers are reevaluated on a quarterly basis.

Before the massive growth in computational power, researchers investigating narrative dynamics for the stock market resorted to crude metrics of manual reading of news, such as measuring headline-letter size (Niederhoffer, 1971). Since then, however, algorithmic advances in textual analysis have aspired to human-level reasoning for detecting relevance and meaning while allowing for exponentially greater volumes of input and faster processing speed. *RavenPack*'s platform is at the forefront of big data news analytics. That said, advances in manual rule-based applications to narrative analyses of the stock market are also discussed in this book and illustrated with a formal Scapegoat analysis of stock returns presented in Chapter 11.

---

[18] Many textual data studies connecting market sentiment to stock returns utilize content analysis programs that employ simple word count or phrase level search algorithms, such as dictionary-based information retrieval systems (Davis et al., 2006; Demers and Vega, 2008; Engelberg, 2008; Tetlock et al., 2008; Loughran and McDonald, 2011; Mangee, 2017, 2018; Tetlock, 2007).

Chapter 7 introduces another set of indices that measure the degree of compositional variation, or diversity, across KU groups over the sample period. Which stock market periods are characterized by many different KU-group narratives concurrently? Which periods are dominated by just a few? How does the diversity in corporate KU groupings evolve over time? Which KU groups are most influential overall for the stock market? These questions and more will be investigated in this chapter.

Chapter 8 introduces the companion data to the corporate micro KU indices by tracking the unscheduled macro events related to the US over the sample period. Although macro KU events are dwarfed by the frequency of corporate KU events, there are numerous findings from this chapter that show a close connection between the two realms of nonrepetitive events. The two baseline indices share a very high correlation as do the first principal components of micro and macro narrative proxies that include sentiment, novelty, relevance, and inertia, suggesting that the two levels of uncertainty share common narratological threads. Furthermore, there is evidence that the macro KU events statistically lead to micro events, which implies that unforeseeable change at the systemic level cascades and spills over onto lagging corporate novelty and associated smaller-scale instability.

However, the macro KU indices are shown to exhibit considerably less variation in both event count and group diversity over the sample period as compared to corporate indices. High narrative intensity periods connected to macro events fail to approximately align with those connected to micro events that are explicitly reported as influencing corporate prospects and share prices. Furthermore, the macro indices are unable to convincingly improve upon any of the empirical tests of stock market outcomes conducted in Chapters 9 and 10 when substituted for micro KU information. One interpretation is that corporate KU events are a more immediate and intimate lens into stock market instability because they track the nonroutine change that is churning on a smaller scale while simultaneously capturing the large-scale instability trickling (or rushing) down from major historical events. Taken together, the findings from this chapter give confidence that unscheduled corporate events are the more informative source for assessing narrative dynamics related to stock market instability and, therefore, are used for empirical analyses conducted in Chapters 9, 10, and 12.

## I.6   STATISTICAL ANALYSIS OF KU AND NARRATIVE DATA

Chapter 9 presents the first set of empirical findings involving the micro KU indices generated in Chapters 5 through 7 and establishes a statistical and economically meaningful connection between novel corporate events and stock market relationships. Nonparametric correlation tests suggest that the baseline KU and KU variation indices share a statistical relationship with market outcomes at the aggregate and individual firm level, often with the correct hypothesized sign. For instance, a negative correlation is found between micro KU indices and SP500 prices and valuation ratios that implies an uncertainty premium may exist.

Furthermore, correlation and statistical "causality" tests find that the micro KU indices are inversely related to and "lead" the variance in analysts' long-term projections of growth in earnings per share for the thirty firms in the *Dow Jones Industrial Average*. These results suggest that unscheduled corporate events may exert an informational effect whereby analysts glean more qualitative information about future returns from greater increases in the count and variation in KU events. For large enough subsets of KU events whose interpreted impacts on expected returns are believed to be directionally consistent with each other, the bounds of analysts' long-run growth estimates are narrowed. Narrative threads that connect the groups of nonrepetitive corporate events would then serve to shape and clarify the overall degree of bullishness versus bearishness of the full information set for investor return forecasts.

Chapter 10 offers the second set of formal empirical tests, but now explicitly focusing on the relationships between corporate KU events, narratives, and stock market instability. An expanded structural break analysis of commonly-modeled stock market relationships describing aggregate and firm-level returns, market volatility, trading volume, and equity fund flows is conducted. One test allows for the periods of highest narrative intensity from Chapter 6 to be imposed as potential breakpoints in stock market relationships. Other instability tests are conducted that leave open the timing and magnitude of potential breakpoints for comparative analysis. The results suggest that structural breaks in factor-model relationships of aggregate and firm-level stock returns approximately align with periods of greatest narrative intensity based on interactions of relevance, novelty, and sentiment connected to the KU events. There is also supportive evidence for NNH applied to stock market volatility and ETF (exchange traded fund) flows.

Chapter 11 presents a manual rule-based narrative analysis of Scapegoat effects and instability in the stock market. Based on information contained in *Bloomberg News* stock market wrap reports, formal empirics show the dramatic variation in investor attention across a range of macroeconomic and financial factors for the stock market. Increases in attention around particular narratives, that is, Scapegoat factors, are found connected to fundamentals' autoregressive data-generating process. One interesting finding is that investor narratives involving interest rates tend to comove positively with levels of underlying data on market-wide rates such as the 3-month Treasury bill yield. That is, when rates are historically high, stock market narratives involving interest rates increase substantially and vice versa. Results from the manual Scapegoat analysis provide insights into the close, but highly irregular, connection between stock market narratives and observed trends in conventional data on fundamentals.

Development of the macro and micro KU indices and subsequent narrative intensity analyses offer a range of possible applications for researchers and investors to consider for their own future work. Chapter 12 presents a case study applying the narrative frequency of the "dividends-earnings" corporate KU category to the present value model of aggregate stock market prices through a cointegrated vector autoregression (CVAR) analysis. The results suggest that adjusting for KU effects improves upon the statistical connection between aggregate prices and dividends. Moreover, a simple trading strategy that sells short (buys long) the aggregate market portfolio when narrative intensity is high (low) is shown to beat the market (albeit not adjusting for transactions costs) over the twenty-year sample period.

## I.7  THE FUTURE OF MACRO FINANCE

Chapter 13 offers thoughts about the future of macro-finance based on the need for incorporating historically novel events and associated narratives more broadly into economics and finance research. Whether a potential Kuhnian paradigm shift toward narrative-based modeling approaches under uncertainty is commencing is discussed (Kuhn, 1970; Mangee, 2015). For Kuhn, scientific revolutions occur when the statistical toolkits adopted, views of the world, and questions posed are challenged from within a scientific community. Ultimately, the researchers at large deem what is worthy of scientific status.

Throughout the chapter, emphasis is placed on extant methodological approaches to modeling aggregate outcomes that allow for historical events to change asset-price relationships in unforeseeable ways. A comparison of probabilistic versus nonprobabilistic representations of structural change in macro-finance models will be made in Kuhnian terms. In doing so, statistical frameworks for modeling revisions in participants' expectations that stop short of being fully prespecified are brought to the forefront (Frydman and Phelps, 2013; Frydman et al., 2019).

A brief Chapter 14 offers some main takeaways, concluding thoughts, and directions for future research. Lastly, Appendix B provides any reader, researcher, or student with the toolkit to conduct a manual, rule-based narratological analysis of unstructured stock market text under KU. The project includes a classification dictionary of fundamental, psychological, technical, and KU-specific factors along with a pretabulated Excel spreadsheet (available at the author's website) for scoring. The project's methodological approach enables the generation of unique time-series data on the influence of a wide array of factors deemed relevant for the stock market day-to-day Importantly, the project allows for contextualized meaning and unforeseeable change in price relationships at all times, past, present, and future. The project can be applied to any financial text, offering limitless application to trading strategies and future research.

# 2    Unpredictably Unstable

## 2.1    INTRODUCTION

This chapter is about time-varying relationships driving stock price fluctuations and volatility and how novel events and narrative dynamics may be at play. First, this chapter will address the role of narratives within the context of stock market outcomes, illustrated by recent novel events. Second, it will look at the variability and impact of investor sentiment in narrative dynamics when nonrepetitive events occur. And, third, the chapter discusses two stylized facts within the literature on structural change in financial markets, namely regime-switching and parameter nonconstancy, as frameworks for illuminating the connection between narrative dynamics and stock market instability.

## 2.2    NARRATIVES AND UNFORESEEABLE CHANGE

Epistemologically speaking, the emergence, transmission, and evolution of popular narratives are now considered part of the fields of "narratology" and "narrative science." How financial markets transmit and process information is, in part, about stories. In virtually every communication thread involving financial professionals and retail investors alike, humans are forced to simplify the relations that are actually pushing security prices this way and that. Consequently, though the vast majority of stories endure because of support from the underlying stream of micro events, scheduled and unscheduled, there is a more speculative component to narratives reflecting uncertainty about the future. "It's tough to make predictions, especially about the future."[1] Forward-looking markets rely on our imagination about

---

[1] Many variants of this quote exist throughout literature. Its origin is unknown, but has been traced at least to the Danish artist/writer Robert Storm Petersen (1882–1949). Others have

what may happen. It is doubtful that many would object to the view that imaginations, themselves, are temporally unstable and change in ways that would be difficult to foresee.

Stories about financial markets are told by analysts, investors, the media, researchers, politicians, government officials, central bankers, and the public. Virtually every individual now has some skin in the game and the potential "narrative" connection between investment professionals and retail (i.e. Main Street) investors is as significant as ever. Just consider that 6.5 million people are employed in the finance and insurance industry (NAICS 52), over 44 percent of all households own mutual funds (56 million individuals), 2,766 registered broker-dealers serve retail investors with $3.8 trillion in assets under management (AUM) across nearly 139 million accounts, 8,200 registered investment advisers (IAs) serve 32 million nonhigh-net-worth individuals with $4.8 trillion in AUM, and 8,000 registered IAs serve 4.8 million high-net-worth individuals with $6.15 trillion in AUM.[2] Interaction within the community of investment professionals and the correspondence between professionals and retail investors is channeled as much through story as through numbers, if not more so.

Professional conversations naturally extend beyond quarterly performance figures and sentiment tone is always part of the communication's content and delivery (Shiller and Pound, 1989). Narratives connecting the economy, politics, armed conflicts, oil prices, central bank decisions, and tax policy to current investment positions and future prospects likely permeate the air. Investment professionals and their clients participate in narrative dynamics whether they

traced the quote to the Danish politician Karl Kristian in the 1948 book *Farvel Og Tak*. Still others believe that Mark Twain is the original author. The quote is often falsely attributed to Yogi Berra.

[2] Employment in the Finance and Insurance sector (NAICS code 52) data is collected from the Bureau of Labor Statistics for March 2019. Mutual fund data is collected from the ICI 58th Edition 2018. Broker-dealer and investment advisor data is collected from Rel. No. 34-86032 *Form CRS Relationship Summary*; Amendments to Form ADV for December 2018 and is based on those BDs and IAs registered with the SEC.

are aware of it or not. If a fund manager, broker-dealer, or investment advisor was aware that narrative information was relevant for particular investment prospects and forecasting strategies it would behoove them to incorporate that information into their analysis. High stakes and cut-throat competition dictate such behavior. No doubt the technology and housing bubbles of the late 1990s and mid-2000s, respectively, were associated with narratives of exceptional investment performance connected to particular industries and the leveraging of specific financial instruments with (erroneously) perceived minimal downside risk (Shiller, 2000; Tuckett, 2009).

Consider again the COVID-19 crisis, a stark example of a nonrepetitive event that caused instability in the stock market and narrative dynamics to emerge. Narratives were of uncertain times, Depression-like unemployment and economic standstill, social isolation, government stimulus measures, under-supplied medical equipment, growing case numbers, high death tolls, potential second waves, pernicious origins of the virus and so on. It was a period of unprecedented anxiety over a highly contagious virus. The rapid changes in labor market data, business activity, domestic and international travel, and institutions at large by the end of March 2020 suggest that structural breaks in the relationships driving stock market outcomes occurred quickly. Public concern also supports this view. Google Trends searches for "virus" narratives from January 2004 through March 2020 are plotted in Figure 2.1.

Figure 2.1 shows that searches for the general term "virus" were virtually nonexistent until late January 2020, indicating relatively little public interest in "virus" during the 2009–2010 H1N1 swine flu pandemic. Attention to the virus narrative then exploded, reaching peak interest during the week of March 15, 2020. This specific week was witness to historical damage to the US stock market as illuminated in the *Bloomberg News* market wrap report discussed in Chapter 1. The figure suggests that the impact of the coronavirus on society at large was unique and fast-acting.

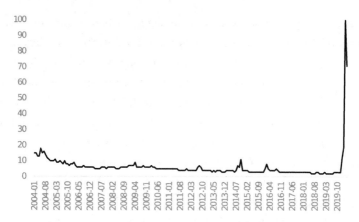

FIGURE 2.1 The figure plots the US Google Trends searches for "virus" during the period January 2004 through March 2020. The vertical axis measures search interest.

The narrative of "trade war" with China is also applicable to the Novelty–Narrative Hypothesis (NNH) for stock market instability. Prior to 2018, trade wars and weaponized tariffs were not considered important enough for stock market investors to monitor closely because they did not occur with enough frequency or veracity.[3] Ever since tariff threats and impositions began in March 2018, there have been many instances where story-line kernels have swayed the overall narrative trend up or down taking stock market prices with them. These kernels may come in the form of statements by government officials, presidential comments or tweets, or third-party nation maneuvers. When in conjunction with the more routine fundamental data releases, like earnings announcements, the narrative threads may coalesce around quantitative data causing a dramatic movement in prices for the day, or even week.

For example, the trade-war narrative took another turn sending stock prices broadly lower on July 30, 2019. Just before US delegates,

---

[3] The most popularized US-imposed tariff is arguably the Tariff Act of 1930, most commonly known as the Smoot–Hawley Tariff. Post-WWII retaliatory tariffs have declined in the US due to the General Agreement on Tariffs and Trade (renamed World Trade Organization) and the North American Free Trade Agreement.

including Treasury Secretary Steven Mnuchin and Trade Representative Robert Lighthizer, were to meet in Shanghai to resume trade talks, President Trump emboldened the trade-war narrative through a series of tweets early Tuesday morning, before markets opened. Mr. Trump tweeted,

> China is doing very badly, worst year in 27 – was supposed to start buying our agricultural product now – no signs that they are doing so. That is the problem with China, they just don't come through. Our Economy has become MUCH larger than the Chinese Economy is is (sic) last 3 years . . . My team is negotiating with them now, but they always change the deal in the end to their benefit. They should probably wait out our Election to see if we get one of the Democrat stiffs like Sleepy Joe. Then they could make a GREAT deal, like in past 30 years, and continue to ripoff the USA, even bigger and better than ever before. The problem with them waiting, however, is that if & when I win, the deal that they get will be much tougher than what we are negotiating now . . . or no deal at all. We have all the cards, our past leaders never got it!
>
> *(@ realDonaldTrump, 7:10 a.m. July 30, 2019)*

On market opening on Tuesday, *Bloomberg News* led with the headline, "Stocks Fall on Earnings, Trade Talk." The trade-war narrative was bolstered as "The S&P500 slumped, with overnight trading reaching lows after President Donald Trump criticized China just as negotiators start talks in Shanghai." Thursday was much of the same. In response to President Trump announcing new China tariffs, *Bloomberg News* led with, "US stocks tumble on Fresh Tariffs." The *Dow Jones Industrial Average* (DJIA) was down 1.05 percent on the day. Equity markets sank on Friday for the fourth consecutive day. Figure 2.2 shows the unprecedented increase in public attention to "trade wars" through Google Trends searches. The increase in concern beginning in 2018 aligns with the beginning of US–China tariff-policies, ensuing negotiations, and not infrequent presidential tweets and was maintained at a high level through mid-2019. Could the narrative dynamics of a US–China trade war be related to fluctuations and instability in stock market behavior?

Narratives are related to the frequency and direction of actual underlying events: When numerous tech-laden firm initial public

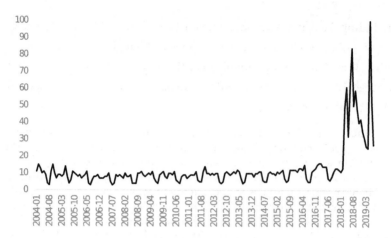

FIGURE 2.2 The figure plots the US Google Trends searches for "trade war" during the period 2014 through 2019. The vertical axis measures search interest.

offerings (IPOs) are announced and subsequently brought to market, narratives about information-age transformations of future productivity through automation and artificial intelligence are fueled. However, understanding the role of popular stories for stock market instability requires a recognition that narratives are fluid, amorphous, malleable, persistent, contagious, slippery, and potentially very powerful and manipulative. In short, narratives themselves are unstable and a source of uncertainty. They can be based firmly in reality or take on more of an imaginary shape. The stories humans tell about the economy, to social constructs, to international affairs, to the stock market are naturally interspersed with simplifications, but also with half-truths, bent reasoning, and even alternative facts often messaged and echoed by political institutions, government officials, corporations, and the media. Throughout history narratives have been promoted at different times to serve as interference from culpability. In reality, though they spawn from the occurrence of market events, narratives are likely a combination of fact and fiction; this combination is what allows them to survive. Narratives about data breaches are a good example of a potentially disproportionate story thread connected to novel events that is seemingly disconnected from trends in the raw underlying data, but impacts stock returns in unique ways nonetheless. This may indicate that the narrative is being influenced by alternative interpretations of the data or from the unfolding of other related events.

Since 2005, there have been over 9,015 publicly reported data breaches in the US with a combined total of 10,387,398,893 records breached over the period.[4] Data breaches have reentered the media cycle with recent news about the early-2019 Capital One data breach where over 100 million consumer accounts involving Social Security numbers, bank records, and credit applications were hacked. The reports were released roughly one week after the Federal Trade Commission (FTC)'s announcement of the class-action settlement from the Equifax consumer and financial data breach back in 2017.[5] The timing and severity of the two events likely compounded the data-breach narrative.

Figure 2.3 plots the Google Trends results from "data breach" searches. The two major, and heavily reported, events involving Equifax and Capital One are indicated by the sharp spikes in public attention. However, there have been thousands of other data breaches that have occurred since 2005 and 172 of them have involved a breach of 1 million records or more. Figure 2.4 plots the number of data breaches for the period January 2005 through July 2019 where it is evident that the period with the most data breaches was from 2010 to 2016. By contrast, the year 2019 experienced the lowest number of data breaches since 2005–2006.

The Google Trends data and the underlying economic data do not display similar patterns. However, since the magnitude and scope of information hacked in the data breach are not captured in

---

[4] The publicly available data is collected from the Privacy Rights Clearinghouse and may be accessed at www.privacyrights.org/data-breaches.

[5] For the FTC statement on the Equifax Data Breach Settlement see www.ftc.gov/enforcement/cases-proceedings/refunds/equifax-data-breach-settlement.

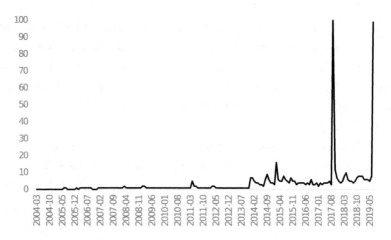

FIGURE 2.3  The figure plots the US Google Trends searches for "data breach" during the period 2005 through 2019. The vertical axis measures search interest.

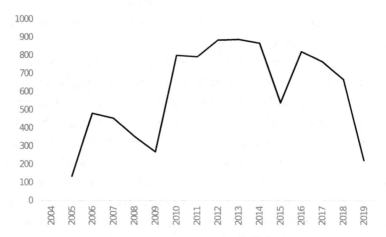

FIGURE 2.4  The figure plots actual reported data breaches in the USA or for US-based companies abroad during the period 2005 through 2019.

Figure 2.4, Figure 2.5 plots the number of data breaches involving more than 1 million records. The clear upward trend in the data suggests that public attention and potential narratives of data breaches are partially a function of the severity and magnitude of the events.

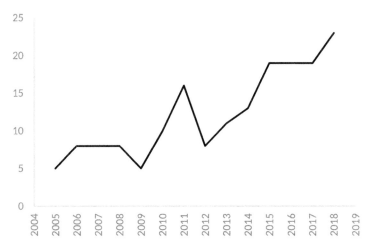

FIGURE 2.5 The figure plots the number of data breaches in the US involving more than 1 million records.

Tracking the time-series properties of underlying data in support of a popular narrative is an important starting place for analysis. Chapter 11 provides a textual scapegoat analysis of stock price fluctuations wherein market participants pay the greatest attention to various fundamental factors which have recently experienced dramatic and historical movements in their own underlying data series. Consequently, a changing array of "headline" fundamentals that underpin the most gripping narratives in any given period will become a part of investor forecasting strategies. As different fundamentals enter and exit this process unforeseeable structural change in stock return relationships will unfold.

Neither the COVID-19 virus, trade-war, nor data-breach narrative was a primary concern for the public prior to 2017. All three novel events, however, displayed sharp spikes in public interest thereafter. Dramatic increases in interest in these stories may contribute to different subnarratives buttressing the upward trending recession narrative presented in Figures 1.1 and 1.2 that, in turn, may feed back into other subnarratives connected to economic contractions. The systemic nature of these events and their linkages to different industries make them prime candidates for causing larger-scale instability between stock market outcomes and fundamentals with the potential to cascade into unanticipated change at the micro level. In fact, Chapter 8 provides empirical evidence that Black Swan events cause future Grey Swan events in the stock market.

Stock market narratives also arise when the cause of, or motivation for, a novel event is largely unknown or difficult to rationalize *ex post*. When this is the case, groups of media outlets can fuel particular narratives especially if there are large gaps of incomplete information. Researchers can trace how a firm was acquired, how a product was recalled, and how oil refinery spills, airplane crashes, and other industrial accidents occur. They can somewhat trace a firm's bankruptcy, an IPO failure, a new patent's acceptance, or an executive's resignation. But when the underlying causes are unsettled, such as armed conflicts, terrorism, mass shootings, political elections, and even COVID-19, the evolution of novel events can be manipulated into desired narratives with ulterior motivation.

The 2019 back-to-back mass shooting attacks in El Paso, Texas and Dayton, Ohio on August 3 and 4, respectively, serve as examples of this effect. The shootings catalyzed competing narratives about prospective gun regulation and the potential behavioral links from exposure to video game violence. The narratives were fueled by little more than public statements from President Trump and other government officials combined with news media's *ex post* rationalizations for the deadly acts. No one knew whether tighter federal gun control measures such as enhanced background checks, red flag laws, delayed purchases, bans on high-capacity magazine or assault rifles would soon become federal legislation; history suggests that such proposals would have faced stiff pushback on many fronts (Lott, 2010).

The gun control narratives, however, drove Smith and Wesson (now American Outdoor Brands) and Sturm Ruger up as much as 7.3 percent and 3.1 percent, respectively, throughout Monday,

August 5.[6] Alternatively, the video game narrative led shares of Activision and Electronic Arts down 6 percent and 4.6 percent, respectively, at market close the same day. The SP500 closed the day's trading session down 2.9 percent. There have been many studies investigating a potential connection between video game violence and behavioral tendencies among adolescents. Any cursory review of the literature will be quickly confronted with highly mixed evidence: Some studies claim conclusive evidence in support of a linkage while other studies claim conclusive evidence against it.[7] Arguing for a causal effect through a survey of the extant literature, Anderson (2004, p. 113), for instance, writes, "An updated meta-analysis reveals that exposure to violent video games is significantly linked to increases in aggressive behavior, aggressive cognition, aggressive affect, and cardiovascular arousal, and to decreases in helping behavior. Experimental studies reveal this linkage to be causal. Correlational studies reveal a linkage to serious, real-world types of aggression."

In fact, the American Psychological Association in 2015 released an updated and revised *Resolution on Violent Video Games* in which the APA states,[8]

> Multiple meta-analyses of the research have been conducted. Quantitative reviews since APA's 2005 Resolution that have focused on the effects of violent video game use have found a direct association between violent video game use and aggressive outcomes ... The link between violent video game exposure and aggressive behavior is one of the most studied and best established. Since the earlier meta-analyses, this link continues to be a reliable finding and shows good multi-method consistency across various representations of both violent video game exposure and aggressive behavior.

[6] Early trading stock market data is collected from the August 5 report from *Business Insider* at https://markets.businessinsider.com/news/stocks/gun-stocks-rise-after-dual-weekend-shootings-calls-for-laws-2019-8-1028418220#. By market close, American Outdoor Brands and Sturm Ruger posted 2.25% and −1.4% returns from the previous trading day.

[7] For studies concluding there exists a connection between exposure to video game violence and negative behavioral outcomes and desensitization to violence see Anderson (2004) and references therein. For studies concluding the lack of any convincing link see Przybylski and Weinstein (2019).

[8] For further details, see the APA's 2015 resolution at www.apa.org/about/policy/violent-video-games and references therein.

Yet, Przybylski and Weinstein (2019, p. 1), a study touted as being one of the most comprehensive studies on the subject to date declare,

> Following a preregistered analysis plan, multiple regression analyses tested the hypothesis that recent violent game play is linearly and positively related to carer assessments of aggressive behaviour. Results did not support this prediction, nor did they support the idea that the relationship between these factors follows a nonlinear parabolic function. There was no evidence for a critical tipping point relating violent game engagement to aggressive behaviour.

One of the authors to this study has commented further, in a 2019 University of Oxford News Release, that, "The idea that violent video games drive real-world aggression is a popular one, but it hasn't tested very well over time. Despite interest in the topic by parents and policy-makers, the research has not demonstrated that there is cause for concern."

This is a complicated topic to be sure. Every person has a view about this issue whether from personal experience, anecdotal evidence, intuition, training, political affiliation, or otherwise. Yet, canyon-wide disagreement about whether a fundamental connection exists appears to define the state of research from professional social scientists on this important issue. When there is lack of consensus, data-driven or simply perceived by the public, about how and why particular novel events unfold there is relatively more room for narrative dynamics to fill the unsettled space.

This narrative effect has, to some degree, been witnessed in the climate change debate, the policy use of Temporary Assistance for Needy Families (TANF) and other forms of government assistance in society, the role of the US in international affairs, the benefits of tax cuts for corporations and the wealthy, the state's decision whether or not to reopen the COVID-19-stricken economy and so on. These topics are dynamic, nonlinear, and riddled with novelty and uncertainty. However, the amount of disagreement concerning their validity, one way or another, has portrayed them, rightly or wrongly, as being grossly unsettled issues. Insofar as these complex factors impact stock market fluctuations in unforeseeable ways, which they obviously do, narratives will swirl through professional and public discourse, filling the gaps of knowledge and interpretation, eventually to become ensnared in market instability.

## 2.3    INVESTOR SENTIMENT AND INSTABILITY

A key hypothesis advanced in this book, and quantitatively analyzed in subsequent chapters, is that novelty, instability, popular narratives, and investor sentiment are inextricably connected as implied by NNH. When novel events occur, there is unforeseeable structural change. When there is unforeseeable change, investors face inherent ambiguity contemplating both the odds of possible future states and the most appropriate model for forecasting returns conditional on their occurrence. In doing so, individuals are prone to rely on stories that simplify relevant relationships for cognitive tractability, particularly those stories infused with the greatest emotion. Psychological considerations and feelings give narratives life and shape that provide investors the perception of a more complete picture of the process driving outcomes when relationships have changed in unforeseeable ways. Given the interconnected complexities of capitalistic markets and investors' imperfection of knowledge, real-world decision-making would be paralyzed otherwise. This process is at the core of NNH for asset markets under instability and Knightian uncertainty (KU).

Knight recognized the inextricable and pragmatic connection between sentiment, calculation, and the novelty of most business decisions. For Knight (1921, p. 226), the "degree of confidence" underpinning business decisions "cannot be ignored, for it is of the greatest potential significance" since it necessarily assists individuals in dealing with "unanticipated, dynamic changes." Keynes echoes Knight's views and eloquently spells out this dynamic relationship:

> We are merely reminding ourselves that human decisions affecting the future, whether personal or political or economic, cannot depend on strict mathematical expectations, since the basis for making such calculations does not exist; and that it is our innate urge to activity which makes the wheels go around, our rational selves choosing between the alternatives

as best we are able, calculating where we can, but often falling back for our motive on whim or sentiment or chance.

*(Keynes, 1936, pp.162–163)*

Knight and Keynes both trace the necessary role of "confidence" to the natural ebbs and flows in situations involving uncertainty when "the basis for making such calculations does not exist." Keynes clarifies his notion of uncertainty, in a similar spirit as Knight, in stating,

> By "uncertain" knowledge, let me explain, I do not mean merely to distinguish what is known for certain from what is only probable. The game of roulette is not subject, in this sense, to uncertainty; nor is the prospect of a Victory bond being drawn. Or, again, the expectation of life is only slightly uncertain. Even the weather is moderately uncertain. The sense in which I am using the term is that in which the prospect of a European war is uncertain, or the price of copper and the rate of interest twenty years later hence, or the obsolescence of a new invention, or the position of private wealth owners in the social system in 1970. About these matters, there is no scientific basis on which to form any calculable probability whatever. We simply do not know.
>
> *(Keynes, 1936, pp. 213–214)*

Like Knight, Keynes recognizes the role of novel events for investor forecasts under uncertainty by relating historic instances of systematic concern that are largely unforeseeable, such as "war" and "new inventions," to the inability to form "calculable probability." He then connects this argumentative thread involving sentiment, ambiguity, and novelty to "instability underpinning investment decisions":

> There is the instability due to the characteristic of human nature that a large proportion of our positive activities depend on spontaneous optimism rather than on a mathematical expectation, whether moral or hedonistic or economic. Most, probably, of our decisions to do something positive, the full consequences of which will be drawn out over many days to come, can only be taken as a result of animal spirits – of a spontaneous urge to action rather than inaction, and not as the outcome of a weighted average of quantitative benefits multiplied by quantitative probabilities.
>
> *(Keynes, 1936, p. 161)*

Keynes' excerpts portray a financial market environment where investment decisions confronting true uncertainty – whether manifested through historical events or the time lag for decisions' consequences to become apparent – naturally depend on sentiment mattering right alongside calculation. This view is in opposition to the standard approach of investor sentiment as reflecting irrationality in many behavioral noise trader models.[9] Sentiment-infused narratives enable market participants to "do something positive" when the prospects of today's investment under uncertainty are "drawn out over many days to come." This may be the case following novel events such as mergers, acquisitions, IPOs, partnerships, capital expenditures, firm reorganization and so on. M&As, for instance, are consistently in the top ten most-identified corporate KU groups during different subperiods in the US stock market (Chapter 7). Therefore, when analysis finds that overall sentiment for KU groups is related to aggregate stock market outcomes (Chapters 6, 7, and 9) and structural change (Chapter 10), M&As and other frequently identified KU groups, whether associated with optimism or pessimism, are contributing a relatively greater effect.[10]

Consider, for instance, the Department of Justice's July 2019 approval of the mega $26 billion merger between telecommunications firms T-Mobile and Sprint, effectively reducing industry competition alongside market titans Verizon and AT&T. With the merger, the new conglomerate captures 30 percent of the market share. How might an investor consider the cash flow prospects one, two, ten, or even twenty years hence? There are many moving pieces and contingent impacts related to novel events to consider that limit the benefit of relying on past data. First, both Sprint and T-Mobile must divest enough telecom assets to allow the relatively smaller Dish to replace Sprint and become the fourth national carrier (as per the M&A terms of agreement). Dish will be offered retail spaces and up to seven years of access to T-Mobile's network while it establishes its own grid.

---

[9] For a seminal study on noise trader models in the stock market, see De Long et al. (1990).

[10] For the close connection between M&A announcements and investor sentiment in the stock market see, for instance, Rosen (2006).

The approved merger is intended to advance firm investment into the development of, and broad access to, 5G network capabilities. Will the Federal Government consider future regulations involving 5G? Will regulation mandate broadband access in rural areas? The divestiture is intended to enhance competition by allowing Dish and other potential new entrants to compete with the now Big Three. But it is estimated that the top three telecommunications firms will now represent 95 percent market concentration that may lead to higher prices and fewer services demanded in the future. The 2018 revenues for T-Mobile and Sprint were $43 billion and $32 billion, respectively, eclipsed by Verizon's and AT&T's respective revenues of $130 billion and $170 billion. However, what about hundreds of billions of dollars recently levied in tariffs on China, a key supplier of intermediate technologies relied upon for production by the US telecommunications industry? Jessica Rosenworcel, an attorney and member of the Federal Communications Commission (FCC), has recently stated, "All the building blocks of 5G wireless – from modems to antennas to semiconductors – are subject to this new tax. It's not good for consumers, innovation or US leadership."[11]

How will the dynamics from this major industry shake-up play out in terms of future revenues, earnings, investor perception, market concentration and the like? How can the moving pieces, economic, social, political, and geopolitical in nature, be factored into stock market expectations of future returns? Which forces will dominate? "We simply do not know" (Keynes, 1936). There is inherent ambiguity about the future earnings prospects of this novel event that itself would have been difficult to anticipate just five years ago. Investor forecasts will have to rely on soft information, narrative accounts, and degrees of confidence in opinions to determine whether or not to put capital at stake, if so, how much, and which side of the market to take bets on.

---

[11] This excerpt is from Jessica Rosenworcel's Twitter feed on May 14, 2019.

Sentiment influences the weights investors attach to various pieces of news when assessing different forecasting strategies and is, therefore, a function of the news content of market information itself (Frydman and Goldberg, 2011). Generally, good, or better-than-expected, news generates positive sentiment and vice versa. Economics and finance researchers, however, tend to ignore the inherent interaction between the news about fundamentals and the sentiment surrounding its interpretation. Those studies that recognize this interaction effect, usually through a textual-based proxy for sentiment from market news reports, find very interesting results.

For instance, using *Dow Jones Newswire* and *Wall Street Journal* feeds, Tetlock et al. (2008) find that when the sentiment tone of textual information is interacted with explicit mentions of individual firm earnings the high frequency impact is five times greater in contemporaneous and predictive return regressions. Using the same textual data source as Tetlock et al. (2008), Boudoukh et al. (2013) report significant increases in market $R^2$ values for firm- and industry-level return regressions on "news" versus "no news" trading days once the tone of information is taken into account.[12] Similarly, Garcia (2013) uses word tone from *New York Times* stock market reports to show that daily predicted return sensitivity for the DJIA is amplified during recessions when there are greater levels of market pessimism.

These studies notwithstanding, there has been scant investigation relating the sentiment–fundamentals interaction effects explicitly to structural change. However, Frydman et al. (forthcoming), using a sentiment proxy from the *Wall Street Journal Abreast of the Market* columns, reveal a novel channel through which market

---

[12] See also Uhl et al. (2015) who use *Thomson Reuters'* linguistic algorithm interacting news events and textual tone surrounding them to measure sentiment of identified macro- and firm-level events for improving portfolio asset allocation strategies. Mian and Sankaraguruswamy (2012) interact high/low sentiment proxies with good/bad firm-level news on dividends, earnings announcements, and stock-splits. The authors' sentiment proxy is based on the Baker and Wurgler (2006) index constructed to be intentionally orthogonal to fundamentals.

participants' sentiment influences how they forecast stock returns: Their optimism (pessimism) affects the weights they assign to fundamentals. If good (bad) news about dividends and interest rates coincides with participants' optimism (pessimism), the news about these fundamentals has a significant effect on participants' forecasts of future returns with expected signs (positive for dividends and negative for interest rates). In models without interactions, or when market sentiment is neutral or conflicts with news about dividends and/or interest rates, this news often does not have a significant effect on *ex ante* or *ex post* returns, suggesting that these models (absent of interactions) experience structural change.[13] When market sentiment is found to influence aggregate stock returns, it does so in highly irregular ways in terms of both timing and magnitude.

## 2.4   THE NATURE OF STOCK MARKET CHANGE

It is now well documented that posited relationships driving asset market behavior undergo change over time. Descriptive accounts on the instability of stock markets have been provided by Knight (1921), Keynes (1936), Minsky (1986), Soros (1987, 2008), Akerlof and Shiller (2009), Frydman and Goldberg (2011) among others. A large empirical literature on structural change in relationships driving stock markets is outlined in Sections 2.4.1 and 2.4.2 below. Commenting on the empirical record of instability in predictive regressions, Pesaran and Timmermann (2002, p. 495), for instance, state that breaks between stock returns and fundamentals "could arise due to a number of factors, such as major changes in market sentiment, the burst or creation of speculative bubbles, or regime switches in monetary and debt management policies." Other plausible sources may be

---

[13]   Baek (2016) studies structural change in a cointegrated vector autoregression (CVAR) model that includes market returns, earnings, and sentiment, as measured by the Baker–Wurgler index. Cointegration is only found between sentiment and earnings. However, once a structural break is allowed in the analysis, sentiment-based predictions of medium-run earnings are further improved.

institutional, regulatory, technological, social and so on.[14] There are many forms of temporal instability in stock market models, such as short-run changes in parameter estimates, outlier events, omitted variables, and alternative longer-run functional forms that can all lead to forecasting failures, spurious regressions, and fat-tail kurtosis in return distributions.

In order to relate change in stock market behavior to novelty and narratives, the analysis must first ask, what does change look like in the stock market? What stylized regularities concerning instability have been found? Indeed, researchers have uncovered substantial evidence of temporal instability in the relationships driving asset prices and volatility. The findings broadly point toward asymmetric change connected to different stages of the business cycle, different fundamentals mattering for outcomes during different periods of time, and an important role for rare disaster events. One of the key findings central to the present thesis is that instability triggered by novel events, such as the appointment of a new Federal Reserve chair, could not have been anticipated by financial market participants, let alone researchers (Kaminsky, 1993). This is an example of unforeseen change as implied by NNH.

The next two subsections survey this literature with a focus on two concepts of instability in stock market relationships. The first is based on regime-switching approaches where model parameters shift between (usually) two states describing outcomes. The second is based on direct tests for parameter nonconstancy, or structural change, in market relationships attempting to identify the location and number of potential breakpoints during a particular period.

Both concepts of instability lend themselves to NNH. First, the importance of narrative factors in explaining stock market activity

---

[14] Of course, there remains great debate over the causes of changing relationships driving fluctuations in stock, and other asset, markets, and the most appropriate prescriptive response by the state. See, for example, Frydman and Goldberg (2011) for discussions on this topic. For a focus on instability and state response during crises see, for instance, Claessens et al. (2013) and Aliber and Kindleberger (2015) and references therein.

under uncertainty can fit readily into a framework of multiple regimes that switch over time. As illustrated in the financial news excepts presented throughout this book, narratives tend to assimilate themselves as a collection of informational and emotional threads that all share a consistent perceived qualitative impact, whether bullish or bearish, on future stock returns. Second, NNH implies that periods characterized by greater novelty and narrative intensity might align with the location of breakpoints in the processes driving stock market outcomes. Both regime-switching models and tests for structural breaks imply that the relationships driving asset returns and volatility have changed in statistically meaningful ways. Whether such change reflects time-varying weights investors attach to explanatory factors, nonlinearities in the functional form, psychological considerations, or rare disasters, NNH implies that much of the change is unforeseeable and can be best understood at the intersection of nonrepetitive events and narrative dynamics under uncertainty.

## 2.4.1   Regime-Switching

First, consider the stylized facts from empirical studies on stochastic (i.e. probabilistic) regime shifts in the stock market. Ang and Timmermann (2012) provide a comprehensive survey of the Markov-switching approach, popularized by Hamilton (1988, 1989), as applied to equity, bond, and currency markets. Their review concludes that allowing for different regimes offers a much better characterization of the underlying data-generating process for stock returns rather than assuming stable parameters across a singular sample period. Because stock returns display kurtosis, skewness, serial correlation, heteroskedasticity, and nonlinearities, allowing for regime changes based on different distributions can better match the underlying data-generating process. However, by dismissing the role of unforeseeable change, determinate models of stochastic instability, such as the Markov-switching class of models, have underestimated the presence, and sources, of structural change in stock market relationships. Nevertheless, the evidence from this well-developed literature overwhelmingly rejects the hypothesis of stable stock market returns behavior over extended periods of time.

Several findings have emerged from regime-switching studies relevant for the subsequent empirical chapters against which the narrative findings may be compared: (i) the probability of regime shifts is best characterized as time-varying; (ii) regimes may be viewed as nonrecurring and ever-expanding; (iii) impacts on returns, volatility, and cross-correlations are asymmetric across economic expansion/contraction and bull/bear regimes; (iv) uncertainty about future regimes is connected to the asymmetry, persistence, and clustering in stock market volatility; and (v) major historical events help to explain additional regime shifts. Each one of these stylized facts is important to investigate further in the context of NNH as applied to the stock market.

Most regime-switching studies on stock price fluctuations allow for shifts in either the drift or variance of the endowment process measured by dividend or consumption growth in which the probability of entering a different regime is a function of being in the current regime and is typically fixed over time (Driffill and Sola, 1998; Gabriel and Martins, 2011; Gutierrez and Vazquez, 2004). Finding (i), however, suggests that allowing for time-varying transition probabilities provides a better description of stock returns and volatility (Schaller and van Norden, 1997).[15] Moreover, the presence and influence of nonrepetitive events implies there is no basis for knowing the timing or magnitude of such shifts in financial market behavior *ex ante*. In an important study, Kaminsky (1993), for example, shows that changes in transition probabilities due to the appointment of a new Federal Reserve chair could not have been anticipated in a Markov-switching model of the exchange rate.

---

[15] Macroeconometric studies on Markov-switching have connected time-varying transition probabilities to the duration of time spent on one regime (Durland and McCurdy, 1994) and to variation displayed by different fundamental variables (Diebold et al., 1994; Filardo, 1994).

Related to (i), Timmermann (2001) shows an improved fit for stock return and volatility estimates when shifts in the dividend process follow an expanding set of nonrecurring regimes where each regime distribution is unique, that is, finding (ii).[16] After each break in the endowment process, a new set of parameters arise increasing investor uncertainty and rendering past observations irrelevant. This representation of instability is particularly useful for shifts related to historically unique events such as "technological change and certain types of legislative or political changes that are irreversible or unlikely to repeat" (Ang and Timmermann, 2012). The highest degree of uncertainty occurs immediately following a regime shift implying that return variance is also the highest immediately following the break. This leads to the close relationship between stylized findings (iii) and (iv).

It is now clear that stock returns and volatility behave differently across bull versus bear markets and various stages of the business cycle.[17] Veronesi (1999) links the finding of asymmetric regimes to greater economic uncertainty, Pastor and Veronesi (2009a) to technological uncertainty, and Bittlingmayer (1998) to political uncertainty. The well-known "peso problem" implies that market participants face increased uncertainty during bad times about whether the regime has changed, how large of a shift has occurred, if it will survive and, if so, for how long.[18] In addition to the already present uncertainty about future growth in the endowment process, instability serves as an additional source of uncertainty. Consequently, return volatility is countercyclical with the business cycle and clustered around bull market downturns. The studies of Gennotte (1986), Timmermann (1996, 2001), Brennan (1998), and Adam et al. (2015) explain asymmetric effects in financial markets through investor learning

[16] The Chib (1998) change-point process allows for nonrepeating regimes to occur and has been applied to the stock market by Pastor and Stambaugh (2001) and Pettenuzzo and Timmermann (2011).

[17] See, for example, Campbell and Hentschel (1992), Calvet and Fisher (2007), Pagan and Sossounov (2003), and Liu et al. (2012).

[18] Evans (1996) provides a survey of the Markov-switching literature on peso problems.

when parameters driving outcomes are uncertain but clarified over time by observing new data points.[19]

Stylized finding (v) suggests that shifts across multiple regimes in stock return relationships may be triggered by major historical episodes such as changes to fiscal or monetary policy, oil price shocks, and financial crises or simply from nonrepetitive firm events such as stock splits (Brown et al., 1985). Calvet and Fisher (2007), Mangee (2016), and others provide empirical evidence suggesting there is indeed a larger number of different regimes in the stock market than the two typically allowed for in most studies and that the timing of shifts may correspond to important macroeconomic events.[20] However, researchers underestimate the presence and destabilizing impacts of nonrepetitive events by framing them as rare "disasters" approximated by extreme left-tail shocks to the endowment process even if the probability of "disaster risk" is allowed to vary over time (Wachter, 2013). Such a framing necessarily misses the high degree of novelty and unforeseeable change in stock market relationships argued for throughout this book.

David and Veronesi (2009) allow for positive and negative rare events corresponding to good and bad states, respectively, in addition to the more prevalent "normal" regime. Stock prices are highest (lowest) in the good (bad) regime and are driven by "directional," perhaps narrative, information that is perceived overall as "good" or "bad" for stocks. Uncertainty is the greatest in both good and bad regimes since the probability of exiting back into the normal, neutral, regime is very high, especially when exiting the bad regime (Barro, 2006). Rare disaster events can have a large impact on returns and volatility because bad regimes, like negative narratives, garner a greater amount of investor attention. While there are many potentially positive narratives about the stock market, and many instances of both positive and negative narratives concurrently unfolding, the most palpable and

---

[19] See Pastor and Veronesi (2009b) for a review of learning models applied to asset markets.

[20] For evidence of more regimes in the foreign exchange market see, for instance, Stillwagon and Sullivan (2019).

visceral are negative ones. Similarly, there is also much evidence on the disproportionate weight of negative versus positive psychological considerations for decision-making under uncertainty (Chapter 3).

### 2.4.2   Parameter Nonconstancy

Now consider the statistical evidence of structural breaks, or parameter nonconstancy, in univariate and multivariate stock market relationships and in the endowment process itself. Referring to the parameter that has determined mean stock returns since 1926, Brennan (1998, p. 301) states, "there are good reasons to doubt that this parameter has remained constant for almost three quarters of a century which has witnessed the most dramatic economic, technological and social change of any comparable period in history."

Viceira (1997) reports structural breaks in the process driving expected returns in a univariate setting. For multivariate models, structural change in how fundamentals drive returns has been documented in many studies for both *ex post* and *ex ante* outcomes.[21] This is unsurprising since so many of the underlying macroeconomic and financial variables themselves undergo structural change over time (Stock and Watson, 1996). Indeed, often-cited periods of breaks in the endowment process of dividend or consumption growth involve the Great Depression, WWII, the large oil price shocks of the mid and late 1970's, stagflation of the early 1980's, the technology-infused run-up in asset prices and wealth in the late 1990s, the bursting of the IT bubble and subsequent recession of the early 2000s, the expansion in household and private sector credit and housing boom in the mid-2000s, the global financial crisis and subsequent Great Recession beginning in 2007, the early-2010s sequestration and debt ceiling crisis, the historic Tax Cuts and Jobs Act of 2017, and now the COVID-19 global pandemic and Great Lockdown Recession. These

---

[21] See, for example, Pastor and Stambaugh (2001), Timmermann (2001), Nasseh and Strauss (2004), Paye and Timmermann (2006), Rapach and Wohar (2006), Pettenuzzo and Timmermann (2011), and Mangee (2016) for studies on *ex post* returns and Frydman and Stillwagon (2018) for *ex ante* returns.

are just the most conservative episodes of potential structural change that researchers have found in stock market data and underestimate the full range of potentially destabilizing events connected to novel corporate events (Chapters 5 through 7).

Using a recursive structural change analysis based on an extended present value stock price relation, Mangee (2016) connects numerous breaks in out-of-sample predictive regressions to major historical events. For example, breaks at 1970:05 and 1981:09 match roughly the beginning of National Bureau of Economic Research (NBER)-dated economic recessions commencing in 1969:Q4 and 1981:Q3, respectively. The breakpoint found at 1978:08 precedes the second Organization of Petroleum Exporting Countries (OPEC) oil shock of 1979:03 by six months. Additionally, return forecasts may have shifted from the introduction in April 1999 of the Gramm–Leach–Bliley Act repealing the Glass–Steagall Act and eliminating barriers between commercial and investment banking activities; the act's introduction in the Senate lags the breakpoint found at 1999:01 by three months.

Other breakpoints identified in Mangee (2016)'s structural change analysis correspond to reversals in stock price swings. The break found at 1981:09 aligns with the period where the SP500 price-to-earnings ratio reversed from a low, commencing one of the longest historical stock market upswings lasting until December 1999. The break in 1997:05 aligns nearly perfectly with the Asian Financial Crisis beginning in July. The break at 2002:07 lags by four months the trough of US stock market prices, initiating one of the greatest bull runs in financial market history. Finally, the break found at 2008:10 aligns perfectly with the systemic collapse of the stock market following the September bankruptcy of financial intermediary Lehman Brothers – the largest bankruptcy in US history, sparking the early stages of the global financial crisis. In total, Mangee (2016) finds eleven breakpoints from 1959 through 2013.[22]

---

[22] Other empirical studies match points of instability in stock market behavior to major events. For example, Pettenuzzo and Timmermann (2011) trace eight breakpoints in

Structural change tests have also informed asymmetries in returns and volatility behavior through time. Henkel et al. (2011), for instance, shows that multivariate return predictability is absent in expansions, but present in contractions. Relatedly, the directional relationship between economic data and stock returns appears to vary across stages of the business cycle: Returns share a positive relationship with good macroeconomic news during contractions but share a negative relationship with such news during expansions.[23] There is ample evidence of asymmetric narratives during different stages of economic and financial cycles, such as stories of ever-increasing stock prices, wealth, and leverage during the mid-2000's and tax-cut-fueled run-ups in 2017 (Chapter 4). This effect is particularly evident during the most excessive peaks and troughs in equity valuations – periods when the diversity of nonrepetitive events is relatively high (Chapter 9).

Much research has established that the strength of stock return predictability based on fundamental factors has varied considerably over time. Campbell and Thompson (2008), in response to Goyal and Welch (2008)'s results that nothing can beat the historical mean in forecasting the equity premium out-of-sample, find that a time-varying information set of fundamentals significantly improves the predictive ability of macroeconomic and financial regressors. Furthermore, Pesaran and Timmermann (2002), Ang and Bekaert (2007), and Goyal and Welch (2008) document that constant parameter multivariate predictability of stock returns vanished during the 1990s, a period characterized by narratives about IT firms' unbounded earnings potential and floods of industry M&As. It is likely that this finding is driven by structural change in the relationships driving returns due, in part, to the omission of relevant variables.[24] This

present value relations for stock price fluctuations from 1926 through 2005 to major macroeconomic and financial events.

[23] See, for instance, Pearce and Roley (1985), McQueen and Roley (1993), Boyd et al. (2005), and Mangee (2014).

[24] For surveys on predictive regression instability in stock market data see Paye and Timmermann (2006) and Rapach and Wohar (2006).

book provides evidence that, in addition to the time-varying equity premium documented throughout the literature, there is a time-varying uncertainty premium in the stock market and it is connected to the novelty of a wide array of corporate events.

This chapter aimed to accomplish three things. First, the role of narratives in the stock market was discussed and illustrated by recent events. Second, the influence of investor sentiment was explored under NNH. Third, the nuanced evidence on temporal instability was surveyed through the lens of NNH. The next question is, what have researchers in other social sciences found about the presence and variation in narrative dynamics under uncertainty? How might findings from outside disciplines help researchers approach quantitative analysis of novelty and narratives in financial markets? These are the topics of Chapter 3.

# 3 Narratology and Other Disciplines

What is narratology? How might stock market instability from novel events be better understood under the light of narratological findings from disciplines outside of economics and finance? How narratives emerge and ripple through society is a complex and time-varying process. Social scientists do not fully understand what makes certain narratives more captivating than others nor how they survive, propagate, change, and either die off or manifest themselves in future narratives. What connections have other disciplines been able to make between the roles of uncertainty, emotions, and novelty in answering these questions?

Storytelling has been around for as long as humans have roamed the earth. It is accepted as an essential act for our generational progress as a civilization. Thousands of studies across psychology, sociology, linguistics, and stylistics have investigated the narrative features within our communicative dynamics. Yet, the fields of economics and finance have largely ignored the influence of narratives in explaining aggregate market outcomes. Authoritative findings from other disciplines' research on narratives, arrived upon by asking different questions and employing different analytical lenses, may help to shed light on the instability of stock market behavior under uncertainty.

Where there is novelty there is instability. Where there is instability there is uncertainty. Where there is uncertainty there are narratives – narratives are the currency of uncertainty. Other disciplines have caught on to this dynamic through their respective treatments on the formation of individual beliefs and expectations. The evidence presented here will focus on the role of affective states and emotions driving expectations when confronted with new information and on the social dynamics of contextualized narratives that parallel the evolution of people. A brief background on how economics and finance researchers have treated novelty under uncertainty will first be provided.

The narrative mode framework of Bruner (1986), which explores the unsystematic part of the mind used to create imagined realities of possible states of the world, will be discussed along with other cognitive-psychological and neurological views on the power of stories. A sociological perspective will be offered on the basis of "endogenous animal spirits" (DiMaggio, 2002), "emotional embeddedness" (Bandelj, 2009), and "creative action theory" (Joas, 1996; Whitford, 2002) as they may be applied to uncertainty and unanticipated change in decision-making parameters. Finally brief findings from stylistics and linguistics on the importance of conditioning narratives within context and zeitgeist are presented (Toolan, 1992).

## 3.2   HOW ECONOMISTS DEAL WITH NARRATIVES AND NOVELTY

"Economists have predicted nine out of the last five recessions." This quote, often attributed to Paul Samuelson, the grandfather of contemporary economics, reflects the profession's poor track record in predicting major downturns in the macroeconomy. Other missed calls have included the global financial crisis, the Great Recession, the Trump election, Brexit, and the Great Lockdown Recession. Conventional economics' inability to foreshadow major events stems, in part, from the presumption that human behavior, and the markets that reflect it, can be modeled with the same predictive and mathematical precision as the natural sciences.[1] Under such determinate

---

[1] See, for example, Lo and Mueller (2010) for a discussion on "physics envy" in finance academia. Prominent economist John Cochrane recently quipped on his blog, *The Grumpy Economist*, that,

Others bemoan "too much math" in economics, a feeling that seldom comes from people who understand the math. The fact is, we have too little math in economics. There are so many phenomena we'd like to capture, so many frictions and real-world complications we would like to add and understand, but just don't have the tools to do it. Especially in

frameworks, nothing genuinely new can ever happen that has not been prespecified by the researcher. Investors' understanding of the returns process evolves over time, yet a determinate model implies that knowledge growth is fixed by the structure of the researcher's model *ex ante*. When novelty cannot unfold and knowledge and understanding cannot grow, instability, uncertainty, and narrative dynamics cannot be readily investigated.

Traditional macro and finance economists have constructed determinate accounts of change in which the evolution of participants' expectations of future prices and returns is a strict output of the model's structure, that is, its informational variables, functional form, coefficients, decisions-rules, preference rankings, etc. That is, any change in individuals' beliefs or understanding about future investment prospects that the researcher cannot fully capture in their model *ex ante* cannot be allowed save for a stochastic shock to the error term. Because their model is presumed to provide an adequate representation of reality, expectations from traditional approaches are drawn from a single overarching probability distribution. Knightian uncertainty (KU) involving multiple probability distributions that are not quantitatively known *ex ante* is, therefore, typically swept aside.[2] This is one reason why traditional time-invariant accounts of stock market risk premia have performed so poorly when confronted with the data (Mehra and Prescott, 1985).

For example, when researchers include a financial sector in Dynamic Stochastic General Equilibrium (DSGE) models, major

finance, policy discussions go on and on about channels that we have very little clue to model.

*(June 20, 2017)*

The issue is not an insufficient amount of math (just open any top economics or finance journal), but rather that we do not employ the right kind of math, the kind that allows for novelty, unforeseeable change, and true uncertainty in describing the nonmechanical processes driving market outcomes. Perhaps positing less mathematical precision and sharp prediction can allow for more nonroutine change to unfold, change that often characterizes real-world financial market relationships. Chapter 13 will elaborate more on this.

[2] For an expansive discussion on risk and uncertainty in economics and finance, see Friberg (2015) and references therein.

episodes of crisis or institutional change are proxied by random shocks drawn from objective probability states. Reliance on such approaches is one reason why economists' models failed to explain the systematic risk surrounding the global financial crisis (Colander et al., 2009). One would suspect that the COVID-19 pandemic's impacts on the macroeconomy in a DSGE model would be represented in a similar way – only future studies will tell.

The popular DSGE modeling approach generates sharp stochastic predictions of change precluding any and all novel event outcomes whose likelihood of occurrence cannot be foreseen and quantitatively approximated in advance. Thus, the nonroutine instability of associated narrative dynamics does not fit well into the standard DSGE modeling framework. The uniqueness of a nation's institutions, monetary policy, fiscal and regulatory structure, social context, or political trajectory implies little basis for estimating future states based solely on past data that assume major events repeat themselves to some degree. Indeed, the importance of nonrepetitive events and the unforeseeable change and narrative dynamics they engender for the stock market is inadmissible under the frequentist approach. Chapters 4 through 8 show that the vast majority of all events related to stock market outcomes are unscheduled in nature.

One reason an economist might defend modeling structures based upon determinate change in financial market relationships is that research suggests market participants have a strong distaste for ambiguity in choice-decisions. The importance of narratives for stock markets, however, is closely related to the finding of "ambiguity aversion." When investors face ambiguity about the likelihood of possible future outcomes under uncertainty they invoke narratives that assist in their interpretations of novel events' impacts on future returns. Much evidence presented in subsequent chapters shows that when uncertainty can be given informational value, it can offer explanatory power for future earnings growth prospects and returns (Chapter 9).

The classic Ellsberg paradox (Ellsberg, 1961) is that predictions based on preferences, formed either by Bayesian updating or Savage's subjective expected utility, are violated when there is ambiguity about certain information sets.[3] In taking bets, people "prefer the devil they know." Even when payoffs from unknown probabilities clearly dominate – say from a guaranteed win with unknown likelihood – individuals consistently prefer the identified, known quantities – say with low but known likelihood of a win. Unsurprisingly, Ellsberg (1961, p. 643) traces the paradox to scenarios "when *a priori* calculations were impossible; or when the relevant events were in some sense unique." Individuals do not like ambiguity. Therefore, they develop, communicate, and rely on narratives in attempts to reduce the ambiguity of particular situations even though it can never be completely removed.

Allowing for subjective preferences has spawned much research into ambiguity aversion, but, there too, studies have not fully considered the implications of true uncertainty.[4] There is no formal model of uncertainty, but rather models that *allow* for unforeseeable change and KU driving aggregate market outcomes. All observers of financial markets face model ambiguity where the probabilities driving outcomes are simply unknown. Historically novel events, such as new production processes or corporate scandals, which Knight and others argue cannot be reduced to measurable notions of risk, carry information about future stock prices, above that which necessarily translates into net income. Only contingently, or partially, open representations of change within an economist's model of outcomes can grasp the unique impacts of novel events while maintaining empirical relevance.

[3] Both Bayesian updating and subjective preference formation as applied to decision theory assume known probabilities underpinning possible outcomes. Bayesian updating determines a posterior probability governing a hypothesis as a function of a prior probability and independent and conditional likelihoods based on the new information. Subjective preferences involve axiomatic relationships between the individual expected utility of an outcome and the probabilities of each possible event state weighted by corresponding utilities of the individual.

[4] By dropping the completeness of preferences ranking assumption in Savage (1954)'s framework, Bewley (1986) allows for a set of probability distributions under uncertainty but prespecifies those quantitative distributions.

Overarching rules governing what researchers can know about the likelihood of market outcomes before they occur ignore the subtleties and nuance inherent to real-world financial market decision-making. Investors have imprecise beliefs about which firms have the best prospects for future cash flows. Who knows today what a potential bailout for airline firms stymied by plummeting demand due to the COVID-19 pandemic means for the industry five, ten, or thiry years hence? Hertz just declared bankruptcy; what does the Great Lockdown Recession mean for the transportation industry in general moving forward? Firms have imperfect assessments themselves of *ex ante* distributions due to their own management shake-ups, technological innovations, and capital investment projects. Firms' ability to foresee their own return on investment, let alone anticipate future consumer demand, future supply channels, future economic conditions, future regulations, future monetary and fiscal policy, and so on, is murky at best. Chapters 6 through 8 show that there are both systemic macro and firm-level micro novel events whose interdependence is important for understanding the US stock market.

It is no secret that economists draw on other disciplines in the social sciences for research ideas, but rarely do so for subject matter authority.[5] As Northwestern University president Morton Shapiro and professor Gary Morson, authors of *Cents and Sensibility: What Economics Can Learn from the Humanities*, have remarked, "There's a lot we leave on the table. It's a great field, but it could be so much better if we were less insular" (Morson and Schapiro, 2017).[6] To be fair, economists are not conventionally trained to think about the behavior of popular narratives, the inherent instability of financial markets, or the imperfection of knowledge under true uncertainty. The popular representative agent framework tied to the Rational

---

[5] New areas of research have emerged in the fields of neuroeconomics (Camerer et al., 2005) and evolutionary and biological economics (Lo and Zhang, 2018).

[6] For further detail, see https://news.northwestern.edu/stories/2017/july/cents-and-sensibility/.

Expectations Hypothesis implies that the market's expectation (a representative average of all individuals') will follow the expectation implied by the structure of the economist's model. But, as previously discussed, it is likely that narrative dynamics arise when there is unforeseeable change that prompts model ambiguity about which tomorrow will come to fruition and greater diversity of forecasting strategies, two issues rooted in the more anthropological, sociological, and psychological facets of society.

Indeed, narratives are inextricably tied to the zeitgeist and culture of the times. The stories people tell are often the stories other people told them and depend on the perspectives they share about how the world works or ought to work. Popular narratives depend on experiences, training, intuition, and emotional faculty. Such matters, however, cannot be assumed to remain fixed during all periods of time or across various populations at a point in time or even within one individual over time. The United States is a great example of vast regional differences across hard and soft characteristics of life, economics, culture, politics, religion, education, and health. Humans are social creatures and societies change in function and form.

> You need to be able to put yourself in the position of the people you are trying to study. Culture and values will differ, people won't respond the same way to the same measures. Different disciplines don't just deal with different subject matter, they see the world differently; their whole vision of people is different and quite often they don't understand each other.
> *(Morson and Schapiro, 2017)*

Economic recession has likely shaped many individuals' views about the precariousness of economic and financial markets and the tenuous grasp on employment. Living through the COVID-19 crisis has certainly impacted perceptions of how societal structures, business protocols, and healthcare system capabilities will evolve. Experiencing the worst of the pandemic will likely influence the anxiety and mental health of many moving forward. This "living-through-it" effect contributes to instability of beliefs, risk assessments, risk aversion, and decision-making under uncertainty. For example, findings from survey questionnaires dating back to 1989 show that risk assessments of US institutional investors are impacted by news headline narratives, natural disasters, and other major events that they have personally experienced throughout their lifetimes (Goetzmann et al., 2016). Malmendier and Nagel (2011, 2014) find similar connections at the household level whereby recent, lived-through adverse macroeconomic events negatively impact willingness to invest in the stock market.

In addition to Shiller (2017, 2019, 2020), there exist a few studies applying narratology to economics and finance with the aim of understanding major historical events and how they may influence individual beliefs. Akerlof and Snower (2016), for instance, have advanced a central role of narratives in decision-making to better understand the political economy of the Soviet Union in the twentieth century. The authors hone in on the ways in which narrative dynamics necessarily aid decision-making in an indeterminate world by emphasizing that narratives help simplify and communicate complex, interdependent economic and social relationships. The study elucidates the view that narratives at their core provide information and meaning by conveying underlying motives, beliefs, understanding, and hierarchical power positions that characterize the multidimensional dynamics of decision-making environments under ambiguity and uncertainty.

Tuckett (2009) relies on narrative analysis based on interviews of international equity fund managers to investigate their motivations for and beliefs about particular investment decisions and adopted strategies surrounding the 2008 financial crisis. Testimony reveals distorted beliefs about achieving and maintaining exceptional performance held broadly across the sample of "53 highly experienced and senior fund managers working for 16 asset management houses in Boston, Edinburgh, London, New York and Paris" (p. 9). The fund managers all imagined lofty rewards while vocally minimizing the downside risks associated with their speculative strategies. The most interesting finding in Tuckett (2009) involves the stories investors told themselves (and presumably others) as revealed through the interviews. The author states,

The major finding of the interview study is that fund managers gained confidence by developing both general stories to explain their general strategy and specific stories that enabled them to feel both excited and comfortable about each individual decision. These stories involved weaving facts together within an imaginative context that made emotional sense – that felt true. The specific stories managers told me about the individual securities they chose to buy, sell or hold, were thus woven to legitimate the sense that their choices were linked to their general strategy as well as having a reasonable chance of working out. They had to create the emotional conviction both to allow them to tie the initial knot when making the investment and then to allow them to tolerate impatience and doubt so that they could remain attached to their decisions for the length of time necessary to let things work.

*(Tuckett, 2009, p. 14)*

Tuckett suggests narratives are necessary for speculative decisions to make "emotional sense" whereby investors invoke stories to help "legitimate" their own cognitive understanding of the processes driving asset prices in an internally coherent way. This finding fits with the cognitive consistency of narrative formation under uncertainty discussed in Chapter 1 and analyzed empirically in Chapters 7 and 9. From an academic standpoint, investigating the "stories" referenced in Tuckett's quote can be framed under emotional finance (Pixley, 2012) – a fertile strand of literature for investigating narrative dynamics in financial markets. Emotional finance deals with physiological stimuli from investment decisions and trading floor behavior (Abolafia, 1996; Lo and Repin, 2002), trust processes in client-based investment interactions (Pixley, 2004), and the neurological synapses triggered in activities involving money and wealth (Zweig, 2007). Narratological studies of cognitive and physiological feedback during high volatility periods, for example, would fit naturally into this promising literature.[7]

---

[7] Emotional finance differs from behavioral finance in numerous respects. One area of distinction is that mainstream behavioral finance maintains the same standard for so-called rational behavior as first formulated by Muth (1961)'s Rational Expectations Hypothesis tying the evolution of individual expectations to the probabilistic structure of an economist's "true" model. For a survey of behavioral finance see Barberis and Thaler (2003).

Large-scale analysis of popular narratives can be a powerful tool in reflecting a society's culture, history, social values, ethos, and zeitgeist (Michel et al., 2011). Such considerations captivate human attention and influence preferences over today's choices and beliefs about tomorrow. Economists have studied fads and fashions in social dynamics that react to trends in underlying economic data through feedback effects (Shiller, 1984). The rise in Socially Responsible Investing (SRI) and Environmental, Social, and Governance (ESG) investment criteria are just two recent examples of the interaction between social movements and financial markets. To the author's knowledge, there are no extant theoretical models of financial markets that bring narrative analysis to the forefront in describing outcomes.[8] Recent theoretical approaches based on Knightian Uncertainty Economics (KUE) (Frydman et al., 2019) have been advanced that, while they do not explicitly model narrative factors, do allow for their indeterminate impacts on market outcomes under ambiguity and investor uncertainty.[9]

The distinguishing feature of macroeconomic and finance models based on KUE is how they treat instability *ex ante*: Unlike changing relationships in the Markov-switching framework, KUE models do not imply stochastic representations of change that prespecify future distribution states upon which potential outcomes are based. To generate testable predictions, KUE models impose intervallic constraints on parameters relating fundamentals to asset price behavior at a point in time. For instance, the Knightian Uncertainty Hypothesis developed by Frydman et al. (2019) constrains parameters, say earnings' impact on stock prices, to lie *within* some stochasti-

---

[8] Akerlof and Shiller (2009) do not analyze narratives, but, rather, use a narrative mode of analysis to relate aggregate outcomes in macroeconomics and finance to evidence from behavioral studies.

[9] Knightian Uncertainty Economics develops the theoretical framework for allowing unforeseeable change and the KU and model ambiguity it engenders to drive asset price fluctuations. Numerous studies based on imperfect knowledge have shown that the empirical struggles of traditional asset pricing models stem from the inability of probabilistic approaches to capture unforeseeable change (Frydman and Goldberg, 2007, 2011, 2013, 2015).

cally constrained interval bounds. Within these bounds, expectational parameters may be drawn from myriad unknown distributions in open ways allowing for forecasting diversity, ambiguity, unforeseeable change, and therefore narrative dynamics, in stock price relations while still generating empirical relevance. Consequently, narrative dynamics infused by culture, social context, and institutions, given the constraints of the models, are allowed to influence outcomes observed in financial markets in contingently open ways past, present, and future (more on this in Chapter 13).

The next sections discuss some of the evidence from other disciplines on the temporal behavior of narratives, the role of sentiment, and the importance of relational context under uncertainty.

## 3.3  EVIDENCE FROM OTHER DISCIPLINES

The study of narratives, or narratology, has been explored from the perspectives of psychology (Bruner, 1986), philosophy (Carr, 1986), religion (Nelson, 1987), sociology (Polletta et al., 2011), anthropology (Maggio, 2014), history (Michel et al., 2011), law (Brooks, 2006), linguistics and stylistics (Toolan, 1992), just to name a few.[10] Psychology and brain researchers, interested in cognition and emotional stimuli, treat narrative dynamics as impulses on our thoughts and feelings. Sociologists and anthropologists, interested in societal interactions and exchanges that advance and shape popular stories, treat narratives as evolutionarily parallel to human progress. Linguisticians and stylisticians, concerned with the patterns in language conditioned on context, treat narratives as a reflection of the communicative zeitgeist of the era. English fiction writer Neil Gaiman argues stories are akin to living, evolving organisms as part of a symbiotic relationship between narratives and human beings.[11] "Stories grow, sometimes

---

[10] For a comprehensive treatment of theoretical narratology, see Bal (1997). See also Stanzel (1984), Onega and Landa (1996), and Herman (2002).

[11] Maria Popova's "Brainpickings" interview of Neil Gaiman can be found at www.brainpickings.org/2015/06/16/neil-gaiman-how-stories-last/.

they shrink. And they reproduce – they inspire other stories. And, of course, if they do not change, stories die."

### 3.3.1  The Psychological View of Narratology

Although often debated, the origins of narratives are frequently traced either to psychological or anthropological considerations.[12] The onto-genetic, or psychological, view of narratives suggests their formation may be intertwined with cognitive and neurological functions, impulse responses of emotion and thought ingrained in our physical and mental being. Neurologists, for instance, have documented the von Restorff effect that the brain tends to focus on abnormal events, or outliers, which are surprising, odd, or weird. This is consistent with the attention garnered by outlier corporate (mis)behavior and the ensuing impact on share prices. Recent examples might include fake bank accounts created by Wells Fargo in 2016, United Airlines dragging a bloodied sixty-nine-year-old passenger off an overbooked flight in 2017, or the 2018 video interview of Elon Musk apparently consuming marijuana as an SEC lawsuit unfolded claiming the CEO made false statements on Twitter about plans to take Tesla private at $420 per share. These were all somewhat strange events that conjured up a litany of emotions and quickly led to sharp declines in corporate share prices.

Consider the Wells Fargo example. Narratives surrounding the financial services company in late 2016 involved many negative corporate superlatives including fraud, scandal, conspiracy, abuse, and racketeering that were fueled by news of Congressional hearings, DOJ subpoenas, regulatory investigations, and Labor Department violations. Of all the Wells Fargo-specific news reported in *Dow Jones Newswire* feeds during September 2016, the majority involved either the legal and regulatory issues facing the company or the numerous marketing conferences it organized in hopes of combating the bearish narrative with a bullish one. Amazon's termination of its

---

[12] For a deeper discussion on the epistemological origins of narratives, see, for instance, Cobley (2001).

student-loan-based partnership with Wells Fargo in early September was likely motivated by a desire to sidestep the best it could associations with the swarm of negative stories on the horizon. The process driving Wells Fargo stock returns had changed in an unforeseeable way. The multitude and scope of alleged corporate illegalities was such a historical event that some even advanced visceral narratives comparing Wells Fargo's gross misconduct to Enron's irreverent criminal behavior – just ask Elizabeth Warren.

The psychological view argues that narratives cannot be understood without recognizing the role emotions play when novel change exposes incomplete information about the fundamental process. Or, that "affective states influence how actors cope with informational vacuums" (DiMaggio, 2002, p. 80). When novel events cause the environment's parameters to change in unforeseen ways, there is incomplete information and imperfect knowledge about the most appropriate forecasting strategy to employ. Consequently, individuals rely on narratives and the associated emotions to help organize their framework of reasoning. Emotions help fuel narratives and narratives help humans manage emotions.

Positive affective states can increase the amount of confidence in judgments necessary for actionable decision-making under uncertainty. However, if drastic enough, they may also cause individuals to underestimate risk and overestimate the likelihood and payoff from speculation.[13] Shiller (2000) famously describes "irrational exuberance" as a feedback result involving affective cognitive factors, such as overconfidence and euphoria, which render equity prices excessively volatile and often overvalued relative to market fundamentals. Psychologically-driven self-fulfilling expectations about being able to sell stocks at a higher price next period with more-or-less certainty increases demand, and thus prices, today.

---

[13] For a review of psychology literature on this issue see Aspinwall (1998) and references therein.

Mainstream economists tend to focus on explaining the effects of extraneous sentiment, the so-called biases plaguing our decision-making when one is befallen by psychological maladies. By contrast, sociologists and psychologists are more concerned with the social and cognitive dynamics, or heuristics, that lead to the rise and diffusion of internal affective states occurring naturally in our minds and in our social interactions. Our (albeit limited) emotional capacity required for dealing with unanticipated change in decision-making parameters is built-in and continuously at work. Though not all affective states operate in stories, the most captivating ones function alongside our imaginative capabilities. Financial trading platforms for retail investors such as E*TRADE use marketing campaigns that tickle the mind into imagination of a wealthier life – "Don't get mad, get E*TRADE" – because, not only is your brother-in-law richer than you, "There are dogs with better lives than you."

Imaginative cognitive states are the basis for Bruner (1986)'s popular book *Actual Minds, Possible Worlds*, a psychological account of the fantastical side of functional thinking for everyday action. The prominent cognitive psychologist teaches us that thought processes, like affective states, are made up of two modes: paradigmatic argumentation, aka logico-scientific, and imaginative, aka narrative. He states that the "two modes of thought, each provide distinctive ways of ordering experience, of constructing reality. The two (though complementary) are irreducible to one another. Efforts to reduce one mode to the other or to ignore one at the expense of the other inevitably fail to capture the rich diversity of thought" (p. 11). Bruner's psychological approach implies that we as humans are primed and prepped for a propensity to create and sustain narrative while seeking to understand the shifting world around us.

Our minds think rationally through images and symbols that trigger positive or negative feelings, what Damasio (1994) calls "somatic markers." The reality of one's world is shaped and determined within our mind and the mind operates in stories. Individuals become writers of their own interpretation of events.

They construct the narrative. They assess its characteristics within the context of the experiences, feelings, thoughts, and impulses that it produces within them; a mapping into a unique reality of their own. This world is defined by the most influential events – those that conjure up the greatest emotions about palpable issues of justice, humanity, compassion, empathy, tragedy, heroism, violence, life, and death. Such issues shape our economies, our values, our corporate ethos, our politics, our laws, and our capital markets. For some, the narrative surrounding Tesla stock's prospects is inextricably connected to the images of Musk as a liability, a rebel, and an unstable CEO. Other minds cultivate a narrative of rogue, tech-savvy entrepreneur, visionary who does not conform to political correctness, and "it's his company, he can do as he pleases."

The psychology literature is peppered with examples of probability-based prediction being violated for judgments under uncertainty. And, there is good reason to believe that narratives are the key to understanding the role of imagination when elevated degrees of ambiguity in choice decisions are present. Tversky and Kahneman (1983)'s famous "Linda the Bank Teller" case, or simply the "Linda" problem, illustrates the phenomenon that respondents have a propensity to attach a higher probability to the occurrence of conjunction events that exceeds the perceived probability of one of its constituents, a scenario that cannot be true under basic probability theory. When provided a description of a liberal-sounding woman, individuals are asked to assess which is more likely, that she is a bank teller or that she is a bank teller and a feminist activist.[14] The so-called conjunction fallacy occurs when individuals have an easier time imagining the conjunction of two events when representative and availability heuristics are present, two psychological states that

---

[14] Tversky and Kahneman (1983, p. 297) provide the description: "Linda is 31 years old, single, outspoken, and very bright. She majored in philosophy. As a student, she was deeply concerned with issues of discrimination and social justice, and also participated in anti-nuclear demonstrations. Which is more probable? (1) Linda is a bank teller (2) Linda is a bank teller and is active in the feminist movement." Respondents overwhelmingly choose option (2).

readily lend themselves to narrative influence through the stories people tell each other. Moreover, narrative subcomponents such as linguistic framing, meaning extraction, and semantic understanding have all been offered as explanations of the conjunction fallacy (Fiedler, 1988; Hetwig et al., 2008; Politzer and Noveck, 1991).

When a situation is characterized by uncertainty about possible outcomes and their respective likelihoods, imagining a greater probability when multiple events are combined is itself a form of narrative construction – the events coalesce in individuals' minds to tell particular stories that offer a more articulated plot than events held in isolation. Determining whether the stock market is approaching a bull or bear market phase, or is due for a correction, will necessarily combine multiple factors that relate to each other through various narratological threads. As analysis in subsequent chapters shows, forecasting returns for a single firm entails the simultaneous consideration of a wide array of unscheduled events, such as labor strikes, executive resignations, regulatory issues, acquisition denials, and industrial accidents, whose interpreted impacts on expected profits would be difficult to foresee.

As narratives permeate the imaginative sides of our psyches, the complexities of financial market decisions are compounded once we recognize that not only do investment professionals – institutional investors, investment advisors, and broker-dealers alike – create internal realities that live in emotion-infused story, they must simultaneously form expectations of returns based on which narrative lenses they think others think about the world through. There are always higher orders of uncertainty akin to Keynes' beauty contest and narrative diffusion creates an additional source of uncertainty.

Keynes (1936)'s famous chapter 12 describes a newspaper beauty contest based on the pictures of a hundred women's faces. Contestants were asked to pick the six most beautiful faces where the prize is awarded to the contestant whose selections most closely match the preferences of all players as a whole. Contest participants would be best off not by selecting the faces that they deem to be most beautiful themselves, but, rather, by selecting the faces that the other contestants deem most beautiful. If other participants also share this strategy then the expectations of others are of even higher order, that is, what the average opinion expects the average opinion expects the average opinion, and so on, to be.

This process of higher order expectations is analogous to the stock market investor who must not select the corporation that they deem to have the best cash flow prospects to invest in, but rather they must select the corporation they believe others will believe has the best investment prospects. Popular narratives will naturally influence this process as people tell the stories that people tell them and must consider which stories others have heard and told.[15] Chapter 8 supports the view of higher order narrative dynamics by providing evidence that the more common stories connected with macro uncertainty events feed into future subnarratives connected to corporate, or micro, uncertainty events specific to the stock market.

### 3.3.2   The Anthropological View

The second treatment of narratives in the social sciences is based on the phylogenetic, or anthropological, view that argues for a more cultural and evolutionary source of narratives, one intimately connected to the elapsing of time. Narratives coalesce and spread because in isolation we know very little about the feeling of personal interaction; the experiences with others, whether in person or digital, are the building blocks of narratives. Life is a story whose plotline is characterized by connecting links, or building blocks, of cause and effect, not randomized chaos (Bruner, 2004; Carr, 1986). Practical action theory would imply that over time, fragments of stories are picked up through all sorts of interactions, whether personal, business, or social, and a narrative thread emerges or an existing thread is extended (Bourdieu, 1980). Humans spend a tremendous amount of

---

[15] See, for example, Allen et al. (2006) for an application of higher order expectations à la Keynes' beauty contest to a traditional stock-pricing model.

time, perhaps unbeknownst to many of us, crafting particular stories through the daily communicative behaviors of talking, listening, and processing ideas.

Financial market decisions involve a massive amount of communication since profit-seeking is an inherently creative process in which the outcomes and the interactions process toward achieving them are both vast in possibility and unknown to the individual at the beginning of the investment decision (Bandelj, 2009; Whitford, 2002). Narrative-based emotion may emerge throughout the process either clarifying the goals that are desirable (improvisational) or altering the set of desirable goals (situational adaptation). Corporations are very cagey in the ways they manipulate their narrative campaigns through client communication and interaction.

Goldman Sachs, for instance, was likely well aware of the narrative influence its May 27, 2020 release to clients, leaked on social media, would have as it compared Bitcoin's fundamentals, or lack thereof, to the popular Dutch tulip mania of the 1600s, one of the most extreme examples of historical asset-price bubbles. Essentially, Goldman Sachs rejected the digital currency as a viable investment tool, or even as a portfolio-worthy asset at all.[16] Through this interaction with the professional world, the investment bank's statements added a link to the existing narrative that Bitcoin is a purely speculative asset compared to stocks and bonds and that its other most salient feature is as "a conduit for illegal activity." Investment professionals, and retail investors, with experience interacting with Bitcoin in their portfolios will have a different emotional connection to Goldman Sachs' statements. Those with only limited knowledge of cryptocurrencies will have alternative emotions triggered and will likely cultivate an entirely different story thread that may extinguish their willingness to ever hold the digital currency.

---

[16] Supporters of cryptocurrency were quick to point out, among other things, that Goldman Sachs pursued opening a crypto-division and trading desk in 2018.

All of the interactions train us, whether we harness its power or succumb to it, that emotional management is key to the countless decisions humans make throughout their lifetimes (Damasio, 1994). Emotions help humans to think strategically about decisions; they help us to simplify in identifying informational relevance under uncertainty; helping to assess which choices and outcomes should garner the most attention and how they might be ranked. Those with higher degrees of emotional intelligence through increased inter- actions of life's experience will be more successful in preference formation and decision-making (Cherniss et al., 1998).[17]

The arrival of novel information leads to greater uncertainty and a rise in "endogenous animal spirits," the innate "emotional feeling states" present in the conduct of economic activity above what cold calculation would imply (DiMaggio, 2002). Such affective states are open to differing interpretations when parameters attached to future circumstances and outcomes are more uncertain. Consequently, the more interactions one has involving business, and life, decisions, particularly those that are somewhat unique, the better equipped one will be with emotional management skills. The more individuals are exposed to nonrepetitive situations the more apt they become at adapting to shifting environmental parameters. It is, of course, odd that many large financial decisions that provoke the most emotion when forming judgments – think purchasing a home or selecting a retirement plan – are those that are experienced relatively infre- quently.

Novelty, emotion, and change give narratives fuel but, under the anthropological view, so does the passage of time. Narratives are temporal in nature. They are about familiarity and familiarity depends on time. Narratives reflect an elapsed time (short or long) and explain the events' magnitude and collective inertia throughout time. For French philosopher Paul Ricoeur, narratives are the continuous bridge between humans and time (Ricoeur, 1986). Narratives change people,

---

[17] For a review on emotional intelligence see Bar-On and Parker (2000) and references therein.

whether they participate in advancing them or not. Narratives need us to endure, but we, as humans with cognitive needs, also rely on narratives for our own endurance. Stories help us make sense of the world. They help us to imagine the unknown future as much as they help us to get away. They also help us to act. Having the confidence to take speculative positions in the stock market, with such high stakes and even greater competition, sometimes requires stories that invoke "a spirit of confident adventure" (Veblen, 1923).

Sociologists subscribing to the phylogenetic view of narrative dynamics might also argue that "interactive ritual chains" can explain narrative transmission through the lens of social movement theory and collective identity (Collins, 2005). The situations we are consistently drawn to in our day-to-day lives reinforce our emotions and thought processes. For better or worse, narratives are given a more refined shape when interactions increase along the lines of social networks, institutions, politics, and culture that typically carry with them the most sensational emotions of the period (Granovetter, 1985).[18] The high frequency of daily interactions on these mediums become framed within demographic, religious, familial, and political tracks of our lives entrenching an affective belief that current conditions, or in the case of financial markets, stock valuations, relative returns, asset allocation, or corporate ethos may be unjust, inequitable, or immoral (Snow et al., 1986). Narratives shape and spread through digital social movements and interactions by picking up nuanced exchanges that reinforce collective identities and their boundaries, mostly through self-selection (Polletta and Jasper, 2001).

Since everyone participates in the economy, it is highly plausible that narratives are present in the majority of day to day consumer and household decisions. Might personal investment decisions, such as which types of stocks to invest in, which investment plans to adopt, which fund managers to select, or whether to self-direct your

---

[18] For a review on the link between sociological considerations, emotion, and reasoning in economic judgments see, for example, Berezin (2005).

retirement portfolio, be intertwined with the narratives that people tell to each other and to themselves? Or the narratives corporations or the government perpetuate? Might institutional investors and other financial professionals be just as influenced? It is likely that there are narrative threads coursing through one's mind when contemplating these decisions, whether they voice them or not, whether they are making the decisions for a household or for a Fortune 500 company. In order to investigate the underlying narratives woven into the fabric of our daily lives, social scientists in humanities often turn to literature and other unstructured text for creating the environment within which stories reflect what we do, how we think, and why.

### 3.3.3   Linguistics and Narratives

For decades, literary and linguistic scientists have concerned themselves with the multidimensional nature of patterns in language across time, space, and meaning. Stylistician Michael Toolan's seminal work *Language, Text and Context* (Toolan, 1992) illuminated the empirical possibilities of linguistic textual patterns across social science and humanities disciplines when context was taken into account.[19] After the "contextualized" turn, social scientists in applied linguistics were now documenting textual evidence of instability over time – whether historical, institutional, demographic, or political in nature – rather than attributing the changing patterns to nuances of the author's voice. Relationships between linguistic text and context were now understood to fundamentally change over time (Duranti, 1992; De Fina and Georgakopoulou, 2012).

Labov and Waletzky (1967)'s seminal work on narratology emphasized the importance of experiential and anecdotal exchanges in language discourse when exploring the nature of enduring stories. Narrative fragments, or even sub-narratives, which may seem

---

[19] For a collection of essays extending, and in honor of, Toolan (1992) to reflect interdisciplinary updates in digital mediums and empirical advances in textual analysis and corpus stylistics with an emphasis on contextualization, see the 2019 handbook *Rethinking Language, Text and Context* edited by Page, Busee, and Nrgaard.

innocuous at first glance to researchers, are the product of an intricate web of relational complexities; our human minds lacking the capacity to full understand (Cobley, 2001). Assessing the way story fragments evolve into full-fledged narratives, or the way large narratives spill over into smaller subnarratives, within individuals' minds is a challenging task to say the least.

Finance researchers' ability to foresee which narratives may become important for explaining tomorrow's outcomes is contingent on their willingness to focus on the regularities of stories' inner dynamics during different sub-periods of time. "That we do not anticipate [narratives] is usually because we do not attend to the network of relations in which a story resides" (Cobley, 2001, p. 2). In this spirit, the textual analyses conducted in Chapters 5 through 12 rely on the inner classifications of millions of novel corporate events and the changing patterns their interactions with emotion, relevance, and inertia share with stock market instability.

One main takeaway of narratology from disciplines outside economics and finance is that narrative dynamics evolve in unforeseeable ways – that narratives themselves are unstable. The studies cited connect the emergence, behavior, and importance of narratives to considerations that are experiential, cognitive, institutional, cultural, social, generational, and political in nature. They are humanistic. They are higher order in structure. Just as these aspects of life change in unanticipated ways, so too must the narratives that tag along.

## 3.4   DATA SOURCES AND METHODOLOGIES CONSISTENT WITH THE EVIDENCE

The previous section discussed some features of narratology, emotion, and instability under uncertainty as applied by disciplines outside economics and finance. The studies cited suggest that narratives are intimately connected not only to human thought, but to communication and interaction within the societal and institutional zeitgeist. No one knows how such factors will unfold over time. If narrative dynamics are unforeseeable and unstable how can researchers, particularly those studying financial markets, approach their analysis in scientific ways? The answers may lie in mediums that allow for informational content to change in open ways, that is, those sources which allow broad data to speak freely, and those that are able to track emotion, relevance, story inertia, etc.

Survey, interview, and questionnaire findings may elicit the views of investors and financial market professionals to reveal patterns related to narratives. Informational responses based on this format, however, are somewhat predetermined and potentially muddied through response bias, question framing, and even delivery approach, which can alter the interactions between story-lines and narrative analysis (Ryan, 2004). Morson and Schapiro (2017) believe that understanding the time-varying nuances of culture, values, and ethics is best done through literature. This approach allows for diversity of events and views to matter, albeit at the expense of constraining the researcher to accept the author's perspective that can only be observed to a certain degree.

Technological advancements combined with social media offer a vast landscape upon which narrative analysis may be conducted (Page et al., 2019). Narratology now draws upon video blogs and YouTube, Twitter and Facebook feeds, Reddit, and chatroom discussion boards. Social media platforms offer oceans of longitudinal data that, in theory, could offer valuable insights into the narratological threads of various groups over time. Digital media platforms, however, may lack a certain degree of scientific structure or objectivity. This leaves room for analytical advancements toward social and digital media to flesh out the underlying regularities in financial market story threads and linguistic context in meaningful ways.

Alternatively, narrative analysis conducted in the upcoming chapters is based on stock market reports constructed daily by the world's most prominent financial news analytics firms. The big data analysis is based on millions of intra-day financial news reports from the *Dow Jones Newswire*, *The Wall Street Journal*, *Barron's*,

*MarketWatch*, and *Bloomberg News*. Using both algorithmic and expertise scoring techniques, the textual analysis is able to identify unscheduled events and quantify their inertia, relevance, emotion, and historical novelty. Chapter 4 argues that textual analysis of these stock market reports is a sensible approach to reveal the dynamism of narratives associated with unscheduled macro and micro events and the unforeseeable change they engender in relationships driving stock market outcomes day-to-day.

# PART II  News Analytics as a Window into Stock Market Instability

# 4 News Analytics

## Novelty, Narratives, and Nonroutine Change

### 4.1 INTRODUCTION

There now exists a well-developed literature connecting information contained in unstructured financial text to outcomes in the stock market.[1] News analytics have been used to measure stock market returns, volatility, investor sentiment, expected earnings, idiosyncratic and systematic risk, and even uncertainty. Popular sources for extracting informational content and tone from financial text have included *The Wall Street Journal, New York Times, Dow Jones Newswire* feeds, *Thompson Reuters NewsAnalytics, Bloomberg News* market wraps, corporate earnings releases, IPO prospecti, 10-k reports, and finance message boards.[2] Loughran and McDonald (2011, 2016) and Li (2010a) provide excellent reviews of textual studies in accounting and finance, Mitra and Mitra (2011) present *The Handbook of News Analytics in Finance*, while Das (2014) surveys the literature with an emphasis on technical linguistic approaches.

---

[1] It is odd to attach the term "unstructured" to textual data that has already been written to be intelligible, organized, and crafted for coherence and meaning. The content is already in a narrative form that, by definition, is structured to formulate a story with entities, description, plots, and subplots. But the author digresses, since the term "unstructured" in textual circles refers to any information that is not already compartmentalized into an ordered format, such as Gross Domestic Product (GDP) data per period, ready to be imported directly into an Excel spreadsheet, say from the Bureau of Economic Analysis (BEA) website.

[2] The news analytics literature is too large to list exhaustively. For *Bloomberg News* reports see Mangee (2011, 2014, 2017, 2018, 2019) and Frydman et al. (2015). For the *New York Times* see Garcia (2013). For *The Wall Street Journal* see Tetlock (2007), Tetlock et al. (2008), and Mangee (2018). For *Dow Jones Newswire* feeds see Tetlock et al. (2008) and Boudoukh et al. (2013). For *Thomson Reuters News Analytics* see Leinweber and Sisk (2011) and Uhl et al. (2015). For corporate earnings releases, 10-k, or IPO prospecti, see Davis et al. (2006), Demers and Vega (2008), Engelberg (2008), Li (2008, 2010b) and Feldman et al. (2011). For finance message boards see Antweiler and Frank (2005) and Das and Chen (2007).

Why do researchers turn to unstructured financial text to better understand stock market behavior? How can stock market news reports help to reveal novel events and associated narratives while allowing for unforeseeable change and true uncertainty? This chapter discusses the particular features of textual analysis that are attractive to researchers investigating these questions. The benefits of soft information, broader and richer information sets, textual tone, unstructured data, and novel event identification are all discussed within a narratological framework under the Novelty–Narrative Hypothesis (NNH). Focus will be paid to the textual data sources of stock market news reports released by *Dow Jones*, *The Wall Street Journal*, *Barron's*, *MarketWatch*, and *Bloomberg News*.

Word clouds from *Bloomberg News* stock market wrap reports based on a lexicon dictionary of Knightian uncertainty (KU) entities and events for the last twenty-seven years are presented with accompanying histograms of event frequency. The word clouds track the importance of the Mexican peso crisis, the North American Free Trade Agreement (NAFTA), President Clinton's presidency, the Russian debt crisis, the battery of mergers in the late 1990s, the global financial crisis, debt sequestration, and US fiscal cliff, the Tax Cut and Jobs Act of 2017, President Trump's trade war with China, Brexit, and the COVID-19 crisis. The word clouds' illustrative variation in frequency and composition of KU terms reported as impacting the stock market is fascinating and indicative of the novel events and instability likely underpinning investor narratives from year to year. Lastly, the chapter offers a cost/benefit comparison of algorithmic versus manual methodological approaches to textual analysis foreshadowing how both approaches are applied in subsequent empirical chapters.

## 4.2 BENEFITS OF TEXTUAL ANALYSIS UNDER UNCERTAINTY

Researchers employing textual analysis in finance, regardless of information source, are essentially interested in the underlying narratives of the content. Textual analysis presents numerous benefits for dealing with novelty, popular human-interest stories, and their roles in driving stock market instability when market participants (and researchers) face inherent ambiguity and uncertainty about the actual process driving returns. Uncertainty, however, is different than risk. There are many papers utilizing textual analysis of corporate disclosures to assess risk attributes such as liquidity risk (Bodnaruk et al., 2015), litigation risk (Ganguly, 2018), systematic risk (Kravet and Muslu, 2013), and investor risk perceptions (Huang and Li, 2008). The few textual studies that focus on uncertainty, however, primarily use a bag-of-words approach tracking "uncertain" and "weak" words (Friberg and Seiler, 2017; Kim, 2018).

To start, consider the narrative of uncertainty itself, as proxied by the public's interest in search queries for it. Figure 4.1 plots the Google Trends results for searches of "uncertainty" over the past five years. The time-series properties of "uncertainty" searches exhibit strong patterns of cyclical behavior. Peak queries occur at the end of the third quarter (September) with trough queries occurring at the end of second and fourth quarters (June and December,

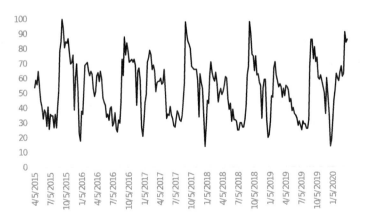

FIGURE 4.1 The figure plots the US Google Trends searches for "uncertainty" during the period April 2015 through March 2020. The vertical axis measures search interest.

respectively). Why are searches for "uncertainty" peaking at the end of each summer? Researchers have found that September is a historically poor-performing month for stock market returns. Those who track financial markets may also recall that "some of the most turbulent recent events have arrived in the late summer, including Augusts of 1989, 1998, 2007, 2011 and 2015."[3] The late-summer events in chronological order are, 1989: the first operating loss in the Federal Deposit Insurance Corporation (FDIC)'s history ($4.2 billion) related to the Savings and Loan Crisis; 1998: the emerging markets financial crisis involving several East Asian nations and Russia's debt default; 2007: the subprime mortgage and credit crisis; 2011: US Government sequestration and fiscal cliff and European sovereign debt crisis; 2015: China's stock market crash and "Black Monday" US stock selloff.

The patterns in search interest could be connected to the Federal Government's fiscal year and budgetary process (Joyce, 2012), the precarious weather pattern of natural disasters during hurricane season (Lobell et al., 2007; McLay et al., 2016), the decrease in the nation's economic activity during the summer months (Bloom, 2014), or even industry-specific inventory management practices (Eroglu and Hofer, 2011). One thing is clear, the only other period that experiences the annual peaks of August/September/October is March 2020 corresponding to the COVID-19 crisis. In fact, 2020 is the only year in which March measures of "uncertainty" interest were greater than those in the preceding August–September months. If the public is searching for it, they are thinking about it, talking about it, and writing about it. Textual analysis is an exceptional candidate for investigating impacts of novelty, narratives, and uncertainty on stock market instability.

First, finance research based on textual analysis allows for iden-tification of broader information about financial market outcomes

---

[3] For a discussion, see www.nytimes.com/2019/08/12/upshot/august-financial-troubles-history.html?smtyp=cur&smid=tw-nytimes.

above what is gleaned strictly from hard data like quarterly earnings or employment figures. So-called soft information includes unconventional, or novel, fundamental factors at both the macro level, such as presidential speeches, Fed chair comments, terrorist attacks and natural disasters, and the micro corporate level, such as product recalls, management shake-ups, legal issues, and merger announcements. Importantly, soft information also reflects the tone surrounding investor interpretations of such events' impacts on future outcomes. As highlighted by the psychological and anthropological views in Chapter 3, narratives naturally involve emotions and nuanced qualitative factors that are inherent to cognition and experience. Soft information from financial text allows for these considerations to matter for financial markets in organic, and open, ways.

With a broader information set involving novel events and emotional interpretations thereof, textual approaches are then able to identify "news" versus "no news." Not all available information is relevant for stock market participants' forecasts of future returns. As referenced earlier, Boudoukh et al. (2013), investigating the informational content of daily *Dow Jones Newswire* feeds, shows that textual analysis is able to "identify relevant news, both by type and by tone. Once news is correctly identified in this manner, there is considerably more evidence of a strong relationship between stock price changes and information." These text-based findings are consistent with Bruner's view that individuals discriminate across information through both imaginative and logico-scientific cognitive states, two modes of thought constantly at work as the mind creates a unique reality of its own in determining which information matters and which does not.

Second, textual analysis has the ability to distinguish the ways relevant factors may matter for investor forecasting strategies. Financial text is essentially a story involving hard and soft information, interpretations and responses, and underlying relationships posited as driving outcomes. News analytics can reveal directional interpretations of events' impacts on expected returns by providing the story links that comprise the larger narratives at play. How? Financial text predetermines neither the set of information that investors deem relevant nor the qualitative ways in which such information may matter.

For instance, textual analysis allows for the same fundamental factor to matter with different directional sign for stock returns during different periods of time – a conservative indication of structural change. The plotline is not predetermined one period to the next. Conducting a textual analysis of *Bloomberg News* wrap reports, Mangee and Goldberg (2020) show that the directional relationship several macro fundamentals share with stock market returns changed in unforeseeable ways during the period 1993 through 2009. For example, factors associated with economic activity were interpreted by market participants as sharing a positive relationship with stock price fluctuations 60 percent of the time they were mentioned while oil prices mattered negatively 54 percent of the time (more on this finding in Section 4.5).

Third, in addition to detecting how broader information matters for stock market outcomes in open ways, textual data detects how an event may matter to investors days or weeks after its occurrence. Tetlock (2011), for instance, uses *Dow Jones* and *Wall Street Journal* reports to show that investors trade more aggressively on stale data – retail investors in the same direction as the news, institutional investors in the opposite direction. Why? One reason is because unforeseeable change implies that prior news' impacts on returns may vary over time and become more easily interpreted as the unfolding of other relevant events and data provide greater interpretive meaning and contextualization. Even cursory observers of stock markets can attest that certain news may not matter much to investors until future information triggers its importance. News impact studies that rely on decomposing contemporaneous returns into so-called abnormal and normal components necessarily miss this dynamic temporal feature of capital market instability.

Consider, for instance, that the weight investors attached to BP's long-term debt position likely changed after the 2010 Deepwater Horizon oil spill. The novel event caused a dramatic shift in the importance of the oil giant's existing net debt position. Previously released data on firm debt was now being viewed through a different interpretative and contextualized lens due to the unfolding of unanticipated events. Stale news still matters because novel events clarify its meaning in nonroutine ways when forecasting future returns under uncertainty. BP stands today as one of the most highly leveraged firms in the industry and is still paying off its financial settlements from the industrial accident.[4]

Once deemed collectively relevant, the bundles of hard data and nonrepetitive events eventually coalesce into investor beliefs and forecasting strategies. How? Soft information connects novelty and routine data releases to one another, and eventually to expected returns, with interwoven story threads, and relational narratives. This interactive process may take time, but combining it with findings that investors are slower to update their beliefs about returns surrounding "qualitative" events compared to hard data (Demers and Vega, 2008) may offer insight into the post-announcement earnings drift documented throughout the event studies literature (e.g. Sadka, 2006). These findings are consistent with the anthropological view that narratives are honed over time through many rounds of interaction with the surrounding environment.

Every time an unscheduled macro or micro event hits the market, another iteration of experience and informational exchange requiring emotional management is added to investors' memory rolodex. Each historical event gives investors another chance to reinterpret previous events' expected impacts on returns in an updated light. Each iteration conditions narrative threads and offers researchers a window into the higher-order dynamics of both

---

[4] For December 31, 2019, the ratio of long-term debt to stockholder's equity for BP, Exxon Mobil, and Chevron was 0.58, 0.13 and 0.16, respectively, implying that BP is over three times more leveraged than its industry peers.

story diffusion and investor expectations as discussed in Chapter 3. Textual approaches account for the overlapping influences of multiple events, and the overlapping investor interpretations they catalyze. For example, using textual data on news searchers from *Bloomberg* terminals and the Google Search Volume Index, Sheng (2019) finds significantly higher stock returns when investor attention to concurrent macroeconomic news events is interacted with firm earnings announcement dates.

Fourth, textual analysis allows for all of the forms of instability in stock market relationships documented in Chapter 2. Novel events triggering large-scale shifts and those associated with smaller, more continuous, forms of structural change are both allowed under textual analysis to drive stock returns in open ways. Uncertainty surrounding how these dynamics unfold is recognized by the indeterminate nature of posited relationships as detected by textual analytics platforms. The central thread across the psychological and anthropological views of narrative dynamics and the work following Toolan on narrative context and meaning, is that stories are fundamentally unstable.

Financial text data uniquely allows for researchers to explore these temporally contingent issues in financial market behavior with more tractability, and a larger toolkit, than conventional data permits. It is not clear whether Knight or Keynes had textual news analytics in mind when discussing the precariousness of business decisions and investor forecasts facing uncertainty, but the benefits from its methodological toolkit are consistent with their insights. Different questions can be asked because the data speaks more freely, because the data captures the time period, the culture, the contextual relations, the emotions, and the stories. Consider the following string of financial news text.

In the early morning of August 23, 2019, China imposed retaliatory tariffs on an additional $75 billion worth of US goods. Within hours of the opening bell on Wall Street, President Trump delivered a series of tweets wherein he attacked the Federal Reserve, saying,

"My only question is, who is our bigger enemy, Jay Powell or Chairman Xi?" and continued that "Our great American companies are hereby ordered to immediately start looking for an alternative to China" (10:59 a.m., August 23, 2019). Chapter 2 suggested that the US–China "trade war" narrative has garnered a high degree of the public's, and Wall Street's, attention recently. The *Dow Jones Industrial Average* (DJIA) plummeted after the president's comments, ending the trading day down 2.4 percent.

Responding to the policy instability of August 23, Neil Irwin, senior economics correspondent for the *New York Times*, sums up the US–China trade war situation, stating, "A single news cycle makes vivid how these different areas of policy can influence one another in unpredictable ways." Irwin quotes Julia Coronado, president of *MacroPolicy Perspectives*, who offers a similar view: "The escalation, the unpredictability, the erratic nature of policy developments is central to what is going on, and these aren't things you can plug into an economic model. Something is breaking. It's very dangerous."[5] These excerpts illustrate the volatile nuance of narratives about domestic and foreign "enemies," executive "orders" for US corporations to take "action," and the undeniable interaction of novel events that "influence one another in unpredictable ways." Textual analysis is one way to illuminate the visceral nature of narrative dynamics and underlying wrinkles enveloping investor beliefs as capital markets digest large gulps of unanticipated information above that gleaned from stand-alone conventional data.

Textual data approaches help circumvent the constraints facing econometricians who must determine which information set to bring to the data and under which functional forms to relate it to market outcomes. Textual data is not limited in such a way and, therefore, allows for nonrepetitive events and associated narratives in the marketplace to impact stock returns in open ways. Consequently,

---

[5] For more details, see www.nytimes.com/2019/08/24/upshot/global-economy-political-chaos-risk.html.

textual news analytics, as a subfield of unstructured financial text, is a strong candidate for assessing the Novelty-Narrative Hypothesis (NNH) central to this book. Typically, financial market studies based on textual analysis of news reports adopt either an algorithmic or manual methodological approach. Both analytical frameworks offer their own distinct benefits and limitations for investigating narrative dynamics from stock market news. These issues are discussed in Section 4.3.

## 4.3   STOCK MARKET NEWS REPORTS AND NARRATIVES

It is well recognized that news plays an important role in driving financial market outcomes. As mentioned above, Mitra and Mitra (2011) provide a handbook on the financial news analytics literature. The present book focuses on stock market reports from the news analytics firms of *Dow Jones* and *Bloomberg L.P.* These are the two primary data sources from which statistical analysis of NNH will be tested under stock market instability and uncertainty. Why are news reports excellent sources for a narratological investigation of the stock market? A big data textual analysis from major financial news outlets makes scientific sense for many reasons.

With readership in the millions, the two major financial news analytics firms have a long-established history of delivering comprehensive, detailed, and reputable analysis of market behavior. *Dow Jones & Company* was established in 1882 while *Bloomberg L.P.* incorporated in 1981. Both *Dow Jones* and *Bloomberg* have a tremendous amount of capital and labor resources for following up-to-the-second news and popular stories that move stock, and other financial, markets day-to-day.[6] With thousands of employees located across the globe, journalists and equity market analysts are able to track the full spectrum of novel events and their high and low frequency impacts on stock prices. To the author's best knowledge, *Dow Jones Newswires*

---

[6] *Bloomberg* and *Dow Jones* employ approximately 20,000 and 8,000 workers, respectively.

and *Bloomberg News* are the predominate news sources for major financial institutions and professional investors.[7]

When domestic and international events occur, at the macro global and corporate level, analysts and journalists from *Dow Jones* and *Bloomberg News* can see the markets react in real time. By plugging into the resources on business data analytics and financial platform technologies, stock market reports from *Dow Jones* and *Bloomberg News* capture a granular assessment of corporate news' impacts on returns, details that are so often overlooked by mass media coverage. Furthermore, these firms have a deep rolodex of hundreds of fund managers, traders, analysts, and other market professionals whose forecast projections and daily testimony are routinely included in stock market reports.[8] In this sense, the reports generated by both news analytics firms serve as a window into the marketplace of events and the views of professionals whose trading decisions actually drive stock price fluctuations.

Both financial news firms generate billions of dollars in revenue annually, in part, by offering a highly sophisticated menu of software, news analytics tools, proprietary market data, and indicators used by virtually every major financial institution in the world and featured in every major business school. Stock market traders routinely access continuous news feeds and proprietary data tools that have been shown to improve risk management and portfolio allocation. *Bloomberg News*, for example, generates its *"Bloomberg Estimates,"* that is, *"B-est,"* forecasts of future firm- and market-level factors, data that will be used in empirical analysis in Chapter 9 and often featured in its stock market wrap reports.

The sheer volume of news threads tracked by both firms is all-encompassing; *Dow Jones Newswire* and *Bloomberg News* feeds

---

[7]  See Fang and Peress (2009) for the relative degree of comprehensive coverage offered by *Dow Jones Newswire* feeds for US equity markets.

[8]  Mangee (2011)'s dataset based on *Bloomberg News'* end-of-the-day stock market wrap reports consistently contained testimony from a revolving cohort of 100–200 fund managers, traders, and other professional players directly connected to stock market behavior.

aggregate and disseminate the news reports produced by other major financial news outlets. For example, *Dow Jones* equity reports include all news stories released by *The Wall Street Journal*, *Barron's*, and *MarketWatch*. Big data news analysis of these feeds, thus, provides a rich dataset for assessing the relevance of stock market novelty and narratives across millions of news articles.

Furthermore, both outlets offer a daily column that serves as a market summary describing the factors driving stock prices during a particular trading day. For *Dow Jones* (*The Wall Street Journal*) and *Bloomberg News*, these reports are titled *Abreast of the Market* and *Market Wrap*, respectively.[9] As the seminal study on textual analysis in finance, Tetlock (2007) is based on the pessimistic tone of daily *Abreast of the Market* content in predicting (temporary) short-run declines in returns in the DJIA. Social psychologists have even used the *Abreast of the Market* columns to show the impact journalist descriptions of market relationships, that is, their narrative and tonal assessments, can have in perpetuating bullish or bearish trends in investor expectations (Andreassen, 1987). The narrative datasets generated in Chapters 5 through 8 include the *Abreast of the Market* columns (though the focus is on the millions of up-to-the-second equity-specific corporate news reports) while Chapter 11 offers a scapegoat analysis of stock price behavior specifically based on the *Bloomberg News* wrap reports.

## 4.4   NEWS-BASED MEASURES OF UNCERTAINTY

Dealing with uncertainty is an important task for all researchers investigating decision-making and outcomes in financial markets. Bloom (2014) finds that economic and financial proxies for uncertainty are time-varying within and across different definitions of "news." Textual data approaches are keenly able to extract macro- and

---

[9] Other studies based on *Abreast of the Market* columns include Tetlock et al. (2008), Mangee (2018), and Frydman et al. (forthcoming). For studies based on *Bloomberg News* market wraps, see, for example, Mangee (2011, 2014, 2017, 2018, 2019), Frydman et al. (2015), and Mangee and Goldberg (2020) .

corporate-level information on uncertainty, beyond that which enters into standard assessments of risk, and connect it to historical events that, as discussed in previous chapters, are important for narratives' impacts on stock market outcomes. In practice, textual news analytics has used classification dictionaries and bag-of-words to measure uncertainty and risk (Friberg and Seiler, 2017; Li, 2006), machine learning to identify uncertainty from major "disaster" events (Manela and Moreira, 2017) and from high frequency "jumps" in stock prices (Baker et al., 2019), and human auditing to reveal economic policy uncertainty (Baker et al., 2016).

The next question for conducting a narratological investigation of stock market news under NNH involves the trade-offs between applying a manual versus algorithmic analytical approach. Advances in text processing tools and expansions in financial news coverage have increased the volume of textual information available and machine learning has improved the interpretability of large-scale analysis. Yet, some researchers argue that "these approaches are (at present) inferior to human auditors" (Baker et al., 2019). Since there are numerous benefits and limitations associated with both manual and algorithmic textual analysis, the subsequent empirical investigations of Chapters 5 through 10 and 12 are based on a sophisticated *hybrid* approach from the *RavenPack* news analytics platform applied to *Dow Jones Newswire* feeds, *Wall Street Journal*, *Barron's*, and *MarketWatch* equity market reports.

The *Bloomberg News* stock market wraps briefly discussed in Section 4.2 are prime candidates to apply an initial screening for potential narratives related to historical, or Knightian uncertainty (KU), events, that is, those that are somewhat nonrepetitive in their occurrences. *Bloomberg* mini-wraps are written throughout the day and released in full form at the end of each trading session detailing the major events driving broad index and firm-level stock prices.[10]

---

[10] See Mangee (2011), Frydman and Goldberg (2011), and Frydman et al. (2015) for more information on the wrap report characteristics.

Appendix B provides a detailed textual analysis project based on a manual rule-based scoring of stock market wrap reports, but which can be applied to any financial text, with accompanying factor classifications involving conventional and KU fundamentals, and psychological and technical trading considerations.

Here, a simple automated bag-of-words search will be implemented as a first analytical pass. It is interesting to document the frequency of KU factors from the *Bloomberg News* wrap reports for each year over the twenty-seven-year sample period January 1993 through March 2020 by generating word clouds from each year's reports (roughly 250 trading days per year). The terms are based on a KU lexicon dictionary available at the author's website.[11] The lexicon dictionary is not perfect: It does not contain every nonroutine event that occurred from 1993 through 2020, nor does it detect context or clarify meaning, but the illustrative dynamics make a compelling case for NNH in shedding light on inherent instability in the US stock market.

The KU lexicon dictionary contains roughly 500 terms corresponding to influential persons, such as US presidents, prominent CEOs, and Fed chairpersons, domestic policy shifts, such as tax cuts, bailouts, and stimulus, and international events, such as Brexit, war, nuclear agreements, and tariffs. However, the KU dictionary also tracks micro corporate events such as bankruptcy, default, credit issues, stock buybacks, and mergers and acquisitions. To be sure, constructing the lexicon dictionary benefits from hindsight: Terms such as "sequestration," "default," "Brexit," and "virus" were included with the *ex post* knowledge that these factors played influential roles in driving financial markets during subperiods of the data sample. It is, however, likely that these novel factors contributed to popular narrative dynamics impacting stock market outcomes.

---

[11] The lexicon dictionary can be downloaded at www.taskstream.com/ts/mangee/ NicholasMangee.

The word cloud program is run in R software using the text mining package "tm." The code to produce a word cloud from any .txt file using the KU lexicon dictionary is provided in Appendix A. Of course, following a simple bag-of-words approach misses the importance of meaning and relational context. The more advanced narratological analysis of Chapters 5 through 10 and 12 is based on the *RavenPack* news analytics hybrid platform that offers the ability to interact macro and micro novel KU events with sentiment, novelty scores, inertia, and relevance to identify periods of high and moderate narrative intensity. Nevertheless, the automated word cloud program applied to *Bloomberg* stock market wraps has the capability of assessing which nonrepetitive events (and unique entities) from the lexicon across the more than 6,000 reports are most often reported as driving fluctuations in stock market prices day-to-day. As is customary in word clouds, the terms with the greatest frequency are relatively larger in size. Word clouds were generated for each year from 1993 through 2020. Due to space constraints, word cloud graphics for even years (and 2017) are included in Figures 4.2 through 4.16.

FIGURE 4.2 The figure plots the *Bloomberg News* word cloud of KU events based on the stock market wrap reports for 1994.

FIGURE 4.3  The figure plots the *Bloomberg News* word cloud of KU
events based on the stock market wrap reports for 1996.

FIGURE 4.4  The figure plots the *Bloomberg News* word cloud of KU
events based on the stock market wrap reports for 1998.

The results from the figures paint a vivid picture of the unique
events, issues, and entities garnering stock market attention that are
most likely to have contributed to underlying narratives. An hour's
time could be easily spent dissecting the historical stories behind each
of the factors in just one year's word cloud. One evident feature of the
output is that the composition of terms and their relative frequency

FIGURE 4.5 The figure plots the *Bloomberg News* word cloud of KU events based on the stock market wrap reports for 2000.

FIGURE 4.6 The figure plots the *Bloomberg News* word cloud of KU events based on the stock market wrap reports for 2002.

exhibit dramatic variation during different sub-periods, suggesting that these terms, people, organizations, policies, or events may be connected to unforeseeable change in the relationships driving US stock market outcomes. The following are just some of the most frequent considerations identified in the wrap reports during different years in the sample.

FIGURE 4.7 The figure plots the *Bloomberg News* word cloud of KU events based on the stock market wrap reports for 2004.

FIGURE 4.8 The figure plots the *Bloomberg News* word cloud of KU events based on the stock market wrap reports for 2006.

In 1994, stock market reports frequently mentioned the Mexican peso crisis and results (presumably) from the NAFTA trade "agreement" signed prior to. Merger narratives entered the scene in 1994 and increased in relative frequency in 1996 and 1998. Narratives about Fed Chairman Greenspan increased in frequency in 1996, likely capturing his famous December 5 assessment of stock market valuations as

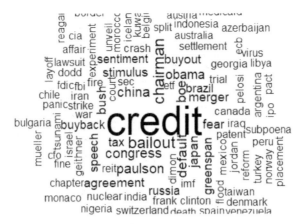

FIGURE 4.9 The figure plots the *Bloomberg News* word cloud of KU events based on the stock market wrap reports for 2008.

FIGURE 4.10 The figure plots the *Bloomberg News* word cloud of KU events based on the stock market wrap reports for 2010.

"irrationally exuberant." His relative importance for the stock market experienced a surge in 2004, likely reflecting his role in continuing to loosen monetary policy – the Fed Funds rate reached a decades-long trough in 2003–2004. Both the Japanese and Russian financial crises narratives are evident in 1998.

The Iraq war narrative is evident in 2002 as is Iran's nuclear arms advancement in 2006. Credit market narratives emerge in 2000

FIGURE 4.11 The figure plots the *Bloomberg News* word cloud of KU events based on the stock market wrap reports for 2012.

FIGURE 4.12 The figure plots the *Bloomberg News* word cloud of KU events based on the stock market wrap reports for 2014.

and take center stage in 2008 aligning with the global financial crisis. This is also the time that bailouts and stimulus narratives become much more prevalent in the stock market. China-related issues become important in 2010. This is also the time when default, stimulus, and fiscal issues in the US increase in frequency. The years 2012 and 2014 show that stimulus narratives played a dominant

FIGURE 4.13 The figure plots the *Bloomberg News* word cloud of KU events based on the stock market wrap reports for 2016.

FIGURE 4.14 The figure plots the *Bloomberg News* word cloud of KU events based on the stock market wrap reports for 2017.

role in the wrap reports relating to the US debt crisis, sequestration, and sovereign downgrade. Brexit narratives were found in the 2016 wrap reports. China narratives play a large role in 2016 through 2020. The word cloud for 2017 is included to show just how much attention President Trump and the Tax Cut and Jobs Act received in the stock market during the year. The heightened frequency of the term "war" in 2018 could relate to trade war narratives with China

FIGURE 4.15 The figure plots the *Bloomberg News* word cloud of KU events based on the stock market wrap reports for 2018.

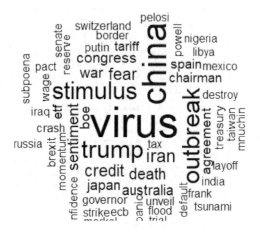

FIGURE 4.16 The figure plots the *Bloomberg News* word cloud of KU events based on the stock market wrap reports for 2020.

and/or a possible military war with North Korea. Unsurprisingly, terms involving President Trump, China, and tariffs were also evident in 2018. Though not reported, the 2019 word cloud looks very similar to that for 2018. The word cloud for 2020 only extends to March 31 so it is no surprise that the most frequently mentioned KU terms involve "virus," "outbreak," "stimulus," and "China" associated with the

COVID-19 global pandemic. It is rather eerie that "death" and "fear" are so often mentioned in the 2020 stock market reports.

Looking across the years' word clouds, terms involving US presidents Clinton, Bush, Obama, and Trump were often reported in the stock market wraps. The term "congress" waxes and wanes in frequency over the sample. The UK and European central banks, the Bank of England (BOE) and the European Central Bank (ECB) respectively, were often mentioned in the wrap reports from 2000 on. Combined with the frequency of terms such as "Greenspan," "chairman," "Paulson," and "Draghi," the BOE and ECB mentions suggest that monetary policy-makers and government/Treasury officials, both domestically and abroad, are often discussed in the context of US stock market analysis.

The KU lexicon dictionary also includes a few considerations related to investor sentiment and market momentum. As previously discussed, and to be analyzed later in the *Dow Jones* textual analysis, psychological factors play an important role in sparking, fueling, and sustaining stock market narratives. Both psychological and technical factors are considered unscheduled and would be part of any expanded measure of financial market uncertainty. The word cloud for 2016 shows a clear presence from "sentiment" and "momentum" in the wrap reports.

Granted they are appealing to the eye and provide a relative gauge of importance within the list of novel events, the word clouds plotted do not explicitly report how frequent the KU lexicon terms appear in the *Bloomberg* wraps. Absolute mentions of terms are masked by the relative size of words in the cloud. However, simple frequency histograms are able to shed light on the absolute count of KU terms per year. Figures 4.17 through 4.19 plot several selected histograms of KU word frequency for the years 1998, 2008, and 2018.

One immediate takeaway from the histogram plots is how frequent the KU terms are mentioned. There are approximately 250 trading days in a given year, and thus approximately 250 wrap reports, and the most reported KU lexicon factors mattered hundreds of times

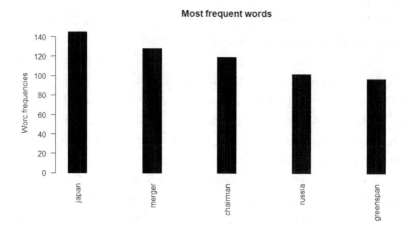

FIGURE 4.17 The figure plots the *Bloomberg News* histogram of KU events based on the stock market wrap reports for 1998.

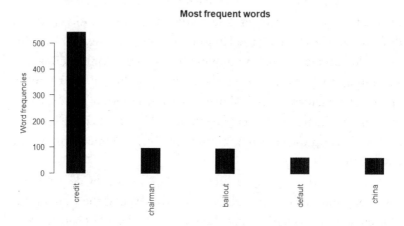

FIGURE 4.18 The figure plots the *Bloomberg News* histogram of KU events based on the stock market wrap reports for 2008.

annually. There were over 500 mentions of "credit"-related issues in 2008 and 250 mentions of "China" and "Trump" in 2018. The histogram for 1998 is included to show how the level of mentions of individual KU terms has increased in recent years. In 1998, the most frequent KU terms were mentioned fewer than 150 times, though the frequency was rather similar for the top five KU terms.

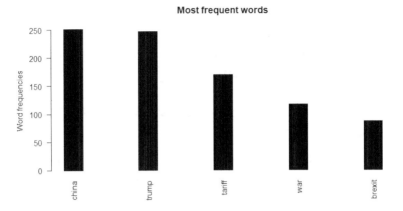

FIGURE 4.19 The figure plots the *Bloomberg News* histogram of KU events based on the stock market wrap reports for 2018.

By contrast, highest-frequency KU terms eclipsed 250 mentions each for numerous years at the end of the sample. There is much evidence presented in Chapters 5 through 8 showing that different measures of KU events deemed important for the US stock market have increased in recent years. While the bar graphs do not reflect the distribution within a given year or the magnitude of impact on stock returns, they do suggest that identified KU factors mattered quite often for stock market outcomes and that their importance displays high variation year-to-year.

The word cloud and histogram analysis is a rudimentary glance at the topics underpinning potential narratives year-to-year in the US stock market. Though the word clouds are a crude depiction of the importance of narrative KU factors, they offer an initial window into the kaleidoscope of investor information sets beyond conventional measures of earnings and interest rates. They also demonstrate the power of algorithmic and automated approaches in analyzing thousands of financial news articles and identifying terms based on a lexicon dictionary of hundreds of entries, all within seconds of time. Overall, the results underscore the view that nonrepetitive events and unique entities impacting the stock market change at times and in ways that would be difficult to fully foresee. Section 4.5 considers the strengths and limitations of manual textual analysis approaches to understanding novelty, narratives, and the instability of stock market relationships under uncertainty.

## 4.5   MANUAL APPROACHES TO NARRATIVE ANALYSIS OF NEWS

Manual approaches to textual analysis of financial market news have been around for decades and offer features in the way of capturing context and detecting meaning that some automated approaches may lack. Li (2010a) offers a survey that includes early studies employing manual approaches to textual analysis of equity market behavior. Niederhoffer (1971) was perhaps the first textual analysis of stock return responses to major events based on a manual scoring of the news. Using *New York Times* reports, the author was able to connect the textual attributes of actual headlines – their event type, "good" versus "bad" classifications, historical novelty, concurrence with other events, and even size of letters – to movements in stock market prices over the following days. The beauty of manual analysis applied to financial news is the benefit of human judgment and capacity for higher orders of thought and reasoning processes in assessing relational context and linguistic meaning. Human readers can often feel the underlying narratives at play, sensing the subtext, interpreting how words and situations are framed in ways that automated techniques are challenged by.

As a case in point, Mangee (2011) and Mangee and Goldberg (2020) manually score *Bloomberg* wraps showing that the directional relationship between macro fundamentals and stock prices depends on the market's expectation. If quarterly firm earnings increase, but by less than expected, stock prices decline even though earnings increased in absolute terms. This method of textual analysis is the basis for the KU project detailed in Appendix B. The approach allows for any factor – whether conventional fundamental, KU, psychological, or technical trading – to matter for stock market price fluctuations while allowing for unforeseeable change at every point in time. Moreover, the author's rule-based manual approach is also able to discern whether the posited directional relationship a single fundamental factor shares with stock prices has changed over time conditioned on the market's expectation – a conservative indication of temporal instability in the processes driving stock prices. As mentioned earlier, factors associated with economic activity and oil prices were interpreted by market participants in time-varying ways with stock price fluctuations over the period 1993–2009.

Figures 4.20 and 4.21 illustrate this variation in the directional relationship between the economy and oil prices, respectively, and stock prices based on the *Bloomberg News* data. For both series, periods are identified where the reported directional relationship crosses the 50 percent threshold and maintains its new directional relation with the stock price.

The economy, for instance, mattered positively more than half the time from 1993:01 to 1994:08, (mostly) negatively from 1994:09 to 2000:10 and positively again from 2000:11 through the end of the

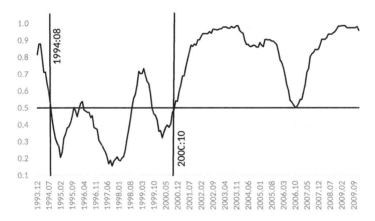

FIGURE 4.20 The figure plots the proportion of days per month that the economy shared a positive sign with stock prices (12-mo MA). Source: Mangee and Goldberg (2020)

FIGURE 4.21 The figure plots the proportion of days per month that oil prices shared a negative sign with stock prices (12-mo MA). Source: Mangee and Goldberg (2020)

sample in 2009:12. Oil prices mattered negatively more than half of the time from 1993:01 to 1994:10, positively from 1994:11 until 2002:12, negatively again from 2003:01 to 2007:06, and positively again throughout the rest of the sample. The combined results from the economy and oil price sign-changes are then plotted against the SP500 Composite Index price in Figure 4.22. The identified points of change, denoted by vertical bars, are strikingly synchronized with major reversals in stock market price swings around late 2000, early 2003, and late 2007.

These results, and those from other news studies showing asymmetric effects across different stages of economic and financial cycles, suggest a bullish/bearish narrative that includes similar investor interpretations of different events' impacts on returns tied to the cycle-specific subperiod.[12] Manual approaches are keenly able to pick up this temporal nuance in tractable ways. However, even though researchers may follow a strict set of rules for scoring financial news reports, their consistency can come at the expense of implicit bias

[12] For this literature (also referenced in Chapter 2), see, for instance, Pearce and Roley (1985), McQueen and Roley (1993), Boyd et al. (2005), and Andersen et al. (2007).

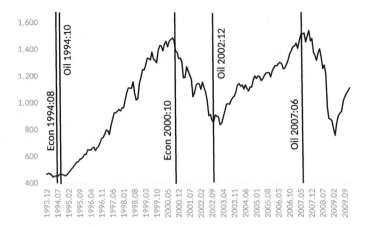

FIGURE 4.22 The figure plots the periods of directional inflection with the 50% mark against the SP500 Index price. Source: Mangee and Goldberg (2020)

or slight subjectivity of how relational content is interpreted. This is one drawback of manual approaches. Baker et al. (2019) address this by employing a team of human readers to "objectify the content" of news reports within context.

However, the most obvious drawback of manual approaches to textual analysis of financial news is the sheer limitation in speed and capacity of data processing compared to algorithmic approaches. Not every researcher has the time, or motivation, to read 4,206 multipage stock market wrap reports while scoring all content for each factor explicitly mentioned as driving daily stock prices (Mangee, 2011). Of course, current technological capabilities are light-years ahead of human processing speed. This is one reason, in particular, why machine learning and other advanced linguistic processing techniques have gained such popularity in the finance literature.

## 4.6 ALGORITHMIC APPROACHES TO NARRATIVE ANALYSIS OF NEWS

The bag-of-words search of *Bloomberg News* wrap reports for KU terms is a rudimentary way of assessing the composition and temporal dynamics of potential narrative topics in the stock market. The analysis, however, did not capture any meaning or relational context underpinning stock price behavior. Can algorithms read like humans? Can they detect the underlying narratives at play? Can they allow for relationships within the text to unfold in nonroutine ways over time? Can they deal with uncertainty? Stylisticians and linguisticians have been grappling with these questions for years. The short answer to all the questions seems to be, "Yes, mostly."

Researchers in textual analysis accept the costs of employing subhuman readers (computers) given the benefits and scope of information processing. However, to be sure, the ultimate objective of computerized information processing of text is to "automate human thinking" (Mitra and Mitra, 2011). To conduct a narratological analysis, an automated textual approach must be able to deal in word phrases, handle double negatives, interpret word meaning, and identify the passage of time outside and inside the report in order to assess the overall context within which narratives live. Moreover, automated approaches must simultaneously incorporate the emotion enveloping the text that gives salience and richer meaning to the embedded relationships. The *RavenPack* news analytics platform used in Chapters 5 through 10 and 12 is able to meet these demands.

When researchers have used lexicon and machine learning platforms in conjunction with event identification analysis, hybrid approaches such as those employing the *Thomson Reuters News Analytics* database (Healy and Lo, 2011; Leinweber and Sisk, 2011; Uhl et al., 2015) and the *Stock Sonar* (Boudoukh et al., 2013; Feldman et al., 2011) appear to capture more accurately the context within which stock market relationships are reported to unfold.[13] This is because most hybrid approaches utilize some combination of both algorithmic and manual techniques in processing text. A comprehensive narratological textual analysis of financial news reports for the

---

[13] See also Baker et al. (2016) and Baker et al. (2019) for hybrid approaches to textual analysis of stock market behavior.

stock market would, therefore, benefit from employing all three areas of lexicon-based, machine learning and manual approaches.[14] Why is this so?

First, a narrative investigation of stock market news requires context and sentiment. As first documented by Loughran and McDonald (2011) (LM), situations of negative connotation in layperson terms may not carry the same connotation within the parlance of finance. Put differently, generic word lists from a psychosocial standpoint can misclassify finance-related terms, such as "crude (oil)" or "vice." LM advanced the field of lexicon-based research by developing a dictionary that categorizes terms based on finance-specific connotation. The authors, along with Mangee (2018), have produced empirical evidence suggesting that the LM dictionary is superior to the Harvard IV-4 General Inquirer psychosocial classification dictionary at explaining stock market outcomes, such as returns, volume, volatility, and unexpected earnings.

Second, a narrative investigation of stock market news reports under uncertainty requires macro and corporate event identification and assessments of associated event novelty. The scope of machine learning capabilities can easily trace whether various market events have been reported to matter in recent news feeds and, if so, how far back in time they were first mentioned. When combined with human reading of training data, machine learning can assess the market circumstances and relational contexts surrounding the events. Finance experts are now commonly involved in informing the priors upon which classifiers, such as Bayesian updating, are based. Manually tagged textual data is then run through the updated classifier generating predictions about future classification probabilities from unstructured text within seconds. Clearly, this process should be informed by the researcher, and by theoretical priors, to establish which relational

---

[14] For techniques and limitations using Bayesian text classification see Kim et al. (2006). For benefits and limitations of both lexicon-based approaches and machine learning in finance see, for instance, Guo et al. (2016).

content is of particular importance for various hypotheses being investigated in the data (Baker et al., 2019).

The subsequent empirical chapters employ *RavenPack*, a sophisticated news analytics platform that encompasses lexicon-based, machine learning, and human expertise techniques, making it an excellent candidate for an assessment of NNH based on stock market news reports. Chapters 5 through 8 will discuss the key features of the *RavenPack* data platform that track and identify historical events, associated novelty, sentiment, inertia, and relevance at both the macro and micro level.

## 4.7 INTRODUCTION TO *RAVENPACK* NEWS ANALYTICS

The *RavenPack* news analytics platform generates proprietary, explanatory, and predictive data from extensive textual analysis of the universe of *Dow Jones Newswire*, *Wall Street Journal*, *MarketWatch*, and *Barron's* news reports. News indicators and other textual information produced by *RavenPack* have been used by financial professionals and academics for evaluating high frequency trading signals, risk-adjusted return models, alpha-capture, asset and risk management and so on.[15] The information tracks thousands of influential people, over 40,000 companies, 3,000 organizations, and 240 traded currencies and commodities all across 135,000 key geographic locations in 200 countries around the world.

The analysis involves *RavenPack*'s "Dow Jones Edition – Equities Events" and "Dow Jones Edition – Global Macro Events" datasets that identify in real time the relevant corporate- and macro-level events, respectively, reported from *Dow Jones Newswire* feeds, the *Wall Street Journal*, *Barron's*, and *MarketWatch*. Though both datasets detect and score events from the news sources, the equities events dataset explicitly identifies events mentioned in connection to a particular corporation's overall prospects and/or its share price

---

[15] For news-based applications of *RavenPack* data to business and investment strategies and other research findings, see *RavenPack* News Analytics 2018 and www.ravenpack.com/research/browse/, respectively.

whereas the global macro events dataset does not make this explicit connection (more on this distinction in subsequent chapters).

The *RavenPack* platform is based on three proprietary methodologies – traditional, expert consensus, and market response – used to assess macro and micro events, associated entities, underlying sentiment, novelty, relevance, event inertia, and whether the expected impacts on stock market outcomes may be viewed as positive or negative. These are important features for investigating narrative dynamics because, as mentioned throughout previous chapters, these considerations help shape the soft information narratives are connected to and revealed through over time.

The algorithms reach far beyond strict bag-of-words dictionary-based approaches to textual analysis. The most important capability of the *RavenPack* data platform for this book and NNH, however, is the classification of market news into "scheduled" versus "unscheduled" events. Because they are unscheduled, this category will proxy for nonrepetitive events and will be used to generate various indices based on macro and corporate KU used in the subsequent empirical investigations. These are the novel events that will be further analyzed based on their narrative components. As examples, GDP and nonfarm payroll data releases are considered scheduled while labor strikes, natural disasters, and corporate legal issues are considered unscheduled.

The traditional component of the *RavenPack* platform uses prescored words, phrases, and definitions with over 12,000 text combinations designed to match stories, events, and sentiment classification from samples of 75,000 financial news articles. Randomly selected stock market news stories are evaluated for consistency against the "Rule Base," and larger story datasets can be compared in an automated fashion. Expert consensus entails training classification algorithms on the results of financial experts manually tagging stories. Experts tag large sets of news articles as having positive, negative, or neutral tone while noting the effects on the stock price of a given company in the hours immediately following an identified event. The manually constructed training sets, 28,000 in total, are used as the basis for automated classification using a proprietary updater such as a Bayes network. The market response component measures the degree of impact a news item has on the market over the following two-hour period. The classifier was trained on several years of news archives (30,000 stories total) based on a set of global companies, their relative volatility, and the time of day in which the story arrived.

Because story sampling is based on a limited data range, there always exists the possibility that new economic terminology, trends, types of reporting, and new market forces may emerge after the sample period. As argued throughout the book, changes in context and relational meaning underpinning narratives unfold over time in unforeseeable ways, as do a nation's institutions, social values, politics, economic structure, corporate ethos, and, therefore, events' perceived impact on expected returns. In order to account for these natural temporal changes, all classifiers are reevaluated by *RavenPack* on a quarterly basis.

In short, *RavenPack*'s news analytics methodologies are exceptional tools for investigating NNH underpinning stock market instability. The platform is keenly able to detect, track, and generate measures of stock market narratives because they identify nonrepetitive events, track their novelty, relevance, sentiment, and inertia while relying on both automated classifiers as well as human expertise scoring. All of this while allowing for the underlying informational and relational content to be open to unforeseeable change and the KU it engenders in driving stock market outcomes.

Chapter 5 introduces the micro KU index based on unscheduled corporate-specific events identified in the *Dow Jones, Wall Street Journal, Barron's,* and *MarketWatch* stock market news reports. Initial statistical analysis of the corporate KU index is conducted focusing on the index's univariate time-series properties. A detailed analysis of the KU event identification and scoring methodology is provided with examples based on Lehman Brothers' historic bankruptcy declaration (the largest in US history) during September 2008.

# 5 The Corporate Knightian Uncertainty Index

## 5.1 INTRODUCTION

The preceding chapters set the stage for the subsequent empirical investigation of novel events and associated narratives as they relate to unforeseeable structural change in the processes driving stock market outcomes under Knightian uncertainty (KU). The present chapter accomplishes several goals. First, a general description of the *Dow Jones* events data classification method is provided. One table classifies different event groups (within which event categories are classified) by broader topic of "Business," "Economy," "Environment," "Politics," and "Society." The relatively high proportion of event categories, whether macro or corporate, classified as unscheduled within each group taxonomy is reported.

Second, description of the corporate KU events dataset commences (macro global events are discussed in Chapter 8). Future chapters show that unscheduled corporate events share a high correlation with their macro event counterparts and even reflect macro-based narrative dynamics (Chapter 8). However, unlike macro events, unscheduled corporate events are found to share economically meaningful correlations with stock market outcomes and analyst forecast dispersion of long-run firm growth prospects (Chapters 7 and 9). Moreover, narrative intensity periods based on corporate KU events (Chapter 6) are shown to approximately align with periods of structural change found in major stock market relationships with fundamentals (Chapter 10). The present chapter motivates the overarching and relative power of corporate novelty in explaining structural change, reflecting KU, and contributing to narrative dynamics in the US stock market.

Third, an example of a *RavenPack* unscheduled corporate event record is provided to illustrate the output source of the data, which involves thirty-two total metrics for each identified event. Of particular interest is the classification of KU events by "novelty," "relevance," "sentiment," and "volume/inertia" scores. These are the output factors that will be interacted to identify narrative intensity periods and generate narrative proxy variables against which stock market outcomes and structural change dynamics will be compared. These metrics are discussed in detail.

Fourth, the baseline KU index and summary statistics are introduced based on unscheduled corporate events with accompanying time-series plots of level-count data and as a proportion of total corporate events. A battery of autoregressive tests is conducted to inform which statistical properties best describe the events' data-generating process. Lastly, the chapter concludes with an examination of historical stock market events that align with major shifts in the index. Hereafter, when referring to the index of unscheduled corporate events, the terms micro event index, corporate event index, and baseline KU index will be used interchangeably.

## 5.2   DATA DESCRIPTION: EVENT CLASSIFICATION AND CORPORATE KU EVENTS

*RavenPack* classifies all identified events (corporate and macro) into categories, categories into groups, and groups into topics.[1] A central feature of *RavenPack*'s news analytics platform for this book is the classification of event categories as scheduled or unscheduled. In total, there are 2,065 event categories over the sample period January 1, 2000 through March 31, 2020, the majority of which (1,395 or 67 percent) are classified as unscheduled and, thus, are considered somewhat nonrepetitive, or novel, in their occurrence. These are the categories into which all identified KU events (corporate and macro)

---

[1]  There are also classifications by type, subtype and property, but, as will be shown, those are less important for the book's main thesis.

are first classified. Appendix D lists all 1,395 unscheduled event categories by group.

Unscheduled corporate events include mergers and acquisitions, patent filings, bankruptcy, regulatory issues, debt restructuring, capital projects, corporate scandals, labor strikes, product recalls, CEO turnover, share issuances, buybacks and splits, industrial accidents, IPOs, executive compensation, legal issues, and many more. Such corporate events are considered unanticipated since they do not follow any calendar schedule of release like quarterly earnings or revenue announcements. Unscheduled macro events (discussed in detail in Chapter 8) may include central bank stimulus measures, presidential actions, terrorist attacks, and natural disasters as compared to scheduled macro events such as releases of GDP or unemployment rate data. Indices based on unscheduled events reflect KU due to the lack of *a priori* information on an objective probability distribution describing the events or possible future outcomes arising from their occurrence.[2] When such events occur the probabilities underpinning stock market outcomes are unknown to all observers. Table 5.1 shows how *RavenPack*'s event taxonomy classifies groups of total events, all of which contain at least one event category (corporate or macro) that is considered unscheduled. The table lists event groups by topic of "Business," "Economy," "Environment," "Politics," and "Society" where the proportion of unscheduled event categories within each group is reported in parentheses.

Within the fifty-one groups listed in Table 5.1, most have a majority proportion of unscheduled versus scheduled event categories and some groups are totally comprised of unscheduled event

---

[2] Merriam-Webster defines the word "unscheduled" as "not appointed, assigned, or designated for a fixed time." The unscheduled events in the analysis have no designated calendar release of information. Whether an individual can anticipate an unscheduled event might be considered a more philosophical question. In financial markets, a person who trades securities based on knowledge about a particular unscheduled event – think product recall, failed pharmaceutical trial, company default or bankruptcy – that is yet to become public information is referred to as engaging in illegal insider trading. However, not all insider trading is illegal. This is discussed in future chapters.

Table 5.1 *Groups within topic of KU events*

| | | | |
|---|---|---|---|
| **Business**[a] | | | |
| acquisition–mergers (0.81) | analyst ratings (1) | assets (0.81) | bankruptcy (1) |
| commodity prices (1) | credit (0.91) | credit ratings (1) | dividends (0.4) |
| earnings (1) | equity actions (0.82) | exploration (1) | indexes (1) |
| industrial accidents (1) | insider trading (1) | investor relations (0.33) | labor issues (1) |
| marketing (0.25) | order imbalances (1) | partnerships (1) | price targets (1) |
| products–services (0.97) | regulatory (0.77) | revenues (0.3) | stock prices (1) |
| technical analysis (1) | | | |
| **Economy** | | | |
| balance of payments (0.43) | business activity (0.5) | consumption (0.38) | credit (0.56) |
| domestic product (0.61) | employment (0.36) | foreign exchange (0.84) | housing (0.44) |
| interest rates (0.33) | production (0.36) | public finance (0.44) | taxes (1) |
| **Environment** | | | |
| natural disasters (1) | pollution (1) | | |
| **Politics** | | | |
| elections (1) | foreign relations (0.6) | government (0.88) | |
| **Society** | | | |
| aid (1) | civil unrest (1) | corp. responsibility (1) | crime (1) |
| health (1) | legal (0.93) | security (1) | transportation (1) |
| war–conflict (0.95) | | | |

[a] *Note:* The table reports the groups that contain at least one KU (unscheduled) event across the universe of *Dow Jones* news outlets during the period January 2000 through March 2020.

categories. Topics of Business, Environment, Politics, and Society all have high proportions of unscheduled event categories listed within groups of products–services, equity actions, assets, acquisitions–mergers, and bankruptcy reporting 97, 82, 81, 81, and 100 percent proportions, respectively. Even groups containing routine firm-level data releases still involve unscheduled event categories. For instance, the earnings group contains 15 percent unscheduled event categories, such as earnings misstatements or revisions, earnings guidance announcements, or earnings revisions from outside entities (much more on the description of KU events within each category to follow).

Unsurprisingly, the Economy topic has the lowest proportion of unscheduled event categories per group reflecting the prevalence of categories involving formal data on key economic indicators released on a calendar frequency from Federal Reserve banks and other government entities such as the Bureau of Economic Analysis (BEA), Bureau of Labor Statistics (BLS), and the Treasury. The Employment group, for instance, contains only 36 percent unscheduled event categories. By contrast, 100 percent of the event categories classified within the Environmental groups natural disasters and pollution are considered unscheduled. Similarly, event categories within groups in the Society topic are virtually all unscheduled. A majority of identified macro events discussed in Chapter 8 are classified under the Economy, Environment, and Politics topics while a majority of corporate events belong to the Business and Society topics. Of course, having a high or low proportion of unscheduled event categories within a group does not necessarily translate to high or low numbers of unscheduled events identified in the news reports. A comprehensive and detailed breakdown of the variation in individual corporate KU event categories is presented in Chapter 7. Taken together, the evidence from Table 5.1 makes a strong preliminary case for the many possible cases of novelty, unforeseeable change, and KU impacting the US stock market.

Once identified, *RavenPack* then connects the events to other proximate entities such as (other) corporations, people and their

professional positions, geographic locations, organizations, currencies, commodities, and other micro and macro entities to inform the
story dynamics and news analytics output. As discussed in Chapter
4, the *RavenPack* platform employs hybrid techniques incorporating
both algorithmic and human expertise approaches to distinguish
across granular levels of news' informational content in assessing
both meaning and context surrounding an underlying corporate or
macro event.

The focus of descriptive and empirical analyses under the
Novelty–Narrative Hypothesis (NNH) will be placed primarily on
unscheduled corporate events. The *Dow Jones Equities* (DJ-EQ)
edition of *RavenPack*'s news analytics platform will be the core data
source that identifies and tracks all events explicitly connected to a
US corporation's investment prospects and/or share price as reported
in *Dow Jones Newswire* feeds, *The Wall Street Journal*, *Barron's*, and
*MarketWatch* for the twenty-year sample period.

Subsequent chapters identify periods of narrative intensity and
generate proxies of narrative variables by interacting the unscheduled
events with their associated event sentiment, novelty, relevance,
and volume/inertia, to give an expanded view of the complexities
surrounding KU in the US stock market. This approach is in contrast to textual studies on stock market uncertainty tracking bag-of-
word terms "explicitly associated with subjective probabilities (e.g.
'believe,' 'perhaps'), ambiguous outcomes (e.g. 'ambiguous,' 'indeterminate') or Donald Rumsfeld's memorable term unknown unknowns
(e.g. 'sudden,' 'unforeseen')" (Friberg and Seiler, 2017, p. 610). For each
event, the *RavenPack* platform is able to hone in on the accuracy,
detail, and description of how the event actually unfolds in relation
to corporate and share price prospects – a critical feature for assessing
the multidimensional nature of narrative dynamics.

For example, the corporate-laden group of acquisitions–mergers
contains fifty-five unique categories of unscheduled events delin-
eated, for instance, by "acquirer," "acquiree," indicating whether the
M&A event was a "bid," or whether it was "delayed," "blocked,"

"completed," "failed," "rejected by Government authority," or simply reflected "interest" on behalf of a firm. Moreover, the classification indicates whether there was "regulatory opposition," "approval," or "scrutiny" surrounding the merger or acquisition or whether it was based simply on "rumors." Delineating categories of novel events with this much qualitative detail, or soft information, offers a rich and nuanced view into the major stories and associated subtext traveling through the stock market day-to-day.

## 5.3 EVENT RECORD EXAMPLE

Chapters 1, 2, and 3 argued from various perspectives that stock market narratives under temporal instability and uncertainty naturally involve the interaction of nonrepetitive events with investor emotion in ways that would be difficult to foresee in advance. The following news story and subsequent event record provide information that allows for narratological assessment through this lens. The event is the famous declaration of Chapter 11 bankruptcy filing by Lehman Brothers Holdings Inc. that became public information on the morning of September 15, 2008 and all but set US financial markets ablaze as the global financial crisis hit home. Here is the full article tracked by *RavenPack* and the associated event record of output in Table 5.2 from the DJ-EQ data.

---

**Lehman Brothers To File For Chapter 11 Bankruptcy**
2008–09-15 01:00:00 ET

**DOW JONES NEWSWIRES**
**Lehman Brothers Holdings Inc. (LEH)** Monday said it intends to file a petition under Chapter 11 for bankruptcy protection. In a statement, **Lehman** said that none of its broker-dealer subsidiaries or other subsidiaries would be included in the bankruptcy filing and will continue to operate. The ailing investment **bank** is continuing efforts to sell its broker-dealer subsidiaries, as previously announced, and is in advanced discussions with potential buyers for its investment management division. "**Neuberger Berman**, LLC and **Lehman Brothers**

Asset Management will continue to conduct business as usual and will not be subject to the bankruptcy case of its parent, and its portfolio management research and operating functions remain intact," it said. **Lehman**, a 158-year-old firm that started as an **Alabama** cotton brokerage, failed to find a buyer after the **U.S. government** refused to provide a financial backstop to potential buyers.

(END) **Dow Jones Newswires**
September 15, 2008 01:00 ET (05:00 GMT)

---

There are several features of output from Table 5.2 beneficial for the subsequent analysis and necessary for assessing NNH advanced throughout this book.[3] First, it is important to be able to identify the categorical nature of unscheduled events that unfold daily in the stock market. The "Category" row is a unique tag to label, identify, and recognize a particular entity-specific news event. In the case of Table 5.2, the category of the corporate KU event is "bankruptcy." The event taxonomy delineates identified events from largest classification to smallest following: "topic," "group," "type," "sub-type," "property," and "category." This event's particular taxonomy takes the form: business (topic) → bankruptcy (group) → bankruptcy (category) → Lehman Brothers Holdings Inc. (entity).

Second, narratives reflect information that investors, other market participants, and the public at large consider to be relevant today for thinking about future returns. Narratives are not fueled and transmitted by mentioning them merely in passing. They reflect topics, issues, and situations that matter to people, governments, and corporations for extended periods of time. There are two entities mentioned in the news story: Lehman Brothers Holdings Inc. and the Government of the United States. A nation's stock market can spend months weighing the impacts from historically unique events that unfold in unforeseeable ways over time. Moreover, as discussed in

---

[3] The definitions of each output field are provided in Appendix C.

Table 5.2 *Example event record output*

| Headline: "Lehman Brothers to File for Chapter 11 Bankruptcy" | |
| --- | --- |
| Timestamp_UTC[a] | 2008–09-15 5:00:00 AM |
| Entity_Name | Lehman Borthers Holdings Inc. |
| Entity_Type | COMP (Company) |
| RP_Entity_ID | A78640 |
| Position_Name | N/A |
| RP_Position_ID | N/A |
| Country_Code | U.S. |
| Relevance | 100 |
| Topic | business |
| Group | bankruptcy |
| Type | bankruptcy |
| Sub_type | N/A |
| Property | N/A |
| Evaluation_Method | N/A |
| Maturity | N/A |
| Category | bankruptcy |
| Event sentiment (ESS) | 7 |
| Aggregate event sentiment (AES) | 65 |
| Aggregate event volume (AEV) | 346 |
| Similarity key | 79D48EF9BFD7D193823A3A1EA0DCC18C |
| Novelty (ENS) | 24 |
| Novelty similarity gap | 0.01181 |
| Novelty ID (ENS_KEY) | 4C446D3731E254471F1A84C0DAFFDA42 |
| Novelty elapsed time | 21960000 |
| Global novelty (G_ENS) | 8 |
| Global novelty similarity gap | 0.00694 |
| Global novelty ID (G_ENS_KEY) | 4C446D3731E254471F1A84C0DAFFDA42 |
| Global novelty elapsed time | 21960000 |
| News_Type | Full Article |
| Source | B5569E (Dow Jones Newsfeed) |
| Product_Key | DJ-EQ |
| RP_Story_ID | 9316A53C6A45CDD5CC5BD84C647B719B |

[a] *Note:* The table displays the output fields from an identified unscheduled event by *RavenPack*. A detailed description of each field is provided in Appendix C.

Section 4.2, advanced textual analytics is both able to distinguish when multiple events overlap in their relevance for future returns and to discern how an event's impact may change over time as other information arrives and circumstances evolve. To deal with this,

*RavenPack*'s event record provides a "relevance" score indicating how important an identified event is for the larger news story thread (i.e. the rest of the news article), even if the same event is mentioned in multiple news reports during different periods of time.

Each identified event from a news story receives its own relevance score. The metric ranges from 0 to 100 where values greater than 75 are considered "significantly relevant." Events mentioned merely in passing in the news, or simply mentioned at the end of the report, may be considered irrelevant and receive a lower score (usually 20 or below). Relevance score is also hierarchical in text: the sooner the event is mentioned in the story the more prominent it is and the higher the score it will receive. Thus, it is unsurprising that the corporate KU event "bankruptcy" receives a relevance score of 100 for the example stock market story.

*RavenPack*'s relevance score uses an automated classifier connecting the entities mentioned within the story (Lehman Brothers Holdings Inc. and the Government of the United States), and their posited contextualized roles, to the identified event. For instance, a news story headlined "Amazon Finalizes Acquisition of Whole Foods" would identify the entity Amazon as the "acquirer" while Whole Foods receives the category tag "acquiree." If a story reads, "IBM Files Lawsuit against Zillow over Patented Home Estimate Technology," it would be categorized as a patent-infringement: IBM receives the tag "patent-infringement-plaintiff" while the entity Zillow is assigned "patent-infringement-defendant."

*RavenPack*'s classifier algorithms contain information about an entity's relationship to an event, including "short-names, long names, abbreviations, securities identifiers, subsidiary information, and up-to-date corporate actions data," which improves upon the determination of entity roles, event meaning, and situational and relational context. For example, *RavenPack* "maps countries to membership organizations such as the European Union, the Eurozone, G20, OPEC, OECD, and NATO or to trading blocs such as NAFTA, MERCOSUR, or The League of Arab States through relationships which are point-in-time sensitive keeping track of when entities join (or leave) any given membership."

Third, the event record produces a sentiment score for each identified event. Novel events that have more extreme sentiment – optimism or pessimism – associated with them may have a greater propensity for catalyzing popular narratives and may lead to more powerful narratives, both in magnitude and duration. The Event Sentiment Score (ESS) ranges from 0 to 100 where values above or below 50 indicate positive or negative sentiment, respectively, and a value of 50 is considered neutral. Event Sentiment Scores are enhanced by volumes of survey data from "industry experts with extensive backgrounds in finance and economics" to match stories based on similar entity-event composition to assess whether events may be viewed as having a positive or negative effect on corporate prospects and shorter-run stock price fluctuations. The survey data is then interacted with the textual content surrounding the news event.

To this end, Event Sentiment Scores are based on automated classifiers that detect relationships and meaning from the story. For instance, the *RavenPack* algorithms attach sentiment to events that reflect interpretations of "actual figures, estimates, ratings, revisions, magnitudes, and recommendations disclosed in news stories." That is, ESS is capable of detecting the differences between actual and expected values of dividends, earnings, revenues, or macroeconomic data releases. What is more, the ESS, whether positive or negative, is amplified by the percentage by which actual data figures exceed or fall short of consensus estimates. That is, a quarterly earnings report that beat market estimates by 40 percent per share would increase the ESS by a greater amount than one which beat estimates by 5 percent per share, ceteris paribus. Although events that have market and analyst "expectations" are likely classified as scheduled, they will often interact with and impact narratives involving unscheduled corporate and macro events alike whose narratives, in turn, interact with each other (Chapter 8).

Moreover, there are numerous automated transformations of story data, which allow for event sentiment to be compared across similar data categories. For example, the algorithm standardizes the three credit ratings scales across Moody's, S&P, and Fitch to allow for intensity impact comparisons. Similarly, the sentiment platform is able to account for the various analyst ratings scales employed by over 150 different brokerages, investment banks, and credit ratings agencies. A downgrade from "strong buy" to "strong sell" is a larger downgrade and will consequently have a greater negative effect on sentiment than a more moderate downgrade from, say, "hold" to "weak sell." Subsequent chapters will reveal how important large revisions in credit and analyst ratings and price upgrades and downgrades are for corporate novelty and stock market instability.

The ESS score also reflects the intensity of emotional language surrounding the event within the story text. The emotional factor scale has five rankings, or magnitudes, (i) low, (ii) moderate, (iii) substantial, (iv) severe, and (v) critical. Whether positive or negative, these classifications provide a sense of the event's potency impacting investor emotion. For example, "moderate" may include "nothing much" or "fairly flat." "Critical" may include "devastation," "super colossal," or "most damaging." In fact, the algorithm is nuanced enough to interpret the Richter scale of an earthquake or the number of casualties in a terrorist attack. The ESS for the Lehman Brothers Holdings Inc. bankruptcy news story is 7, indicating that the event is associated with extremely pessimistic sentiment.

Fourth, the degree of event novelty is reported in the record output. Novelty is a critical component of narrative dynamics and the temporal instability unscheduled events engender in stock market relationships. *RavenPack*'s automated classifiers produce an Event Novelty Score (ENS) based on the news sources covered, ranging from 0 to 100 (higher values indicate more novel), which captures how "new" the event is for an identified entity within the previous twenty-four-hour window of all preceding news output. A global score detects similar events from all of the international news outlets *RavenPack* covers. Once the window has elapsed, a new sequence would begin and the event, if reported again in connection to the same entity, would receive a novelty score of 100. If the algorithm can match the same event with the same entities across multiple news stories within the time window the events would be considered similar and lead to a lower novelty score, following a decay function, for the more recent event recording. However, a chain of similar event entities can span a time frame greater than twenty-four hours as long as no two consecutive event-entity matches occur more than twenty-four hours apart.

If two similar event-entity matches occur, but over a period of time greater than twenty-four hours, the novelty similarity gap will inform us about the time since last reporting. If the similarity gap score is lower, the similar events have occurred in close proximity – a value of 0 implies the exact same timestamp. A value of 100 indicates one of the similar events has occurred at least a hundred days or more in the past. The ENS for the Lehman Brothers bankruptcy story and event record of Table 5.2 is 24, which indicates that the public news event of Lehman Brothers' bankruptcy declaration on September 15, 2008 at 1:00 A.M. ET (or 5:00 Coordinated Universal Time – UTC) is not scored by *RavenPack* as being particularly novel.[4] This is not an error. The chapter has thus far presented the "Full Article" of Lehman's Chapter 11 bankruptcy declaration; many headline news events about Lehman's pending bankruptcy on September 14, 2008 precipitated the full article on the 15th. Put differently, Lehman's bankruptcy event is a novel event, in a descriptive or categorical sense, since it is unscheduled, but the degree of event novelty is given a temporal score based on its earliest reporting across the *Dow Jones* news outlets as captured by ENS. The novelty score will help track the timing and degree of information leakage likely connected to associated narrative dynamics over time.

The *RavenPack* news types span (i) "Hot News Flash" where the entity event was identified in only a headline with the phrase

---

[4] Greenwich Mean Time (GMT) is a synonym for Coordinated Universal Time (UTC).

"Breaking News," (ii) "News-Flash" where the entity event was identified in only a headline without the phrase "Breaking News," (iii) "Full Article" where the entity event was identified in a full-length news article, (iv) "Press Release" where the entity event was identified from a press release by another entity such as a corporation or organization and disseminated to the public through one of the news outlets tracked by the DJ-EQ edition, or (v) the entity event was identified in the "Tabular Release" involving data-intensive news presented in table form. All five mediums may contain more than one identified event. More than one outlet or news medium can contain the same entity associated with the same event just at different time periods (though the actual timestamps will likely be relatively close). For example, consider the following "Hot News Flash" involving Lehman Brothers Holdings Inc. (and Barclays) from September 14, 2008 at 1:17 P.M. ET:

---

**BREAKING NEWS**

**WSJ: Barclays Is Walking From Lehman Deal - Sources**
2008–09-14 13:17:00 ET

(MORE TO FOLLOW)**DOW JONES NEWSWIRES**
September 14, 2008 13:17 ET (17:17 GMT)

---

The nullification of the Barclays–Lehman Brothers contract follows the event taxonomy of: business (topic) → products-services (group) → business-contract (category) → Barclays PLC contract (entity); Lehman Brothers Holdings Inc. contract (entity).

Though seemingly simple, this headline news flash offers a tremendous amount of information through *RavenPack*'s analytical platform that helps to provide an assessment of identified events' underlying novelty and narrative dynamics. The "Hot News Flash" communicated that Barclays is no longer interested in the rescue takeover of Lehman Brothers' deteriorating balance sheet. If you followed these corporations' activities and the proposed rescue agreement, you would have gleaned from the headline that it was likely the failure of the US Government to back the $300 billion of exposed assets that nullified the deal, prompting Barclays to walk. Since the two entities are involved in the same identified event, namely a nullified business contract, the ENS key for the two separate event records (one for Barclays PLC and one for Lehman Brothers Holdings Inc.) is the same. The ENS similarity gap for both records is 100 since news of this event broke with the "Hot News Flash" headline (i.e. that "the most recent similar entity event occurred more than 100 or more days in the past"). The *RavenPack* story ID will also be equal across records.

However, the Aggregate Event Sentiment (AES) and the Aggregate Event Volume (AEV) for the two records are different since AES "represents the ratio of positive events reported on an entity compared to the total count of events measured over a rolling 91-day window from a particular *RavenPack* package." The AEV "represents the count of events for an entity measured over a rolling 91-day window in a particular *RavenPack* package." Since Barclays PLC and Lehman Brothers Holdings Inc. had different identified news events and corresponding sentiment over the previous three months, the two entities would have different AES and AEV scores for the two records involving the same event captioned, "Barclays is Walking from Lehman Deal."

For the Lehman bankruptcy event, it is now understood why the ENS from Table 5.2 is not 100. Consider the news event occurring on September 14, 2008 at 6:54 P.M. ET in which Lehman Brothers was first identified with the event category tag "bankruptcy" with corresponding event record of output in Table 5.3.

---

**BREAKING NEWS**

**Lehman Brothers To File For Bankruptcy Protection - Sources**

2008–09-14 18:54:00 ET

(MORE TO FOLLOW)**DOW JONES NEWSWIRES**

September 14, 2008 18:54 ET (22:54 GMT)

---

Table 5.3 *First news event identifying Lehman Brothers' bankruptcy*

Headline: "Lehman Brothers to File for Bankruptcy Protection – Sources"

| | |
|---|---|
| Timestamp_UTC[a] | 2008–09-14 10:54:00 PM |
| Entity_Name | Lehman Brothers Holdings Inc. |
| Entity_Type | COMP (Company) |
| RP_Entity_ID | A78640 |
| Position_Name | N/A |
| RP_Position_ID | N/A |
| Country_Code | U.S. |
| Relevance | 100 |
| Topic | business |
| Group | bankruptcy |
| Type | bankruptcy |
| Sub_Type | N/A |
| Property | N/A |
| Evaluation_Method | N/A |
| Maturity | N/A |
| Category | bankruptcy |
| Event sentiment (ESS) | 7 |
| Aggregate event sentiment (AES) | 66 |
| Aggregate event volume (AEV) | 341 |
| Similarity key | 79D48EF9BFD7D193823A3A1EA0DCC18C |
| Novelty (ENS) | 100 |
| Novelty similarity gap | 100 |
| Novelty ID (ENS_KEY) | 4C446D3731E254471F1A84C0DAFFDA42 |
| Novelty elapsed time | 0 |
| Global novelty | 100 |
| Global novelty similarity gap | 100 |
| Global novelty ID (G_ENS_KEY) | 4C446D3731E254471F1A84C0DAFFDA42 |
| Global novelty elapsed time | 0 |
| News_Type | Hot News Flash |
| Source | AA6E89 (Wall Street Journal) |
| Product_Key | DJ-EQ |
| RP_Story_ID | 4C446D3731E254471F1A84C0DAFFDA42 |

[a] *Note:* The table displays the output fields from the first *RavenPack* record of Lehman Brothers' bankruptcy declaration.

Table 5.3 shows that the "Hot News Flash" concerning Lehman Brothers' bankruptcy declaration on September 14, 2008 at 6:54 P.M. ET, which precipitated the "Full Article" about the bankruptcy on September 15, 2008 at 1:00 A.M. ET, generates different output for the event record. For instance, the ENS score (and global ENS score) is 100, as opposed to 24 in the full article, indicating that it is indeed the first story reporting a categorized event (bankruptcy) about one or more entities (Lehman Brothers). In fact, there were ten news releases between 6:39 P.M. on September 14, 2008 and 1:00 A.M. on September 15 that involved the entity Lehman Brothers Holdings Inc. Second, the ENS (and global ENS) similarity gap is 100, implying that the most recent similar event occurred a hundred or more days in the past. This makes perfect sense since this is the first of any news in the DJ-EQ package to report the identified event category of "bankruptcy" in association with the identified entity "Lehman Brothers Holdings Inc."

Taken together, these four metric areas – category, relevance, sentiment, and novelty – associated with an identified unscheduled event will help to inform NNH applied to stock market instability under KU. In many ways, narrative structure can be decomposed into these four areas (Toolan, 1988). The next chapter uses these metric areas and more to proxy for periods where the intensity of narratives is considered the greatest. By taking above-average relevance, the highest and lowest sentiment, and the highest novelty, Chapter 6 identifies the most conservative periods of high narrative intensity against which the structural change tests of stock market relationships can be compared in Chapter 10. Next, the baseline corporate KU Index is presented.

## 5.4   BASELINE CORPORATE KU INDEX

For a given month, across the DJ-EQ news outlets, there were an average of 64,926 total identified corporate-related events (scheduled and unscheduled) over the sample (or 2,164 events per day). The maximum and minimum number of total events was 110,091 and 9,709, respectively, per month with a standard deviation of 21,390.83. Again, because the core hypothesis surrounds novelty, narratives, and stock market instability under KU, the statistical analysis will focus on unscheduled events identified across the *Dow Jones* financial news outlets. In total, the *RavenPack* platform identified 11,156,359 unscheduled events explicitly reported as important for corporate prospects and associated share prices over the twenty-year period January 2000 through March 2020. The typical month contained roughly 45,911 unscheduled corporate events. The summary statistics for the monthly count of unscheduled corporate events where,

$$KU = \#unscheduled\ corporate\ events \qquad (5.1)$$

are reported in Table 5.4.

The distribution of the corporate KU Index is statistically nonnormal and displays fat and asymmetric tails as evidenced by a significant Jarque–Bera value rejecting the null hypothesis of normality with a *p*-value = 0.019 and skewness and kurtosis values different from zero and three, respectively. One interpretation of these findings is that the frequency of KU events does not approach any expected value as time elapses – there are many outlier months in which KU events are highly irregular in timing and magnitude away from the (time-varying) mean value both from above and below. This is unsurprising since KU events are, by definition, unscheduled events associated with novelty of occurrence. The nature of KU events implies they are nonrepetitive and, as such, are precluded from following the frequentist approach of historically and identically drawn observations fluctuating in distribution around an objective

Table 5.4 *KU Index summary statistics*

| Mean[a] | Median | Min/Max | $\sigma$ | Skew. | Kurt. | J.B. |
|---|---|---|---|---|---|---|
| 45,910.94 | 47,158 | 5,919/79,897 | 16,644.81 | −0.313 | 2.376 | 0.019 |

[a] *Note:* The table reports summary statistics for the corporate KU Index over the sample period January 2000 through March 2020. Data is monthly. $\sigma$ denotes standard deviation. Skew. and Kurt. denote skewness and kurtosis, respectively, while J.B. denotes the *p*-value for the Jarque–Bera test against the null hypothesis of a statistically normal distribution.

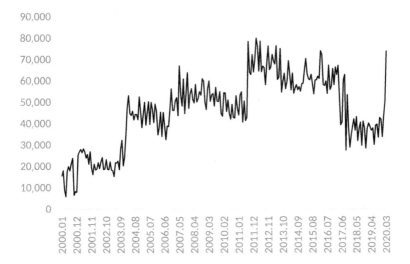

FIGURE 5.1 The figure plots the monthly count of corporate KU events reported as relevant for driving US stock market behavior across the *Dow Jones* financial news outlets over the period January 2000 through March 2020.

expected value toward which values converge over time. Figure 5.1 plots the corporate KU Index over the sample period.

There are numerous results from the graph worth noting. First, there is a clear outlier spike in corporate KU events in 2020 due to the COVID-19 crisis – yet more evidence of the increase in novelty and KU in corporate America and in financial markets due to the onset of the global pandemic. Second, the index of unscheduled events appears nonstationary. For example, the index takes on values approximately near 20,000 events per month for the first four-year period 2000 through 2003 while increasing to 60,000 events per month from 2012 through 2016 only to hover around 40,000 events per month for the last three-year period 2017 through 2020.

Third, and related to the other graphical observations, the corporate KU Index has trended upward over the twenty-year sample period. A linear trend-line through the index generates the equation $y = 133.66x + 29,604$. There are several interpretations and conjectures about this finding. It may be the case that the information set of fundamentals that investors deem the most important for forecasting future returns is growing in composition to include more novel events over the years (Frydman and Goldberg, 2011; Mangee, 2011). Maybe more KU events have occurred over recent years or that similarly grouped KU events could have mattered more themselves. Many of the Google Trends graphics of nonroutine events presented in previous chapters have suggested an increase in KU events in recent years (think "trade war," "data breach," "recession," and "virus"). Chapter 7 will shed more light on these conjectures.

The fourth, and perhaps most striking, regularity from Figure 5.1 is the display of mean-shifts in the level of the KU Index. The approximate number of monthly unscheduled corporate events oscillates within a relatively narrow range for, say, three to five years, only to undergo a sharp spike immediately entering a new range of values for another three to five years. For example, the number of corporate KU events per month deemed relevant by stock market participants hovered around 50,000 from 2007 through 2011. From July to August of 2011, the monthly value skyrocketed from 43,000 to 78,000 relevant events where it then hovered around 65,000 for five years. Similarly sized shifts occurred in 2003/2004 and 2017/2018. It is interesting that virtually all of the spikes leading to a new range of values reflect increases in corporate uncertainty; the one decrease occurs at 2017/2018.

Univariate statistics also suggest that the corporate KU Index has a time-varying mean over the sample period. A traditional Augmented Dickey–Fuller (ADF) test for the null hypothesis that the KU Index contains a unit root (i.e. is nonstationarty) generates a $t$-statistic ($p$-value) of $-2.256$ $(0.187)$ failing to reject the null.[5] However, the ADF unit root-with-break test rejects the null hypothesis generating a $p$-value $= 0.025$ with a break identified at 2000:12.[6] This suggests

---

[5] A constant term was included in the ADF test specification with two lags included based on Schwarz information criterion (SIC).

[6] The break specification of the test allows for a break in the intercept term.

that there are structural breaks in the autoregressive process of the KU Index, but also that the series may be mean-reverting within subintervals between breakpoints. The 2020 COVID-19-induced spike in corporate KU could signal another regime of micro-level uncertainty, but more data must be analyzed. Might variation in the corporate KU Index be connected to stock market outcomes and potential instability in the fundamental processes driving them? These questions are empirically addressed in Chapters 9 and 10, respectively.

The dramatic shifts in micro-level KU may hold potential clues about the timing of potential change in stock market relationships. Timing of the shifts in the KU Index does appear to match that of major historical events. The first noticeable shift in the KU Index at 2003:11–2004:03 aligns approximately with the ramp-up to the US–Iraq War. The shift in 2006:07–2006:11 aligns approximately with the hiring of new Secretary of the Treasury Henry Paulson, the thwarted terrorist attack on a flight from the UK to the US, the *Dow Jones Industrial Average* eclipsing 12,000 for the first time, Democrats winning over both houses of Congress after mid-term elections, and the bursting of the housing bubble as historic numbers of foreclosures filed in the US increased 42 percent from 2005 to 2006.

The shift in 2011:06–2011:08 aligns with the US debt ceiling crisis and historic Federal Reserve policy accommodations. In August, legislation of the Budget Control Act of 2011 was signed into law by President Obama, raising the debt ceiling in hopes of dampening the crisis. The same month, the *Dow Jones Industrial Average* fell over 5.5 percent in response to *Standard and Poor*'s historic downgrade of US sovereign debt and the Federal Reserve's announced commitment to "quantitative easing."

Lastly, the shift in 2017:02–2017:09 aligns with the beginning of the Trump presidency and the corresponding changes to numerous cabinet appointments and economic and social policies. The Tax Cuts and Jobs Act was introduced in November and passed in December (the 2017 word cloud from Chapter 4 showed just how important these two events, the Trump presidency and new corporate tax policy,

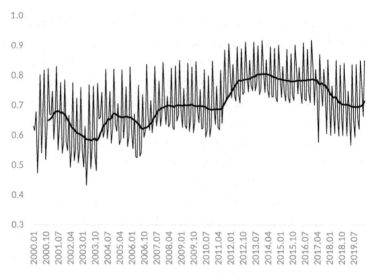

FIGURE 5.2 The figure plots corporate KU events as a proportion of total corporate events per month as reported across the *Dow Jones* financial news outlets from January 2000 through March 2020.

were to the stock market). In February 2017, the new president signed an executive order aimed at rolling back many features of the Dodd–Frank Wall Street Reform and Consumer Protection Act. North Korea launched ballistic missiles in April and July after which President Trump declared that the totalitarian country "will be met with fire and fury" and that "all options are on the table." In June, President Trump announced that the US would withdraw from the Paris Agreement on international commitments to reduce greenhouse gas emissions. Chapter 8 demonstrates how macro uncertainty events such as these spill over into corporate uncertainty in the stock market.

Of course, it may be the case that the level count of corporate KU events is changing, but that the proportion of total corporate events (scheduled plus unscheduled) is remaining constant. To address this concern, Figure 5.2 plots KU events as a proportion of total identified corporate events. The darker solid line plots the twelve-month moving average of the series.

The results are visually clear. First, KU events as a proportion of total equity news undergoes significant variation over the twenty-year sample period; there are subperiods where the proportion is closer to 60 percent, such as 2002 through 2004. Then, there are subperiods where the proportion is closer to 70 percent (2008–2012 and 2018–2019) or 80 percent (2013–2016). This figure reinforces the relative importance of unscheduled versus scheduled corporate events. Second, and related to the first observation, the proportion of KU events appears to have increased to a new, higher threshold after mid-2011 – further evidence suggesting that nonrepetitive events and KU have increased in corporate America and in the stock market over the last five to ten years relative to the early 2000s. Third, the variance of corporate KU events is quite high, but appears to be consistent over the sample period, suggesting that KU events may be bounded in their proportion to scheduled events. That is, when investors are determining the information sets they deem relevant during a particular period of time for forecasting returns, there is always a substantial proportion of information connected to unscheduled events (at least 40 percent in the early 2000s or at least 70 percent in the mid-2010s), though the volatility period-to-period is high. The general concept of subperiod boundedness in uncertainty is similar to the findings reported earlier in Figure 4.1 based on Google Trends searches for the term "uncertainty."

The textual analytics presented thus far have identified the unscheduled events reported as being relevant for corporate outcomes and stock market prices across the *Dow Jones* family of equity-specific news reports. Figure 5.1 suggests that the monthly counts of unscheduled events fluctuate over time, have increased over the last twenty years, and have displayed apparent mean shifts in their frequency. Figure 5.2 suggests that KU events as a proportion of total corporate events also undergoes substantial variation over the sample period, but that the variation at a point in time may be bounded. The next chapter begins the empirical assessment of narrative dynamics and instability under KU in the stock market by interacting the corporate KU Index with events' sentiment, novelty, and relevance in order to generate proxies for narrative intensity in the stock market.

# 6 KU Sentiment, Novelty, and Relevance

## 6.1 INTRODUCTION

Chapter 5 introduced the baseline Knightian Uncertainty Index tracking the monthly count of unscheduled corporate events reported as influencing firm and stock market behavior across the family of *Dow Jones* equity news outlets (*RavenPack* DJ-EQ package). As argued in previous chapters, Knightian uncertainty (KU) and narrative dynamics go hand-in-hand since they are both connected to unforeseeable structural change in stock market relationships. The formulation and advancement of narratives in the marketplace, however, requires sentiment, relevance, and further enhancements of event novelty extended to the KU events. This chapter introduces KU indices based on the sentiment, novelty, relevance, and volume/inertia of unscheduled corporate news events.

Graphical analysis and summary statistics of the corporate KU Event Sentiment Score (ESS) Index are presented here. The historical record of US stock market valuation levels (price-to-earnings) over the last twenty years is compared against the time-series plot of the sentiment-based index. KU event-months with the highest/lowest sentiment scores are identified. Similarly, the corporate KU Event Novelty Score (ENS), Aggregate Event Volume (AEV), and Relevance Indices are introduced with graphical and descriptive analysis. Taken together, the three filters for highest/lowest sentiment, highest novelty, and highest relevance are interacted with the baseline KU Index from Chapter 5 to identify periods with the highest narrative intensity. Periods of moderately high narrative intensity are also identified. These points of interest will serve as benchmarks for identified breakpoints found in structural change tests for stock returns, volatility, volume, and equity index fund flow relationships in Chapter 10.

These narrative intensity breakpoints will also be compared against their macro KU event analogs in Chapter 8.

## 6.2 THE KU SENTIMENT INDEX

As discussed in greater detail in Chapter 4, *RavenPack*'s composite ESS is derived from three proprietary methodologies for detecting linguistic meaning and context: traditional, expert consensus, and market response. The traditional component uses prescored words, phrases, and definitions that combine the lexicon-based approach with training data on news events. Expert consensus utilizes classification algorithms informed by financial experts manually tagging news events as having positive, negative, or neutral short-run effects on a company's stock price. The market response uses several years of news archives to measure the degree of higher frequency impact a news item potentially has on the market. The three components allow ESS to better gauge investor interpretations of news and the intensity of emotional narratives embedded within the KU event stories.

What distinguishes the present sentiment extraction approach from others using hybrid approaches is that the ESS estimate focuses exclusively on unscheduled events reported as drivers of corporate prospects and stock market behavior.[1] The present specification for KU event-sentiment (KU_ESS) tracks the monthly average of sentiment explicitly connected to corporate KU events over the sample period January 2000 through March 2020 as measured by:

$$KU\_ESS = \frac{1}{KU} \sum_{i=1}^{KU} ESS_{KU,i} \qquad (6.1)$$

where $ESS_{KU,i}$ denotes the sentiment score for the $i$th KU event. Table 6.1 reports summary statistics for KU_ESS.

Several features of Table 6.1 stand out. First, ESS for corporate KU events is positive on average (52.61), suggesting that such events are typically associated with optimistic feeling, emotions, and

---

[1] Most studies interacting sentiment with fundamentals have not focused on KU events. See references cited in Chapter 2.

Table 6.1 *KU Sentiment Index summary statistics*

| Mean[a] | Median | Min/Max | $\sigma$ | Skew. | Kurt. | JB |
|---|---|---|---|---|---|---|
| 52.61 | 52.46 | 49.08/57.64 | 1.46 | 0.63 | 3.85 | 0.000 |

[a] *Note:* The table reports summary statistics for the corporate KU Sentiment Index (KU_ESS) during the sample period January 2000 through March 2020. Data are monthly. $\sigma$ denotes standard deviation. Skew. and Kurt. denote skewness and kurtosis, respectively, while JB denotes the *p*-value for the Jarque–Bera test against the null hypothesis of a statistically normal distribution.

sentiment about their interpreted impacts on future market outcomes. Keynes remarked that the yield of an asset depends partly on the "future events which can only be forecasted with more or less confidence" through investors' "psychological" beliefs, which he famously refers to as the "state of long-term expectations" (Keynes, 1936, pp. 147–148). Keynes understood the intimate connection between uncertainty and psychological considerations. This is not to say, however, that the most important KU events for the stock market are associated with bullish events. In fact, much evidence presented throughout this book suggests that corporate KU events imply an uncertainty premium for investors, reflecting the psychology necessary, optimism or pessimism, to pursue increasingly excessive, and uncertain, valuations. Second, the high kurtosis of the KU ESS Index implies many outlier observations comprise heavy tails of the distribution. Relatively extreme values will help to identify periods during which narrative intensity may be the highest.

Figure 6.1 plots the corporate KU ESS Index against Shiller's Cyclically Adjusted Price-to-Earnings (CAPE) ratio for the SP500 over the sample period. KU ESS is plotted against the CAPE valuation ratio to shed light on KU sentiment's potential connection with an equity uncertainty premium based on how relatively expensive or cheap the market is trading. When valuation ratios in asset markets become historically high or low, pursuing marginally bullish or

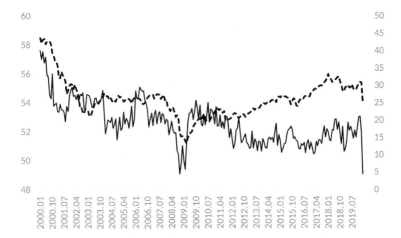

FIGURE 6.1 The figure plots the corporate KU Event Sentiment Score (ESS) Index (solid line, left axis) against Robert Shiller's Cyclically Adjusted Price-to-Earnings ratio for the SP500 Composite Index (dashed line, right axis) for the period January 2000 through March 2020. The CAPE data is available at www.econ.yale.edu/~shiller/.

bearish positions, respectively, becomes more uncertain and requires an additional uncertainty premium to push valuations further into excessive territory. Investor judgment, in turn, requires a greater influence of psychological considerations, such as confidence, to stake an increasingly exposed open position during periods of historical excess.[2] The following excerpt from the *Bloomberg News* stock market wrap illustrates the connection between valuation levels, sentiment, and novel events (in this case, government instability) when an uncertainty premium is present:

> "When your government is in total turmoil, your confidence goes down the chute," said Cummins Catherwood, a managing director of Philadelphia-based Rutherford, Brown & Catherwood, which oversees $570 million. "When your confidence goes down the chute, you're not going to pay 30 times earnings for GE." General Electric Co., the largest company by market value, fell 1 11/16 to 80 3/16.
>
> *(Bloomberg News, September 9, 1998)*

---

[2] See Frydman and Goldberg (2007, 2011) for theoretical underpinnings and empirical evidence of the gap-risk premium approach for asset markets under uncertainty.

Therefore, one would expect sentiment associated with KU events to co-move positively with the CAPE valuation ratio.

The comovement between the two series in Figure 6.1 is evident, particularly from 2000 through 2011. The nonparametric Spearman correlation coefficient between KU ESS and CAPE is 0.151, rejecting the null hypothesis of zero correlation with a $p$-value = 0.018.[3] The close comovement is also displayed by the sharp decline in both variables during the COVID-19 crisis of 2020 – KU sentiment became very pessimistic and stock prices collapsed in mid-March.

The global maximum of positive sentiment over the first six months of 2000 corresponds to the highest historical valuations for the SP500, peaking in late 1999 and early 2000 following the run-up in technology-laden stock prices and the so-called dot.com bubble. The ESS Index reaches a global minimum in late 2008 (October) dropping into pessimistic territory. Of course, this subperiod aligns with the depths of the financial crisis sparked by the largest bankruptcy announcement in US history by Lehman Brothers in September. Interestingly, there appears to be somewhat of an asymmetric relationship between KU ESS and CAPE: When valuations are excessive from above, and risk assessments have been building, stock prices, and thus valuation ratios, plunge, undergoing sharp reversals that appear to comove strongly with the decline in corporate KU sentiment. The two series plunged together during 2001, 2008, and finally during 2020, years coinciding with US economic recessions and the COVID-19 crisis. However, the same strong comovement is less evident during periods of increases in the CAPE valuation ratio.

---

[3] The CAPE is based on an average of the past ten years of earnings in the denominator with the aim of smoothing earnings outliers due to fluctuations in the broader economy. To deal with the recent trend in corporate dividend policy toward share repurchases rather than dividend payments, Shiller's new total return cyclically adjusted price-to-earnings ratio (TRCAPE) accounts for reinvested dividends in the price index and scales earnings per share due to buybacks. Using TRCAPE produces a very similar plot and a weakly significant Spearman correlation coefficient with ESS of 0.107 ($p$-value = 0.095).

## 6.3 THE KU NOVELTY INDEX

Novel events and narrative dynamics are connected through the inherent instability present in stock market relationships. Textual studies of stock market news have found a complex relationship between trading behavior and novelty or, by contrast, the staleness of information. The findings appear to depend on the variance of news' expected impact on future returns. Briefly mentioned in Section 4.2, the study of Tetlock (2011), using *Dow Jones Newswire* feeds, finds that stock returns respond less to the same firm news already publicly reported in a recent release, but that investors trade more aggressively on the stale news as evidenced by the larger imbalance between buy and sell orders. The author shows that returns on stale news days negatively predict one-week returns. This finding, also reported by Birz (2017), is interpreted as evidence of investor overreaction to stale news. Tetlock (2011) considers staleness as the "textual similarity to the previous ten stories about the same firm" (p. 1481). By contrast, the KU novelty score presented here depends on the recent reporting of news by firm-event category that offers a more detailed and nuanced picture of corporate event novelty. What is more, the Novelty–Narrative Hypothesis (NNH) and the empirical findings presented in this book suggest that individuals revise their forecasting strategies in nonroutine ways when confronted by novel events and the unforeseeable change they engender in market relationships. As opposed to systematic "overreaction," investors must now reconsider previously released news in an alternative context as parameters have shifted in unique ways.

In a similar spirit, Fedyk and Hodson (2019), using news streams tracked by *Bloomberg* terminals, find that reports on the same stock market event, based on direct "reprints" of its occurrence (usually at high frequency) leads to less and more uniform trading. However, "recombinations" of an old news event, likely across different sources, with slightly different readings of the news and potentially diverse interpretations for the same event's impact on returns, leads to greater and more differentiated trading activity over the short term. The authors' experimental evidence shows that recombinations of an event are considered significantly more novel forms of stale news as compared to reprints. Taken together, these two studies suggest that the degree of differentiation of views about news' effect on future returns is connected to its perceived novelty by investors.

There are tens of thousands of corporate and stock market news events identified each month through the *RavenPack* platform. Researchers conducting event studies in financial markets all face the challenge of assessing when exactly relevant information becomes available for influencing speculative decisions and which news may still be reflected in prices and volatility over the short run once it is considered stale. The Event Novelty Score (ENS) is a strong candidate for approaching such issues.

Chapter 5 showed that Lehman Brothers' bankruptcy declaration news, which was made public on September 15, actually carried a lower novelty score for the firm event category "bankruptcy" since numerous headline news releases revealed such information in the hours preceding the formal announcement. The more novel the KU event is the more likely it contributes to unforeseeable change in stock market processes and, consequently, the greater uncertainty it produces. For Lehman Brothers' historical Chapter 11 bankruptcy announcement, the novelty came in the late hours of September 14. Similar to the KU ESS Index, the KU ENS Index reflects a monthly average and is measured as:

$$KU\_ENS = \frac{1}{KU} \sum_{i=1}^{KU} ENS_{KU,i} \qquad (6.2)$$

where $ENS_{KU,i}$ denotes the novelty score for the $i$th KU event. Figure 6.2 plots the monthly KU ENS Index for unscheduled corporate events.

The highest values for the KU ENS Index occur in 2000 with a peak in 2000:11. Recall, this was also the break date found from the unit root-with-break test of the baseline KU Index in Chapter 5.

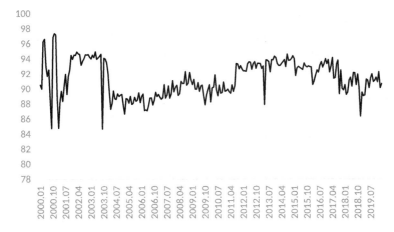

FIGURE 6.2 The figure plots the corporate KU Event Novelty Score (ENS) Index from the *Dow Jones* financial news outlets over the sample period January 2000 through March 2020.

Stock market narratives during 2000 likely involved many novel considerations related to technological advancements such as new hybrid automobiles (Toyota) and new mobile texting platforms (AT&T). Localized high values of ENS occur during the years 2008–2009, 2012–2014, and 2016–2017. There is an evident uptrend in novelty from 2006 through 2009, which aligns with the dramatic upswings in equity and housing prices precipitating the global financial crisis. However, unlike the baseline KU and ESS Indices, the ENS Index appears to display a more stationary process (i.e. time-invariant mean) over the entire sample. The ADF test rejects the null hypothesis of a unit root with $t$-stat ($p$-value) = $-4.310$ (0.001).

## 6.4 THE KU RELEVANCE INDEX

Chapter 5 discussed the motivation for tracking the reported relevance of unscheduled events under NNH. Relevance measures provide a sense of importance for a particular event in terms of the broader context at play and are particularly useful for tracking any event mentioned in a news article or news feed. For example, the last paragraph in a stock market news article might simply list the day's largest advancers and decliners without any elaboration as to the causes or implications. These price movements would, therefore, not be part of the article's central context and underlying narratives. Based on the *RavenPack* metrics, relevance is "a score between 0–100 that indicates how strongly related the entity is to the underlying news story, with higher values indicating greater relevance." That is, the entity that is identified in connection with the unscheduled event receives a higher relevance score if the majority content within the report is related to the entity event. Thus, the relevance score gives cohesion to the KU events within a news article, adding to their associated sentiment and novelty in tracking the entity event's importance for the overarching story and associated subnarratives.

Similar to the KU ESS and ENS Indices, the KU Relevance Index is measured as:

$$KU\_Relevance = \frac{1}{KU} \sum_{i=1}^{KU} Relevance_{KU,i} \qquad (6.3)$$

where $Relevance_{KU,i}$ denotes the Relevance score for the $i$th KU event. Figure 6.3 plots the Relevance Index for corporate KU events over the sample period.

Visual inspection of Figure 6.3 shows that corporate KU events are considered quite relevant: the monthly mean of the series is 92.31 with a min/max = (81.02/97.97). The relevance of KU events peaks early on in the sample in 2000–2001, similar to the KU Sentiment and Novelty Indices, and reaches other heights during the period 2012–2017. Low levels of KU relevance occur during 2002–2003 and from 2018 through 2019. It is fascinating to see that the KU Relevance Index displays such persistence from one period to the next over the sample until 2017–2018 when it exhibits a dramatic decline. Perhaps the decline in 2018 reflects the increase in proportion of unscheduled events over the full sample period as illustrated in Figure 5.2 and the necessary crowding out of each event's relevance for a given news report. Moreover, that Figure 5.1 showed a decline in the overall count of unscheduled events in 2017–2018 may indicate that KU events,

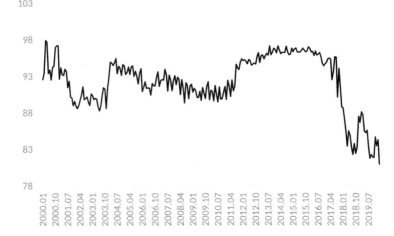

FIGURE 6.3  The figure plots the corporate KU event Relevance Index from the *Dow Jones* financial news outlets over the sample period January 2000 through March 2020.

though decreasing in raw number and overall relevance at that time, are still the most likely type of events to be reported in the financial news as driving stock market outcomes.

Not all KU events are headline worthy and many are not. However, it remains evident that when unscheduled events are identified, the news about stock price fluctuations and firm prospects is very much about such events – the minimum value of the series is 81 and most observations are greater than 92 (the median is 92.6). Put differently, corporate KU events are not mentioned merely in passing; rather, they are centrally important to the underlying news story and posited relationships driving outcomes. This gives confidence that corporate novelty is connected to the narratives swirling about the stock market in ways relevant for market participants' forecasting strategies. Chapter 7 will offer a more detailed correlation comparison across the KU indices presented heretofore.

## 6.5   THE KU AGGREGATE EVENT VOLUME INDEX

A narrative may pertain to any entity whether it be a particular corporation, person, institution, country, or some combination therein.

Each event record identifies the entity or entities involved. *Raven-Pack* tracks the number of events within a three-month window that have been connected to a specific entity and that generate an ESS score above or below, but not equal to, 50. This value is referred to as the Aggregate Event Volume (AEV). Because AEV tracks the volume of an entity's importance for corporate KU events and stock market behavior over time it can help shed light on entity-specific narrative dynamics that may unfold in persistent ways, gaining or losing strength during different subperiods. This is also why AEV is a proxy for entity-story inertia. After all, as discussed in Chapter 3, the passing of time offers narratives the chance to grow and take shape by developing and reinforcing entity-specific associations within people's minds. Figure 6.4 plots the AEV Index measured as the monthly average for corporate KU events over the sample period.

The graph shows that the number of stories citing the same entity for any given corporate KU event rises with the housing fueled run-up in stock prices from 2004 through 2007, peaks during the Great

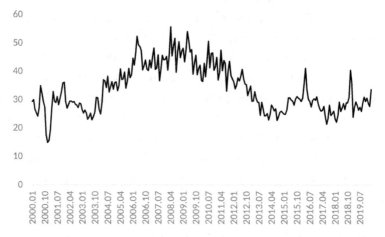

FIGURE 6.4 The figure plots the corporate KU Aggregate Event Volume (AEV) Index from the *Dow Jones* financial news outlets over the sample period January 2000 through March 2020. AEV measures the monthly average of the number of unscheduled events connected to a particular corporation over the previous ninety-one days.

Recession and financial crisis of 2008 through 2010 with over fifty stories for an entity on average, and declines during the economic recovery period before flattening out from 2015 through 2020 save for two spikes in 2016:04 and 2018:12. This graph suggests that there is persistence in the news about a particular entity in connection with unscheduled corporate events and that this persistence may increase during the subperiods of dramatic stock market instability such as those surrounding financial crises.

## 6.6  IDENTIFYING NARRATIVE INTENSITY

Nonrepetitive events cause financial market instability and narrative dynamics help investors cope with unforeseeable change and model ambiguity. To facilitate the narrative-instability analysis of Chapter 10, the KU event-months with the highest and lowest ESS are identified along with the highest ENS and Relevance values. The top/bottom 10 percent of ESS, the top 10 percent of ENS, and top 50 percent of Relevance month-value observations are tracked within the separate five-year subperiods 2000–2004, 2005–2009, 2010–2014, and 2015–2020 to allow for time-varying effects. Unlike sentiment and novelty, the issue of event relevance is less continuous and more binary; either an event is considered relevant or it is not. Consequently, the Relevance Index threshold separates the top/bottom 50 percent of observations within each five-year subperiod. Dates are identified during which corporate KU events were jointly in the top/bottom thresholds of ESS *and* the top threshold for ENS *and* the top threshold for Relevance. These are the criterion for highest-intensity narratives. The results are plotted in Figure 6.5, where a value of 1 implies the criteria are fully met and 0 otherwise.

Considering Figure 6.5, the most likely dates of highest narrative intensity in the US stock market based on corporate uncertainty occur at 2000:03–04, 2000:10, 2008:08, 2013:11, and 2016:08. These are the primary dates against which structural change tests in relationships driving stock market prices, returns, volatility, trading volume, and equity fund flows will be compared in Chapter 10.

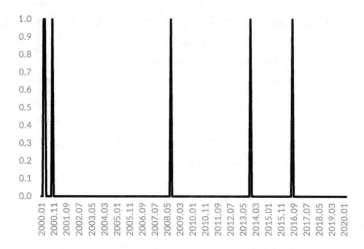

FIGURE 6.5 The figure plots the dummy variable equal to 1 for extreme high/low values of the ESS Index high values of the ENS Index, and high values of the Relevance Index relating to corporate KU events from the *Dow Jones* financial news outlets over the period January 2000 through March 2020.

A second tier of identified periods correspond to moderate narrative intensity. These periods are identified by relaxing the threshold criterion to capture the top (bottom) 25 percent of ESS, the top 25 percent of ENS, and (still) top 50 percent of Relevance month-value observations tracked within the same five-year subperiods 2000–2004, 2005–2009, 2010–2014, and 2015–2020. The results are plotted in Figure 6.6.

The periods identified cluster at the beginning of the sample (2000:03–04, 2000:10), at the financial crisis period (2008:02, 2008:05, 2008:08), and are scattered throughout the remainder of the sample (2013:05, 2013:11, 2014:08, 2014:11, 2015:08–09, 2016:08, 2016:11, 2017:01, 2017:03). That the narrative intensity periods bunch together suggests that underlying stories connected to nonrepetitive corporate events are interacting and being shaped by related dynamics in the marketplace. Chapter 8 reveals similar narratological linkages between micro and macro KU events and over time.

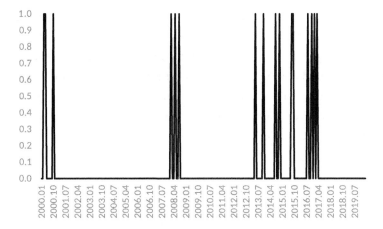

FIGURE 6.6 The figure plots the dummy variable equal to 1 for moderately high/low values of the ESS Index, moderately high values of the ENS Index, and high values of the Relevance Index relating to KU events from the *Dow Jones* financial news outlets over the period January 2000 through March 2020.

Interestingly, when various thresholds of the KU AEV Index were included in the joint analysis with ESS, ENS, and Relevance, there were no identified dates in common. That is, when periods during which the AEV Index values were in the top 10 or top 25 percentile of the distribution, there were no common periods matching the requisite thresholds for the other KU indices. The findings hold for high and moderate intensity criterion. There is not a clear explanation for this. More research is required. Chapter 8 finds that although both the corporate and macro AEV indices are informative for constructing narrative proxy variables under NNH, AEV values are significantly higher for unscheduled macro events (more on this later).

This chapter introduced the ESS (sentiment), ENS (novelty), Relevance, and AEV (volume/inertia) Indices for unscheduled corporate events identified as driving stock market and firm-level behavior across the *Dow Jones* financial news over the period January 2000 through March 2020. The indices serve a key role in the empirical analyses of Chapters 7 through 10. The next chapter introduces the KU var Index, tracking the diversity of unscheduled corporate event groups, which serves as a proxy for subnarrative variation during different periods of time in the stock market. Analysis shows that changes in the composition of corporate KU event groupings offer insight into several areas of stock market inquiry above what the baseline KU Index is able to explain.

# 7   Diversity of Corporate Uncertainty Events

When novel events occur, they lead to unforeseeable change in the relationships driving stock market outcomes imparting Knightian uncertainty (KU) and ambiguity onto investor forecasts over which model may be most appropriate for thinking about future returns. At each stage of this process, narrative dynamics are unfolding. When individual novel events belong to a common group their collective impacts may become concurrently denser. For instance, if, concurrently, a prominent firm considers an IPO, another invests in a new business project, and yet another increases its investment stake in another corporate entity, the instances all contribute to the group of unscheduled "Equity Actions."

By contrast, when different groupings of novel events occur over a stretch of time, interactive narratives exert a combinatory effect in their relevance for stock markets. The increase in diversity of unscheduled corporate event groups may lead to an elevated degree of uncertainty about how investors will interpret the unanticipated news' impacts on future returns and more reason to suspect that instability is unfolding in marketplace relationships. The more dissimilar the KU event groupings are the greater potential for model ambiguity to rise. Even if diversity is high, the more qualitatively similar the KU group-events are, however, the more information may be gleaned about the underlying change.

This chapter introduces the KU Diversity, or Variation, Index (KU var) that considers to what degree there are different unscheduled corporate event groups occurring simultaneously during a particular subperiod of time in the stock market and how this composition changes over time. The top ten groups of unscheduled KU events from the fifty-one listed in Table 5.1 will be ranked across each of the four five-year subperiods over the data sample based on proportion of total corporate KU events. Changes in composition and ranking of the groupings will be discussed. Detailed descriptions of each novel event category within the highest ranked groups are provided. Case studies of three large-cap US firms are presented during the dramatically volatile days of March 2020 corresponding to the COVID-19 crisis to illustrate the importance of unscheduled corporate events, particularly in times of market turmoil and instability. The chapter closes with time-series plots of numerous KU event groups of interest such as products–services, assets, legal issues, and price targets.

## 7.2 KU EVENT DIVERSITY

Chapter 2 discussed various strands of literature documenting empirical evidence of instability in stock market relationships with macro fundamentals and risk. One of the stylized findings suggests that different fundamental factors matter for stock market prices and volatility during different periods of time. Faced with ever-imperfect knowledge and model ambiguity, evidence suggests that investors cope with uncertainty by altering their forecasting strategies in ways that would be difficult to foresee – that model pluralism is more the rule than the exception.

Numerous studies have found that investor rankings of the importance of different fundamental factors for stock, and other asset, markets are time-varying.[1] And, narrative dynamics are likely related to the shifting composition of investor information sets. The KU dataset of fifty-one different groups from Table 5.1 enables investigation into whether the ranking of importance for unscheduled corporate events in the stock market varies over time, offering temporal clues about the make-up and dynamic nature of narrative instability. Table 7.1 displays the top ten groups of unscheduled events for each of

[1] See Chapter 2 for studies of time-varying investor information sets in the stock market. For currency markets, see Fratzscher et al. (2015).

Table 7.1 *ku event groups as a proportion of total KU events*

| 2000–2004 | 2005–2009 | 2010–2014 | 2015–2020 |
|---|---|---|---|
| analyst (0.14)[a] | insider trading (0.18) | technical (0.32) | technical (0.26) |
| labor issues (0.10) | order imbalances (0.14) | insider trading (0.18) | insider trading (0.22) |
| insider trading (0.09) | analyst (0.12) | analyst (0.08) | analyst (0.10) |
| order imbalances (0.09) | labor issues (0.08) | credit ratings (0.06) | price targets (0.08) |
| M&A (0.08) | products–services (0.08) | order imbalances (0.06) | credit ratings (0.07) |
| equity actions (0.07) | credit ratings (0.06) | equity actions (0.05) | labor issues (0.05) |
| stock prices (0.06) | M&A (0.06) | products–services (0.04) | equity actions (0.05) |
| credit ratings (0.06) | equity actions (0.05) | labor issues (0.04) | M&A (0.04) |
| technical (0.04) | price targets (0.05) | M&A (0.03) | stock prices (0.04) |
| revenues (0.03) | stock prices (0.04) | stock prices (0.03) | investor relations (0.03) |

[a] *Note:* The table reports particular corporate KU event groups as a monthly proportion of total corporate KU events whose average for each subperiod is reported in parentheses.

the four five-year subperiods from January 2000 through March 2020 based on the groups that contribute the highest proportion of total corporate KU events.

Findings from Table 7.1 show that while the total composition of top ten KU event groups remains relatively consistent, the internal rankings by proportion changed across every five-year period. The groups reported as constituting the highest proportions of KU events every period include analyst ratings, labor issues, insider trading, M&A, equity actions, stock prices, and credit ratings. It is unsurprising that, unlike the Economy, Environment, and Politics topics, the groups with highest contribution to corporate KU events are those which are classified under the Business topic and most directly relevant for firm outcomes. To provide a clearer picture of the underlying factors included within the more common KU groups, the list presented here reports the individual KU event categories within the most important groups of Acquisitions–Mergers, Analyst Ratings, Credit Ratings, Equity Actions, Insider Trading, Labor Issues, Order Imbalances, Stock Prices, and Technical Analysis, with descriptions about what each corporate KU event category entails.

**Acquisitions–Mergers**

acquisition-acquiree: The Company announces its shares or assets are being acquired by another entity

acquisition-acquirer: The Company announces it will acquire the shares or assets of another entity

acquisition-bid-rejected-acquiree: The Company rejects an offer for being acquired or merged by another entity

acquisition-bid-rejected-acquirer: The Company's bid to acquire or merge the shares or assets of another entity is rejected

acquisition-blocked-acquiree: The acquisition of the Company is blocked by a governing or regulatory body

acquisition-blocked-acquirer: An acquisition by the Company is blocked by a governing or regulatory body

acquisition-delayed-acquiree: The acquisition of the Company is delayed or postponed

acquisition-delayed-acquirer: An acquisition by the Company is delayed or postponed

acquisition-failed-acquiree: The acquisition of the Company fails or is terminated by the parties

acquisition-failed-acquirer: An acquisition by the Company fails or is terminated by the parties

acquisition-interest-acquiree: The Company is a target firm for being acquired or merged by another entity

acquisition-interest-acquirer: The Company is interested in acquiring or merging the shares or assets of another entity

acquisition-merger-termination-fee: The Company agrees to a termination fee in case the merger or acquisition is not completed

acquisition-opposition-acquiree: The acquisition of the Company is opposed by its board of directors, shareholders, or staff

acquisition-opposition-acquirer: An acquisition by the Company is opposed by the board of directors, shareholders, or staff

acquisition-regulatory-scrutiny-acquiree: The acquisition of the Company is being investigated by a regulatory body

acquisition-regulatory-scrutiny-acquirer: An acquisition by the Company is being investigated by a regulatory body

acquisition-regulatory-scrutiny-authority: The Entity that investigates the acquisition

acquisition-rumor-acquiree: The Company is rumored to be the target firm for its assets being acquired by another entity

acquisition-rumor-acquirer: The Company is rumored to be interested in acquiring the shares or assets of another entity

acquisition-rumor-denied-acquiree: The Company denies a rumor that its shares or assets are being acquired by another entity

acquisition-rumor-denied-acquirer: The Company denies a rumor that it is interested in acquiring the assets of another entity

merger: The Company agrees to merge part or all its assets with another entity

merger-blocked: The Company's planned merger is blocked by a governing or regulatory body

merger-delayed: The Company's planned merger is delayed

merger-failed: The Company's planned merger fails or is terminated by the parties

merger-opposition: The Company's merger is opposed by the board of directors, shareholders, or staff

merger-regulatory-scrutiny: A merger involving the Company is being investigated by a regulatory body

merger-regulatory-scrutiny-authority: The Entity that investigates the merger

merger-rumor: The Company is rumored to be interested in merging with another entity

merger-rumor-denied: The Company denies a rumor that it intends to merge with another entity

stake-acquiree: The Company sells part of its stock to another entity

stake-acquirer: The Company buys part of the stock of another entity

unit-acquisition-acquiree: A unit or division of the Company is acquired by another entity

unit-acquisition-acquirer: The Company acquires a unit or division of another entity

unit-acquisition-bid-rejected-acquiree: The Company rejects an offer for one of its units or divisions to be acquired by another entity

unit-acquisition-bid-rejected-acquirer: The Company's bid to acquire a unit or division of another entity is rejected

unit-acquisition-blocked-acquiree: The acquisition of one of the Company's units is blocked by a governing or regulatory body

unit-acquisition-blocked-acquirer: An acquisition by the Company of a unit of another entity is blocked by a regulatory body

unit-acquisition-delayed-acquiree: The acquisition of the Company's unit or division is delayed or postponed

unit-acquisition-delayed-acquirer: An acquisition of a unit or division by the Company is delayed or postponed

unit-acquisition-failed-acquiree: The acquisition of the Company's unit or division fails or is terminated by the parties

unit-acquisition-failed-acquirer: An acquisition of a unit or division by the Company fails or is terminated by the parties

unit-acquisition-interest-acquiree: The Company's unit or division is a target for being acquired or merged by another entity
unit-acquisition-interest-acquirer: The Company is interested in acquiring or merging a unit or division of another entity
unit-acquisition-opposition-acquiree: The acquisition of the Company's unit is opposed by its board of directors, shareholders, or staff
unit-acquisition-opposition-acquirer: An acquisition of a unit by the Company is opposed by the board of directors, shareholders, or staff
unit-acquisition-regulatory-scrutiny-acquiree: The acquisition of the Company's unit or division is being investigated by a regulatory body
unit-acquisition-regulatory-scrutiny-acquirer: An acquisition by the Company of a unit or division is being investigated by a regulatory body
unit-acquisition-regulatory-scrutiny-authority: The Entity that investigates a unit or division acquisition
unit-acquisition-rumor-acquiree: The Company's unit or division is rumored to be acquired by another entity
unit-acquisition-rumor-acquirer: The Company is rumored to be interested in acquiring a unit or division of another entity
unit-acquisition-rumor-denied-acquiree: The Company denies a rumor that its unit or division is being acquired
unit-acquisition-rumor-denied-acquirer: The Company denies a rumor that it is interested in acquiring a unit or division of another entity
unit-acquisition-termination-fee: The Company agrees to a termination fee in case the unit acquisition is not completed

**Analyst Ratings**
analyst-ratings-change-negative: The Company's stock is downgraded
analyst-ratings-change-negative-rater: The rating Entity downgrades a company's stock
analyst-ratings-change-neutral: The Company's stock is rated unchanged
analyst-ratings-change-neutral-rater: The rating Entity leaves unchanged the company's stock

analyst-ratings-change-positive: The Company's stock is upgraded

analyst-ratings-change-positive-rater: The rating Entity upgrades the company's stock

analyst-ratings-history-negative: The Company's stock was previously rated negative

analyst-ratings-history-negative-rater: The rating Entity previously reported a negative rating for the company's stock

analyst-ratings-history-neutral: The Company's stock was previously rated neutral

analyst-ratings-history-neutral-rater: The rating Entity previously reported a neutral rating on a company's stock

analyst-ratings-history-positive: The Company's stock was previously rated positive

analyst-ratings-history-positive-rater: The rating Entity previously reported a positive rating for a company's stock

analyst-ratings-set-negative: The Company's stock is initiated as negative

analyst-ratings-set-negative-rater: The rating Entity initiates a company's stock as negative

analyst-ratings-set-neutral: The Company's stock is initiated as neutral

analyst-ratings-set-neutral-rater: The rating Entity initiates a company's stock as neutral

analyst-ratings-set-positive: The Company's stock is initiated as positive

analyst-ratings-set-positive-rater: The rating Entity initiates a company's stock as positive

**Credit Ratings**

credit-rating-action: The Entity's bond rating is reviewed by a rating entity

credit-rating-action-rater: The rating Entity reviews an entity's credit rating

credit-rating-affirmation: The Entity's bond rating is reviewed and no change is deemed necessary credit-rating-affirmation-rater: The rating Entity reviews a bond rating and deems no change necessary

credit-rating-confirmation: The Entity's bond rating is removed from a watch list and is formally confirmed

credit-rating-confirmation-rater: The rating Entity removes a rating from a watch list and formally issues a confirmation

credit-rating-corrected: The Entity's bond rating is corrected due to error

credit-rating-corrected-rater: The rating Entity reviews and corrects a bond rating

credit-rating-downgrade: The Entity's bond rating is downgraded

credit-rating-downgrade-rater: The rating Entity downgrades a bond rating

credit-rating-expected: The Entity's bonds are anticipated or expected to be rated

credit-rating-expected-rater: The rating Entity anticipates or expects to assign a bond rating

credit-rating-matured: The Entity's bonds reach the end of their repayment term and rating coverage is discontinued

credit-rating-matured-rater: The rating Entity discontinues the coverage of a bond rating as it has reached the end of its repayment term

credit-rating-no-rating: The Entity's bonds are not rated due to lack of request, insufficient information or policy

credit-rating-no-rating-rater: The rating Entity decides not to rate a bond due to lack of request, insufficient information or policy

credit-rating-outlook-developing: The Entity's bond rating is developing and may change contingent on an event

credit-rating-outlook-developing-rater: The rating Entity issues an opinion on a bond rating as developing or contingent on an event

credit-rating-outlook-negative: The Entity's bond rating may be lowered

credit-rating-outlook-negative-rater: The rating Entity expects a bond rating to be lowered

credit-rating-outlook-positive: The Entity's bond rating may be raised

credit-rating-outlook-positive-rater: The rating Entity expects a bond rating to be raised

credit-rating-outlook-revision: The Entity's credit rating outlook is expected to be updated

credit-rating-outlook-revision-rater: The rating Entity expects to update a bond rating outlook

credit-rating-outlook-stable: The Entity's bond rating may be unchanged

credit-rating-outlook-stable-rater: The rating Entity expects a bond rating to be unchanged

credit-rating-outlook-unchanged: The Entity's credit rating outlook is left unchanged

credit-rating-outlook-unchanged-rater: The rating Entity leaves a credit rating outlook unchanged

credit-rating-paid-in-full: The Entity's bond rating coverage is discontinued as it reaches maturity

credit-rating-paid-in-full-rater: The rating Entity discontinues the rating coverage of a bond as it reaches maturity

credit-rating-provisional-rating: The Entity's bond receives a provisional rating

credit-rating-provisional-rating-rater: The rating Entity issues a provisional rating to a bond

credit-rating-publish: The Entity's bond rating is published on the rating entity's website

credit-rating-publish-rater: The rating Entity issues a public announcement of a bond rating on its website

credit-rating-reinstated: The Entity's previous bond rating is restored

credit-rating-reinstated-rater: The rating Entity restores a previous bond rating

credit-rating-revision-enhancement: The Entity's bond rating is placed under review, commonly when its rated security becomes insured

credit-rating-revision-enhancement-rater: The rating Entity places a bond rating under review, commonly when a rated security becomes insured

credit-rating-set: The Entity's bond receives an initial rating

credit-rating-set-rater: The rating Entity initially rates a bond

credit-rating-unchanged: The Entity's bond rating is reconfirmed at the existing level

credit-rating-unchanged-rater: The rating Entity reconfirms a bond rating at the existing level without change

credit-rating-upgrade: The Entity's bond rating is upgraded

credit-rating-upgrade-rater: The rating Entity upgrades a bond rating

credit-rating-watch: The Entity's bond rating is placed on watch

credit-rating-watch-developing: The Entity's bond rating is estimated to be raised, lowered, or affirmed due to an event

credit-rating-watch-developing-rater: The rating Entity estimates a bond rating may be raised, lowered, or affirmed typically due to an event

credit-rating-watch-negative: The Entity's bond rating may be lowered due to an event

credit-rating-watch-negative-rater: The rating Entity estimates a bond rating may be lowered due to an event

credit-rating-watch-positive: The Entity's bond rating may be raised due to an event

credit-rating-watch-positive-rater: The rating Entity estimates a bond rating may be raised due to an event

credit-rating-watch-rater: The rating Entity places a bond rating on watch

credit-rating-watch-removed: The Entity's bond rating watch has been removed

credit-rating-watch-removed-rater: The rating Entity removes a watch on a bond rating

credit-rating-watch-unchanged: The Entity's bond rating on watch remains unchanged

credit-rating-watch-unchanged-rater: The rating Entity leaves unchanged a credit rating watch

credit-rating-withdrawn-rating: The Entity's bond rating is withdrawn

credit-rating-withdrawn-rating-rater: The rating Entity withdraws a bond rating

**Equity Actions**

bought-deal: The Company announces a securities offering where an investment bank commits to buy the entire offering

buyback-suspended: The Company suspends the repurchase of stock or bonds it had issued previously

buybacks: The Company repurchases stock it has issued previously

capex-guidance: The Company announces capital expenditure (CAPEX) guidance figures or projections

capex-guidance-down: The Company announces a decrease in CAPEX guidance figures or projections

capex-guidance-up: The Company announces an increase in CAPEX guidance figures or projections

capital-increase: The Company announces a capital increase

capital-increase-approved: The board members or shareholders of the Company approve a capital increase

equity-shelf-registration: The Company announces a stock offering that may entitle multiple public offerings with the same registration statement

expenses-charge: The Company announces a one-time charge against earnings

fundraising: The Company announces a new round of financing

going-private: The Company converts from a publicly traded company into a private entity

investment-investor: The Company invests in a new business project

investment-location: The Place where an investment for a new business project is realized

investment-recipient: The Company receives investment for a new business project

ipo: The Company announces an Initial Public Offering (IPO)

ipo-considered: The Company is considering an IPO

ipo-delayed: The Company's IPO is delayed or postponed

ipo-extended: The Company's IPO is extended

ipo-failed: The Company's IPO is canceled or terminated

ipo-issuance-decrease: The Company decreases the share size of its IPO

ipo-issuance-increase: The Company increases the share size of its IPO

ipo-opposed: The Company's IPO is opposed by its board of directors or shareholders

ipo-price-decrease: The Company decreases the share price range of its IPO

ipo-price-increase: The Company increases the share price range of its IPO

ipo-pricing: The Company prices the shares of its IPO

ipo-regulatory-approval: A regulatory body approves the Company's IPO

ipo-regulatory-approval-authority: The Entity approves the IPO of a company

ipo-regulatory-scrutiny: A regulatory body opens an investigation into the Company's IPO

ipo-regulatory-scrutiny-authority: The Entity investigating the IPO of a company

ipo-rumor: A rumor circulates that the Company is starting an IPO

ipo-rumor-denied: The Company denies a rumor that it is starting an IPO

ipo-unit: The Company announces the IPO of one of its units

ipo-unit-considered: The Company is considering an IPO of one of its units or divisions

ipo-unit-delayed: The IPO of one of the Company's units or divisions is delayed or postponed

ipo-unit-extended: The IPO of one of the Company's units or divisions is extended

ipo-unit-failed: The IPO of one of the Company's units or divisions is canceled or terminated

ipo-unit-rumor: A rumor circulates about the Company starting an IPO of one of its units

ipo-unit-rumor-denied: The Company denies a rumor that it is starting an IPO of one of its units

name-change: The Company changes its official corporate or registered name

ownership-decrease-held: Another entity decreases its investment or stake in the Company

ownership-decrease-owner: The Company decreases its investment or stake in another entity

ownership-increase-held: Another entity increases its investment or stake in the Company

ownership-increase-owner: The Company increases its investment or stake in another entity

private-placement: The Company announces a private placement of its shares

private-placement-suspended: The Company suspends or cancels a private placement of its shares

public-offering: The Company announces the sale of equity shares or other financial instruments to the public

public-offering-delayed: The Company delays or postpones the sale of equity shares or other financial instruments to the public

public-offering-suspended: The Company withdraws the sale of equity shares or other financial instruments to the public

reorganization: The Company announces a reorganization of its business

reorganization-approval: The Company's reorganization plan is approved by a governing or regulatory body

reorganization-considered: The Company is considering a reorganization of its business

reorganization-costs: The Company announces the cost of its reorganization plan

reorganization-delayed: The filing or announcement of the Company's reorganization plan is delayed or postponed

reorganization-denied: The Company denies a reorganization plan

reorganization-failed: The Company's reorganization plan is canceled or terminated

reorganization-rejection: The Company's reorganization plan is rejected by a governing or regulatory body

reorganization-savings: The Company announces savings from its reorganization plan

reorganization-unit: A unit or division of the Company announces a reorganization plan

reorganization-unit-approval: A reorganization plan of a unit, division, or assets of the Company is approved by a governing or regulatory body

reorganization-unit-rejection: A reorganization plan of a unit, division, or assets of the Company is rejected by an affiliate or regulatory body

reverse-stock-splits: The Company reduces the number of shares outstanding without altering its equity capital

rights-issue: The Company announces a rights offering or issue

rights-issue-suspended: The Company withdraws a rights offering or issue

savings: The Company announces savings in operating costs or other savings figures

savings-guidance: The Company announces a cost reduction program or figures for how much it expects to save over a given period of time

shareholder-rights-plan: The Company adopts or extends a shareholder rights plan as a type of defensive tactic against a takeover

shareholder-rights-plan-suspended: The Company withdraws or suspends a shareholder rights plan

spin-off: The Company sells part of its business forming a new organization or entity

spin-off-suspended: The Company suspends plans to spin off part of its business

stock-splits: The Company's existing shares are divided into multiple shares increasing the number of shares outstanding

trading-delisting: The Company's securities are removed from trading in a particular market or exchange

trading-delisting-review: The Company's securities are reviewed for eligibility of continued listing on an exchange

trading-halt: The Company's shares are temporarily not traded on a listed exchange

**Insider Trading**

insider-buy: An executive of the Company buys corporate stock

insider-gift: An executive of the Company gives away corporate stock, usually as a charitable donation

insider-sell: An executive of the Company sells corporate stock

insider-sell-registration: An executive of the Company registers to sell corporate stock

insider-surrender: An executive surrenders shares back to the Company typically to pay taxes or cover the cost of an option exercise

insider-trading-lawsuit-defendant: An executive of the Company is charged with illegal insider trading

insider-trading-lawsuit-plaintiff: The Company is the plaintiff in a lawsuit or in litigation regarding illegal insider trading

**Labor Issues**

executive-appointment: The Company appoints or promotes an executive

executive-compensation: The Company discloses additional pay or bonuses paid to an executive

executive-death: An executive of the Company dies

executive-firing: The Company suspends, dismisses, or fires an executive

executive-health: An executive of the Company suffers health problems

executive-resignation: An executive of the Company resigns

executive-salary: The Company discloses the wages or compensation paid to an executive

executive-salary-cut: The Company reduces the pay or compensation of an executive

executive-salary-increase: The Company increases the pay or compensation of an executive

executive-scandal: An executive of the Company is involved in a public scandal

executive-shares-options: The Company grants shares or options to an executive

hirings: The Entity announces new employment or hire for work

hirings-location: The Place where the hiring occurs

layoffs: The Entity announces job cuts or massive layoffs

strike: The Entity's personnel stops work in order to press employment demands

strike-ended: The Entity's personnel end or cancel a planned work strike

strike-ended-location: The Place where the worker strike has ended or been canceled

strike-location: The Place where the worker strike occurs

union-pact: The Entity makes a formal agreement with a worker's union

union-pact-rejected: The Entity and a worker's union reject or fail to reach a formal agreement

workforce-salary-decrease: The Entity reduces the pay or compensation of its workforce

workforce-salary-increase: The Entity increases the pay or compensation of its workforce

**Order Imbalance**

buy-imbalance: An exchange reports an excess of buy orders for the Company's stock that cannot be matched to orders of the opposite type

delay-imbalance: Extreme order imbalance results in the temporary suspension of trade of the Company's stock

mkt-close-buy-imbalance: An exchange reports an excess of Market On Close (MOC) buy orders for the Company's stock that cannot be matched to orders of the opposite type

mkt-close-sell-imbalance: An exchange reports an excess of MOC sell orders for the Company's stock that cannot be matched to orders of the opposite type mkt-open-buy-imbalance: An exchange reports an excess of Market On Open (MOO) buy orders for the Company's stock that cannot be matched to orders of the opposite type

mkt-open-sell-imbalance: An exchange reports an excess of MOO sell orders for the Company's stock that cannot be matched to orders of the opposite type

no-imbalance: An order imbalance for the Company's stock is resolved

no-mkt-close-imbalance: An MOC order imbalance for the Company's stock is resolved

sell-imbalance: An exchange reports an excess of sell orders for the Company's stock that cannot be matched to orders of the opposite type

**Stock Prices**

stock-gain: The Company's share price rise from a previous level makes headlines

stock-loss: The Company's share price drop from a previous level makes headlines

**Technical Analysis**

relative-strength-index: Information on the Relative Strength Index (RSI) of an Entity is released

relative-strength-index-overbought: The price of the Entity is considered overbought and becoming overvalued according to the RSI

relative-strength-index-oversold: The price of the Entity is considered oversold and becoming undervalued according to the RSI

relative-strength-index-rater: The Entity that issues RSI information

technical-price-level-resistance-bearish: Technical analysis indicates the Entity's price has approached a resistance level where traders are typically willing to sell

technical-price-level-resistance-bullish: Technical analysis indicates the Entity's price has approached a resistance level where traders are typically willing to buy

technical-price-level-resistance-rater: The Entity that issues technical price level information

technical-price-level-support-bearish: Technical analysis indicates the Entity's price has reached a support level where traders are typically willing to sell

technical-price-level-support-bullish: Technical analysis indicates the Entity's price has reached a support level where traders are typically willing to buy

technical-price-level-support-rater: The Entity that issues technical price level information

technical-view: Technical analysis information on the Entity's price is released

technical-view-bearish: Technical analysis indicates the Entity's price will depreciate or lose value

technical-view-bullish: Technical analysis indicates the Entity's price will appreciate or gain value

technical-view-overbought: Technical analysis indicates the Entity's price is overbought and a correction is due

technical-view-oversold: Technical analysis indicates the Entity's price is oversold and a rally is due

technical-view-rater: The Entity that issues technical analysis information

There is vast delineation within each group listed capturing virtually every conceivable way an unscheduled event within these common KU groups may unfold. Indeed, "Business decisions deal with situations which are "far too unique" (Knight, 1921, p. 231). For example, credit ratings detect whether a corporation's bond rating is "initial," "provisional," "discontinued," "assigned," "updated," "unchanged," "raised/lowered," "placed under review," "on/removed from a watch list," or "contingent on an event." Like other groups, credit ratings communicate forward-looking considerations, such as "expected" bond ratings, their "outlook," how rating decisions are "developing" across *Moody's*, *Standard and Poor's*, and *Fitch*, whether the ratings are "under review," or whether the ratings process for a firm's debt has simply been "initiated," is based only on "opinion," or that there is currently "no rating" at all.

Who could fully foresee these debt-related events or their importance for corporate prospects and the stock market? The public now knows the role that credit rating agencies played in the subprime mortgage crisis predating the global financial meltdown. And, *Standard & Poor's* credit rating downgrade of US sovereign government debt from AAA to AA+ on August 5, 2011, was certainly a major historical event in the fiscal crisis and debt sequestration of 2011.

Even those factors traditionally associated with narrative dynamics are detected by KU categories involving "ipo-rumor," "unit merger rumor," "acquisition rumor" and so on. Rumors are important features of narrative dynamics, and may lend themselves to explain the role of super-spreaders in extensions of the Kermack and McKendrick (1927) model to better understand the contagion properties of story diffusion. *MarketWatch*, for instance, has a section of news analysis dedicated to "Rumors" that often contains stories about investor whispers connected to KU events such as mergers or acquisitions. The October 31, 2020 Rumors section, for example, contains a lead report titled, "Centene Stock Tumbles After Humana Dismisses Rumors of a Takeover."

The KU group of "Labor Issues" is also deeply informative for potential narratives and stock market instability. The year 2018 witnessed a record number of labor strikes in the US amounting to nearly 500,000 workers who were either involved in walkouts or whose work was shut down by employers due to strikes. Corporations rely on labor inputs in their production process and labor strikes can result in millions of cumulative days off the job.[2] The KU event

---

[2] The largest strike in US history was the United Mine Workers of America strike lasting from April 1 through December 7, 1946 involving 400,000 strikers and 70,400,000 cumulative workdays lost. The largest US labor strike to occur in the last fifty years involved the Screen Actors Guild–American Federation of Television and Radio Artists union representing 135,000 video game voice actors. The strike lasted from May 1 through October 30, 2000 costing 17,280,000 work days. One of the largest corporations in the video game industry, Sony Corp (SNE) with market capitalization at the time of this writing of $108 billion, witnessed its share price fall from $114.25 on July 31, 2000 to

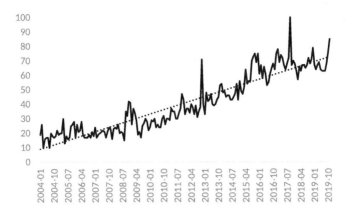

FIGURE 7.1 The figure plots the US Google Trends searches for "CEO salary" during the period 2004 through 2019 with line-of-best-fit (dotted line). The vertical axis measures search interest.

classification tracks "strikes," their initial and ending "location," and whether a corporation has made a formal "union-pact" agreement.

But labor issue narratives also swirl around the employment circumstances of management and executives. Narratives involving such entities tend to fall into two camps: either stories reflect executives who are "appointed," "fired," have "resigned" or passed away ("death"), or the narratives are about their "compensation." The news analytics platform further delineates whether the salary was disclosed, cut, or increased or whether share options have been allotted. There is even a category dedicated to "executive scandal."

Figure 7.1 plots the Google Trends searches for "CEO salary" from 2004 through 2019. There is a clear upward trend in the data; a linear trendline fitting the series generates the equation "CEO salary"_searches = 8.7196 + 0.3352x. There are noticeable spikes in 2012 and 2017, years in which reporting of historically high executive salary structures rippled through the US news: "In Executive Pay, a Rich Game of Thrones" (New York Times, April 7, 2012); "CEO Pay is

$74.50 on November 1, 2000. For information on the strikes, see www.usatoday.com/ story/money/2020/04/08/31-largest-worker-strikes-in-american-history/111460504/.

380 Times Average Workers" (*CNN*, April 19, 2012); "CEO Pay: How It Got out of Control and How to Rein It in" (*Fortune*, April 19, 2017); "Top 10 Highest Paid CEOs in 2016" (*USA Today*, May 23, 2017).

Of course, when thinking about the emergence and fueling of stock market narratives, it is imperative to consider firm-specific stock market-related decisions, or "equity actions." The textual analytics platform is able to detect events concerning "buybacks," "capital expenditures," "shareholder or board approvals," "capital reorganization," or "investment in new business projects." Such considerations are often communicated to shareholders and other financial market participants through corporate 10-K and 8-K disclosure reports. Investigating how firms engage in "equity actions" – the type, timing, composition, and complexity of such events – serves as fertile ground for detecting relevant narrative information and, of course, for assessing future corporate share prospects.

Like other top KU groups' category delineation, "equity actions" contain all the permutations of IPO considerations such as whether one is "considered," "delayed," "extended," or "failed." The categories can discern whether issuance shares being offered increased or decreased, whether the offering price increased or decreased, or whether the capital funds stem from "private placement" or a "public offering." IPO decisions are always closely watched by the market and are known for influencing some of the most visceral narratives about corporate prospects and potential returns. Underwriters of IPOs charge hefty fees (the largest IPO cost) for not only determining when a firm goes public with new shares, how many shares to offer and at which initial price, but also for marketing the offering to large investment firms and high-rollers. When investment banks shop around their upcoming IPOs they naturally and necessarily craft particular narratives about the prospects of getting in early. The number of US IPOs peaked in the mid- to late 1990s and 2000. IPOs during the twenty-first century experienced high clustering in

2004–2007 and 2013–2014 and a slight resurgence in the last few years.[3]

The top corporate KU event groups also include stock price changes up or down *if* they are included as a headline event in a news article. These are important categories for NNH. Indeed, the most popular description of financial market euphoria or panic is one that is precipitated by news events of dramatic price increases or decreases, respectively. The price change is so noteworthy, and somewhat historically unique, that the fluctuation itself becomes a KU event. Volumes of studies have been written about investors who abruptly alter their asset demand for stock due to recent dramatic price movements and the extrapolative belief for ever-increasing or -decreasing prices tomorrow. Indeed, many popular models of technical and momentum trading in the field of behavioral finance connect historical trends in prices and earnings to behavioral tendencies such as over- and underreaction to price news.[4]

Figure 7.2 plots the proportion of corporate KU events across the seven groups routinely ranked in the top ten – Analyst, Credit Ratings, Equity Actions, Insider Trading, Labor Issues, Mergers and Acquisitions, and Stock Prices. The figure shows that even within the subgroups with the highest contribution to corporate KU events on average, there is considerable variation over time.

For example, Insider Trading events, such as insider-buys and registrations to sell, did not matter at all for 2002–2003, but reached over 20 percent of total corporate KU events for 2004–2005 and 2007–2008 and nearly 40 percent for 2018–2019. Credit ratings peaked in 2003, 2009–2010 and from 2017 through March 2020, comprising over 10 percent of KU events during each subperiod, but mattered less than

---

[3] For IPO statistics see, for instance, https://site.warrington.ufl.edu/ritter/files/IPOs2019Statistics.pdf.

[4] For a seminal study connecting past stock price data to extrapolative expectations through behavioral considerations, see De Long et al. (1990). For a seminal study connecting past earnings data to stock prices through the behavioral tendencies of over- and underreaction, see Barberis et al. (1998).

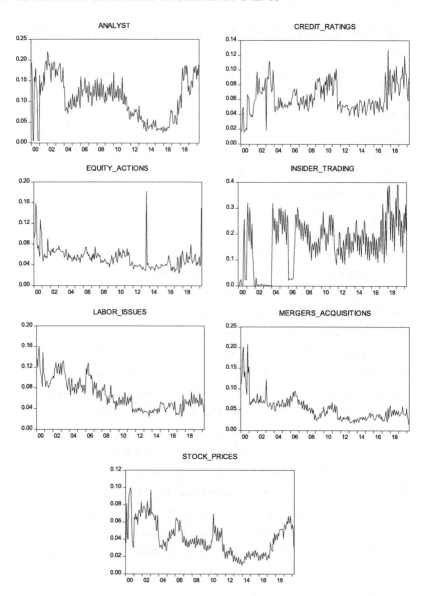

FIGURE 7.2 The figure plots the top groups by proportion of corporate KU events in the *Dow Jones* financial news reports over the sample period January 2000 through March 2020.

5 percent in the early 2000s. Newsworthy changes in Analyst Recommendations – a potential source of small continuous revisions in
investor forecasting strategies – constituted approximately 20 percent
of total KU events from 2003 to 2004. Its importance then dropped
to less than 5 percent from 2014 through 2016 only to increase near
20 percent again in 2018 through 2020. Mergers and Acquisitions
constituted over 20 percent in 2000 (supporting the word cloud
findings from Chapter 4), but mattered less than 5 percent from 2012
through 2020. Equity Actions displays a dramatic spike in frequency
increasing from less than 4 percent in 2012 to over 16 percent in 2013,
declining to 4 percent in 2014, but displaying another spike near 12
percent in February and March 2020 due to the COVID-19 pandemic.

The KU event group Stock Prices mattered often for total
corporate KU events in the early 2000s and during the second half
of the prolonged upswing in index prices from 2014 through 2020 –
a period coinciding with the Tax Cuts and Jobs Act of 2017 and
frequently acclaimed stock market performance. However, headline
stock price changes were not a high proportion of KU events during
the Great Recession and financial crisis period, suggesting there may
be an asymmetric effect from such considerations.

Whether through transitory spikes or persistent swings, all
seven groups display some form of significant variation in their
contributed proportion of total corporate KU events over the twenty-
year period. This variation in the diversity of micro-level novelty
is likely connected to time-varying narratives influencing market
outcomes during different subperiods of the sample. But how different
are the KU groups? And is there evidence that particular stock market
relationships are impacted when the different groupings are more
similar? More dissimilar? These questions will be explored in the
following chapters.

For now, consider a case study conveying the importance of
particular corporate KU event groups during the historic March 2020
stock market turmoil for three large-cap equities: Amazon, American
Airlines, and Verizon. Though all identified corporate events are

Table 7.2 *Total identified events for Amazon (AMZN)*

| Date | Position | Group | Category | Unscheduled |
|------|----------|-------|----------|-------------|
| 3/2[a] | VP | insider trading | insider sell-registration (3) | yes |
| 3/4 | Chairman | insider trading | insider gift | yes |
| 3/12 | Executive | labor issues | executive resignation (2) | yes |
| 3/12 | | products–services | business contract | yes |
| 3/16 | | partnerships | partnership | yes |
| 3/16 | | revenues | revenue up | no |
| 3/16 | | labor issues | hirings (2) | yes |
| 3/16 | | labor issues | workforce salary increase | yes |
| 3/17 | | labor issues | hirings (2) | yes |
| 3/17 | | analyst ratings | ratings change neutral | yes |
| 3/19 | | stock price | stock price gain (2) | yes |
| 3/20 | | labor issues | hirings | yes |
| 3/22 | | labor issues | hirings | yes |
| 3/23 | | labor issues | hirings (5) | yes |
| 3/24 | | assets | facility close (2) | yes |
| 3/26 | | price targets | target downgrade (2) | yes |
| 3/26 | | analyst ratings | ratings change neutral | yes |
| 3/26 | | partnerships | partnership (2) | yes |
| 3/30 | | labor issues | workers strike | yes |

[a] *Note:* The table reports the corporate KU events by group and category for Amazon (AMZN) during March 2020. Total instances of the same event are reported in parentheses next to the event category.

listed, virtually all are classified as unscheduled and appear connected to the COVID-19 outbreak and economic lockdown in late Q1. These events are chronicled by firm in Tables 7.2 through 7.4.

There are several notable features of Tables 7.2 through 7.4. First, approximately 94 percent of the total identified events are classified as unscheduled. That is, for these three firms, nearly all of the events identified in the *Dow Jones* news outlets contribute to potential instability and KU driving corporate prospects and stock market outcomes during March 2020. Second, not only is there a range of different KU groups across the three firms for the month, but the range of bullish versus bearish events within individual firms varies considerably over the month. For example, from Table 7.2, Amazon had numerous days of hiring events, a business partnership agreement, and even a workforce salary increase. Yet, the firm also

Table 7.3 *Total identified events for American Airlines (AAL)*

| Date | Position | Group | Category | Unscheduled |
|------|----------|-------|----------|-------------|
| 3/2[a] | | transportation | transportation disruption | yes |
| 3/3 | Director | insider trading | insider buy (2) | yes |
| 3/6 | | stock price | stock loss | yes |
| 3/10 | | products–services | products discontinued | yes |
| 3/10 | | stock price | stock gain | yes |
| 3/10 | | earnings | earnings guidance suspended | yes |
| 3/13 | | credit ratings | ratings watch negative (4) | yes |
| 3/16 | | price targets | target downgrade | yes |
| 3/16 | | equity actions | trading resumed | yes |
| 3/17 | | equity actions | trading resumed | yes |
| 3/18 | | stock price | stock loss | yes |
| 3/19 | | credit | extension provider (3) | yes |
| 3/19 | | credit | loan recipient | yes |
| 3/20 | | stock price | stock gain (2) | yes |
| 3/20 | | credit rating | rating downgrade (9) | yes |
| 3/23 | | analyst ratings | ratings change negative | yes |
| 3/23 | | analyst ratings | ratings change neutral | yes |
| 3/23 | | price targets | target downgrade | yes |
| 3/25 | | price targets | target downgrade (2) | yes |
| 3/25 | | credit | loan recipient | yes |
| 3/26 | | analyst ratings | ratings change neutral | yes |
| 3/26 | | price targets | target upgrade | yes |
| 3/27 | | analyst ratings | ratings change negative | yes |
| 3/27 | | price targets | target set | yes |
| 3/27 | | credit | rating downgrade (3) | yes |
| 3/30 | | analyst ratings | ratings change neutral | yes |
| 3/30 | | price targets | target downgrade | yes |
| 3/31 | | credit rating | rating action (2) | yes |

[a] *Note:* The table reports the corporate KU events by group and category for American Airlines (AAL) during March 2020. Total instances of the same event are reported in parentheses next to the event category.

experienced an executive resignation, an insider sell registration by an executive, the closure of a facility, a price target downgrade, and even a worker's strike. It would be difficult to fully foresee any of these somewhat unique events, let alone assign a quantitative probability governing future prospects of the firm based on their occurrences *ex ante*.

The rapidly evolving debt position of American Airlines is evident from Table 7.3 through credit rating downgrades, a negative

Table 7.4 *Total identified events for Verizon (VZ)*

| Date | Position | Group | Category | Unscheduled |
|---|---|---|---|---|
| 3/2[a] | | analyst ratings | ratings change positive | yes |
| 3/2 | | price target | target set | yes |
| 3/2 | CFO | marketing | conference participant | yes |
| 3/2 | | stock price | stock gain (2) | yes |
| 3/3 | VP | insider trading | insider buy | yes |
| 3/5 | | dividends | dividend | no |
| 3/5 | VP | insider trading | insider buy (5) | yes |
| 3/6 | | investor relations | conference call | yes |
| 3/6 | VP | insider trading | sell registration | yes |
| 3/10 | Chair, VP, CFO | insider trading | insider buy (9) | yes |
| 3/12 | | equity actions | capex-up (5) | no |
| 3/12 | | equity actions | capital increase | no |
| 3/13 | | labor issues | executive resignation | yes |
| 3/13 | CEO | labor issues | executive resignation | yes |
| 3/16 | | analyst ratings | ratings change positive | yes |
| 3/16 | | price targets | target set | yes |
| 3/18 | | credit rating | rating set (3) | yes |
| 3/23 | | equity actions | fundraiser | yes |
| 3/23 | | products–services | product release | yes |
| 3/30 | | analyst ratings | ratings change neutral | yes |
| 3/30 | | price targets | target downgrade | yes |

[a] *Note:* The table reports the corporate KU events by group and category for Verizon (VZ) during March 2020. Total instances of the same event are reported in parentheses next to the event category.

credit watch, increased loans, and credit extension. Trading of shares for American Airlines was halted after circuit-breaker and single-stock limit up-limit down rules were triggered due to share price volatility.[5] From Table 7.4, Verizon also experienced an executive resignation, but had analyst ratings upgraded to positive, unveiled

---

[5] The volatility in the broad market and in individual share prices clustered during the months of February and March. The SP500 and NYSE halted trading on March 9, 12, and 16. Level 1 thresholds for the broad market require a drop of 7 percent from the previous day's closing price that halts trading for fifteen minutes unless the drop occurs after 3:25 P.M. or there is a Level 3 halt. The Level 2 threshold requires a 13 percent drop for a fifteen-minute halt unless occurring after 3:25 P.M. or a Level 3 halt. Level 3 thresholds require a 20 percent drop that halts trading for the rest of the day. It appears trading for individual shares was halted because stock price bands were violated under the limit up-limit down rule. See https://personal.vanguard.com/pdf/limit_up_limit_down_rule.pdf?cbdForceDomain=true for Vanguard's explanation of the single stock rule.

new products, and had the chairman, CFO, and VP engage in insider-buy and -sell activities. Though not reported, smaller capitalization firms such as Wayfair Inc. displayed more consistently negative KU events at the end of Q1 2020. Unlike the hiring implemented by Amazon, Wayfair Inc. engaged in large labor layoffs – 3 percent of its global 17,000 workers – in mid-February (labor issues). Like many other small-cap traded firms, share prices for Wayfair Inc. were extremely volatile, causing on seven occasions (mostly in March) circuit-breaker rules halting all trading to be triggered due to dramatic price declines (equity actions).[6]

These findings motivate the question of whether and by how much the composition of unscheduled corporate events changes over the twenty-year sample period. Figure 7.3 plots the number of KU event groups that constitute more than 2 percent of total corporate KU events each month. This measure of KU diversity/variation is a proxy for how many potentially different subnarratives there may be in the stock market at a given point in time, noting that the number of larger narratives could be more, less, or the same depending on the subnarratives' directional connection to them. This conjecture is explored in Chapter 8.

Figure 7.3 shows that there is substantial variation in the number of KU groups reported as driving firm prospects and stock market prices over time. Interestingly, the number of groups increases steadily from nine KU groups in 2000:01 up to fifteen groups in 2006:05. The number of KU groups then decreases to hover around eleven from 2007 through 2012 only to decrease again to approximately nine from 2014 through 2017 and increases to approximately ten from 2018 through March 2020. Though corporate KU events as a proportion of total events has increased over the last ten years (Figure 5.2), the group diversity has declined. The KU Variation Index (KU var) will be used in the empirical analyses of Chapters 8 and 9,

---

[6] Wayfair Inc. and other stocks with share prices above $3 (National Market System Tier I) will have the trading of their shares halted for five minutes if the price moves above or below 5 percent bands based on continuously updated average price movements.

FIGURE 7.3 The figure plots the number of groups that constitute more than 0.02 of total corporate KU events.

connecting it and other KU-based indices to stock market returns, volatility, trading volume, and equity fund flows.

## 7.3   OTHER KU GROUPS OF INTEREST

Ranking the KU event groups that contribute the greatest share of total corporate KU events does not imply that there are no other KU event groups that could underpin narrative dynamics connected to stock market instability. Figure 7.4 plots twenty other KU groups involving Assets, Balance of Payments, Bankruptcy, Civil Unrest, Crime, Dividends/Earnings, Government, Indexes, Industrial Accidents, Legal, Partnerships, Pollution, Price Targets, Products–Services, Regulatory, Revenues, Security, Taxes, Transportation, and War–Conflict.

Though their contribution to total corporate KU events may be relatively low, the graphs show that the importance of certain groups of KU events varies considerably over time. Some spike early in the sample period (i.e. Indexes, Regulatory, and Taxes), some spike in the middle of the sample (i.e. Balance of Payments, Civil Unrest, and Government), and some at the end (i.e. Transportation, War–Conflict, Industrial Accidents, and Crime).

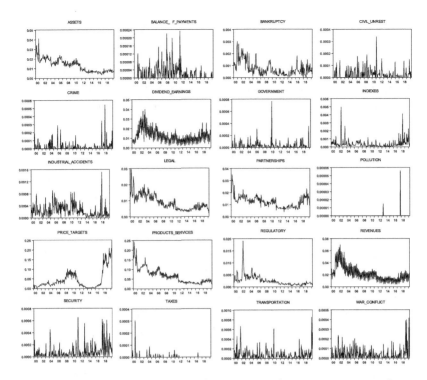

FIGURE 7.4 The figure plots the proportion of corporate KU events for twenty groups from *Dow Jones* news reports for the period January 2000 through March 2020.

The importance of corporate Civil Unrest events, for instance, spiked in February 2011. Digging into the news reports reveals that during the month there was a rash of evacuations of civilians and employees by several oil and gas drilling firms caught in the Egyptian Civil War. The US firms identified with the evacuation events included National Oilwell Varco Inc., Diamond Offshore Drilling Inc., and Occidental Petroleum Corp. One story, for example, reads:

---

**MARKET TALK: Natl Oilwell Evacuates Employees From Egypt**
2011–02–03 10:09:27 EST
10:09 (Dow Jones) National Oilwell Varco (NOV) has evacuated expatriates and foreign nationals from Egypt "except for a few safe on

offshore rigs," CFO Clay Williams says. The civil-strife-ridden North African nation accounted for $47M of the Houston oil-and-gas equipment maker's 2010 revenue. "Like many, we are watching the events in Egypt closely," Williams tells investors on a conference call. "We don't yet know what the financial impact of events will be in the first quarter."

---

It would be very difficult to anticipate such an event let alone foresee how investors will interpret its impacts for firm cash flow prospects and share prices. The Egyptian civil-war situation carried much uncertainty across geopolitical, economic, and social fronts all unfolding in historically unique ways. Investors would have had to rely on much incomplete information and narrative threads to assess what the events might mean for the companies in both the short and medium run. When novel events hit the stock market even the CEOs "don't yet know what the financial impact of events will be."

The Government KU group also displayed a spike near 2010/2011 coinciding with the unfolding of the US debt ceiling and sequestration crisis. Recall, however, that the micro-level KU data identifies unscheduled events that are explicitly connected to stories involving corporate entities. While macro KU events like the debt sequestration and fiscal cliff certainly spill over into micro KU events (Chapter 8), mining into the corporate-specific data reveals that the timing of the spike in Government is primarily associated with testimony of Goldman Sachs' CEO Lloyd Blankfein before a congressional senate panel. The testimony was in response to regulatory investigations in which the "SEC Charges Goldman with Fraud in Structuring and Marketing of CDOs Tied to Subprime Mortgages" on April 16, 2010. GS stock declined over 12 percent from the previous day's closing price.

One could even imagine that the significance of the often-stand-alone spikes displayed by numerous KU event groups across Figures 7.2 and 7.4 are suggestive of potential instability in the way factors' impacts on future stock returns are interpreted by investors. Here is some brief discussion on select narrative groups peaking during just the last five years of the sample.

The frequency of corporate KU events grouped into Transportation spiked to its highest level across the entire sample in February and March 2020 from global disruptions in airline travel due to the COVID-19 outbreak. The entire airline industry suffered from travel bans, restrictions, and the collapse in demand for flights. For instance, one identified KU event "transportation disruption" on March 2, 2020 headlined with the corporate announcement, "MW Delta, American Airlines will Suspend Flights to Milan Amid Coronavirus Outbreak." The stock price for American Airlines (AAL) and Delta (DAL) declined by 5.3 percent and 2 percent, respectively, between March 2 and March 3.

Events in the Security group increased from March 2018 through March 2020 – evident were both more dramatic spikes and an increase in underlying trend. The group involves KU events such as border control issues, cyber-attacks, travel warnings, and weapons testing, all areas of public and policy concern in recent years. The Crime Group contains the category "shooting" along with "robbery," "kidnapping," "piracy," "assassination" and so on. The KU group experienced a large increase from mid-2017 through mid-2018 peaking in April 2018 from the shooting at the YouTube headquarters in San Bruno, California on April 4.

Industrial Accidents also spiked in April 2018 in response to the Southwest Airlines plane whose blown engine forced an emergency landing in Philadelphia. The firm's share price (LUV) lost over 6 percent over the next five weeks. The War–Conflict group increased in late 2018 through the end of the sample with spikes in March 2019 and January 2020. The group includes categories that are macro-intensive such as "military action," "peace process," "bombing," "terrorism," "violence" and so on (see Chapter 8), but it also includes conflict between nations over economic rules such as import embargoes that directly impact particular firms. For instance, 2020 headline news articles on March 12 and March 26, respectively, read, "France Bars

Boeing 737 MAX Planes from Its Airspace," and "ITC Rules in Qualcomm's Favor in Apple Patent Dispute, Some iPhone Models Face Import Ban." Boeing's stock (BA) declined over 18 percent from the previous day's close. All of these unscheduled events impacted corporate prospects and share prices in significant, difficult to anticipate ways.

It is also interesting to observe the persistence displayed by other corporate KU groups (i.e. Assets, Dividends/Earnings, Legal, and Revenues). The Dividends/Earnings and Revenues groups, for instance, exhibit very similar patterns throughout the sample period. First, both series' proportion of total corporate KU events oscillate from one period to the next within a +0/0.005 band. Second, the oscillating patterns observed by both series undergo persistent swings increasing in value from 2000, reaching a peak in 2003, reversing course, and steadily diminishing through 2017 only to display a localized hump shape from 2017 through 2020. The close comovement of the two series can be seen by their correlation coefficient of 0.828. One explanation for this behavior is that unscheduled sales events are likely related to unscheduled corporate dividend and profit events such as unscheduled announcements about corporate guidance projections and quarterly figures. The corporate KU Dividends/Earnings series will be applied to a cointegration analysis of an uncertainty-adjusted present value model in Chapter 12 to show one way in which nonrepetitive firm events can be incorporated into existing models of stock price fluctuations.

Lastly, a note on the four technical-related KU factor groups: (i) Technical Analysis, (ii) Stock Prices, (iii) Price Targets, and (iv) Indexes. Technical Analysis corporate KU events involve the reporting on relative strength indicators, resistance and support levels, and bullish/bearish trend reports. Recall, the group Stock Prices involves dramatic share price fluctuations from previous levels that make headline news. Price targets involve an entity's announcement of a projected price or the upgrade/downgrade of such a price target for a corporation. Index KU events involve the rebalancing of market portfolios due to the addition or removal of a company from an index, rebalancing for stock splits, or if a company that manages a particular index makes headline news. Note that all four of the technical-related KU event groups are only identified if they are reported in headlines or deemed relevant for a particular corporation's investment prospects.

Technical trading factors are KU events because they are unscheduled. It is difficult to assess when such factors may enter the information sets of investors. Bullish/bearish technical signals such as Relative Strength Indices or resistance/support levels can be interpreted to some degree with historical data on similar occurrences, but, ultimately, no two periods of bullish/bearish price, valuation, or volatility metrics are the same. There are two other reasons for corporate-level technical factors to be considered KU events. First, stock price trends, or day-to-day fluctuations, if significant enough can constitute a stand-alone event – think of the severe, and unexpected, collapse in stock market prices on October 19, 1987 (i.e. "Black Monday").

Second, stock market momentum, upward or downward, has been a prominent subnarrative (if not a primary one) for every major upswing and downswing in recent memory. From the run-up in tech-fueled prices during the dot-com upswing, to the increases in housing and equity prices from 2004 through 2007, to the plummeting prices associated with the global financial crisis from 2008 through 2009, to the ten-year bull market stymied by the COVID-19 pandemic in March 2020, stock price trends have been part of every bullish or bearish narrative.

What is more, stock price trends tend to dominate movements in valuation ratios such as Shiller's popular CAPE measure of the expensiveness of the broad equity market as proxied by the SP500. No two price-level periods, however, can really be compared on similar grounds as the importance of other macroeconomic and financial variables must be assessed within the time period to make sense of what the price, or valuation, behavior actually means. For example, the stock market reached record highs in December 2019, yet the CAPE stood at 28.9, a low value compared to the 44.2 valuation ratio

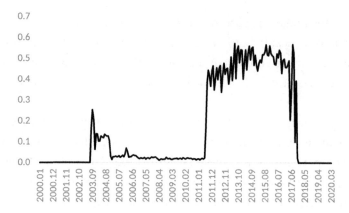

FIGURE 7.5 The figure plots corporate Technical Analysis considerations as a proportion of total corporate KU events from the *Dow Jones* financial news reports over the period January 2000 through March 2020.

reached in December 1999. Historical context and KU events matter to this interpretation.

Given the passage of time, the ten-year average of earnings in the denominator of Shiller's CAPE valuation metric has finally excluded the collapse in profits during the financial crisis/Great Recession period of 2008–2009 that is now dragging down current CAPE values. Others have questioned the role of historically low interest rates when interpreting the current levels of valuation ratios like CAPE.[7] Adding to Table 7.1, Figure 7.5 shows the time-varying importance of unscheduled technical analysis events.

Technical Analysis events mattered very little (less than 5 percent of total corporate KU events) from 2005 through 2010, but the proportion increases dramatically to over 50 percent of total KU events from 2013 through 2017 only to collapse in importance from 2018 through March 2020. The figure suggests that, like other KU event groups, the importance of unscheduled technical events for

---

[7] For a recent discussion on the context necessary for interpreting valuation ratios such as Shiller's CAPE measure, see https://finance.yahoo.com/news/doubt-about-a-nobel-prize-winners-valuation-ratio-111015056.html.

corporate prospects and share prices, unfolds in nonroutine ways over time.

## 7.4 HOW THE KU INDICES RELATE TO EACH OTHER

Thus far, there have been six indices developed based on the unscheduled, or KU, corporate events identified through textual analytics of *Dow Jones* financial news for the US stock market, (i) the KU Index, (ii) the KU ESS Index, (iii) the KU ENS Index, (iv) the KU AEV Index, (v) the KU Relevance Index, and (vi) the KU Variation Index. Comparing the correlations across indices offers additional insights potentially relevant for narrative dynamics. One of the assumptions of the traditional Pearson correlation coefficient is that the variables are univariate normally distributed. Chapters 5 through 7, however, suggest that the corporate KU indices may have nonnormal distributions. Therefore, since stock market outcomes also display nonnormality, all correlation analyses rely on the nonparametric Spearman rank-order test that deals with nonnormal variables and time-variant means through monotonic rank correlations between two series. The Spearman test is also robust to potential nonlinearities in the data (another violated assumption of the traditional Pearson correlation test) that may be present in the relationships between corporate KU variables and stock market outcomes. Table 7.5 reports the Spearman rank correlation statistics across the six indices.

There are several results worth mentioning, and one must, as always, recognize that correlation does not imply causality. First, the correlation between the baseline KU Index and the KU var Index is negative and significant. This suggests that when there are more KU events by absolute count, there are fewer groups of KU events being represented. One interpretation is that KU events are persistent in their occurrence and similarity, that is, that the events are related and potentially connected to similar larger narratives. Second, when there are more groups of KU events, there is less novelty. These two findings support the view that narratives connected to corporate uncertainty grow over time and are fueled by the clustering of similar KU events

Table 7.5 *Spearman correlation tests for corporate KU indices*

|  | KU[a] | KU var | ESS | ENS | AEV | Relevance |
|---|---|---|---|---|---|---|
| KU | 1.000 |  |  |  |  |  |
|  | N/A |  |  |  |  |  |
| KU var | **−0.358** | 1.000 |  |  |  |  |
|  | (0.000) | N/A |  |  |  |  |
| ESS | **−0.726** | **0.533** | 1.000 |  |  |  |
|  | (0.000) | (0.000) | N/A |  |  |  |
| ENS | 0.101 | **−0.328** | **−0.144** | 1.000 |  |  |
|  | (0.117) | (0.000) | (0.025) | N/A |  |  |
| AEV | **0.197** | **0.466** | **0.128** | **−0.516** | 1.000 |  |
|  | (0.002) | (0.000) | (0.047) | (0.000) | N/A |  |
| Relevance | **0.570** | **−0.370** | **−0.374** | **0.247** | −0.189 | 1.000 |
|  | (0.000) | (0.000) | (0.000) | (0.000) | (0.003) | N/A |

[a] *Note:* The table reports Spearman rank-order correlation coefficients with $p$-values for the null hypothesis of zero correlation in parentheses. Bold values indicate significance at the 5% level.

within group. Third, when there are more KU events by count there is much more pessimism generating a significant negative correlation coefficient of −0.726. When there are more groups of KU events, there is more optimism generating a significant positive correlation coefficient of 0.533. This suggests that when there are qualitatively similar unscheduled corporate event groups (i.e. less KU diversity) there is greater pessimism (i.e. lower ESS). These two findings support the view that corporate KU serves an informational role pointing toward lower corporate growth prospects in the future and a higher uncertainty premium today. Chapter 9 provides empirical evidence in support of both of these hypotheses.

This chapter discussed the variation observed in different groups of corporate KU events over the sample period. The top KU groups per five-year subperiod were identified to show which are the most important for stock market investors and how this composition evolved over the last twenty years. The KU var Index was introduced showing that the number of KU groups varies considerably over time. Numerous KU groups were plotted over time revealing dramatic spikes for some groups but persistent trends in others. Correlation coefficients across KU indices suggest that when novel corporate events increase in raw terms so does the clustering of KU events by group, implying that narrative dynamics may be unfolding. The next chapter incorporates macro KU events into the analysis and offers an extensive comparison against the corporate micro KU events with a particular focus on the time-series narrative dynamics between the two realms of unscheduled considerations.

# 8    Macro versus Micro Novelty

## 8.1    INTRODUCTION

Many of the studies referenced in Chapter 2 document that the timing and magnitude of structural change may be connected to major historical events that cause large-scale shifts in stock market relationships and increase investor uncertainty in forecasting future returns. However, there is a dearth of studies assessing the degree to which higher orders of structural change – think interdependence between large- and small-scale shifts in returns processes – may unfold in financial markets. Chapter 3 presented evidence from other social sciences arguing that individuals deal with novel and uncertain situations by developing hierarchical plotlines that prompt thinking in multidimensional narratives when making decisions.

However, the time-varying dynamics of narratives themselves introduce a form of uncertainty into the marketplace since people are telling each other what other people are telling them, leading to higher orders of thinking. Therefore, it is difficult to predict which narratives will become dominant, which may change abruptly, and which may die off. Combining the evidence from Chapters 2 and 3 motivates the view that large narrative threads buttressed by major macro-level Knightian uncertainty (KU) events may interact with subnarratives associated with smaller-scale micro-level KU events. This is the topic of the present chapter.

Chapters 5 through 7 presented data on the prevalence and diversity of novel corporate events in the stock market. These unscheduled news events were explicitly connected to corporate entities and/or share price fluctuations. Findings from these chapters have shown how major unanticipated macro events, such as financial crises and economic recessions, are lurking behind many of these corporate KU events. The recent COVID-19 pandemic and Great Lockdown Recession, for instance, have had a clear impact on corporate KU events, as supported by findings from firm case studies reported in Tables 7.2 through 7.4 and elsewhere. These results suggest that effects from unscheduled macro events, which may or may not have a direct connection to a firm's earnings prospects, may spill over onto corporate novelty and micro-level uncertainty. The present chapter aims to empirically investigate this hypothesis.

Conversely, if qualitative interpretations for future returns are similar enough, novel events at the micro level can accumulate sufficiently so as to feed the growth and transmission power of larger narratives through time and space. When fractures in a particular industry expand and become revealed to outsiders, they have the potential to topple even the most advanced economies. Volumes of ill-advised IT IPOs, predatory subprime mortgage loans, and excessive household debt positions are just recent examples whereby the concentration of micro novelty, and the associated subnarratives, spread vertically to damage larger parts of the economy proliferating uncertainty and stories with greater reach across public and policy spheres. Can researchers say anything about macro versus micro novelty and narrative interactions therein to better understand instability in the US stock market?

This chapter explores higher order relations of stock market stories by focusing on the dynamics between overarching narratives and the subnarratives coursing through the market or, put differently, between macro novelty and micro novelty. Specifically, the unscheduled macro events data from *Dow Jones* financial news outlets is introduced that serves as a companion to the unscheduled corporate events analyzed in Chapters 5 through 7. There are several key findings reported in the present chapter that shed light on the overall Novelty–Narrative Hypothesis (NNH) and inform the relative importance of nonrepetitive corporate events for the upcoming empirical chapters involving stock market outcomes and formal structural change tests.

First, the absolute count of unscheduled macro events reported for the US is dwarfed by its firm-level KU counterparts. However, unscheduled macro events as a proportion of total macro events for the US is remarkably large. Second, the macro KU indices share many of the same internal relationships as the corporate KU indices do. Both KU macro and micro count data display similar signs of correlations between their associated Event Sentiment Score (ESS), Relevance, and Event Novelty Score (ENS) Indices, suggesting that both narratives and subnarratives may have a common internal narratological framework. Third, the diversity in unscheduled macro events is less than that for unscheduled micro groups, suggesting that compositional variation of micro novelty may offer further insight into structural change in stock market relationships. Fourth, the ESS, Relevance, ENS, and Aggregate Event Volume (AEV) Indices for KU macro and micro events are interacted through principal components analysis to create a KU micro "narrative" proxy series and a KU macro "narrative" proxy series. The comovement of the two new variables over time is striking, suggesting that macro narratives and micro (sub) narratives are positively related.

The fifth key finding is that there is strong statistical evidence of "causality" only in the direction from unscheduled macro events to unscheduledd corporate events. Results hold for narrative proxy variables. This finding supports the view that there are novelty, instability, and uncertainty spillover effects from the macro to the micro level in the stock market. Sixth, the highest narrative intensity periods of corporate KU events previously identified do not align with the highest narrative intensity periods of macro KU events identified here based on the same threshold conditions. Moreover, KU macro indices offer virtually no improvement to any of the investigations connecting nonrepetitive events to stock market outcomes in subsequent chapters – all of the explanatory power appears to stem from variation in corporate KU events. One conclusion from the evidence presented here is that, while macro novelty is a catalyst for explaining a portion of micro firm-specific novelty, a stronger connection between stock market dynamics and temporal instability stems from the more intimate effects, and subnarratives, at the corporate level.

## 8.2 KU MACRO INDICES

Table 5.1 showed the fifty-one groups within which there exist unscheduled corporate and macro events reported across the *Dow Jones* news reports. The equities events data presented thus far is based on stock market-specific news that explicitly identifies and connects unscheduled events to a corporate entity and/or its share price. Unsurprisingly, the categories of events most frequently mentioned in the equities data belong to the Business topic of Table 5.1, which includes bankruptcy, earnings, stock prices, credit ratings, dividends, equity actions and more. By contrast, while the macro KU events may be reported in relation to company activities from time to time, they stem primarily from unscheduled occurrences stretching into the other four KU topics of Economy, Environment, Politics, and Society. Though they often influence corporate prospects and share prices, novel macro events, such as natural disasters, pandemics, terrorist attacks, congressional activities, political campaigns, judicial appointments, Fed Chair comments, and so on, are mostly identified in connection to countries, cities, central banks, government branches, organizations, committees, agencies, and institutions. A comprehensive index of all unscheduled events, corporate and macro, is included in Appendix D.

Of course, there are instances of macro and micro KU overlap within group. But, now, when stories of unscheduled events involving mergers and acquisitions are identified, they may involve the Federal Communications Commission (FCC) as a regulatory authority. Credit ratings now relate to changes in the riskiness of a government's sovereign debt. Products–services may now reflect the Food and Drug Administration (FDA) granting approval of a regulated product. Or, that a military branch has secured government contract for a particular product. Taxes may now refer to US congressional approval

FIGURE 8.1  The figure plots the total monthly count of US-related macro unscheduled events reported across *Dow Jones* news outlets for the period January 2000 through March 2020.

of, say, the Tax Cut and Jobs Act of 2017. Technical analysis now refers to a nation's or region's currency behavior.

The KU macro data is tracked by *RavenPack*'s *Dow Jones Global Macro* (DJ-GM) edition of identified news events. Although the platform tracks and classifies any macro event on a global scale, the current analysis focuses on those unscheduled macro events that are identified as having a connection to the US. This includes any unscheduled macro event occurring within a US geographic location, but it also includes unscheduled macro events directly involving the US, or US-owned assets, abroad. For example, unscheduled austerity measures implemented by the Parliament of Greece are not included in the data, but a violent attack by the Islamic State targeting US forces in Iraq is included. A cyclone natural disaster in Bangladesh is not included, but the US Government's lifting of an embargo on a foreign nation is. Figure 8.1 plots the macro KU Index for the sample period January 2000 through March 2020.

Compared to Figure 5.1 for monthly counts of KU corporate events, Figure 8.1 shows that the KU macro events occur significantly less often – the average month experiences approximately 46,000 unscheduled US corporate events compared to only 2,400 unscheduled US macro events. That corporate novelty occurs, and is reported to matter, much more frequently than macro novelty may not be too surprising, but that it is nineteen times more likely to be reported seems a significant difference. Evidence presented in Section 8.4 will elaborate on this disparity by arguing that macro KU events for the US cause an avalanche of unscheduled events at the micro level. The macro KU Index displays its highest event count during the period 2006–2017, that is similar to the highest count months for the corporate KU Index occurring during the period 2012 through 2018. Both series are nonstationary over the sample and a unit root-with-break test for macro KU events identifies virtually the same breakdate (2000:12 for macro KU vs. 2000:11 for micro KU).

Like corporate KU events, variation in the raw count data for macro KU events could reflect changes in the overall macro event count as opposed to relative changes in the proportion of unscheduled events. As an analog to Figure 5.2, Figure 8.2 plots unscheduled macro events for the US as a proportion of total identified macro events for the US over the sample period.

The most obvious feature of the macro KU proportion series is how high the values are: For an average month, over 83 percent of all identified macro events for the US are unscheduled. That is remarkably high and a higher proportion than that of unscheduled events at the corporate level (67 percent). The distribution (not illustrated) is highly nonnormal (Jarque–Bera [JB] $p$-value = 0.000) and has a very long and fat left-tail reaching a minimum value of 52 percent in 2000:11, the same approximate date for identified breaks in the micro and macro count series. Though the count data for macro KU events is much lower than that at the corporate level, the high proportion suggests that macro novelty is a salient feature for the US as a whole. Fifteen of the most reported and interesting macro KU event groups will be presented graphically and discussed in Section 8.3.

The second feature of Figure 8.2 is that, barring the lower values at the beginning and end of the sample, the proportion of unscheduled

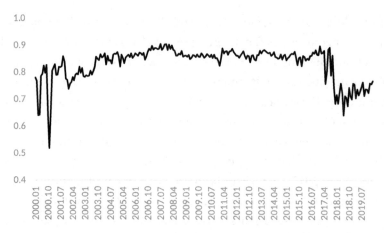

FIGURE 8.2 The figure plots unscheduled macro events for the US as a proportion of total macro events for the US as reported across the *Dow Jones* news outlets during the period January 2000 through March 2020.

events for the US appears fairly flat from 2004 through 2016. However, there is evidence of nonstationarity over the full sample with a mean shift occurring in 2017, perhaps related to the US presidential election, new federal policies such as the Tax Cut and Jobs Act, and numerous shake-ups in cabinet appointments. In fact, the ADF unit root-with-break test finds the series' autoregressive process achieves stationarity around the most likely breakpoint identified at 2017:08. Though the macro KU proportion of total US macro events from Figure 8.2 will be used in subsequent empirical analysis, significantly high proportions of unscheduled macro events beg the question of what the proportion compared to global events looks like.

Figure 8.3 plots unscheduled macro events for the US as a proportion of total macro events (US plus global). The series displays a visual upward trend over the sample period, reaching its highest values in 2019 and 2020, which may suggest that US macro uncertainty from nonrepetitive events has increased over recent years relative to the rest of the world. Dissecting the interdependence of event novelty and associated narratives within a global economic and financial context is left for future research.

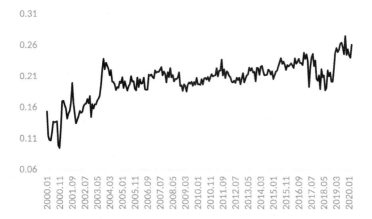

FIGURE 8.3 The figure plots unscheduled macro events for the US as a proportion of total macro events (US plus global) as reported across the *Dow Jones* news outlets during the period January 2000 through March 2020.

One key takeaway from both Figures 8.2 and 8.3 is that the macro KU proportion series is considerably less volatile than its micro counterpart period-by-period (Figure 5.2), a disparity obvious from visual inspection. A simple test of equality of variance across the corporate and macro proportion series, for US and global denominators, provides strong evidence of statistically unequal variances – micro variance is over $1.5\times$ that of the US proportion series and $3\times$ that of the global proportion series – rejecting the null hypothesis of equality with $p$-value $= 0.000$ for both comparisons. Chapter 12 shows how the additional volatility from corporate KU events, specifically unscheduled dividends and earnings events, can help reveal a much stronger fundamentals-based relationship driving stock market prices over time.

Both specifications, level count and proportion, suggest that unscheduled corporate events may offer relatively greater explanatory variation as applied to narrative dynamics and structural change in stock market relationships. However, the high proportion of novelty in macro events likely offers additional information. Empirical analysis presented in this chapter shows how the two realms of considerations are related to each other and how micro events are able to pick up the variation of large-scale novelty displayed at the macro level. The next comparative analysis considers the ESS, ENS, Relevance, and AEV subindices for macro KU events. First, the macro KU subindices are considered. Second, the relationships within macro KU subindices will be compared to those within the micro KU subindices. Third, relationships across micro and macro KU indices will be compared.

## 8.3 CORPORATE VERSUS MACRO KU INDICES

Several findings have already been presented on the importance of the ESS, ENS, and Relevance subindices for corporate KU events. Figure 8.4 plots the three series, plus the AEV Index, for unscheduled macro events for the US over the twenty-year sample period. Similar

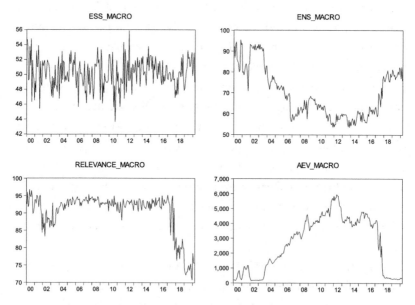

FIGURE 8.4 The figures plot indices related to macro KU events identified in the *Dow Jones* news reports during the period January 2000 through March 2020.

to the micro KU indices, the macro indices measure the monthly average for sentiment, novelty, relevance, and aggregate event volume for unscheduled events identified by the *RavenPack* analytics platform for the same *Dow Jones* news outlets.

The results in Figure 8.4 can be preliminarily compared to the analogous figures for micro KU, namely Figures 6.1 through 6.4. For example, the macro KU ESS Index displays less drift and more volatility than its micro counterpart. In fact, the macro ESS Index is strongly stationary (JB test $p$-value = 0.419) whereas the micro ESS Index displays nonstationary behavior. Moreover, the macro ESS Index does not significantly comove with stock market valuation ratios such the Cyclically Adjusted Price-to-Earnings (CAPE) ratio like the corporate ESS Index does – ESS macro generates a Spearman test $p$-value = 0.259 failing to reject the null hypothesis of zero correlation with CAPE. It is also odd that pessimistic values for the macro ESS Index spike in September 2010, over one year after the end of the Great Recession and global financial crisis. Finally, the macro ESS Index exhibits substantially greater pessimism, reaching a minimum value of 43.7 and mean of 50.2 compared to the corporate ESS minimum of 49.1 and mean of 52.6, while macro versus micro event optimism reaches max values at 55.9 and 57.6, respectively. This suggests that unscheduled macro events are associated with more pessimistic narratives and a more negative framing of contextualized meaning compared to micro unscheduled events. This finding is consistent with the "rare disaster events" literature in financial markets referenced in Chapters 2 and 4.

The macro ENS series exhibits substantially greater range than its micro analog. The former displays persistent drift spanning values between 53.5 and 95.4 compared to the min and max of 84.7 and 97.4 for corporate ENS events that, though also persistent, exhibit large downward spikes periodically. The two relevance indices are graphically very similar in tracking dramatic declines beginning at the end of 2017 and extending through to the end of the sample. Comparing the AEV indices reveals a stark difference, however, between macro versus micro unscheduled events. Mean values for the macro AEV

Index are over seventy-five times that for the micro events. Recall that the AEV tracks the volume of news events reported to involve the same entity within a three-month window. One explanation is that the unscheduled macro events involve entities that, in comparison to corporations, are much larger in scope and scale on an aggregate level – think US Congress, the SEC, the White House, or the US Federal Reserve – and therefore would be involved in many news events, some related and some not, over the ninety-one-day AEV window.

There are two sets of correlation statistics generated. The first (not reported here) is based on Spearman correlation coefficients *within* the KU macro indices and is a companion to the output presented in Table 7.5. Here are some key findings. Similar to the micro KU relations, when there are more unscheduled macro events (higher KU macro) there is more pessimism (lower ESS macro), greater relevance (higher Relevance macro), and higher ninety-day entity volume (higher AEV macro). All of these internal macro correlation coefficients are significant at the 1 percent level except ESS macro, which is insignificant. Consistent signs and majority significance between KU events and their respective Sentiment, Relevance, and Volume subindices could reflect the inner workings of narrative dynamics since the correlation findings hold across both micro and macro realms of unscheduled events.

The second set of correlations are based on the coefficients *across* micro versus macro KU indices and are reported in Table 8.1. The KU indices correspond to those from Chapters 5 through 7 and are given the "micro" labels simply for ease of comparative interpretation with macro KU indices.

The main results from Table 8.1 are reported along the diagonal that pairs the corresponding micro and macro KU indices. Four out of these six correlations are statistically significant and all four are positive. Of mention is the very high correlation of 0.845 between the count of micro and macro events per month (KU micro and KU macro), suggesting a very close relationship between unscheduled

Table 8.1 *Spearman correlation tests between KU micro and macro indices*

| | KU[a] macro | KU macro prop | ESS macro | ENS macro | Rel. macro | AEV macro |
|---|---|---|---|---|---|---|
| KU micro | **0.845** | **0.609** | 0.094 | **−0.858** | **0.340** | **0.820** |
| | (0.000) | (0.000) | (0.142) | (0.000) | (0.000) | (0.000) |
| KU micro prop | **0.382** | **0.219** | 0.031 | **−0.409** | 0.067 | **0.378** |
| | (0.000) | (0.001) | (0.635) | (0.000) | (0.300) | (0.000) |
| ESS micro | **−0.493** | **−0.228** | −0.103 | **0.553** | −0.014 | **−0.490** |
| | (0.000) | (0.000) | (0.109) | (0.000) | (0.832) | (0.000) |
| ENS micro | −0.015 | **−0.140** | **0.152** | −0.035 | **−0.231** | 0.034 |
| | (0.812) | (0.030) | (0.018) | (0.587) | (0.000) | (0.598) |
| Rel micro | **0.446** | **0.392** | **0.120** | **−0.550** | **0.445** | **0.510** |
| | (0.000) | (0.010) | (0.062) | (0.000) | (0.000) | (0.000) |
| AEV micro | **0.422** | **0.461** | **−0.131** | **−0.286** | **0.412** | **0.400** |
| | (0.000) | (0.000) | (0.041) | (0.000) | (0.000) | (0.000) |

[a] *Note:* The table reports the Spearman rank-order correlation coefficients between micro and macro KU events identified in the *Dow Jones* news over the sample period January 2000 through March 2020. KU macro prop is the proportion of unscheduled macro events for the US compared to total macro events for the US.

events at both levels. KU proportions also share a significantly positive correlation. Moreover, when unscheduled macro events are deemed relevant so too are unscheduled micro events as evidenced by the significant Relevance correlation of 0.445. Put differently, it is not the case that one type of novelty is driving the stories while the other type is merely mentioned in passing at the end of the article; macro novelty and micro novelty are collectively relevant. The key takeaway from Table 8.1 is that not only are the counts and proportion of unscheduled events occurring at the corporate level related to those occurring at the macro level, but the relevance and inertia at both levels are positively correlated with one another as well. Taken as a whole, the evidence points to joint, or higher order, novelty and associated uncertainty unfolding in the stock market, which may be manifested through common threads connecting narratives to subnarratives. This hypothesis is explored further in Section 8.4.

## 8.4    MACRO DIVERSITY, NARRATIVE INTENSITY, AND CAUSALITY

Ample evidence from Chapters 5 through 7 showed that the importance of corporate KU events changes at times and in ways that would be difficult to foresee. For instance, Figure 7.3 showed that there is substantial variation in the number, or diversity, of corporate KU groups reported as driving firm prospects and stock market behavior over time. Figure 7.4 illustrated that this variation comes in different forms, some KU groups drift in one direction or another in persistent ways while other groups display sharp spikes in importance. Moreover, Chapter 7, in reflecting on the variation exhibited by Figure 7.3, remarked that KU group diversity is a proxy for how many potentially different subnarratives there are in the stock market at a given point in time, noting that the number of larger narratives could be more, less, or the same depending on the subnarratives' directional and qualitative connection to them. This section explores this conjecture by first presenting different representations of macro KU group variation.

A natural starting point is to generate the analog to Figure 7.3 by tracking the number of different macro KU groups per month that exceed 2 percent of total contribution to total macro KU events for the US. Thus, Figure 8.5 is a proxy for how many potentially different overarching narratives there are swirling in the US at a given point in time.

The results from Figure 8.5 show that there is a considerable range for macro KU group diversity – the minimum value is zero groups that exceed the 2 percent threshold (2004:06) while the maximum value is 13 (2000:10 and 2000:12). However, virtually all of the observations fall between 4 and 13 groups, as the zero observation is an outlier. Like its micro KU counterpart, the group variation in

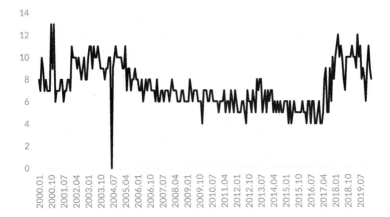

FIGURE 8.5 The figure plots the number of macro KU groups that constitute more than 0.02 of total macro KU events per month for the period January 2000 through March 2020.

macro KU events displays persistence from period to period. The global maximum values seem to predate the short-lived US recession in 2001 that lasted from March through November, during which time the series declines sharply from 13 to a range of 6–8. This may reflect a consolidation in larger narratives as the macro economy garnered relatively more attention during this period. Like the comparisons of macro versus micro KU indices reported in Table 8.1, the event variation indices also produce evidence of comovement between micro and macro considerations sharing a significant positive correlation of 0.282 ($p$-value = 0.000).

However, there are also several differences between the diversity indices across micro and macro KU groups. Though the correlation is positive and significant, not all subperiods experience the same magnitude of comovement. For example, Figure 8.5 displays a dramatic increase in the number of different macro KU groups during the last three years of the sample whereas micro KU diversity appears flat from mid-2017 and on. Moreover, we can simply look at the lower mean value of 7.3 macro KU groups compared to the average of 10.7 micro KU groups to infer that there are more subnarratives and greater

diversity in corporate novelty than overarching narratives and macro
novelty for an average month. This finding adds support to the view
that structural change in US stock market relationships may be more
closely connected to unscheduled corporate events than unscheduled
macro events.

The second way to infer changing variation in macro KU event
groups is to consider the group-specific graphs as an analog to Figure
7.4. Figure 8.6 plots fifteen of the most identified (as a proportion
of total macro US events) and interesting unscheduled macro event
groups. There are several features of Figure 8.6 worth mentioning.
First, similar to the micro KU group counterparts, there are some
groups that display persistence, such as Domestic Product, Government, and Products–Services; while others display outlier spikes in
frequency, such as Transportation and Taxes. The dramatic spike in
unscheduled macro Health events in March 2020 reflects the COVID-
19 pandemic. Natural disaster events display intermittent spikes in
occurrence throughout the sample with a clustering of highest month
values from 2017 through 2020 likely reflecting hurricanes Irma,
Harvey, Florence, and Michael, flooding in Houston and Maryland,
and the western wildfires and mudslides. The rise in the Taxes group
during the end of the sample corresponds to the Tax Cuts and Jobs Act
of 2017.

Some KU macro groups, such as Regulatory, Government, War–
Conflict, Security, and Taxes matter relatively more for macro versus micro unscheduled events. However, Credit Ratings, Products–
Services, and Technical Analysis are commensurately important for
both realms of considerations.

Looking at the frequency of unscheduled US-related macro
events, however, paints a rather incomplete picture of their connection to narrative dynamics and temporal instability in the stock
market. As discussed in earlier chapters, narratives may be part
novelty, part sentiment, and part relevance. To identify periods of the
highest narrative intensity for macro KU events, Figure 8.7 plots the
analog to Figure 6.5 by considering only those points in time where

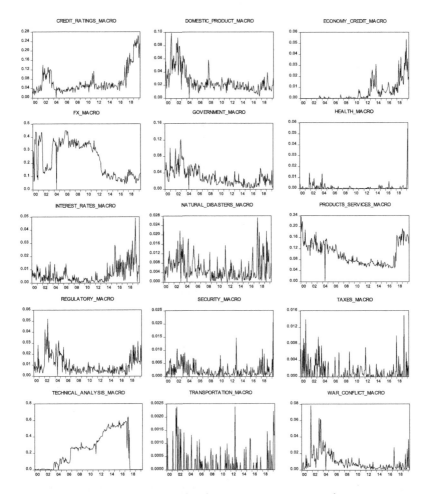

FIGURE 8.6 The figures plot the macro KU event group frequencies as a proportion of total US macro events per month identified in the *Dow Jones* news reports over the sample period January 2000 through March 2020.

the conditions that the top/bottom 10 percent ESS, top 10 percent ENS, and top 50 percent of Relevance for macro KU events within five-year subperiods are jointly met.

The joint conditions of extreme optimism/pessimism, high novelty, and high relevance for macro KU events are met during the periods 2000:12, 2005:05, and 2010:05. These three months are less by

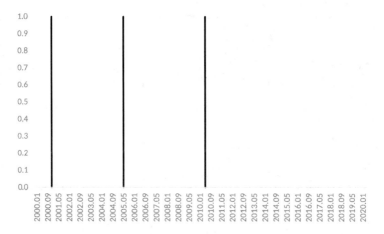

FIGURE 8.7 The vertical bars denote dummy variables equal to one for
the joint condition that macro KU events constitute the highest/lowest
values of ESS, highest values of ENS, and high values of Relevance for a
given period from January 2000 through March 2020.

count than the six months of highest narrative intensity documented
for micro KU events. Moreover, only the narrative intensity period
of 2000:12 approximately aligns with any of the identified intensity
points for corporate events (2000:10). However, 2000:10 is the approximate date on which both macro KU and micro KU count indices
experience the most significant breakpoint in their autoregressive
processes. The other two periods of high macro narrative intensity are
thirty-nine months and twenty-one months apart from their closest
micro counterpart period. Extending the analysis to include moderate
narrative intensity points akin to Figure 6.6 yields clustering around
the years 2005 and 2010, both years absent from moderate narrative
intensity periods for micro KU events.

Table 8.1 reports the very high correlation coefficient of 0.845
between count values of micro KU and macro KU events per month.
In the context of narratives and subnarratives, it would be informative to assess whether there is "statistical causality" between the
two realms of novelty and associated uncertainty. Granger causality
tests do not prove that one variable directly causes another. Rather,

the tests investigate whether lagged values of one variable jointly help explain contemporaneous values of the other variable. The null hypothesis is that the coefficients on the lagged variables are jointly equal to zero. If the null is rejected, past information of one variable is considered useful for explaining future variation in the other variable. The $p$-value for the null hypothesis that KU macro does not Granger cause KU micro is 0.006; the $p$-value for the null hypothesis that KU micro does not Granger cause KU macro is 0.412. The $p$-values for tests based on first-differenced variables to address potential unit roots in the data-generating process are 0.004 and 0.651. The tests suggest that there is statistical causality only in the direction from unscheduled macro events to unscheduled micro events. Micro novelty lags macro novelty, and the latter informs future information contained in the former.

Making empirical inference using the baseline micro and macro KU count data, however, may underestimate the complex narrative influences of sentiment, novelty, relevance, and inertia. One way of getting at the question of how to proxy for narrative dynamics while simultaneously analyzing the relationship between micro and macro novelty involves principal components analysis (PCA). The main idea behind PCA is to reduce the parameters in a system of related variables while maintaining the variation in the data-generating process by using linear combinations, or components, of the variables. Each component, or eigenvector, is orthogonal to the other linear combinations whereby the first principal component makes the largest contribution to the original variance structure with subsequent components making decreasing contributions. To generate narrative proxies each micro versus macro system includes the baseline count of KU events, but also includes the ESS, ENS, Relevance, and AEV variables.[1] Figure 8.8 plots the first principal component for both the micro and macro KU narrative proxies.

---

[1] Since the variables have different measurement scales all data in both information systems are normalized by following $x_{norm} = (x - x_{min})/(x_{max} - x_{min})$ that implies $0 \leq x_{norm} \leq 1$. PCA is performed based on the Spearman rank-order coefficients in the correlation matrix.

FIGURE 8.8 The figure plots the first principal component for both micro KU (solid line) and macro KU (dotted line) events where each PC1 is capturing the greatest variation in the set of ESS, Relevance, ENS, and AEV for each series. All data are normalized.

The comovement between micro PC1 and macro PC1 is apparent from the figure. The Spearman rank correlation coefficient is 0.625 ($p$-value = 0.000). Visually, both series reflect the univariate properties of the corresponding baseline count data of KU events as compared to the ESS, ENS, Relevance, and AEV univariate properties. This finding is also supported through the principal components analysis whereby the count KU data for both macro and micro events is found to be the metric contributing the majority of variance in respective PC1s. This suggests that narrative dynamics, while certainly enhanced by sentiment, novelty, and relevance, are also being picked up by variation in the raw count of unscheduled events.

Though the statistical significance is slightly lessened, the direction of statistical causality after accounting for sentiment, novelty, relevance, and volume and running exclusively from macro KU events to micro KU events still maintains. The $p$-value for the null hypothesis that macro narrative PC1 does not Granger cause micro narrative PC1 is 0.058; the $p$-value for the null hypothesis that micro narrative PC1 does not Granger cause macro narrative PC1 is 0.354.

Lastly, there is a distinction between macro and micro events' connection to stock market volatility worth discussing. The Spearman correlation coefficient between the VIX (the options-implied volatility index for the SP500) and the diversity of macro and micro KU groups is 0.06 ($p$-value = 0.373) and 0.122 ($p$-value = 0.058), respectively. The significant relation between the diversity of micro unscheduled events, but not macro unscheduled events, and SP500 volatility is likely a consequence of the fact that unscheduled micro events are intimately connected to the prospects of corporations and their associated share prices. While major historical macro events cause great instability in financial markets, the evidence presented here increasingly points toward corporate novelty as the key channel through which stock market instability and (sub)narrative dynamics may continuously unfold.

This chapter explored the relational dynamics between macro and micro unscheduled events by assuming that these two groups are associated with stock market narratives and subnarratives, respectively. Although macro KU events are dwarfed by the frequency of corporate KU events, there are numerous findings from this chapter that show a connection between the two realms of unscheduled events. The two baseline indices share a very high correlation, as do the first principal components of micro and macro narrative proxies that include sentiment, novelty, relevance, and volume/inertia. Consistent relations within the macro subindices compared to those within micro subindices suggests the two realms of novelty and uncertainty share common internal narratological structures. Furthermore, there is evidence that the macro KU events lead the micro KU events, implying that unforeseeable change at the macro level may be spilling over onto lagging novel corporate events and ensuing smaller-scale instability.

However, macro KU exhibited considerably less variation in event count and in group diversity over the sample period as compared to micro counterparts. High narrative intensity periods of macro events also failed to approximately align with micro events' analog narrative intensities. Taken together, the menu of findings from this chapter gives confidence that unscheduled corporate events are the preferred source of information for understanding narrative dynamics and stock market instability not only because of the greater variation and diversity, but because they reflect the transmission of lower frequency novelty (and instability) catalyzed at the macro level. This view is supported further by the findings that for every empirical investigation in the next two chapters on stock market outcomes and structural change, none were convincingly improved upon by substituting macro KU for micro KU events.

# PART III Empirical Evidence for the Novelty-Narrative Hypothesis

# 9    Corporate Novelty and Stock Market Outcomes

Chapters 5 and 6 introduced the corporate Knightian uncertainty (KU) Event, Sentiment, Novelty, Relevance, and Volume Indices tracking all unscheduled events connected to firm-level prospects and stock price behavior as reported in the *Dow Jones* financial news outlets from January 2000 through March 2020. Chapter 7 further dissected the data by generating the KU Variation Index tracking the degree of different groupings of unscheduled corporate events over time. Chapter 8 explored the close statistical relationship between micro KU and macro KU events. Though the presence of micro novelty was found to dwarf that of macro novelty, both in count and group diversity, unscheduled corporate events were still able to reflect the key temporal and narratological dynamics occurring at the macro level. The present chapter extends the analysis by presenting a battery of statistical tests aimed at shedding light on the comovements between corporate KU event indices and actual stock market outcomes at both the aggregate and firm level.

The first stage of the analysis is based on correlation statistics between the micro KU indices and the SP500, the Cyclically Adjusted Price-to-Earnings (CAPE) ratio, the VIX options implied volatility index, SP500 trading volume, and equity Exchange Traded Fund (ETF) flows. Findings suggest a strong underlying relationship between novel corporate events and stock market outcomes with many of the hypothesized signs consistent with the overarching Novelty–Narrative Hypothesis (NNH) discussed hitherto. The second stage of the analysis focuses on unscheduled corporate events and the variance in analyst projections of long-term growth prospects for individual *Dow Jones Industrial Average* 30 firms. The analysis is intriguing for

NNH: Results suggest a significant inverse relationship between the dispersion of firm-level analyst forecasts over time and both the count of corporate KU events and variation in KU event groups. Finally, Granger causality tests find that the significance runs from lagged KU event and variation indices to future values of analyst growth estimate dispersion.

## 9.2    CORRELATION BETWEEN KU AND STOCK MARKET OUTCOMES

The micro KU event indices introduced in Chapters 5 through 7 measure the total count of unscheduled corporate events per month (KU), the number of different corporate KU event groups per month (KU var), the proportion of corporate KU events to total corporate events (KU prop), the average corporate KU event sentiment per month (ESS), novelty per month (ENS), relevance per month (Rel), and entity event volume per month (AEV). Prior to taking up the issue of temporally correspondent instability between micro KU narrative intensity and stock market relationships in Chapter 10, the present analysis must first ascertain whether there is evidence of comovement between unscheduled corporate events and stock market outcomes and whether there are economically meaningful signs of correlation and directions of statistical causality.

Aggregate stock market outcomes are represented by the *Standard and Poor's Composite Index* price (SP500), the CAPE ratio for the SP500, the options-implied volatility index for the SP500 (VIX), the trading volume in shares for the SP500 (Vol), and the flow of funds for the SP500 EFT with ticker SPY (Flows). All data are in nominal terms at a monthly frequency.[1]

The following two propositions relate corporate KU indices to the five stock market variables.

---

[1] Data on SP500 closing price (GSPC), Volume, and VIX is collected from www.yahoo.com/finance and CAPE data is collected from Robert Shiller's webpage www.econ.yale.edu/~shiller/. SPY fund flows data is collected from *Bloomberg L.P.*.

**Proposition 1:** *corporate KU events comove negatively with stock market prices and valuation levels.*

When there is a greater degree of potential change, or instability, in stock market relationships due to unscheduled firm events, investors require greater future returns to compensate for the uncertainty and increased ambiguity over which models and forecasting strategies to place the greatest confidence in. Narratives are not bad for the stock market. Rather, they are necessary features in a world of imperfect knowledge. Uncertainty, however, is bearish for stock market prices and returns and requires a premium when the likelihood of future possible states is more ambiguous. That is, when KU is higher, current prices fall as future (required) returns rise. Rare disaster events, such as extreme left-tail shocks to consumption, for instance, have been connected to higher returns (lower contemporaneous prices), a higher (time-varying) equity premium, and greater volatility in the stock market (i.e. Wachter, 2013).

Therefore, when corporate KU events are greater in count and group diversity, implying an uncertainty premium, there is also the need for nuanced investor sentiment, for weighing the prospects of pushing market prices further into excessive valuation territory. Recall, Chapter 6 provided evidence suggesting that investors require greater confidence (through sentiment becoming more optimistic or pessimistic) to stake an increasingly exposed open position when both novel events occur and valuations are historically high. Uncertainty may serve as a bounding force helping to limit excesses in the stock market from both above and below benchmark valuations if a premium is associated with increasing exposure to market reversals, implying a gap-effect. Consequently, increases in unscheduled corporate events and micro uncertainty imply stock prices and index valuation ratios should be lower today and correlation coefficients shared with KU and KU var should possess a negative sign.

The predicted correlation coefficients between ESS and stock prices and valuation levels, however, is ambiguous – it depends on whether uncertainty effects or sentiment effects dominate. While uncertainty pushes stock prices lower, generally speaking, higher sentiment (optimism) connected to higher expected cash flow fundamentals pushes prices higher today and vice versa. The KU Novelty, Relevance, and Volume Indices do not have an economically meaningful hypothesized correlation sign with stock market prices and valuation ratios beyond the negative uncertainty effects discussed above.

**Proposition 2:** *KU events comove positively with stock market volatility.*

Stock market volatility is often considered a "gauge of fear" and has even been treated itself as a proxy for investor uncertainty.[2] When there are more unscheduled events and groups there is greater potential for narrative dynamics related to structural change in the stock market. Beliefs about possible outcomes become more uncertain and stock market price changes become more volatile. This is the standard view of uncertainty and the VIX. Therefore, KU and KU var are predicted to share a positive correlation coefficient with the VIX. However, if an increase in either KU or KU var leads to an increase in qualitatively similar unscheduled events and groups that share directionally consistent interpretations for future returns, then the VIX could decrease. In such a scenario, unscheduled events tracked by KU and KU var are exerting informational effects that dominate the model ambiguity effect. More on this to follow. ESS also has conflicting effects with the VIX. The standard uncertainty effects drive volatility up while optimism and pessimism are predicted to drive volatility down and up, respectively, suggesting an ambiguous predicted correlation sign between ESS and the VIX.[3]

---

[2] For studies treating the VIX as a proxy for market uncertainty through stock liquidity effects see Chung and Chuwonganant (2014), through monetary and other economic policy channels see Bekaert et al. (2013) and Baker et al. (2016), through employment channels see Caggiano et al. (2014), and through political channels see Goodell and Vahamaa (2013) and references therein.

[3] See studies referenced in Chapter 2 for asymmetric effects between stock market volatility and optimism (pessimism) associated with business cycle expansions (contractions).

Corporate uncertainty is hypothesized to increase trading volume in the stock market as investors seek to close large open positions in stock, reduce those which are heavily exposed, or open/increase hedging positions. As part of this process, investors may seek fixed income securities as a safe haven compared to equities. In past episodes thought to be associated with high degrees of uncertainty, such as during the global financial crisis of 2008, trading volume in the US stock market was very high. Consequently, we would expect a positive correlation coefficient between KU/KU var and Volume.[4] Greater pessimism is hypothesized to lead to greater trading volume, predicting a negative correlation between ESS and Volume.

Equity fund outflows (more negative values) into safer asset classes are predicted to increase due to uncertainty, leading to an inverse correlation coefficient with KU and KU var. More pessimism in the stock market leads to ETF outflows, predicting a positive coefficient between ESS and Flows, but more uncertainty also leads to greater outflows, predicting a negative coefficient. Thus, the correlation sign is ambiguous between ESS and Flows. Table 9.1 summarizes the hypothesized signs of correlation between corporate KU event indices and aggregate stock market outcomes based on the two propositions.

Table 9.2 reports the Spearman correlation coefficients for KU event indices and stock market outcomes with associated $p$-values (reported in parentheses) for the null hypothesis of zero correlation between the two variables over the sample period. Bold values denote statistical significance at the 1, 5, or 10 percent level.

Several findings from Table 9.2 emerge in support of NNH. For Proposition 1, three out of four coefficients are of the correct

---

[4] Again, if greater uncertainty is coupled with economic recession or sharp reversal in stock market prices, studies show that trading volume increases. Here, the analysis is focusing on the effects of KU and KU var.

Table 9.1 *Hypothesized relations between KU and stock market outcomes*

|        | SP500[a] | CAPE | VIX | Vol. | Flows |
|--------|----------|------|-----|------|-------|
| KU     | −        | −    | +   | +    | −     |
| KU var | −        | −    | +   | +    | −     |
| ESS    | ±        | ±    | ±   | −    | ±     |

[a] *Note:* The table reports the predicted signs of correlation coefficients between corporate KU event indices and stock market outcomes. The variables are as defined in the text.

Table 9.2 *Correlation between KU and stock market outcomes*

|        | SP500[a] | CAPE     | VIX      | Vol.     | Flows    |
|--------|----------|----------|----------|----------|----------|
| KU     | **0.277**   | **−0.468**  | **−0.184**  | **0.599**   | 0.014    |
|        | (0.000)  | (0.000)  | (0.004)  | (0.000)  | (0.826)  |
| KU var | **−0.608**  | **−0.168**  | **0.122**   | **−0.193**  | **−0.177**  |
|        | (0.000)  | (0.009)  | (0.058)  | (0.003)  | (0.006)  |
| ESS    | **−0.512**  | **0.151**   | **0.285**   | **−0.522**  | −0.020   |
|        | (0.000)  | (0.018)  | (0.000)  | (0.000)  | (0.761)  |
| ENS    | 0.087    | −0.055   | **0.156**   | −0.058   | 0.096    |
|        | (0.177)  | (0.396)  | (0.015)  | (0.369)  | (0.137)  |
| Rel.   | **0.192**   | −0.052   | **−0.255**  | −0.070   | 0.045    |
|        | (0.003)  | (0.419)  | (0.000)  | (0.280)  | (0.487)  |
| AEV    | **−0.367**  | **−0.505**  | **0.167**   | **0.386**   | −0.012   |
|        | (0.000)  | (0.000)  | (0.009)  | (0.000)  | (0.851)  |

[a] *Note:* The table reports the correlation coefficients between the KU event indices and various measures of aggregate stock market behavior. KU var denotes the KU Event Variation Index; Rel. denotes KU Relevance Index; Vol. denotes volume; all of the other variables are as defined in the text. Values in parentheses are *p*-values for the null hypothesis of zero correlation between the two variables. Values in bold indicate statistical significance at the 1%, 5%, or 10% level.

negative sign and statistically significant. Four out of six (67 percent) of the coefficients between ENS, Rel., and AEV and SP500 and CAPE are negative (three statistically significant), giving additional support to the uncertainty effects in these variables. ESS shares a negative correlation with stock market prices, but a positive correlation with CAPE, both significant. That is, for raw prices the uncertainty effect dominates while for valuations the sentiment effect dominates. This finding is consistent with the graphical evidence of comovement presented between ESS and CAPE in Figure 6.1.

For Proposition 2, there is mixed evidence for NNH: Only KU var possesses the predicted positive correlations with the VIX. However, half of the coefficients between KU and KU var and Volume and Flows are of predicted sign and significant. It is interesting that KU var displays the correct sign for every hypothesized correlation coefficient with aggregate stock market outcomes, except with Volume, with three out of five found statistically significant. This suggests that NNH may hold best for the diversity of novel corporate events as opposed to the level count. Finally, for ESS, the uncertainty effect dominates for the VIX, but the sentiment effect dominates with Volume.

### 9.2.1 KU Diversity and the Gap-Effect

As discussed in Chapter 2, many structural change studies report that instability is connected to peaks and troughs in economic and financial cycles and that the impact on return and volatility processes may be asymmetric across these regimes. However, correlation coefficients reported in Table 9.2 and elsewhere assume that the KU variables are picking up the instability in stock market relationships through the timing, magnitude, and diversity of nonrepetitive firm events and associated narratives. Many of the stock market variables listed, however, appear somewhat "bounded" in their movements over time, such as the CAPE valuation ratio that historically has been bounded below 44.2 (December 1999) and above 4.78 (December 1920) for the last 120 years of SP500 data. Is there a connection, possibly

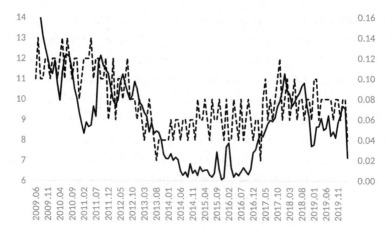

FIGURE 9.1 The figure plots the percentage gap of CAPE from its twenty-year historical average (right axis, solid line) against KU var (left axis, dotted line) for the period June 2009 through March 2020.

asymmetric, between the peaks and troughs of stock market valuation ratios, economic cycles, and novel corporate events?

Figure 9.1 plots the percentage departure of the CAPE valuation ratio away from its arithmetic average (26.15 from 2000:01 through 2020:03), termed CAPE-Gap, against the diversity of novel events as proxied by the variable KU var for the period beginning with the end of the Great Recession (June 2009) and extending through March 2020.[5]

Though not illustrated here, prior to the end of the Great Recession in June 2009 there was no noticeable relationship between CAPE-Gap and KU var whatsoever. Expanding the sample to include the historic economic and financial expansion from 2010 to 2020, however, produces a very different outcome. Figure 9.1 shows a clear comovement between the two variables plotted: When there are peaks or troughs in stock market valuation ratios (i.e. when the CAPE-Gap is high) the number of different KU groups is also high and vice versa. The graph suggests that the diversity of corporate novelty

[5] CAPE-Gap is equal to the absolute value of the difference in log values of CAPE and its mean, $|ln(CAPE_t) - ln(\overline{CAPE})|$.

may be related to periods of excess and subsequent price reversals, or structural change, in the stock market.

## 9.3   KU AND VARIANCE OF LONG-TERM EPS GROWTH FORECASTS

The second stage of analysis focuses on firm-level tests of comovement under NNH. Specifically, data is collected from the *Bloomberg* estimates ("B-est") of analyst forecasts for long-term growth (LTG) of earnings per share (EPS) for the thirty firms from the *Dow Jones Industrial Average* (DJIA).[6] The standard deviation of a six-month rolling window of this series is used as a proxy for the disparity in analyst LTG projections for major stock market firms through time and is compared against corporate KU indices through simple correlation coefficients. Table 9.3 reports the correlation results for each of the thirty DJIA firms against the KU Index (KU), the KU Event Variation Index (KU var), and the KU Proportion Index (KU prop).

First, there is statistical evidence that the dispersion of analyst forecasts over time of firm-level LTG is connected to novel corporate events. Of the thirty firms, the baseline KU Index shares significant correlations with twenty of them, the KU Variation Index shares fifteen significant correlations and the KU Proportion Index shares thirteen. Of those forty-eight significant correlations, forty-three are significant at the 1 percent or 5 percent level, the other five at the 10 percent level. Second, the sign of the correlation coefficient for significant firms is predominantly negative. In fact, thirty-three out of the forty-eight total significant correlation pairings (or roughly 67 percent) are negative.

One interpretation of the result that KU events are negatively correlated with forecast dispersion of growth prospects over time follows from the arguments previously made about uncertainty

---

[6] *Bloomberg L.P.* has growth forecast data for over 15,000 companies worldwide. Approximately 15–25 *Bloomberg* analysts provide estimates of long-term earnings per share growth for each of the 30 DJIA firms. Data was unavailable for the within-period standard deviation of LTG estimates across analysts.

Table 9.3 *Correlation between KU and LTG forecast variance*

| Ticker[a] | KU | KU var | KU prop | Ticker | KU | KU var | KU prop |
|---|---|---|---|---|---|---|---|
| AAPL | 0.062 | **−0.217** | 0.005 | KO | −0.110 | −0.028 | −0.065 |
| | (0.414) | (0.004) | (0.949) | | (0.154) | (0.715) | (0.405) |
| AXP | **−0.222** | **0.210** | **−0.190** | MCD | **0.1919** | −0.040 | 0.074 |
| | (0.003) | (0.006) | (0.012) | | (0.012) | (0.597) | (0.330) |
| BA | **−0.257** | **0.399** | **−0.243** | MMM | 0.095 | −0.079 | 0.030 |
| | (0.001) | (0.000) | (0.002) | | (0.214) | (0.306) | (0.693) |
| CAT | **−0.231** | **0.187** | **−0.228** | MRK | **−0.182** | −0.001 | **−0.141** |
| | (0.003) | (0.015) | (0.003) | | (0.016) | (0.984) | (0.062) |
| CSCO | **−0.238** | 0.050 | −0.065 | MSFT | −0.021 | **−0.352** | 0.042 |
| | (0.002) | (0.516) | (0.400) | | (0.784) | (0.000) | (0.582) |
| CVX | **−0.261** | **0.153** | **−0.190** | NKE | **−0.251** | **−0.288** | 0.064 |
| | (0.001) | (0.044) | (0.012) | | (0.001) | (0.000) | (0.406) |
| DD | 0.138 | 0.089 | −0.080 | PFE | **0.235** | −0.003 | 0.020 |
| | (0.500) | (0.667) | (0.699) | | (0.002) | (0.968) | (0.797) |
| DIS | **−0.263** | 0.111 | −0.099 | PG | **0.428** | **−0.322** | **0.180** |
| | (0.001) | (0.150) | (0.200) | | (0.000) | (0.000) | (0.019) |
| GE | **−0.443** | 0.075 | **−0.164** | TRV | **−0.439** | **0.424** | **−0.329** |
| | (0.000) | (0.324) | (0.031) | | (0.000) | (0.000) | (0.000) |
| GS | **0.253** | **−0.208** | 0.032 | UNH | 0.096 | 0.061 | −0.043 |
| | (0.004) | (0.019) | (0.723) | | (0.205) | (0.421) | (0.574) |
| HD | −0.120 | −0.025 | −0.025 | UTX | **0.137** | −0.040 | −0.057 |
| | (0.115) | (0.743) | (0.743) | | (0.070) | (0.595) | (0.448) |
| IBM | **−0.269** | −0.014 | **−0.142** | V | **−0.334** | 0.001 | **−0.147** |
| | (0.000) | (0.853) | (0.062) | | (0.000) | (0.994) | (0.084) |
| INTC | 0.061 | **−0.227** | 0.050 | VZ | **0.171** | −0.071 | −0.022 |
| | (0.425) | (0.003) | (0.513) | | (0.026) | (0.359) | (0.779) |
| JNJ | **−0.195** | **0.369** | **−0.255** | WMT | 0.061 | **−0.315** | **0.133** |
| | (0.011) | (0.000) | (0.001) | | (0.424) | (0.000) | (0.079) |
| JPM | 0.035 | **−0.390** | **0.147** | XOM | **−0.152** | **−0.224** | −0.028 |
| | (0.649) | (0.000) | (0.056) | | (0.047) | (0.003) | (0.719) |

[a] *Note:* The table reports Spearman correlation coefficients between KU indices and the six-month rolling standard deviation of *Bloomberg* analyst estimates of LTG in earnings per share for the thirty firms listed on the DJIA over the sample period January 2000 through March 2020. Not all B-est LTG firm data go back to January 2000, but all series contain at least 150 observations. *P*-values are reported in parentheses. Bold values indicate statistical significance at the 1%, 5%, or 10% level.

premiums and expanded information sets. Evidence presented in Table 9.3 suggests that KU effects are also present at the firm level. When there are more unscheduled events, by count, by diversity of groupings, and by proportion of total events, there is less variation over time in analyst beliefs about the prospects of longer-run firm-level cash flows. Based on this data and sample period, the informational effect associated with uncertainty appears to dominate the ambiguity effect at both the firm and aggregate level. When combined with the findings in Table 9.2 of inverse correlations between KU events and stock prices and valuation ratios, the findings reported in Table 9.3 suggest greater corporate uncertainty leads to more confidence in (likely) lower growth prospects of EPS per firm.

When there is more KU group diversity, the results suggest that an increasing number of groups' categories share interpreted directional impacts on expected firm returns. For instance, if KU var increases because the groups Analyst Ratings, Credit, Ratings, Credit, and Equity Actions all contain categories of unscheduled firm events that are interpreted as bearish for firm cash flow prospects, then the increase in KU var would lead to a reduction in the variance of analyst projections of long-run earnings growth. The bounds would be narrowed due to the similar qualitative interpretations of unscheduled news' impacts. Narrative links that connect the qualitative interpretations across groups of novel events would then serve to shape and clarify the degree of bearishness versus bullishness of the full information set for return forecasts.

Therefore, the findings in Tables 9.2 and 9.3 suggest that corporate novelty and associated uncertainty may play an informational role in explaining stock market behavior. Taken together, these results, albeit preliminary, may shed light on the large literature documenting that expected returns and varying discount rates explain the largest proportion of variation in stock returns at the aggregate level (Cochrane, 2011); whereas, cash flow effects appear to be the primary driver of stock returns at the firm level (Vuolteenaho, 2002). Uncertainty premiums may be lurking behind both strands of literature and, when combined with results from Chapter 8, offer possible explanation for Samuelson's dictum that stock markets are macro-inefficient but micro-efficient (Jung and Shiller, 2005). Firm returns reflect the information from closely connected corporate novelty and information from previous macro novelty; whereas, aggregate returns predominantly reflect macro novelty. This hypothesis is left for future research.

That correlation coefficients often possess a negative sign begs the question of whether there is a direction of "statistical causality" between the KU indices and variance in analyst forecasts of firm-level growth prospects over time. Granger causality tests offer one way to discern whether lagged values of one variable jointly help explain contemporaneous values of the other variable. Table 9.4 reports Granger causality tests for the thirty DJIA firms (one firm per row) against the KU Index (first column) and the KU Variation Index (second column). Unit root tests for KU event and variation indices from Chapters 5 and 7 suggest that both series are best approximated as nonstationary processes with traditional ADF test $p$-values of 0.187 and 0.591, respectively, against the null hypothesis of a unit root.[7] Consequently, there are two $p$-values reported for the Granger causality tests, one with KU and KU var in levels (first value in parentheses) and one with KU and KU var in first-difference (second value in parentheses). The two columns report $p$-values for Granger causality from KU and KU var indices to the standard deviation of analyst LTG forecasts.

The hypothesis that variation of analyst earnings estimates causes KU events does not have any economically meaningful interpretation. The causality of interest for the present thesis runs from KU events to variance of analyst LTG projections. There are twenty-seven statistically significant cases of Granger causality running from KU Event and KU Variation Indices in levels to the temporal spread of long-run growth forecasts; there are twenty-six significant cases with KU and KU var in first-difference. This is compared to just eight cases in levels and just three cases in first-difference of significant causality running in the opposite direction (not reported). Taken together, the

[7] ADF tests were conducted with a constant and corroborated by the Kwiatkowski–Phillips–Schmidt–Shin (KPSS) unit root test.

Table 9.4 *Granger causality from KU to LTG forecast variance*

| KU Index | KU var Index |
| --- | --- |
| KU ↛ AAPL (0.321, 0.106)[a] | KU var ↛ AAPL (**0.086**, **0.035**) |
| KU ↛ AXP (0.192, 0.386) | KU var ↛ AXP (0.665, 0.118) |
| KU ↛ BA (**0.022**, 0.236) | KU var ↛ BA (0.123, **0.004**) |
| KU ↛ CAT (**0.089**, 0.549) | KU var ↛ CAT (0.976, 0.174) |
| KU ↛ CSCO (**0.003**, **0.000**) | KU var ↛ CSCO (**0.003**, **0.007**) |
| KU ↛ CVX (**0.047**, **0.060**) | KU var ↛ CVX (0.209, 0.277) |
| KU ↛ DD (0.487, 0.942) | KU var ↛ DD (0.883, 0.869) |
| KU ↛ DIS (**0.053**, 0.663) | KU var ↛ DIS (0.544, 0.277) |
| KU ↛ GE (**0.016**, 0.462) | KU var ↛ GE (0.462, 0.382) |
| KU ↛ GS (0.143, 0.361) | KU var ↛ GS (0.163, 0.579) |
| KU ↛ HD (0.229, **0.094**) | KU var ↛ HD (**0.046**, **0.028**) |
| KU ↛ IBM (**0.042**, 0.157) | KU var ↛ IBM (**0.093**, **0.089**) |
| KU ↛ INTC (0.659, 0.894) | KU var ↛ INTC (0.160, 0.414) |
| KU ↛ JNJ (**0.038**, 0.105) | KU var ↛ JNJ (**0.042**, **0.055**) |
| KU ↛ JPM (0.353, **0.005**) | KU var ↛ JPM (**0.010**, 0.315) |
| KU ↛ KO (**0.081**, **0.039**) | KU var ↛ KO (0.498, **0.099**) |
| KU ↛ MCD (0.111, 0.125) | KU var ↛ MCD (**0.062**, **0.024**) |
| KU ↛ MMM (**0.020**, **0.002**) | KU var ↛ MMM (0.119, 0.182) |
| KU ↛ MRK (**0.016**, **0.006**) | KU var ↛ MRK (0.494, 0.379) |
| KU ↛ MSFT (**0.058**, **0.057**) | KU var ↛ MSFT (**0.032**, **0.095**) |
| KU ↛ NKE (0.130, 0.240) | KU var ↛ NKE (0.958, **0.001**) |
| KU ↛ PFE (0.710, 0.310) | KU var ↛ PFE (0.694, 0.220) |
| KU ↛ PG (**0.043**, 0.717) | KU var ↛ PG (**0.037**, 0.128) |
| KU ↛ TRV (**0.005**, 0.337) | KU var ↛ TRV (**0.001**, **0.002**) |
| KU ↛ UNH (**0.053**, **0.030**) | KU var ↛ UNH (0.256, **0.042**) |
| KU ↛ UTX (0.599, 0.249) | KU var ↛ UTX (0.161, **0.079**) |
| KU ↛ V (**0.012**, 0.116) | KU var ↛ V (0.295, 0.174) |
| KU ↛ VZ (0.126, **0.097**) | KU var ↛ VZ (0.194, **0.037**) |
| KU ↛ WMT (0.383, 0.397) | KU var ↛ WMT (**0.015**, **0.044**) |
| KU ↛ XOM (0.136, **0.046**) | KU var ↛ XOM (0.136, 0.342) |

[a] *Note:* The table reports Granger causality tests results between KU indices and the six-month rolling standard deviation of *Bloomberg* B-est LTG forecasts for the thirty DJIA firms over the sample period January 2000 through March 2020. Not all B-est LTG data goes back to 2000:01, but all series contain at least 150 observations through 2020:03. *P*-values are reported in parentheses for the null hypothesis that variable X does not Granger cause variable Y. The first *p*-value in parentheses is based on Granger tests where KU and KU var are in levels; the second *p*-value is based on tests where KU and KU var are in first-difference to obtain stationarity. Bold values indicate statistical significance at the 1%, 5%, or 10% level.

results from Tables 9.3 and 9.4 suggest that increases in both corporate KU events and group diversity therein lead to a reduction in the spread of analysts' long-run growth forecasts over time for individual DJIA firms. Because the DJIA firms are so often reported on in stock market news, the findings also provide support for the view that unscheduled events may serve as a bellwether indicator of future distress in firm-level growth prospects.

## 9.4 KU DIVERSITY AND ECONOMIC TRENDS

Findings from Figure 9.1 and Tables 9.2 through 9.4 suggest that KU var better explains aggregate market outcomes and KU better explains firm long-term earnings prospects. Table 9.5 reports correlation coefficients and $p$-values between KU var and three major macroeconomic and financial indicators: the Industrial Production Index, the 10-year Treasury yield, and the 3-month Treasury yield. If the diversity of unscheduled corporate event groups depresses stock prices and valuation ratios and causes informational effects (likely) bearish for long-term earnings prospects, then economic activity should also be depressed, and interest rates, reflecting a greater uncertainty premium, should be higher in response to higher values of KU var. Therefore, the hypothesized signs for correlation coefficients are negative,

Table 9.5 *KU diversity and economic trends*

|  | Industrial Production[a] | 10-year Treasury Note Yield | 3-month Treasury Bill Yield |
|---|---|---|---|
| KU var | −0.434*** | 0.534*** | 0.364*** |
|  | (0.000) | (0.000) | (0.000) |

[a] *Note:* The table reports correlation test statistics with $p$-values in parentheses for the null hypothesis of zero correlation over the sample period January 2000 through March 2020. Economic indicators are collected from the Federal Reserve Economic Database (FRED) for INDPRO, GS10, and TB3MS; *** denotes statistical significance at the 1% level.

positive, and positive, respectively, for Industrial Production and the 10-year and 3-month Treasury yields. The results are statistically significant and of correct sign for all three macro variables.

This chapter helped to establish an empirical foundation for the view that novel corporate events comove with stock market outcomes at the aggregate and firm level. The chapter presented numerous findings suggesting that the corporate KU and KU var indices are picking up uncertainty premia in the stock market and are good candidates for capturing narrative dynamics. Greater values of KU and KU var were found correlated with lower stock prices and lower valuation ratios. Furthermore, greater KU and KU var are correlated with and Granger cause narrower analyst forecast dispersion over time of long-term EPS growth, implying that qualitatively consistent narrative dynamics may be at play. The next chapter attempts to connect points of temporal instability in aggregate stock market relationships to the narrative intensity periods identified in Chapter 6.

# 10 Narrative Intensity and Stock Market Instability

## 10.1 INTRODUCTION

Chapter 9 presented an empirical analysis supporting a statistical connection between various Knightian uncertainty (KU) indices based on unscheduled corporate events identified in *Dow Jones* news reports and aggregate and firm-level stock market outcomes. Correlation coefficients and Granger causality tests reported significant comovements from KU information to aggregate and firm-level behavior. The core premise of this book is that novel events and associated narratives are related to stock market instability over time. Chapter 2 discussed some stylized facts documented in the literature concerning structural change in stock market relationships driving outcomes. Chapter 6 identified the periods during which micro KU narratives display the highest intensity for the US stock market based on the sentiment, novelty, and relevance of unscheduled corporate events.

The aim of this chapter is to provide insight about whether the periods most likely associated with narrative intensity align with statistical breakpoints identified by formal structural change tests in the relationships driving SP500 and firm-level returns, the VIX, trading volume, and equity Exchange Traded Fund (ETF) flows. Popular breakpoint tests of structural change are applied to each of the stock market relationships based on common fundamental/risk relationships explored in the literature. The Chow test allows for the narrative intensity periods to be imposed *ex ante* in testing for breakpoints. The Bai and Perron unknown multiple breakpoint test identifies the most likely points of structural change in the time-series relations for comparison to the narrative intensity periods without imposing them *ex ante*. The analysis finds that structural breaks, in particular those found in aggregate and firm-level returns regressions, are strikingly aligned with the periods of highest, and moderate, KU narrative intensity from Chapter 6.

## 10.2   MARKET DATA AND INSTABILITY TESTS

The dependent variables that represent a subset of stock market outcomes include SP500 aggregate returns, Dow *Jones Industrial Average* (DJIA) 30 firm-level returns, the VIX, SP500 aggregate trading volume, and equity fund flows for the SP500 ETF (SPY). The aggregate factors are plotted in Figure 10.1.[1] The recent COVID-19 crisis is evident from Figure 10.1: At the end of the sample, SP500 returns plunge, the VIX and trading volume skyrocket, and equity funds experience mass outflows. These findings are consistent with Propositions 1 and 2 in Chapter 9 that hypothesize that unscheduled corporate events will share a negative correlation with stock prices and returns and a positive correlation with volatility and trading volume. Moreover, the corporate uncertainty effect is hypothesized to lead to increased outflows (greater negative values) in ETF funds.

The objective of the present chapter is to assess whether and to what degree the narrative intensity periods identified in Chapter 6 align with potential breakpoints found in returns, volatility, trading volume, and fund flow regressions. There are many structural change tests that can be applied to the regressions considered here and different breakpoint tests may lead to different conclusions about the timing and magnitude of instability. The empirical analysis presented here incorporates two popular tests for structural change. The first is the traditional Chow breakpoint test (Chow, 1960), which allows the structural breakpoint to be imposed by the researcher *ex ante* and tested for its significance. The idea behind the Chow test is to split the

---

[1] For each of the sections to follow, statistical inference of either structural change test relies on assumed stationarity of variables included in the specification. For the sample period January 2000 through March 2020, ADF tests suggest returns and equity fund flows are I(0) (i.e. reject the presence of a unit root) while the VIX and trading volume contain a unit root and, therefore, require first-differencing prior to estimation.

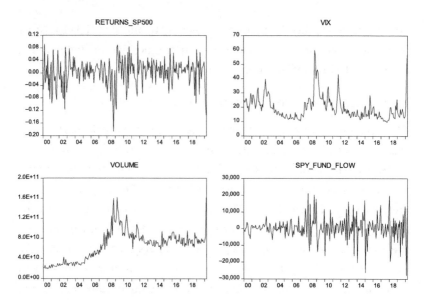

FIGURE 10.1 The figures plot aggregate stock market outcomes from January 2000 through March 2020. Returns_SP500 is the log difference in *Standard and Poor's* 500 Composite Index price (GSPC). VIX refers to the Chicago Board of Options Exchange Volatility Index implied by SP500 Index options. Volume denotes SP500 trading volume in shares. SPY_Fund_Flow denotes the net shares for the SP500 exchange traded fund SPY. Returns, volatility, and volume data are collected from www.yahoo.com/finance while ETF flows are collected from *Bloomberg L.P.* All data are in nominal terms and at a monthly frequency.

sample into smaller subsamples around the hypothesized breakpoint. Significant differences in the estimated models across regimes are suggestive of structural change at the breakpoint. Statistically, the Chow test compares the sum of the squared residuals generated by full sample estimation to the sum of squared residuals from estimating each subsample separately. The Chow test $F$-statistic is computed as:

$$F = \frac{(\varepsilon' - \varepsilon - (\varepsilon'_1 \varepsilon_1 + \varepsilon'_2 \varepsilon_2))/k}{(\varepsilon'_1 \varepsilon_1 + \varepsilon'_2 \varepsilon_2)/(T - 2k)} \qquad (10.1)$$

where $\varepsilon'_i \varepsilon_i$ is the sum of squared residuals for subsample $i$, $T$ is the total number of observations in the entire sample, and $k$ is the number of parameters in the equation. Statistical significance of the breakpoint (or multiple breakpoints) can be assessed as long as the number of observations in each subsample is greater than the number of parameters allowed to vary and that the residuals are serially uncorrelated.

The second structural change test tests for an unknown number and location of breakpoints based on the Bai and Perron sequential break test (Bai and Perron, 1998, 2003). The methodology of BP is based on a global minimization of the sum of squared residuals sequentially nesting potential breakpoints within segments of previously identified breaks.[2] The BP test allows for different distributions in the regressors' process and in the model-based errors. Consider the following linear regression with $m$-breaks ($m + 1$ regimes):

$$y_t = z_t'\delta_j + \varepsilon_t, \qquad t = T_{j-1} + 1, \ldots, T_j \qquad (10.2)$$

for $j = 1, \ldots, m + 1$ where $z_t$ is a ($q$x1) vector of covariates and $\delta_j$ for ($j = 1, \ldots, m + 1$) is the corresponding vector of coefficients and $\varepsilon_t$ is the error term at time $t$. Equation (10.2) is a pure structural change model since all coefficients in $\delta$ are subject to change. The indexing ($T_1, \ldots, T_m$) represents the unknown breakpoints where $T_0 = 0$ and $T_{m+1} = T$. The estimates of $\hat{\delta}_j$ are obtained by minimizing the sum of the squared residuals $S_T(T_1, \ldots, T_m) = \sum_{i=1}^{m+1} \sum_{t=T_{i-1}}^{T} [y_t - z_t'\delta_i]^2$. Let $\hat{\delta}(T_j)$ denote the resulting estimates based on the given $m$-partition ($T_1, \ldots, T_m$) denoted $T_j$. Substituting this estimate into the objective function implies the estimated breakpoints ($\hat{T}_1, \ldots, \hat{T}_m$) follow:

$$(\hat{T}_1, \ldots, \hat{T}_m) = argmin_{T_1, \ldots, T_m} S_T(T_1, \ldots, T_m) \qquad (10.3)$$

where the minimization is taken over all partitions ($T_1, \ldots, T_m$). These test statistics are used for global optimization and sequentially determined breaks in the subsequent analysis. The global breakpoint estimates are based on tests of $l$-breaks versus none. The sequential testing procedure begins with the full sample. If the test rejects the

---

[2] Bai and Perron (1998) develop asymptotic distributions since the iterative truncation of each subsequent sample window prohibits $F$-statistics from converging asymptotically to the standard distribution.

null hypothesis of parameter constancy and identifies a breakdate, single unknown breakpoint tests will be conducted in each subsample. These subsequent tests are a test of $l + 1$ versus the null hypothesis of $l = 1$ breaks. Breakpoints are then added whenever the null hypothesis of constancy is rejected within the newly partitioned subsamples, repeating this procedure until all of the subsamples fail to reject the null hypothesis.

Results from these two key BP breakpoint tests, the global $l$ versus none break test and the sequential break test, will be reported throughout the chapter. Although the BP tests will control for heteroskedasticity and serially correlated residuals allowing for the error distributions to differ across breaks, regressions for each of the two tests applied to returns, volatility, trading volume, and fund flows will be based on the heteroskedasticity and autocorrelation consistent (HAC) adjusted standard errors.[3] Considering both the Chow and BP breakpoint tests provides a sensitivity analysis of instability tests for the posited stock market relationships by allowing for both imposed and unknown breakpoints to assess the correspondence with narrative intensity periods identified in Chapter 6.

## 10.3   STOCK RETURNS AND NARRATIVE INTENSITY

Structural change is understood within the context of an empirical model. To test whether a structural break has occurred in the relationships driving stock market and firm-level returns behavior, the popular Fama and French (FF) multifactor models are first estimated. The objective is not to explain the greatest variance in returns or even to generate significant coefficients (loadings) on risk factors. The aim is to estimate a common returns-based regression, adjust for residual heteroskedasticity and autocorrelation, and assess to what degree temporal instability is present and whether it approximates narrative intensity periods from Chapter 6. Both the three-factor

---

[3] See Bai and Perron (1998, 2003) for details on the various unknown multiple breakpoint tests and the residual properties the tests allow for.

(Fama and French, 1996) and five-factor models (Fama and French, 2015) are explored for both the aggregate stock market and for firm-level DJIA30 returns. Volumes of asset pricing studies have explored the implications of the three-factor and five-factor FF regressions connecting returns behavior to multifactor risk proxies through factor loadings assumed constant through time.[4]

Responding to the empirical struggles of the Capital Asset Pricing Model (CAPM)'s one risk factor ($\beta$) for explaining differences in average stock returns, FF (1996) extend the model to reflect the stylized findings that small-cap and value firms generate higher returns. The "size" effect that smaller firms generate greater returns than large firms is expressed as the average return on small stock portfolios minus the average return on big stock portfolios, or small minus big (SMB). The "value" effect that firms with high book-to-market ratios generate greater returns than firms with low book-to-market ratios is expressed as the average return on value portfolios (high book-to-market) minus the average return on growth portfolios (low book-to-market), or high minus low (HML).

The three-factor model of excess returns for each of the thirty individual companies listed on the DJIA takes the form:

$$R_{i,t} - R_{f,t} = \alpha_i + b_i(R_{M,t} - R_{f,t}) + s_i SMB_t + h_i HML_t + \varepsilon_{i,t} \quad (10.4)$$

---

[4] Like the evidence of structural change in aggregate relationships referenced in Chapter 2, many studies have now documented that asset-specific factor loadings on diversified "size," "value," "profitability," and "investment" return portfolios also vary through time. See, for example, Avramov and Chordia (2006) and references therein. Fama and French (2019) respond to this literature by reformulating the original Fama and MacBeth cross-sectional returns framework into a time-series asset-pricing model for comparison with the three- and five-factor models. The authors take the slope estimates from cross-sectional FM regressions, stack them through time, and interchange them to be the right-hand-side (RHS) factors whose coefficients now capture time-varying characteristics of "size," "value," and so on, in explaining excess returns. Fama and French (2019) state that one deficiency in the three- and five-factor models is that the RHS factors are prespecified, hinting at the benefits from allowing different fundamentals to matter during different subperiods in nonroutine ways. Ultimately, the authors show that a returns model with time-varying loadings based on FM cross-sectional factors outperforms all other models, though the performance is attributed more to cross-sectional than time-varying characteristics.

where $R_{i,t}$ is the return for firm $i$ at time $t$ generated from the one-period difference in log prices $R_{i,t} = ln(P_{i,t}) - ln(P_{i,t-1})$; $R_f$ is the risk-free rate based on the 1-month Treasury bill yield from Ibbotson Associates; $R_M$ is the market return on all Center for Research in Security Prices (CRSP) firms incorporated in the US and listed on the NYSE, AMEX, or NASDAQ; SMB and HML are as described above; $\alpha_i$, $b_i$, $s_i$, and $h_i$ are firm-$i$ coefficients and $\varepsilon_i$ is a mean-zero error term with constant variance.[5] The Chow breakpoint test tests the null hypothesis that there is no breakpoint at each of the individual imposed dates of highest narrative intensity identified in Chapter 6 at 2000:10, 2008:08, 2013:11, and 2016:08.[6] The BP test tests the null hypothesis that there are $l + 1$ breaks versus $l$ breaks.[7] Due to space constraints the BP global $l$ versus none break test and the sequential BP test variants are applied only to aggregate returns later on. Table 10.1 reports the structural change test results from estimating Equation (10.4) for each of the thirty DJIA firms.[8]

The results from Table 10.1 suggest that the points of highest narrative intensity based on corporate KU events are also points associated with instability in firm-level multifactor excess returns relationships based on the FF three-factor model. Chow test results find that the breakpoints at 2000:10, 2008:08, and 2013:11 are strongly significant for every firm's returns regression while three firms display a significant breakpoint at 2016:08. The BP test results reported

---

[5] RHS data for the three-factor and five-factor models are collected from Ken French's website at https://mba.tuck.dartmouth.edu/pages/faculty/ken.french/data_library.html. Firm-level returns are collected from www.yahoo.com/finance.

[6] The earliest points of highest narrative intensity identified at 2000:03–04 are not applicable to the Chow breakpoint test because the number of observations in the first subsample is less than the number of coefficients in the model, invalidating the test. The potential breakpoint at 2000:10 is close, but satisfies the requirements.

[7] Note that BP requires trimming parameters at the beginning and end of the sample – this analysis retains the default of 15 percent; 7.5 at the beginning and 7.5 at the end. Consequently, the KU narrative dates of 2000:03, 2000:04, and 2000:10 are no longer candidates for potential breakpoints in the BP test.

[8] Visa was excluded from the analysis because it was added to the DJIA mid-sample on September 23, 2013.

Table 10.1 *Structural break test for three-factor firm returns*

| | Chow Test | | | | BP Test |
|---|---|---|---|---|---|
| | 2000:10 | 2008:08 | 2013:11 | 2016:08 | $1+1$ vs. $1$ |
| AAPL[a] | **15.600** (0.000) | **22.478** (0.000) | **3.394** (0.010) | 0.976 (0.421) | 2008:10, 2017:03 |
| AXP | **10.132** (0.000) | **43.912** (0.000) | **4.501** (0.002) | 0.689 (0.601) | 2008:08, 2017:03 |
| BA | **8.059** (0.000) | **41.508** (0.000) | **4.096** (0.003) | 0.466 (0.761) | 2008:08, 2017:03 |
| CAT | **15.259** (0.000) | **36.512** (0.000) | **4.450** (0.002) | 0.579 (0.678) | 05:10, 08:11, 17:03 |
| CSCO | **8.560** (0.000) | **38.956** (0.000) | **6.268** (0.000) | **2.022** (0.092) | 05:07, 08:08, 17:03 |
| CVX | **12.017** (0.000) | **43.404** (0.000) | **5.352** (0.000) | 1.432 (0.224) | 2008:08, 2017:01 |
| DD | **10.157** (0.000) | **24.010** (0.000) | **2.884** (0.023) | 0.436 (0.783) | 2009:03, 2017:03 |
| DIS | **10.717** (0.000) | **45.938** (0.000) | **4.699** (0.001) | 0.930 (0.447) | 2008:02, 2017:02 |
| GE | **7.876** (0.000) | **41.066** (0.000) | **4.059** (0.003) | 1.285 (0.277) | 05:07, 08:07, 11:07, 17:01 |
| GS | **9.109** (0.000) | **36.151** (0.000) | **6.979** (0.000) | **2.761** (0.029) | 08:10, 12:07, 17:03 |
| HD | **10.457** (0.000) | **52.178** (0.000) | **4.996** (0.001) | 0.412 (0.800) | 2008:07, 2017:03 |
| IBM | **11.350** (0.000) | **41.009** (0.000) | **4.856** (0.001) | 1.613 (0.172) | 05:01, 08:01, 17:03 |
| INTC | **9.834** (0.000) | **38.785** (0.000) | **6.786** (0.000) | **2.116** (0.080) | 2008:02, 2017:02 |
| JNJ | **11.672** (0.000) | **46.462** (0.000) | **4.655** (0.001) | 0.566 (0.688) | 2008:07, 2017:03 |
| JPM | **12.021** (0.000) | **51.601** (0.000) | **6.772** (0.000) | 1.460 (0.215) | 2008:07, 2017:03 |
| KO | **12.964** (0.000) | **50.457** (0.000) | **4.817** (0.001) | 0.736 (0.568) | 2008:07, 2017:01 |

Table 10.1 *Continued*

| | Chow Test | | | | BP Test |
| --- | --- | --- | --- | --- | --- |
| | 2000:10 | 2008:08 | 2013:11 | 2016:08 | 1 + 1 vs. 1 |
| MCD | **13.761** (0.000) | **46.534** (0.000) | **4.863** (0.001) | 0.705 (0.589) | 2008:02, 2017:03 |
| MMM | **11.809** (0.000) | **45.070** (0.000) | **4.340** (0.002) | 0.638 (0.636) | 2008:07, 2017:03 |
| MRK | **12.060** (0.000) | **51.014** (0.000) | **5.483** (0.000) | 1.334 (0.258) | 05:08, 08:08, 17:03 |
| MSFT | **14.846** (0.000) | **48.638** (0.000) | **6.895** (0.000) | 1.316 (0.265) | 05:05, 08:06, 17:02 |
| NKE | **15.054** (0.000) | **40.070** (0.000) | **4.181** (0.003) | 0.956 (0.432) | 05:07, 08:08, 17:03 |
| PFE | **9.320** (0.000) | **51.877** (0.000) | **4.814** (0.001) | 0.942 (0.440) | 05:07, 08:07, 17:03 |
| PG | **17.775** (0.000) | **45.932** (0.000) | **4.701** (0.001) | 0.440 (0.780) | 2008:07, 2017:03 |
| TRV | **9.188** (0.000) | **47.371** (0.000) | **4.214** (0.003) | 0.754 (0.556) | 05:07, 08:07, 17:03 |
| UNH | **6.378** (0.000) | **41.006** (0.000) | **4.762** (0.001) | 0.575 (0.681) | 05:10, 08:10, 17:03 |
| UTX | **9.860** (0.000) | **44.985** (0.000) | **4.203** (0.003) | 0.429 (0.787) | 2008:07, 2017:03 |
| VZ | **13.356** (0.000) | **47.250** (0.000) | **5.109** (0.001) | 1.498 (0.203) | 05:05, 08:08, 17:01 |
| WMT | **12.422** (0.000) | **45.634** (0.000) | **4.739** (0.001) | 0.776 (0.542) | 05:01, 08:01, 17:03 |
| XOM | **11.560** (0.000) | **41.929** (0.000) | **5.188** (0.001) | 1.759 (0.138) | 08:08, 11:08, 17:01 |

*a*Note: The table reports *F*-statistics and *p*-values (in parentheses) for the Chow breakpoint test at the given points of potential structural change in the estimation of the FF three-factor equation (10.4) for each of the thirty DJIA firms over the sample period January 2000 through March 2020. HAC standard errors are used to compute *p*-values. Significant breakpoints from the Bai and Perron multiple breakpoint sequential *F*-test are reported in the final column. Bold values indicate significance at the 1%, 5%, or 10% level.

in the last column find that the high intensity narrative period of 2008:08, coinciding with the global financial crisis, and all associated novel events, was identified as a significant break for virtually every firm as well. Moreover, every firm's return regression experienced a significant break based on the BP test results occurring between 2017:01 and 2017:03. This finding is not too far from the high narrative intensity period of 2016:08 and aligns perfectly with the two moderate intensity dates identified at 2017:01 and 2017:03. It is interesting to note that thirteen of the firms experience a BP breakpoint at, or approximately near, 2005:05 that is one of the three periods identified as high narrative intensity based on macro uncertainty events from Chapter 8. It is possible that investors were revising forecasting strategies to reflect the transition into the high-octane credit-fueled period of the housing boom.

The FF five-factor model extends the three-factor model to include two "quality" factors: profitability and investment. Fama and French (2015) include the difference between average portfolio returns for firms with robust operating profits and those with weak operating profits (robus minus weak [RMW]). The second extension involves average return differences between conservative investment and aggressive investment portfolios (conservative minus aggressive [CMA]). Both quality factors are expected to increase firm returns, ceteris paribus. The FF five-factor excess returns model for the present application yields:

$$R_{i,t} - R_{f,t} = \alpha_i + b_i(R_{M,t} - R_{f,t}) + s_i SMB_t + h_i HML_t + r_i RMW_t + c_i CMA_t + \varepsilon_{i,t}$$
(10.5)

The FF five-factor model estimated for firm-level returns generated very similar results to those from the three-factor model reported in Table 10.1 and are therefore not presented in the text. For example, for AAPL, the Chow test was able (failed) to reject the null hypothesis of no breakpoint at 2000:10, 2008:08, 2013:11, and 2016:08 with a $p$-value = 0.000, 0.000, 0.033 (and 0.665), respectively, while the BP test identified significant breaks at 2008:10, 2012:10, and 2017:03.

Table 10.2 *Chow test for three- and five-factor aggregate returns*

| | 2000:10[a] | 2008:08 | 2013:11 | 2016:08 |
|---|---|---|---|---|
| $R_M$ | | | | |
| FF three-factor | 5.631*** | 11.826*** | 0.661 | 0.459 |
| | (0.001) | (0.000) | (0.577) | (0.711) |
| FF five-factor | 5.853*** | 4.218*** | 3.419*** | 2.388*** |
| | (0.000) | (0.001) | (0.005) | (0.039) |
| $R_M - R_f$ | | | | |
| FF three-factor | 4.897*** | 13.073*** | 0.691 | 0.474 |
| | (0.003) | (0.000) | (0.558) | (0.700) |
| FF five-factor | 5.285*** | 4.441*** | 3.342*** | 2.343** |
| | (0.000) | (0.001) | (0.006) | (0.042) |

[a] *Note:* The table reports *F*-statistics and *p*-values (in parentheses) for the Chow breakpoint test at the given points of potential structural change in the estimation of three- and five-factor return equations for the aggregate stock market proxied by the SP500 for the sample period January 2000 through March 2020. The top panel reports results for raw returns while the bottom panel reports results for excess returns. All variables appear to be stationary based on ADF and KPSS unit root tests. HAC standard errors are used to compute *p*-values. *, **, *** denotes statistical significance at the 1%, 5%, and 10% levels.

Next, the analysis investigates potential breakpoints in a multi-factor returns regression for the aggregate market portfolio as proxied by the SP500. Because the portfolio is based on the broad market, the first risk factor that is weighted by the market's equity risk premium, $R_M - R_f$, is dropped from the three-factor equation for excess returns, yielding:

$$R_M - R_{f,t} = \alpha + sSMB_t + hHML_t + \varepsilon_t \qquad (10.6)$$

where $R_M$ is the log difference in the SP500 Composite Index price and the left hand side, again, represents the excess return. Table 10.2 reports the first set of structural break test results for three- and five-factor models of both raw and excess returns in the US stock market

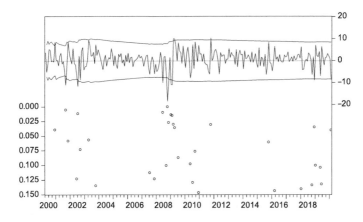

FIGURE 10.2 Recursive residuals are plotted (right axis) with one-step probabilities of parameter nonconstancy below (left axis) for excess aggregate returns based on the three-factor model.

over the sample period January 2000 through March 2020. The second through fifth columns report the test statistics and $p$-values for Chow breakpoint tests based on the periods of narrative intensity identified in Chapter 6. Again, the narrative intensity period of 2000:03–04 yields too few observations to calculate the Chow test statistics and is therefore excluded from the empirical analysis.

The aggregate returns results from the Chow test are supportive of the instability implied by the Novelty-Narrative Hypothesis (NNH).[9] All four narrative intensity breakpoints are statistically significant for the FF five-factor model for both raw and excess returns. The breakpoints for 2000:10 and 2008:08 are significant for the FF three-factor model. The timing and significance of breakpoints can also be assessed by graphical inspection of residual properties from recursive estimation of the returns regressions.

For three- and five-factor models of excess aggregate returns, Figures 10.2 and 10.3, respectively, plot the recursive residuals with standard error bands (above and right axis) and probability value

[9] For the Chow and BP tests on aggregate returns regressions throughout the chapter, the main results are unchanged if Shiller's SP500 prices are used to generate returns instead of GSPC ticker prices.

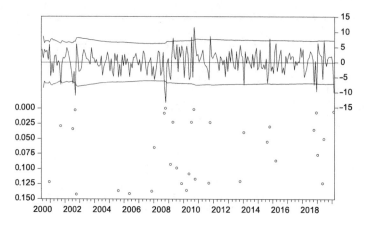

FIGURE 10.3 Recursive residuals are plotted (right axis) with one-step probabilities of parameter nonconstancy below (left axis) for excess aggregate returns based on the five-factor model.

(below and left axis) at or below 15 percent of rejecting the null hypothesis of parameter constancy. That is, the one-step forecast uses each period's error compared with the full sample standard deviation to assess whether the value of the dependent variable at time $t$ came from the model fitted to the data up to that point. The points with $p$-values less than 0.05 correspond to recursive residuals breaking through the standard error bands from either above or below. (Tests for raw returns based on three- and five-factor aggregate returns were also run, but not presented graphically). Sample periods rejecting parameter constancy with a $p$-value less than or equal to 0.025 occur for FF three-factor excess returns at 2001:09, 2002:07, 2008:06, 2008:10, 2009:01, and 2009:02 (raw returns for the FF three-factor model found the same points of parameter nonconstancy) and for FF five-factor excess returns at 2001:09, 2002:07, 2002:09, 2008:09, 2008:10, 2010:09, 2018:12, and 2020:02 (raw returns for the FF five-factor model found the same points).

The findings of Figure 10.3 suggest that the quality-factors extension of the five-factor model is able to pick up the instability in market returns due to the partial government shutdown (2018:12) and COVID-19 pandemic (2020:02) and all ensuing corporate-level KU events occurring late in the sample period. Both periods were characterized by excessive volatility in the stock market due to the increased uncertainty of many macro and micro KU events occurring both domestically and abroad.[10]

The majority of imposed breakdates based on the narrative intensity periods were significant for the Chow test across three-factor and five-factor models for raw and excess returns. Table 10.3 reports results from the Bai and Perron unknown multiple breakpoint tests for aggregate returns. Like the Chow test, the BP break test relies on $F$-statistics under null hypotheses that there are $l+1$ breaks versus $l$ breaks (sequential BP test reported in column 2) or $l$ breaks versus zero breaks (global $l$ versus none test reported in columns 3 and 4) within the sample period.

Column two reports significant breaks identified following the sequential procedure for FF three-factor raw and excess returns at 2003:02, the FF five-factor raw returns model at 2004:04, 2009:01, and 2012:07, and the FF five-factor excess returns model at 2004:05, 2009:04, and 2013:10. The break at 2013:10 approximately aligns with the narrative intensity period of 2013:11. The last two columns report results from the global $l$ BP breakpoint approach. The number of most likely significant breaks is determined by the tests in the third column with the most likely breakdates identified in the last column. The breaks that most closely align with the highest KU narrative intensity occur at 2008:10 (KU at 2008:08), 2013:09 and 2013:10 (KU at 2013:11), and 2016:11 (KU at 2016:08) while those aligning with the moderate corporate KU narrative intensity occur at 2015:12 (KU at 2015:08–09).

---

[10] Of the nineteen trading days in December 2018, the average daily return was −0.5% with ten daily returns greater than or less than 1% (eight negative and two positive). The maximum (minimum) return was 4.8% (−3.2%) on December 26 (4). February 2020 was also quite volatile for stock returns. The average daily return was −0.46%. Six of nineteen trading days were ±1% (two positive and four negative). The maximum (minimum) return was 1.4% (−4.5%) on February 4 (27).

Table 10.3 *Bai–Perron test for aggregate returns*

| | | BP Unknown Breakpoint Test | | |
|---|---|---|---|---|
| | 1 + 1 vs. l | global l vs. none | | |
| $R_M{}^a$ | | | | |
| FF three-factor | 03:02 | 03:02 | seq. breaks: 5 | |
| | | 03:02, 08:10, 12:07 | sig. largest breaks: 5 | |
| | | 03:01, 06:01, 09:01, 12:07, 15:12 | UDmax: 1; WDmax: 3 | |
| FF five-factor | 04:04 | 04:05, 07:06, 10:07, 13:09 | seq. breaks: 5 | |
| | 09:01 | 04:05, 07:06, 10:07, 13:10, 16:11 | sig. largest breaks: 5 | |
| | 12:07 | | UBmax: 4; WDmax: 4 | |
| $R_M - R_f$ | | | | |
| FF three-factor | 03:02 | 03:02 | seq. breaks: 5 | |
| | | 03:02, 08:10, 12:07 | sig. largest breaks: 5 | |
| | | 03:01, 06:01, 09:01, 12:10, 15:12 | UDmax: 1; WDmax: 3 | |
| FF five-factor | 04:05 | 04:05, 07:06, 10:07, 13:09 | seq. breaks: 5 | |
| | 09:04 | 04:05, 07:06, 10:07, 13:10, 16:11 | sig. largest breaks: 5 | |
| | 13:10 | | UDmax: 4; WDmax: 4 | |

$^a$ *Note:* The table reports BP sequential and global unknown multiple breakpoint tests of three- and five-factor models of raw and excess returns for the SP500 over the period January 2000 through March 2020 with 15% trimming. All variables appear to be stationary based on ADF and KPSS unit root tests. HAC standard errors are used to compute *p*-values. BP denotes Bai and Perron unknown multiple breakpoint test based on Bai and Perron (1998, 2003). Breaks from the sequential *F*-statistic are obtained by testing one breakpoint sequentially up to the maximum number allowed (five) until the null of parameter constancy cannot be rejected. The significant *F*-statistic reports the number of largest significant breakpoints. The UDmax test refers to the equal-weighted version of the global *l* vs. none test choosing the alternative that maximizes the *F*-statistic across the number of breakpoints under consideration. The WDmax test applies weights to the individual statistics so that the implied marginal *p*-values are equal prior to taking the maximum. Identified breakpoints are significant at the 5% level.

Many of the identified breakdates from the BP tests for unknown parameter nonconstancy do not match the periods of highest narrative intensity. Of course, this does not imply that novel corporate events interacted with more relaxed sentiment, novelty, and relevance percentiles could not approximately align with the BP identified breaks. Of note, again, from the structural change test results is an identified point of instability (2010:07), which approximately aligns with a high narrative intensity period based on macro KU events (2010:05).

The 15 percent trimming of the sample suggested for the BP test methodology precludes the investigation of highest narrative intensity occurring in March and April 2000, two periods that warrant further discussion. The periods of corporate narrative intensity at 2000:03–04 stand out because they approximate the historical turning points in aggregate stock market prices and valuation ratios. The SP500 reverses an historical upswing of the 1990s, peaking at 1,517.68 in 2000:08. Similarly, the CAPE valuation ratio reaches an all-time high of 44.2 in 1999:12. Turning points in stock market price swings often align with points suggestive of instability in market relationships – as Figure 4.22 shows and other studies document empirically (e.g. Mangee, 2016; Paye and Timmermann, 2006).[11] In fact, the BP sequential $F$-statistic test identifies the period 2003:02 for the FF three-factor and five-factor models of both raw and excess stock returns. The period 2003:02 is the exact month during which the SP500 reaches a trough at 841.15 – where the CAPE also experiences a trough – commencing the dramatic upswing lasting until the global financial crisis.

---

[11] The study of Paye and Timmermann (2006) also uses the Bai and Perron (1998) sequential procedure to test for multiple unknown structural breaks in multivariate regressions of the equity premium on the price-dividend ratio, short-term interest rates, default spread, and the term premium over a sample running from 1952 through 2003. The authors find evidence of pervasive instability by looking at various combinations of multivariate regressions where identified breakpoints are located at points of dramatic financial and economic change.

Finally, the timing of the recent COVID-19 crisis – and associated novelty and narratives – is a prime candidate for a structural break in stock market return relationships. Although its occurrence at the end of the sample period precludes it as a possible break-point in the Chow and BP tests, changes to the stock returns process due to the global pandemic are picked up by the recursive tests of five-factor models as illustrated in Figure 10.3. It is worth pointing out that including this historic unforeseeable event biases against rejecting the null of no breakpoint in previous periods since it causes even greater instability in the partitioned regime for all F-type break tests such as Chow and BP. In fact, virtually all breakpoint tests in the chapter generated higher $F$-statistics and lower $p$-values (i.e. greater likelihood of rejecting the null of parameter constancy) if the sample period ended in 2019:12, just prior to the onset of COVID-19 and ensuing novel events. This provides even further support to the significance of breakpoints that are found throughout this chapter given that the sample period analyzed extends through 2020:03.

Indeed, many future studies will surely investigate the timing and magnitude of instability experienced during the unprecedented pandemic period. Much future work on this topic through the lens of novelty, narratives, and instability must be done.

## 10.4 VOLATILITY AND NARRATIVE INTENSITY

In this section, stock market volatility, as measured by the options-implied VIX, is connected to various measures of risk premia often espoused as influential for understanding financial market outcomes. The class of risk premia involves interest rate spreads. The spread between 10-year ($i^{10y}$, GS10) and 2-year ($i^{2y}$, GS2) Treasury yields represents the maturity risk premium (T10Y2YM); the spread between Moody's Seasoned Baa corporate bond ($i^{Baa}$, BAA) and 10-year Treasury yields represents the default risk premium (BAA10Y); the spread between 3-month LIBOR in US dollars ($i^{LIBOR}$, USD3MTD) and 3-month Treasury bill yields ($i^{3m}$, DTB3) (i.e. the TED spread) represents the interbank (default or credit market) risk premium, and the spread between 10-year Treasury yields and those from 10-year Treasury Inflation Protected Securities ($i^{TIPS}$, TIPS) generates the Breakeven Inflation Rate (T10YIEM) representing the inflation risk premium, or inflation expectations, ten years out.[12] Therefore, the variables used to proxy the VIX relationship, respectively, are,

$$maturity_t^{rp} = i_t^{10y} - i_t^{2y} \tag{10.7}$$

$$default_t^{rp} = i_t^{Baa} - i_t^{10y} \tag{10.8}$$

$$interbank_t^{rp} = i_t^{LIBOR} - i_t^{3m} \tag{10.9}$$

$$\pi_{t|t+10}^{rp} = i_t^{10y} - i_t^{TIPS} \tag{10.10}$$

where the variables are as described above. The maturity risk premium appears to contain a unit root and is therefore expressed in first-difference. The VIX empirical specification takes the following form:

$$VIX_t = \alpha + \beta_1 \Delta maturity_t^{rp} + \beta_2 default_t^{rp} + \beta_3 interbank_t^{rp} + \beta_4 \pi_{t|t+10}^{rp} + \varepsilon_t \tag{10.11}$$

The estimation sample begins in 2003:01 due to data availability for the ten-year Breakeven Inflation Rate, which implies KU narrative intensity periods of 2000:03, 04, 10 are not included in the analysis. Table 10.4 reports results from both the Chow imposed break test and the BP unknown multiple break test. The Chow test finds breakpoints at 2008:08 and 2013:11 to be statistically significant while the breakpoint at 2016:08 is weakly significant at the 15 percent level, providing some empirical support for the connection between the highest narrative intensity periods and instability in the posited relationship underpinning the VIX volatility index.

Although the BP testing procedure finds evidence of numerous periods of structural change, results do not align with the highest

---

[12] Data on interest rate spreads is collected from the Federal Reserve Economic Database (FRED).

Table 10.4 *Chow and BP instability tests for VIX*

| Chow Breakpoint Test | | | | |
|---|---|---|---|---|
| 2000:03–04 | 2000:10 | 2008:08 | 2013:11 | 2016:08 |
| N/A | N/A | 2.115* | 5.783*** | 1.649 |
|  |  | (0.065) | (0.000) | (0.149) |

| BP Unknown Breakpoint Test | | |
|---|---|---|
| seq. $l+1$ vs. $l$ | | global $l$ vs. none |
| 06:08 | seq. breaks: 5$^a$ | 06:08, 09:03, 11:12, 17:09 |
| 09:04 | sig. largest breaks: 5 | 06:08, 09:03, 11:12, 15:02, 17:09 |
| 12:01 | UDmax: 4, WDmax: 5 | |
| 17:09 | | |

$^a$ *Note:* The top panel presents Chow test results for the VIX estimation in Equation (10.11). The bottom panel reports results from the BP test. HAC standard errors are used to compute $p$-values (in parentheses). *, **, *** denotes statistical significance at the 1%, 5%, and 10% levels. All BP identified breaks are significant at the 5% level.

narrative intensity periods for corporate events. However, the BP breakpoint at 2015:02 approximately aligns with both the micro and macro KU moderate narrative period of 2014:11. Like the structural change analysis for returns, the behavior of recursive residuals from the fundamentals-based VIX relationship can also be investigated for clues concerning parameter instability.

Figure 10.4 plots the recursive residuals from the one-step forecast test and standard error bands beyond which the null of parameter constancy is rejected at the 5 percent significance level. There are many significant one-step recursive residuals indicative of parameter nonconstancy – the most significant points occur at 2007:02, 2007:07, 2008:09, 2009:05, 2010:05–06, 2011:08–09, and 2020:02, 03. The breakpoint at 2008:09 approximately aligns with the highest corporate narrative intensity point of 2008:08. The high micro narrative intensity period of 2016:08 approximately matches up with the

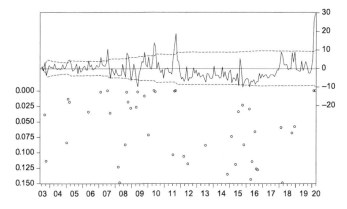

FIGURE 10.4 Recursive residuals are plotted (right axis) with one-step probabilities of parameter nonconstancy below (left axis) for the VIX Index based on Equation (10.11).

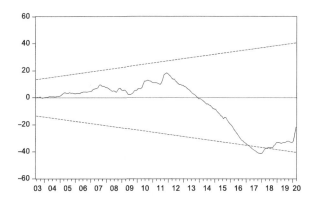

FIGURE 10.5 Cumulative sum of recursive residuals are plotted with 5% significance bands testing the null hypothesis of parameter constancy for the VIX relation.

break at 2016:07, which is significant at the 10 percent level. Again, the recursive residual instability test is able to detect the structural change due to the COVID-19 crisis at the end of the sample.

Figure 10.5 plots the cumulative sum (CUSUM) of the recursive residuals form the VIX estimation from Equation (10.11). When the CUSUM series systematically deviates in one direction, breaking through the standard error bands from above or below, the null hypothesis of statistical parameter constancy is rejected at the

5 percent level (Brown et al., 1975). One benefit of the CUSUM test is that there is no *a priori* breakpoint imposed and structural change in the underlying relationship is allowed to unfold in open ways through time.[13] The results from the CUSUM test show that the series does not fluctuate randomly within the standard error bands. Rather, the series departs systematically away from the zero-line commencing at 2013:11 and breaking through the significance bands at 2016:08. Both of these dates align perfectly with the highest corporate KU narrative intensity points. Overall, the results from investigating NNH for instability in the VIX relationship finds empirical support from the Chow tests, recursive one-step forecast residuals, and CUSUM test, but there was limited support based on the BP test results.

## 10.5   TRADING VOLUME, FUND FLOWS, AND NARRATIVE INTENSITY

One popular approach in the literature modeling stock market trading volume is to connect it to variation in relevant news. Chae (2005), for example, finds that increases in information asymmetry lead to a decrease in trading volume prior to scheduled corporate news announcements, but that volume increases prior to unscheduled corporate events independent of the degree of private versus public information symmetry. These findings suggest that corporate stock market events may be connected to the volume of shares transacted during particular subperiods of time. Following this literature, trading volume for the SP500 is modeled in the present analysis as a function of total corporate news events (scheduled plus unscheduled) identified for the stock market.

Since trading volume and total corporate news events appear to contain a unit root, the first difference of each series is used in the specification. Trading volume, therefore, is estimated as,

---

[13] The CUSUM test of Brown et al. (1975) is preferred to the CUSUMSQ test for contemporaneous (static), as opposed to dynamic, regressions involving stationary variables as specified in Equation (10.11). See Deng and Perron (2008) for a discussion on this.

$$\Delta volume_t = \alpha + \beta_1 \Delta events_t^{DJ} + \varepsilon_t \qquad (10.12)$$

where $events_t^{DJ}$ denotes the total number of events connected to an identified corporate entity reported as influencing firm prospects and stock price behavior from the *Dow Jones* news outlets as described in Chapter 5 and elsewhere.

Based on the specification in Equation (10.12), Table 10.5 reports that Chow and BP breakpoint tests provide no evidence that the highest narrative intensity periods are connected to structural change in the posited relationship driving stock market trading volume. However, the lack of significant breakpoints from the BP test may say something about informational trading effects under KU in response to both scheduled and unscheduled corporate events. This topic is left for future research.

Like trading volume, the equity fund flows into and out of the ETF for the SP500 are modeled as a function of total corporate news events, but the model is augmented with an equity market risk

Table 10.5 *Chow and BP instability tests for trading volume*

| Chow Breakpoint Test | | | | |
|---|---|---|---|---|
| 2000:03–04 | 2000:10 | 2008:08 | 2013:11 | 2016:08 |
| N/A | 0.195 | 1.176 | 0.113 | 0.573 |
| | (0.823) | (0.310) | (0.893) | (0.565) |

| BP Unknown Breakpoint Test | | |
|---|---|---|
| seq. $l+1$ vs. $l$ | | global $l$ vs. none |
| none | seq. breaks: $0^a$ | none |
| | sig. largest breaks: 0 | |
| | UDmax: 0, WDmax: 0 | |

[a] *Note:* The top panel presents Chow test results for the trading volume estimation in Equation (10.12). The bottom panel reports results from the BP test. HAC standard errors are used to compute *p*-values (in parentheses). *, **, *** denotes statistical significance at the 1%, 5%, and 10% levels.

premium. Since investors always have alternative asset allocation choices (e.g. stock versus bonds), the net flows of equity index funds depend on the risk premium associated with stock. Similar to the trading volume specification, the fund flows model includes the first-difference for total corporate-related events. Thus, the specification for fund flows follows:

$$flows_t^{SPY} = \alpha + \beta_1 \Delta events_t^{DJ} + \beta_2 (R_t^M - R_{f,t}) + \varepsilon_t \qquad (10.13)$$

where $flows_t^{SPY}$ and $events_t^{DJ}$ are as defined previously and the RHS term in parentheses denotes the equity risk premium as measured by the Ken French CRSP data library and used earlier in Section 10.3. The results for Chow and BP instability tests are reported in Table 10.6 followed by Figure 10.6, which plots the recursive residual one-step forecast test results.

The results reported in Table 10.6 are supportive of NNH for instability in the posited equity index fund flows relationship.

Table 10.6 *Chow and BP instability tests for ETF fund flows*

| Chow Breakpoint Test | | | | |
|---|---|---|---|---|
| 2000:03–04 | 2000:10 | 2008:08 | 2013:11 | 2016:08 |
| N/A | 0.464 | 2.453* | 6.994*** | 6.995*** |
| | (0.708) | (0.064) | (0.000) | (0.000) |

| BP Unknown Breakpoint Test | |
|---|---|
| seq. $l+1$ vs. $l$ | global $l$ vs. none |
| none | 07:09, 13:05 |
| seq. breaks: $0^a$ | |
| sig. largest breaks: 5 | 03:05, 07:07, 10:07, 13:07, 17:01 |
| UDmax: 2, WDmax: 2 | |

[a] *Note:* The top panel presents Chow test results for the ETF flows estimation in Equation (10.13). The bottom panel reports results from the BP test. HAC standard errors are used to compute $p$-values (in parentheses). *, **, *** denotes statistical significance at the 1%, 5%, and 10% levels. All BP identified breaks are significant at the 5% level.

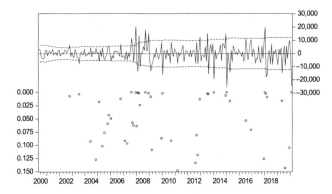

FIGURE 10.6 Recursive residuals are plotted (right axis) with one-step probabilities of parameter nonconstancy below (left axis) for ETF fund flows based on Equation (10.13).

Nearly all narrative intensity periods are significant in the Chow test, particularly those later in the sample. The BP tests find evidence of instability identifying breaks at 2013:05 and 2017:01 (both moderate corporate narrative intensity periods). Once again, one of the break-points identified in the BP procedure (2010:07) approximately aligns with a high narrative intensity period based upon macro uncertainty events (2010:05). The recursive residuals plotted in Figure 10.6 suggest that many periods can be rejecting as coming from the full data sample estimated up to that point. For example, points of statistical parameter nonconstancy include 2008:02, 2008:09, 2013:07, 2014:01, 2014:12, all periods within two months of a high or moderate corporate narrative intensity period. The period 2014:12 also corresponds to the moderate intensity macro narrative period at 2014:11.

The collective empirical analysis of this chapter aimed to explore whether periods of corporate KU narrative intensity for the stock market (as uncovered in Chapter 6) align approximately with significant points of structural change in fundamentals-based relationships driving returns, volatility, trading volume, and fund flows. Many identified/significant structural breaks from the Chow and BP tests matched those for both high and moderate narrative intensity. The strongest connection between corporate narratives and instability was found for firm-level and aggregate stock market returns, based on both the FF three-factor and five-factor models, for raw and excess returns. The analysis also found support for the connection between narratives and instability for the posited VIX relationship for tests including Chow, one-step forecast, and CUSUM, but not for the BP procedure. Breakpoints in the ETF fund flows relationship offered support for NNH, especially for the second half of the sample period. The trading volume results provided no support for the hypothesis. Interestingly, almost every stock market relationship experienced a structural break matching a point of macro narrative intensity, advancing the view that macro and micro narratives are connected through instability triggered by novel events.

Chapter 11 assesses the implications of NNH by presenting formal empirical tests of the scapegoat model for stock prices using manual textual analysis based on the *Bloomberg News* stock market wrap reports discussed in Chapter 4 and elsewhere. The analysis investigates whether instability in aggregate stock market returns can be, in part, explained by micro and macro KU events and concurrent fluctuations in investor narratives surrounding major macroeconomic and financial headline news factors.

# 11 A Manual Novelty–Narrative Scapegoat Analysis

## 11.1 INTRODUCTION

Chapter 4 discussed the basis for using textual news analytics to incorporate novel events and narrative dynamics into understanding instability in stock market relationships. The benefits and limitations of both algorithmic and manual rule-based narrative approaches were explored. Chapters 5 through 10 investigated the behavior of Knightian uncertainty (KU) events and narrative intensity through hybrid approaches based on the *RavenPack* textual analysis platform applied to *Dow Jones* news outlets. This chapter extends the work of Mangee (2011) by applying a manual textual analysis of scapegoat effects in the stock market under the Novelty–Narrative Hypothesis (NNH). Information contained in *Bloomberg News* daily market wrap reports proxy for the story-weights investors place on observable and unobservable micro and macro fundamentals in rationally forecasting future outcomes.[1] The chapter finds that incorporating scapegoat weights and structural change into econometric analysis improves fundamentals' ability to explain aggregate returns. Moreover, time-varying properties of the narrative weights are found to be connected to shifts in the underlying variables' autoregressive processes, implying that narrative dynamics are connected to information on fundamentals in rational ways.

## 11.2 THE SCAPEGOAT HYPOTHESIS

Researchers have offered numerous explanations for what causes the parameters attached to fundamentals in stock price models to vary

---

[1] This chapter is an abridged version of the working paper Mangee (2019).

over time.[2] Bacchetta and van Wincoop (2004, 2006, 2009, 2013) (hereafter BvW) develop a series of models where instability in asset-price (exchange-rate) relations arises from investors placing disproportionately large weight on a varying set of fundamentals when forecasting short-run parameters. The idea in these models is that market participants observing a movement in an asset's price search for a fundamental candidate in a high narrative state to rationalize the price change when the actual causal fundamental factor may be unobservable. When uncertainty about the price-determination process is relatively high, investors respond to the price fluctuation by focusing on an observable fundamental simultaneously involved in "headline" stories, but also economically consistent with the price change, as a "scapegoat" candidate. Over time, trading strategies will place greater weight on narrative intensive scapegoat factors as swings in investor expectations cause the composition of information sets to change, leading to instability in the relationships driving asset-price fluctuations. This chapter applies the scapegoat model to the US stock market.

There is descriptive textual evidence of swaying investor attention toward heightened narratives about a particular fundamental in response to large movements in stock prices. Consider, for instance, an excerpt from a *Bloomberg News* stock market wrap report describing narrative scapegoat behavior of investors:

> U.S. stocks broke out of a two-week slump as a decline in oil prices enabled investors to [finally] look past the biggest increase in inflation since 1980 ... Investors focused on the core rate, which excludes food and energy, according to Michael Sheldon, chief market strategist at Spencer Clarke LLC. That showed a 0.1 percent increase, less than the 0.2 percent economists expected. "Today's calm CPI report, along with lower oil

---

[2] Certain studies focus on shifts in fundamental factors' autoregressive process, such as Markov-switching in dividends (Driffill and Sola, 1998; Gutierrez and Vazquez, 2004; and Gabriel and Martins, 2011). Other studies have considered different sample periods themselves as underpinning changing price relations, such as the "new era" of the 1990s (Goyal and Welch, 2008; Shiller, 2000). Others have argued that there are nonlinearities in the data-relations (Kanas, 2005). See Chapter 2 for a deeper discussion of these studies and others.

prices, takes some pressure off of inflation fears, and that's what the market has been obsessed about the last few weeks," Sheldon said from his office in New York.

*(Bloomberg News, October 14, 2005)*

The excerpt suggests that stock investors narrowly focused on stories about a particular fundamental, in this case inflation, over a stretch of time that has exhibited historic change. Eventually, new scapegoat factors displaying dramatic change (i.e. oil prices in 2005) garner the narrative attention of investors as forecasting strategies and composition of information sets evolve.

There are two main challenges researchers face in testing the BvW scapegoat models; they both involve financial market uncertainty and may be remedied through narrative textual analysis. First, researchers must identify a proxy factor that is both unobservable, or nonroutine, relative to the more conventional government- or firm-data releases, but also economically capable of explaining variation in security prices. Unobservable factors include the non-repetitive, historically novel micro and macro events discussed throughout this book. Some examples consistent with the above excerpt might include resolution to OPEC oil disputes or unilateral shifts in crude production quotas. Second, researchers must find a measure capturing the varying importance market participants attach to stories about alternative fundamentals (i.e. scapegoat weights) over time such as tracking the relevance of oil market activity in stock market news reports. Addressing these two issues presents an obvious challenge to any researcher seeking to understand scapegoat-driven instability in financial markets. Manual rule-based textual news analytics of popular narrative stories offers one path forward.

To proxy for a particular fundamental's narrative intensity, or scapegoat weight, for the stock market, the present analysis employs a unique dataset from *Bloomberg News'* end-of-the-day reports tracking the importance of a wide array of factors mentioned as driving daily stock price behavior. The wrap reports, and associated word clouds, have been discussed and analyzed in Chapter 4. To the author's best knowledge, this is one of the only scapegoat studies for the stock market and the only one testing the implications of NNH.[3] In constructing the reports, journalists rely on contacts with over 150 equity fund managers and other market professionals providing testimony on the drivers of daily price fluctuations. The manual rule-based approach for the narrative dataset spans a sample period of January 4, 1993 through December 31, 2009.

When information hits the market, journalists build intra-day reports as they, investors, and analysts, alike, can see the market react in real time. These reports are then compiled into a final report after market close. Each of the 4,206 reports was manually read and scored by the author to assess context and meaning of fundamental (as well as psychological and technical trading) relationships reported as driving firm-level and aggregate stock prices on a given day.[4] Monthly frequencies generated by the summary wraps serve as a proxy for the narrative weights the broad market attaches to the relevance of a particular scapegoat fundamental for forecasting returns. Importantly, the *Bloomberg* data, and its manual rule-based collection methodology, do not prespecify how or when certain narratives will matter for investors, leaving open the potential variation in popular stories' scapegoat effects to influence investor forecasting strategies in unforeseeable ways.[5]

The unobservable factor required to test scapegoat effects also comes from narrative information contained in the *Bloomberg News* reports and is proxied by the novel events that are categorized by number of story-mentions in Table 11.1. These historically novel

---

[3] Fratzscher et al. (2015) investigate scapegoat instability for the foreign exchange market using survey data from over forty FX fund managers. The authors base scapegoat weights on rankings of a subset of six macroeconomic fundamentals such as country-differentials for interest and growth rates. The unobservable fundamental in their study measures the importance of FX order flows. Unlike the present manual rule-based analysis that leaves open these determinations, Fratzscher et al. (2015) prespecify the six fundamentals and the order flow variable.

[4] The data collection ended at the end of 2009. Updating the *Bloomberg* dataset is left for future research.

[5] For a detailed description of the *Bloomberg* data collection, see Frydman and Goldberg (2011) and Mangee (2011). For other studies using the *Bloomberg* data, see Mangee (2014, 2017, 2018) and Mangee and Goldberg (2020).

Table 11.1 *KU events that moved the market*

| | |
|---|---|
| Mergers and acquisitions (435)[a] | Fed comments/minutes/ communication (369) |
| Legal or accounting issues (286) | Leverage/credit issues (159) |
| Communication by government officials (151) | Armed conflicts (143) |
| Bailouts/nationalization of banks (90) | Business spending (63) |
| Liquidity issues (59) | Political conflict/instability/ corruption (55) |
| Management shake-ups (47) | Bankruptcy (45) |
| Macroprudential policy (40) | Fiscal policy/stimulus plan (40) |
| Large stake/stock splits/share buybacks (38) | Trade agreements (30) |
| Labor layoffs or strikes (25) | Political elections (22) |
| Terrorism (21) | Financial reform (19) |
| Initial public offerings (18) | Natural disasters (11) |
| Healthcare policy (11) | Tariffs/quotas/subsidies (3) |
| Taxes or rules on CEO bonuses (1) | Introduction of Euro (1) |

[a] *Note:* Historically unique factors reported as driving daily stock market prices in *Bloomberg News* wrap reports. Figures in parentheses denote the total absolute number of explicit mentions for each factor in connection with stock price fluctuations over the sample period January 4, 1993 through December 31, 2009. Source: Frydman et al. (2015).

factors, such as management shake-ups, Fed chair statements, or armed conflicts abroad (micro and macro KU factors analyzed throughout the book), also hold explanatory power in forecasting returns behavior. Frydman et al. (2015), for example, use these KU factors to predict the right-side-of-the-market at one-month forecasting horizons showing that dividend- and discount rate-forecasting channels depend on such unobservable fundamentals in the short run, as implied by scapegoat models. Such novel factors are considered unobservable since they typically are unaccompanied by scheduled quantitative, or structured, data released on a calendar frequency.[6]

[6] To be sure, the proxy for unobservable factors is not a measure of stock market risk. However, numerous studies have documented that so-called soft-information events are related to slower information processing by investors and potentially greater risk premia.

The results from Table 11.1 corroborate the importance for stock markets of mergers and acquisitions, legal issues, the government, credit related considerations, and other novel events, as documented in the expanded micro and macro KU data descriptions in Chapters 7 and 8, respectively. The manual rule-based analysis of the *Bloomberg* reports presented here enables one to test, first, whether accounting for narrative scapegoat effects and structural change improves fundamentals' ability to explain movements in stock prices and, second, whether story-intensities of scapegoat weights are largest when concurrent shocks to a scapegoat fundamental and the unobservable factor are large.

### 11.2.1   The Scapegoat Model

Since stock prices and macro fundamentals tend to exhibit nonstationary behavior, consider the first-difference present value equation with unknown, but constant parameters and no risk-premium adjustment:[7]

$$\Delta p_t = \Delta f'_t \left( (1 - \lambda) \beta + \lambda E_t \beta \right) + (1 - \lambda) \Delta b_t \qquad (11.1)$$

where $p_t$ is the log stock market price at time $t$; $f'_t = \left( f_{1,t}, f_{2,t}, \ldots, f_{N,t} \right)'$ is a vector of $N$ macroeconomic fundamentals; $\beta = (\beta_1, \beta_2, \ldots, \beta_N)$ is a vector of actual parameters; $E_t \beta$ is a vector of unknown, but constant parameters; $b_t$ is the unobservable fundamental; $\lambda$ is the discount factor where $(0 < \lambda < 1)$; and $\Delta$ is the first-difference operator. The expression in the first parentheses is a sum of the true and expected structural parameters weighted by the discount factor. In the

See, for example, Demers and Vega (2008) for a textual-based study supporting this view. See Liberti and Mitchell (2018) for a recent discussion on the implications of soft versus hard information in financial markets.

[7] Bacchetta and van Wincoop (2009, 2013) begin with setting the equilibrium value of the exchange rate to the present value of expected future fundamentals where $s_t = (1 - \lambda) \left[ f'_t \beta + b_t + \Sigma_{j=1}^{\infty} \lambda^j E_t \left( f'_{t+j} \beta + b_{t+j} \right) \right] - \lambda \left[ \eta_t + \Sigma_{j=1}^{\infty} \lambda^j E_t \eta_{t+j} \right]$. Assuming no risk premium ($\eta = 0$) sets the last term to zero that then simplifies the relation to Equation (11.1) here.

short run, expectations of the structural parameter can undergo high variation. Since $\lambda$ is near 1, expected, rather than actual, parameters carry virtually all the weight attached to fundamentals, $f_t'$. The $\beta$ term evolves following an interactive learning process (described in BvW) that suggests the term $E_t\beta$ reflects current investor beliefs about $\beta$. Bacchetta and van Wincoop (2009, 2013) show that, in each period, investors receive a signal of $f_t'\beta + b_t$ even though $\beta$ and $b_t$ are unobservable. The derivative of the change in stock price to a change in the fundamental factor is expressed as:

$$\frac{\partial \Delta p_t}{\partial \Delta f_{N,t}} = (1 - \lambda)\,\beta_N + \lambda E_t \beta_N + \lambda f_t' \frac{\partial E_t \beta}{\partial \Delta f_{N,t}} \qquad (11.2)$$

The middle term in Equation (11.2) shows that the impact of scapegoat fundamentals on stock prices depends on the expected structural parameters while the last term expresses the impact that fundamentals have on these expectations. Stock market participants' expectations are diluted by the crosswinds of current information on fundamentals in the short run where variation in these expectations underpin the instability between stock prices and macro fundamentals.

## 11.2.2  Econometric Approach with Fixed Coefficients

The empirical analog to Equation (11.1) assuming fixed coefficients takes the form:

$$\Delta p_t = f_t'\beta + \left(\theta_t \cdot f_t\right)' \varphi + \phi z_t + \epsilon_t \qquad (11.3)$$

where the parameters $\beta$, $\varphi$ and $\phi$ are unknown to individuals; $z_t$ is the unobservable KU fundamental and $(\cdot)$ is the product operator. This model is called the fixed-coefficient scapegoat model (FC-SG). To proxy for expectational (i.e. scapegoat) weights $\theta_t$, the *Bloomberg News* narrative factor frequencies of a fundamental's importance for investors are used. The unobservable factor $z$ captures the novel factors listed categorically in Table 11.1 and can be thought of as a composite (macro and micro) KU factor for the stock market. The narrative-based scapegoat model implies several testable hypotheses based on Equation (11.3). First, including the interaction of fundamental factor $N$ with its corresponding scapegoat weights ($\theta_{N,t} \cdot f_{N,t}$) is predicted to increase the significance of $\beta_N$. Second, the directional sign of $\beta_N$ and $\varphi_N$ should be consistent with each other, implying an amplifying effect from $\varphi_N$ onto $\beta_N$.

Third, the sign of the KU proxy coefficient $\phi$ is ambiguous. As discussed in Section 11.3, a change in $z$ does not carry a predicted directional change in stock prices. This is so for two reasons. First, $z$ is based on novel KU factors not associated with quantitative scales – think Fed chair statements or geopolitical conflicts or election campaigns. Second, $z$ is measured in a binary way capturing whether a historically unique fundamental event mattered for investor trading decisions or not. Thus, $z$ does not reflect whether more or less of a particular event mattered during the day. Consequently, interpretation of the influence of unobservable KU factors will be based partly on whether $\phi_N$ is significantly different from zero.

### 11.2.3    Unknown and Varying Coefficients

When time-varying coefficients are introduced in the scapegoat model Equation (11.1) is extended to:

$$\Delta p_t = \Delta f_t' \left( (1 - \lambda)\, \beta_t + \lambda E_t \beta_t \right) + (1 - \lambda)\, \Delta b_t + \lambda \Sigma_{i=1}^{T} \Delta f_{t-i}' \left( E_t \beta_{t-i} - E_{t-1} \beta_{t-i} \right) \tag{11.4}$$

where $\beta_t = (\beta_{1,t}, \beta_{2,t}, \ldots, \beta_{N,t})$ denotes a vector of time-varying coefficients and $E_t \beta_t$ denotes a vector of expectational structural parameters formed at time $t$. The narrative scapegoat parameters are now allowed to vary over time but are still unknown to investors. Expectations of parameters ($E_t \beta_t$) depend on a combination of investors' understanding of the $\beta_t$s, perhaps based on their longer-run time paths, and the signal received every period in time $f_t' \beta_t = b_t$. The final term on the right-hand side shows that these expectations can change over time, particularly under instability from KU and model ambiguity underpinning investor forecasting strategies.

## 11.2.4 Econometric Approach with Varying Coefficients

The empirical analog to Equation (11.4) takes the form:

$$\Delta p_t = f_t'\beta_t + (\theta_t \cdot f_t)' \varphi + \phi z_t + \epsilon_t \tag{11.5}$$

This model is called the varying-coefficient scapegoat model (VC-SG). The same three predictions involving the parameters $\beta$, $\varphi$, and $\phi$ as outlined for the fixed-parameter case hold here as well. To test whether scapegoat effects strengthen fundamentals' ability to explain stock price fluctuations, benchmark specifications and those that isolate $\theta_{N,t}$ are also tested.

## 11.2.5 Benchmark Models

The benchmark models with fixed and time-varying coefficients, respectively, are expressed as:

$$\Delta p_t = f_t'\beta \tag{11.6}$$

$$\Delta p_t = f_t'\beta_t \tag{11.7}$$

These models are denoted fixed-coefficient benchmark (FC-BM) and varying-coefficient benchmark for Markov-switching (VC-BMMS). The present value model for stock prices is a natural candidate for the benchmark model where the benchmark information set $f_t$ would include dividends and/or earnings and short-rates. Another specification would involve consumption and interest rates as implied by the consumption-based Capital Asset Pricing Model (CAPM).

## 11.3 DATA

Manual rule-based analysis of *Bloomberg News* stock market wraps is highly applicable to testing the narrative-based scapegoat model for stock return instability. The stories leave open which information on fundamentals may influence investor trading decisions at every point in time. The narrative data allows for any fundamental factor, whether observable or otherwise, to exhibit scapegoat effects and enter the information sets of $\theta_t$ and $z_t$ in open ways. As discussed in previous chapters, narrative accounts of social, economic, political, and financial behavior from textual analysis of financial news is an appropriate medium to capture the effects of unforeseeable change from novel events and the KU they engender.

The indeterminate nature of the stock price relationships described in the reports allows for changes in the expectational parameters $(\lambda \sum_{i=1}^{T} \Delta f'_{t-i}(E_t \beta_{t-i} - E_{t-1} \beta_{t-i}))$ to matter for price fluctuations. Modeling changes in expectations, or beliefs, is difficult. Under KU, it is beyond objective frequency assessment *ex ante*. A fundamental factor may impact stock prices today through its expected impact on price forecasts for period $t + 1$ made at time $t$. However, forecasting future prices also involves forecasting future values of fundamentals. It also involves forecasting the forecasts of others. And, shifts in the composition of informational variables likely involves considering the impact of other fundamentals today on a future, potentially different, set of fundamentals. By not predetermining which fundamentals matter and in which ways, the *Bloomberg News* reports allow for higher-order scapegoat effects through various forecasting channels. And, the reports allow for assessment of headline fundamentals upon which the scapegoat weights, and underlying narratives, are based.

### 11.3.1   Scapegoat Weights

The stock market narratives track whether a particular factor was explicitly mentioned as driving stock prices during a given trading day. The narrative-based scapegoat weights $\theta_N$ are measured by the monthly proportion of trading days that a fundamental factor mattered for investors in the story. The data allows for any micro or macro fundamental to display scapegoat effects with stock prices and for this magnitude of narrative-intensity to vary freely over time. For empirical tractability, individual fundamentals such as GDP, Treasury bill yields, or the Consumer Price Index (CPI), for example, are aggregated into "Economic Activity," "Interest Rate," and "Inflation" categories, respectively, for measuring $\theta_N$.[8] This also permits interaction of $\theta_{N,t}$ with $f_{N,t}$ in a straightforward way.[9] Figure 11.1 plots the factor frequencies for six fundamentals. For each factor, the monthly proportion of trading days is plotted over the sample period.

Immediate inspection of Figure 11.1 shows that the narrative weights investors place on a particular fundamental exhibit great variation over the seventeen-year period. For instance, interest rate stories mattered less than 10 percent on average from 2002 through 2003. However, by the end of 2006, interest rates mattered more than 60 percent of the time. Even more striking is the variation in oil price narratives that, on average, mattered very little for investors from 1993 through 2004. By 2005, the importance of oil prices skyrocketed to over 60 percent of monthly trading days. Even fundamental factors that routinely matter for stock prices, such as dividends/earnings and overall economic activity, display substantial variation themselves in the narratives over time. Interestingly, stories about economic activity and consumption both appear to exhibit a mean shift around the beginning of the 2000s, a period associated with the bursting of the dot-com IT "bubble" and a short-lived economic recession.

Such nuanced variation across narratives involving these six factors serves as fertile ground for testing the scapegoat hypothesis outlined above. The dramatic shifts observed in their reported importance would be difficult to anticipate with a rule that predetermines when and in which ways popular stories about particular fundamentals enter stock return forecasts. Thus, the dramatic variation displayed in Figure 11.1 is suggestive of unforeseeable change in stock return relationships. Summary statistics for the *Bloomberg* narrative scapegoat weights are reported in Table 11.2.

---

[8] See Frydman and Goldberg (2011) and Frydman et al. (2015) for a detailed description of the disaggregated fundamental factors included in each broader fundamental category.

[9] Since $0 < \theta_{N,t} < 1$, all variables in the empirical analysis are standardized by subtracting their mean and dividing by their standard deviation.

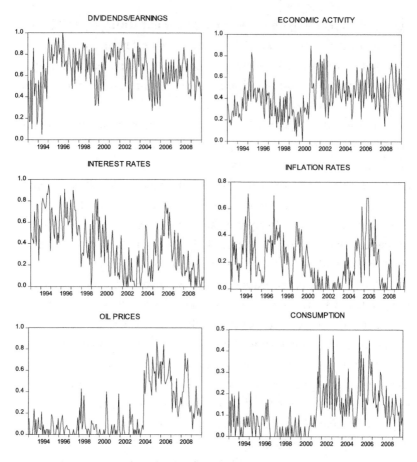

FIGURE 11.1  The figure plots the monthly factor frequency from *Bloomberg News* for a particular fundamental factor. Source: Mangee (2019).

## 11.3.2   The KU Unobservable Factor

The *Bloomberg* dataset contains an extensive record of historically novel events and the narratives about them that unfold over time. Consider the following excerpts that describe how the impacts of unobservable factors (i.e. KU events) are captured in the narrative *Bloomberg* data.

Table 11.2 *Summary statistics for* Bloomberg *factor frequencies*

| Factor[a] | Mean | Min, Max | $\sigma$ |
|---|---|---|---|
| Dividends/Earnings | 0.654 | (0.048, 1.00) | 0.191 |
| Economic Activity | 0.419 | (0.000, 0.895) | 0.176 |
| Interest Rates | 0.383 | (0.000, 0.952) | 0.255 |
| Inflation Rates | 0.197 | (0.000, 0.714) | 0.177 |
| Oil Prices | 0.193 | (0.000, 0.870) | 0.228 |
| Consumption | 0.118 | (0.000, 0.478) | 0.108 |

[a] *Note:* Data is based upon the monthly proportion of trading days that a particular fundamental factor was explicitly mentioned in the *Bloomberg News* wrap reports as driving stock prices; $\sigma$ denotes the standard deviation of the distribution. Source: Mangee (2019).

"The overriding backdrop with the markets is still Iraq," said Jeff Swensen, a trader at John Hancock Advisors, which manages $29 billion in Boston. "The economic numbers only briefly caught the attention of the market, and now we are focused on geopolitical concerns."
*(Bloomberg News, February 7, 2003)*

"The earnings are coming in great, but that is not the focus right now," said Arthur Micheletti, who helps manage $1.5 billion for Bailard Biehl & Kaiser Inc. in Foster City, California. "People are focused on interest rates." Greenspan was "pretty subtle in indicating interest rates are going to rise," he said.
*(Bloomberg News, April 20, 2004)*

U.S. stocks kept the December rally alive, extending the best annual advance since 2003, on takeover speculation that offset concern the Federal Reserve won't lower interest rates anytime soon ... Airlines climbed on an analyst report that UAL Corp., the owner of United Airlines, may announce a merger or acquisition tomorrow. Sabre Holdings Corp., operator of tourism Web site Travelocity.com, and Biomet Inc., a maker of artificial joints, rallied on anticipation they will be purchased ... Announced U.S. deals for 2006 are on a pace to match 2000's record of $1.63 trillion, data compiled by Bloomberg show.
*(Bloomberg News, December 11, 2006)*

"There's still a lot of fear out there because of the fact that this credit contagion is starting to widen out," said Larry Adam, chief investment strategist at Deutsche Bank Alex. Brown in Baltimore, which manages $58 billion. "You're seeing increasing amounts of write-offs by banks, with some of them saying that they're going to be larger for the fourth quarter than the third." ... Financial shares dropped to the lowest since April 2005 after the Federal Reserve said "heightened pressures in money markets" prompted it to take steps to increase the cash available to banks for loans.

(Bloomberg News, November 26, 2007)

The excerpts suggest that unobservable fundamentals such as Fed chair comments, credit issues, macroprudential policy, mergers and acquisitions, analyst reports, and geopolitical tensions abroad impact investor expectations. Frydman et al. (2015) find that 20 percent of the event stories reported in *Bloomberg* wraps as driving stock price fluctuations involve historical events that are somewhat novel such as these.[10] The authors measure the net monthly proportion of positive unobservable events. However, many stories about macroprudential policy or mergers and acquisitions can be interpreted by investors as being either "good" or "bad" for the market, offering no distinct directional priors with stock price movements. Frydman et al. (2015) deal with this by categorizing an historical event as positive or negative if *Bloomberg News* reported it as contributing to a rise or fall, respectively, in stock prices on the given day.[11]

Figure 11.2 plots the net monthly frequency of positive KU events based on manual rule-based narrative analysis along with corresponding Hodrick–Prescott (HP)-trend. Visual inspection suggests that this composite index of nonrepetitive events shares some of the persistence over time as exhibited by the KU indices based

---

[10] The 20 percent figure of KU factors' importance in the *Bloomberg* wrap reports is based on a binary recording whether the factor mattered or not. Therefore, the figure does not capture multiple mentions of the same KU factor, whether connected to the same entity or different ones. Also, the *Bloomberg* data is based on a single wrap report for the stock market per day whereas the data from Chapters 5 through 8 are based on hundreds, if not thousands, of *Dow Jones* financial news reports per day. This explains the disparity of the 20 percent figure reported here and the 67 and 83 percent figures of corporate and macro KU events, respectively, discussed in previous chapters.

[11] For example, if on ten days in a given month at least one KU event was reported as driving stock market prices on each day and six of those days experienced a price increase in, say, the SP500 market price and the other four experienced a market decline and there were twenty-two total trading days in the month, the net monthly proportion of positive KU events would be $6/22 - 4/22 = 0.09$.

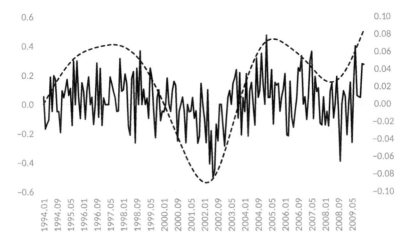

FIGURE 11.2 The figure plots the net positive monthly factor frequency of KU events using manual rule-based textual analysis from *Bloomberg News* (solid line) against the HP-trend (dotted line). Source: Mangee (2019).

on unscheduled corporate and macro events from *Dow Jones* news introduced in Chapters 5 and 8, respectively.

There are several interesting features of the *Bloomberg* KU series of novel events. First, there are not just positive KU or negative KU events over the sample. The mean for the series is 0.022 and the min, max is (−0.500, 0.474). Second, KU events appear to predate major reversals in stock price swings. The *Bloomberg* KU index reverses into a downswing one year prior to the late 1999 peak in stock prices, reverses into an upswing one year before the 2003:02 trough in stock prices, and reverses into a downswing two years prior to the onset of the global financial crisis. Again, as found in Chapters 6 and 9, novel events, narratives, and market uncertainty are related, though not exclusively, to reversals in stock prices and valuation ratios. The findings provide further evidence that novelty-driven KU may help bound periods of excess in the stock market through an uncertainty premium, gap-effect, and associated narrative dynamics.

### 11.3.3   Conventional Data

Data on the 3-month Treasury bill yield comes from the Board of Governors of the Federal Reserve System H.15 Release, denoted $i^S$. Longer-term 10-year yields $i^L$ are taken from Robert Shiller's website along with data on SP500 prices $P$, earnings $E$, and dividends $D$. Personal consumption expenditures (PCE) data comes from the Bureau of Economic Analysis – Personal Income and Outlays Release, denoted $C$; oil price data is West Texas Intermediate (WTI) collected from the Bureau of Labor Statistics, denoted $Oil$, while data on Industrial Production (IP) comes from the Board of Governors of the Federal Reserve System G.17 Industrial Production and Capacity Utilization Release, denoted $Y$. Inflation data, $\pi$, comes from the Bureau of Labor Statistics and is are measured by the log-difference in the CPI. All other fundamentals are expressed in real terms by deflating by the CPI.

## 11.4   EMPIRICAL RESULTS

The empirical results presented in this section are based on monthly data covering the sample period January 1993 through December 2009, yielding 204 total observations. Unless stated otherwise, stock prices and fundamentals are measured in log first-differences. Narrative scapegoat weights $\theta$ and unobserved narrative KU events $z$ are as described previously. The first major scapegoat hypothesis tested is whether narrative accounts of scapegoat effects help fundamentals explain stock price fluctuations. The second hypothesis tests when a fundamental factor may become part of a popular scapegoat narrative.

### 11.4.1   Scapegoat Effects and Fundamentals

The first stage of the analysis seeks to determine which of the potential factors displays greatest potential for being a scapegoat. To this end, the six fundamentals with the largest mean $\theta_{N,t}$ based on the *Bloomberg* factor frequencies reported in Table 11.2 are used. To parse down the number of parameters, a general-to-specific regression approach is followed. The composite regression of scapegoat effects based on Equation (11.5) takes the form:

$$\Delta p_t = \varphi_1 (\theta_{1,t} \cdot f_{1,t})' + \varphi_2 (\theta_{2,t} \cdot f_{2,t})' + \cdots + \varphi_6 (\theta_{6,t} \cdot f_{6,t})' + \epsilon_t \quad (11.8)$$

The general-to-specific reduction process involves estimating Equation (11.8) and dropping the fundamental with the lowest associated $t$-value. The equation is reestimated on five fundamentals, the lowest $t$-value factor is dropped and so on until the only remaining fundamentals are those with $\varphi_{N,t}$ significant at the 10 percent level. Following this approach leaves four fundamental factors: earnings growth, the difference in short-rates, inflation, and consumption growth. This filtered regression is the empirical analog to the fixed-parameter macro model in Equation (11.6). These macro fundamentals are consistent with the present value relation for stock prices and the consumption CAPM. To estimate the fixed-coefficients model, the following equation is estimated:

$$\Delta p_t = \beta_0 + \beta_1 \Delta e_t + \beta_2 \Delta i_t^s + \beta_3 \pi_t + \beta_4 \Delta c_t + u_t \quad (11.9)$$

The estimation results are presented in Table 11.3. Earnings growth and consumption growth are statistically significant with the correct positive coefficients, but short-rates and inflation are insignificant with incorrect signs. The adjusted-$R^2$ for the fixed-coefficient macro fundamentals model is 0.11.

Though not reported, the VC-BMMS model generates significant effects from earnings growth in the first regime, while all other variables are insignificant across both states. The next step includes scapegoat effects and represents the empirical analog to the fixed-coefficient scapegoat model from Equation (11.3). Table 11.4 reports the estimation results for $\beta$, $\varphi$, and $\phi$. First, $\beta_N$ coefficients on earnings and consumption growth remain significant with the correct sign. $\beta_N$ for short-rates and inflation remain insignificant while the scapegoat parameter $\varphi$ on inflation is significant. Second, the consistency in sign between $\beta_N$ and $\varphi_N$ as implied by the scapegoat model holds for earnings growth, short-rates, and consumption growth. Third, the

Table 11.3 *Fixed-coefficient fundamentals model*

| Dep. Var.[a] | | | Fundamental Factors | | | | | |
|---|---|---|---|---|---|---|---|---|
| $\Delta p_t$ | $\Delta d_t$ | $\Delta e_t$ | $\Delta i_t^S$ | $\Delta i_t^L$ | $\Delta y_t$ | $\pi_t$ | $\Delta c_t$ | $\Delta oil_t$ |
| | – | 0.253*** | 0.024 | – | – | 0.046 | 0.215** | – |
| adj-$R^2 = 0.11$ | | (0.096) | (0.075) | | | (0.119) | (0.087) | |

[a] *Note:* Heteroskedasticity and autocorrelation consistent (HAC) standard errors reported in parentheses. Fundamentals for this model are selected based on a general-to-specific testing-down of the regression $\Delta p_t = \alpha_{N,0} + \alpha_{N,1}(\theta_N \cdot f_{N,t}) + \varepsilon_t$ regressing $\Delta p_t$ on all fundamentals $f_{N,t}$ times their expected scapegoat parameters $\theta_N$. All series are standardized by subtracting their mean and dividing by their standard deviation. ***, **, * denote statistical significance at the 1%, 5% and 10% level. Source: Mangee (2019).

parameter $\theta$ on the KU variable $z$ is positive and strongly significant. Finally, the adjusted-$R^2$ for the fixed-coefficient scapegoat model is 0.30, more than twice that of the fixed-coefficient benchmark model.

The next model is the varying-coefficient scapegoat model expressed in Equation (11.5). There are many different ways to test for and model structural change in stock, and other asset, price relationships with fundamentals. Here, a Markov-switching model is considered with constant and dependent transitional probabilities across two regimes. As previously discussed, stochastic representations of change do not allow *ex ante* for unforeseeable instability, as implied by the Novelty-Narrative Hypothesis (NNH) under KU. However, the inclusion of the uncertainty variable $z$ is presumed to be picking up some degree of non-routine change in the relationships driving stock market returns. Furthermore, the results suggest that the Markov-switching approach is underestimating the degree of structural change in the posited relationship, implying a time-varying probability model is better suited to fit the data.

This model with constant transitional probabilities is called the varying-coefficient scapegoat Markov-switching model (VC-SGMS). This specification allows only $\beta_{N,t}$ to vary across regimes, while $\varphi_N$ and $\phi$ remain fixed, as implied by Equation (11.5). For brevity, Table 11.5 reports results for $\beta_{1N,t}$, $\beta_{2N,t}$, $\varphi_N$, and $\theta_N$ under the

Table 11.4 *Fixed-coefficient scapegoat model*

| Dep. Var.[a] | | Fundamental Factors | | | | | | | |
|---|---|---|---|---|---|---|---|---|---|
| $\Delta p_t$ | $\Delta d_t$ | $\Delta e_t$ | $\Delta i_t^S$ | $\Delta i_t^L$ | $\Delta y_t$ | $\pi_t$ | $\Delta c_t$ | $\Delta oil_t$ | $z_t$ |
| $\beta$ | – | 0.248*** | –0.041 | – | – | 0.058 | 0.229*** | – | – |
|  |  | (0.084) | (0.066) |  |  | (0.088) | (0.082) |  |  |
| $\varphi$ | – | 0.129 | –0.083 | – | – | –0.123** | 0.033 | – | – |
|  |  | (0.088) | (0.061) |  |  | (0.062) | (0.028) |  |  |
| $\phi$ | – | – | – | – | – | – | – | – | 0.418*** |
|  |  |  |  |  |  |  |  |  | (0.091) |
| adj-R$^2$ = 0.30 | | | | | | | | | |

[a] *Note:* Coefficient estimates based on the regression $\Delta p_t = f_t'\beta + (\theta_t \cdot f_t)'\varphi + \phi z_t + \varepsilon_t$. HAC standard errors reported in parentheses. All series are standardized by subtracting their mean and dividing by their standard deviation. ***, **, * denote statistical significance at the 1%, 5%, and 10% level. Source: Mangee (2019).

VC-SGMS model. The $\beta$ coefficients are significant for both earnings and short-rates with hypothesized signs in Regime 2. Scapegoat-weighted short-rates, which are not regime-specific, are also significant and of correct sign. The parameter $\phi$ for the KU factors is significant and positive.

One might expect regime-switching behavior (i.e. structural change) under scapegoat effects since the fundamentals being considered, or beliefs about them, may undergo related shifts; earnings and consumption are intimately connected to expansionary/recessionary economic regimes while short-term interest rates and inflation, while also time-varying with the state of economic activity, follow trends in monetary policy set by the Federal Open Market Committee (FOMC). Note that the fixed-transition probabilities reported in Table 11.5 are not very persistent with $P_{11} = 0.34$ and $P_{22} = 0.40$. Though not reported, the expected duration of each regime is 1.51 and 1.67 months for Regimes 1 and 2, respectively. That there are such frequent shifts from one regime to another may suggest a greater degree of instability in the relationship between stock prices and fundamentals than Markov-switching allows for, and that time-varying transition probabilities are a better representation of change than determinate and constant probabilities.

The last test of the first hypothesis of the scapegoat model for stock prices focuses on the in-sample and out-of-sample forecasting ability of the various models. Table 11.6 reports results based on Root Mean Square Error (RMSE) and Mean Absolute Error (MAE) forecasting metrics. The top panel reports in-sample results from estimating over the full sample from 1993:01 through 2009:12 based on one-step-ahead forecasts. The bottom panel reports out-of-sample results from estimating the sample from 1993:01 through 2006:12 and generating one-step-ahead forecasts for the period 2007:01–2009:12. This is a useful sample window since it may shed light on issues related to the global financial crisis. To give all models the benefit of the doubt, actual future values of RHS variables were used, circumventing the need to forecast them separately.

Table 11.5 *Markov-switching scapegoat model* [a]

| Dep. Var. [a] | Fundamental Factors | | | | | | | | |
|---|---|---|---|---|---|---|---|---|---|
| $\Delta p_t$ | $\Delta d_t$ | $\Delta e_t$ | $\Delta i_t^S$ | $\Delta i_t^L$ | $\Delta y_t$ | $\pi_t$ | $\Delta c_t$ | $\Delta oil_t$ | $z_t$ |
| *Regime 1* | | | | | | | | | |
| $\beta_{1t}$ | — | 0.002 | 0.000 | — | — | 0.005 | 0.011* | — | — |
| | | (0.005) | (0.006) | | | (0.006) | (0.006) | | |
| *Regime 2* | | | | | | | | | |
| $\beta_{2t}$ | — | 0.021*** | −0.005* | — | — | −0.004 | 0.005 | — | — |
| | | (0.004) | (0.003) | | | (0.004) | (0.003) | | |
| *Common* | | | | | | | | | |
| $\varphi$ | — | −0.002 | −0.005** | — | — | −0.002 | 0.001 | — | — |
| | | (0.004) | (0.002) | | | (0.002) | (0.001) | | |
| $\phi$ | — | — | — | — | — | — | — | — | 0.014*** |
| | | | | | | | | | (0.002) |
| $P_{11} = 0.34$ | | | | | | | | | |
| $P_{22} = 0.40$ | | | | | | | | | |

[a] *Note:* Coefficient estimates based on the Markov-switching regression model with stochastic transition probabilities for $\Delta p_t = f_t'\beta_t + (\theta_t \cdot f_t)'\varphi + \phi z_t + \varepsilon_t$. All series are standardized by subtracting their mean and dividing by their standard deviation. $P_{ij}$ denotes the probability of being in state $i$ dependent on the previous state $j$. ***, **, * denote statistical significance at the 1%, 5%, and 10% level. Source: Mangee (2019).

Table 11.6 *In-sample and out-of-sample forecasting*

| Dep. Var.[a] | Model Specification | | | | |
|---|---|---|---|---|---|
| $\Delta p_t$ | FC-BM | FC-SG | FC-EXSG | VC-BMMS | VC-SGMS |
| | In-Sample | | | | |
| RMSE | 0.934 | 0.820 | 0.831 | 0.952 | 0.033 |
| MAE | 0.688 | 0.617 | 0.627 | 0.685 | 0.024 |
| | Out-of-Sample | | | | |
| RMSE | 1.428 | 1.390 | 1.300 | 1.657 | 0.064 |
| MAE | 1.055 | 0.963 | 0.956 | 1.141 | 0.047 |

[a] *Note:* FC-BM, FC-SG, VC-BMMS, and VC-SGMS are as described in Section 11.2. FC-EXSG refers to the regression excluding scapegoat effects, but including the KU events, $\Delta p_t = f_t'\beta + \phi z_t + \varepsilon_t$. In-sample forecasts are based on the RMSE and MAE of the one-step-ahead forecasts over the entire sample 1993:01–2009:12. The out-of-sample forecasts are based on an estimation sample of 1993:01–2006:12 where RMSE and MAE correspond to one-step-ahead forecasts for the period 2007:01–2009:12. For both in-sample and out-of-sample forecasts, the actual values of future variables were used. Source: Mangee (2019).

For in-sample results, the lowest RMSEs are for the VC-SGMS. The highest RMSEs are based on the fixed- and varying-coefficient benchmark models (FC-BM, VC-BMMS) that generate similarly high values. To better isolate scapegoat effects, a model is compared that excludes the narrative scapegoat effects but includes the unobservable KU factor. This model is called the fixed-coefficient excluding scapegoat model (FC-EXSG). Although the differences in RMSE and MAE are not dramatic, the model with scapegoat effects performs better (0.820 vs. 0.831 and 0.617 vs. 0.627, respectively). This result, however, does not hold for out-of-sample forecasts where the RMSE for FC-EXSG is 1.300 while that for FC-SG is 1.390. This may reflect the importance of novel events during the financial crisis period. After all, investors were keyed in to comments by the secretary of the Treasury and Fed chair as well as firm M&As, credit issues, bankruptcies, and legal meanderings. The other out-of-sample results are consistent with in-sample: the VC-SGMS produces the lowest forecasting errors while fixed-coefficient and variable-coefficient benchmark models generate the highest forecasting errors.

## II.5 WHEN DOES A FUNDAMENTAL BECOME A POPULAR NARRATIVE?

Chapter 2 presented a case study on the connection between narrative dynamics and US data breaches. The findings suggested that the connection is nuanced. This section tests the longer-run relationships between narrative scapegoat weights $\theta_N$ and the autoregressive behavior of $f_{N,t}$. The analysis hypothesizes that the narrative weights investors place on a particular fundamental's importance for stock prices $\theta_{N,t}$ are directly related to the actual univariate properties of the underlying series. Three subhypotheses are tested:

> $\mathcal{H}_1$: narrative attention $\theta_{N,t}$ covaries positively with the level of $f_{N,t}$
>
> $\mathcal{H}_2$: narrative attention $\theta_{N,t}$ covaries positively with the relative departure of $f_{N,t}$ from benchmark levels, denoted $f_{N,t}^{gap}$
>
> $\mathcal{H}_3$: narrative attention $\theta_{N,t}$ covaries positively with the volatility of $f_{N,t}$, denoted $f_{N,t}^{\sigma}$

The first hypothesis $\mathcal{H}_1$ traces a fundamental's relevance to its magnitude – when the value of $f_{N,t}$ increases so does its narrative weight and vice versa.[12] The second hypothesis $\mathcal{H}_2$ suggests that it is not the absolute magnitude of $f_{N,t}$ that matters for narrative weight, but the relative distance from historically "reasonable" values. The importance of $f_{N,t}$ increases when the underlying data series becomes "too high" or "too low," measured as, $f_{N,t}^{gap} = |ln(f_{N,t}) - ln(\overline{f_{N,t}})|$.[13] The

---

[12] Empirical motivation for $\mathcal{H}_1$ stems from studies that find that good/bad news for the stock market depends on expansionary and contractionary stages of the business cycle. See, for example, Veronesi (1999) and Boyd et al. (2005).

[13] Motivation for $\mathcal{H}_2$ is provided by Keynes (1936, p. 201). When assessing whether to hold cash versus interest-bearing bonds, Keynes notes, "what matters is not the absolute level

third hypothesis $\mathcal{H}_3$ posits that increasing volatility of the underlying data leads market participants to place greater narrative weight on $f_{N,t}$. This is measured by the standard deviation of a twelve-month rolling window where $f^{\sigma}_{N,t} = \Sigma^{12}_{i=0}x_{t-i}/12$ and $x_t = \sqrt{\frac{\Sigma^{12}_{i=1}(f_{N,t}-\overline{f_{N,t}})^2}{n-1}}$.

Visual inspection of Figure 11.1 suggests that the *Bloomberg* factor frequencies may be nonstationary. Formal ADF and Phillips–Perron (PP) tests for the presence of unit roots in the factor frequency data suggest all six fundamental factors are nonstationary.[14] Consequently, we employ cointegration tests to test $\mathcal{H}_1 - \mathcal{H}_3$ for most of the data. For sensitivity and robustness, both Johansen (1995)'s Gaussian Maximum Likelihood VAR-based test as well as the Engle–Granger (1987) two-step cointegration procedure are considered. Further, tests for the null hypothesis of pure adjustment of narrative weights $\theta_{N,t}$ to disequilibrium in the cointegrated VAR (CVAR) are provided. The results for $\mathcal{H}_1$, $\mathcal{H}_2$, and $\mathcal{H}_3$ are reported in Tables 11.7 through 11.9, respectively. The top panel of each table reports the cointegrated VAR and Engle–Granger cointegration test results that correspond to nonstationary behavior of $\theta_{N,t}$ and $f_{N,t}$. When either of the variables are stationary, an unrestricted VAR is estimated and a Wald test statistic for the joint insignificance of lagged values of $f_{N,t}$ on $\theta_{N,t}$ is reported in the bottom portion of the tables.[15]

of $r$ but the degree of its divergence from what is considered a fairly safe level of $r$, having regard to those calculations of probability which are being relied on."

[14] In general, variables bounded within the interval $(0,1)$ do not display explosive unit root behavior when examining longer time periods, say forty years or more. However, this tendency need not necessarily hold for shorter time periods where nonstationary behavior can be the most appropriate statistical characterization of the data-generating process.

[15] For each of Tables 11.7 through 11.9, the value reported under the CVAR is the likelihood ratio trace test statistic. The associated $p$-value against the null hypothesis of no cointegration is reported in parentheses, $r$ denotes the reduced-rank of the $\Pi$-matrix. A restricted constant is included in the cointegration relation. Transitory and permanent intervention dummies are included to deal with outlier residuals until first- and second-order serial correlation is removed. Optimal lag-length for both tests is determined by SIC criterion. E–G denotes the Engle–Granger (1987) cointegration test. The $\tau$- and $z$-statistics are ADF residual-based unit root tests where $\theta_{N,t}$ is the dependent variable. Optimal lag-length is determined by SIC criterion. For the Unrestricted VAR, the value reported is the Wald test for the null of first- and second-lag exclusion of $\theta_{N,t}$ in the $f_{N,t}$ equation in an unrestricted VAR(2). * and ** denote significance at the 5% and 1% level, respectively.

## 11.5.1 $\mathcal{H}_1-\mathcal{H}_3$ and Cointegration

$\mathcal{H}_1$ implies that the narrative weights involving a particular fundamental and the official underlying data comove positively over time.
Table 11.7 reports that the trace test for the null hypothesis of no
cointegration for the CVAR analysis is strongly rejected for both short-
and long-rates and Engle–Granger tests provide strong diagnostic

Table 11.7 *Narrative weights and fundamentals' level*

| Factor | CVAR | | | E–G Test | |
| --- | --- | --- | --- | --- | --- |
| | Trace Test-stat | | $\theta_{N,t}$ adj. | $\tau$-stat | $z$-stat |
| Dividends $(d_t)$ | $r = 0$ | 44.717 (0.000)** | 0.842 | $-2.959$ | $-18.745$ |
| | $r \leq 1$ | 2.561 (0.670) | | (0.125) | (0.065) |
| Earnings $(e_t)$ | $r = 0$ | 39.253 (0.000)* | 0.000 | $-2.791$ | $-17.361$ |
| | $r \leq 1$ | 9.123 (0.050) | | (0.173) | (0.087) |
| Short-Rates $(i_t^S)$ | $r = 0$ | 37.040 (0.000)** | 0.000 | $-4.255$** | $-40.276$** |
| | $r \leq 1$ | 2.755 (0.634) | | (0.004) | (0.000) |
| Long-Rates $(i_t^L)$ | $r = 0$ | 36.017 (0.000)** | 0.001 | $-8.988$** | $-115.932$** |
| | $r \leq 1$ | 3.956 (0.431) | | (0.000) | (0.000) |
| Economic | $r = 0$ | 27.595 (0.003)** | 0.667 | $-4.873$ | $-52.262$** |
| Activity $(y_t)$ | $r \leq 1$ | 3.348 (0.528) | | (0.090) | (0.000) |
| Oil Prices $(oil_t)$ | $r = 0$ | 19.273 (0.067) | – | $-3.469$* | $-27.001$* |
| | $r \leq 1$ | 2.288 (0.721) | | (0.039) | (0.010) |
| Consumption $(c_t)$ | $r = 0$ | 8.436 (0.420) | – | $-2.44$ | $-13.847$ |
| | $r \leq 1$ | 2.511 (0.113) | | (0.309) | (0.176) |

Unrestricted VAR$^c$

| Inflation Rates $(\pi_t)$ | $\chi^2(2) = 11.789(.003)$** |
| --- | --- |

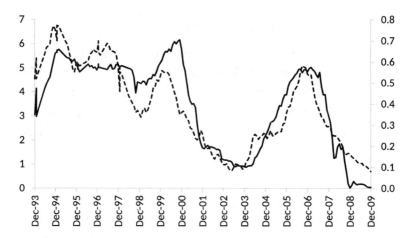

FIGURE 11.3 The figure plots the 12-month moving average of interest rate narrative frequencies from *Bloomberg News* wrap reports (dashed line, right axis) against the 3-month Treasury bill rate (solid line, left axis). Source: Mangee (2019).

support. When market interest rates increase, popular narratives are more likely to be based upon those trends.

Figure 11.3 plots the actual 3-month Treasury bill rate against the narrative weight involving interest rates $\theta_{i,t}$. The comovement between the two series is really striking. Not only do the two series track closely during extended periods of time, but the timing of reversals in 2003–2004 and 2007 is nearly identical. These particular results may help to understand the portfolio balance effects of monetary policy – stock market narratives about interest rates are greater following a tighter monetary policy of higher rates. A similar, albeit less striking, pattern can be seen for oil prices in Figure 11.4. Oil price narratives mattered very little when corresponding crude prices were low. However, starting in 2004, petroleum prices and their associated narratives began to increase dramatically.

Inflation rates, $\pi_t$ and associated narratives, $\theta_{\pi,t}$ are both found to be stationary over the sample period and are, therefore, analyzed with an unrestricted VAR of order two. The coefficient on the first lag of $\pi_t$ for the $\theta_{\pi,t}$-relation is positive and significant at the 1 percent

FIGURE 11.4 The figure plots the twelve-month moving average of oil price narratives from *Bloomberg News* wrap reports (dashed line, left axis) against the price of WTI crude (solid line, right axis). Source: Mangee (2019).

level. Table 11.7 reports a strong rejection of Granger causality (Wald) tests of the null hypothesis that the lagged coefficients on $\pi_t$ are jointly equal to zero for the $\theta_{\pi,t}$ equation. Like interest rate narratives, when inflation rates are higher, investor narratives are more likely to be based upon them. Indeed, visual inspection of the Interest Rate and Inflation Rate series in Figure 11.1 shows a close comovement in timing of peaks and troughs particularly in the second half of the sample. The trace tests also suggest a cointegrating relation between the level of earnings, dividends, economic activity, and the importance of their associated narratives for stock market news. Finally, the analysis fails to reject the null hypothesis of pure adjustment in $\theta_{N,t}$ for dividends and economic activity, suggesting that narratives involving these fundamentals purely respond to disequilibrium movements away from the underlying data. Taken together, Table 11.7 provides rather strong empirical support for the $\mathcal{H}_1$ hypothesis that narrative attention covaries positively with the level of the underlying fundamental.

The second hypothesis implies that narrative weights $\theta_{N,t}$ depend on a fundamental's departure from historical trend values.

Table 11.8 *Narrative weights and fundamentals' gap*

| Factor | | CVAR | | E–G Test | |
|---|---|---|---|---|---|
| | | Trace Test-stat | $\theta_{N,t}$ adj. | $\tau$-stat | $z$-stat |
| Dividends $(d_t)$ | $r = 0$ | 41.522 (0.000)** | 0.040 | −2.796 | −17.626 |
| | $r \leq 1$ | 1.565 (0.852) | | (0.172) | (0.083) |
| Earnings $(e_t)$ | $r = 0$ | 25.717 (0.007)** | 0.207 | −3.224 | −24.499* |
| | $r \leq 1$ | 5.239 (0.268) | | (0.070) | (0.018) |
| Short-Rates $(i_t^S)$ | $r = 0$ | 19.135 (0.070) | – | −3.419* | −25.472* |
| | $r \leq 1$ | 5.476 (0.244) | | (0.044) | (0.015) |
| Economic | $r = 0$ | 22.232 (0.025)* | 0.434 | −4.543** | −47.427** |
| Activity $(y_t)$ | $r \leq 1$ | 0.964 (0.941) | | (0.001) | (0.000) |
| Oil Prices $(oil_t)$ | $r = 0$ | 17.042 (0.132) | – | −2.673 | −14.952 |
| | $r \leq 1$ | 1.924 (0.788) | | (0.214) | (0.142) |
| Consumption $(c_t)$ | $r = 0$ | 63.182 (0.000)** | 0.000 | −1.840 | −6.851 |
| | $r \leq 1$ | 8.177 (0.077) | | (0.611) | (0.578) |
| | | Unrestricted VAR$^c$ | | | |
| Long-Rates $(i_t^L)$ | | $\chi^2(2) = 0.766(0.682)$ | | | |
| Inflation Rates $(\pi_t)$ | | $\chi^2(2) = 0.044(0.978)$ | | | |

When factors are abnormally high or low investors will pay more attention to stories about them. Similar to $\mathcal{H}_1$, $\mathcal{H}_2$ finds empirical support for the extended scapegoat hypotheses. Here, there are significant gap-effects from earnings, dividends, short-rates, economic activity, and consumption. Again, narratives about economic activity, and, now, earnings are shown to purely adjust to deviations away from the cointegrating relations with underlying data. The third hypothesis $\mathcal{H}_3$ connects narrative

Table 11.9 *Narrative weights and fundamentals' volatility*

| Factor | | CVAR | | E–G Test | |
|---|---|---|---|---|---|
| | | Trace Test-stat | $\theta_{N,t}$ adj. | $\tau$-stat | $z$-stat |
| Dividends $(d_t)$ | $r = 0$ | 29.718 (0.001)** | 0.014 | −4.153** | −34.832** |
| | $r \leq 1$ | 2.341 (0.711) | | (0.005) | (0.002) |
| Earnings $(e_t)$ | $r = 0$ | 29.964 (0.001) | – | −4.111** | −34.671** |
| | $r \leq 1$ | 9.519 (0.042) | | (0.006) | (0.002) |
| Inflation Rates $(\pi_t)$ | $r = 0$ | 17.837 (0.105) | – | −1.565 | −7.749 |
| | $r \leq 1$ | 5.027 (0.291) | | (0.738) | (0.504) |
| Oil Prices $(oil_t)$ | $r = 0$ | 17.042 (0.132) | – | −2.408 | −11.957 |
| | $r \leq 1$ | 1.924 (0.788) | | (0.324) | (0.251) |

Unrestricted VAR$^c$

| | |
|---|---|
| Short-Rates $(i_t^S)$ | $\chi^2(2) = 3.064$ (0.216) |
| Long-Rates $(i_t^L)$ | $\chi^2(2) = 0.164$ (0.921) |
| Economic Activity $(y_t)$ | $\chi^2(2) = 3.952$ (0.139) |
| Consumption $(c_t)$ | $\chi^2(2) = 5.764$ (0.056) |

scapegoat coefficients to the twelve-month rolling window of a fundamental's standard deviation. Table 11.9 reports that of the eight narrative weights, seven fail to reject the hypothesis that the variance displayed by a particular fundamental factor does not influence the stories involving them. However, dividend narratives satisfy $\mathcal{H}_3$ for both CVAR and E–G cointegration tests. Taken together, the results for the three subhypotheses $\mathcal{H}_1 - \mathcal{H}_3$ suggest that narrative dynamics as proxied by scapegoat weights depend most on the absolute level of a fundamental and its univariate gap from historical levels.

## 11.6    CONCLUSION

This chapter investigated the narrative weights investors attach to particular fundamentals, or scapegoat effects, in stock return relationships with the use of manual rule-based textual analysis from *Bloomberg News* wrap reports. Manually reading and scoring the wrap reports offers a unique ability to capture time-varying relational meaning and the context within which historically non-repetitive events are interpreted to matter by investors in open ways. Thus, the manual approach offers insight into narrative dynamics involving novel events and associated KU when unforeseeable structural change is present in the stock market.

Evidence presented here suggests that adding historically unique events, narrative weights, and structural change to macro-finance models improves fundamentals' ability to explain stock price fluctuations under uncertainty based on measures of model fit and forecasting accuracy. The results speak to the benefit of allowing returns relationships with fundamentals to change at times and in ways that may be difficult to know in advance. Sometimes a fundamentals' gap-effect may dominate investor stories and return forecasts, other times its level-effect, and still other times both. Showing the diversity of investor forecasting strategies through changing narrative weights, which, in turn, depend on fundamentals' autoregressive processes, implies that narratives are rationally connected to relevant information in ways that probabilistic approaches simply cannot capture. This may be particularly important when the impact of nonrepetitive events is relatively large as during stressful financial periods.

# 12 Applying Novelty and Narratives to Other Research

## 12.1 INTRODUCTION

Chapter 11 conducted a manual rule-based textual analysis of stock market news reports to test the implications of the Novelty–Narrative Hypothesis (NNH) as applied to the scapegoat model for stock price fluctuations under instability and Knightian uncertainty (KU). Chapters 5 through 7 presented the micro KU indices based on unscheduled corporate events tracked by the *RavenPack* news analytics platform across the *Dow Jones Newswire* feeds, *The Wall Street Journal*, *Barron's*, and *MarketWatch*. Chapter 8 introduced the macro KU indices and showed their close connection to corporate novelty and uncertainty. Chapter 9 connected the various corporate indices to stock market outcomes involving aggregate and firm-level returns, volatility, trading volume, and equity Exchange Traded Fund (ETF) flows. Chapter 10 offered statistical tests connecting the highest narrative intensities across the corporate KU indices to periods of parameter instability in the fundamental/risk relationships driving the stock market outcomes.

This chapter will offer some suggestions about how researchers in economics and finance may apply the KU indices and narrative proxies in their own work moving forward. The present value model for the aggregate stock market will be used as a case study wherein the SP500 dividend series is adjusted for the narrative influence from the "dividends/earnings" unscheduled corporate event group presented in Chapter 7. The chapter then applies the corporate narrative intensities to a simple trading strategy that shows enhanced returns through a back-testing example where long and short positions are taken based on moderately high narrative values.

Researchers assessing the implications of NNH in their own research might start by considering ways to incorporate nonrepetitive or unscheduled events into their analyses. There are three pillars of information that hold clues about financial market instability under uncertainty: (i) unscheduled events, (ii) their degree of novelty, and (iii) their associated sentiment for interpreting news' impacts on future returns under model ambiguity. Of course, this can be extended into a fourth pillar by tracking the relevance of such events for investors; a fifth pillar might include entity volume; and a sixth, an entirely higher order of dynamics by incorporating unscheduled macro events and their narratological components. The possibility of applications and approaches is only limited by the creativity of the researcher. This overarching idea will be woven into the present chapter.

## 12.2  NOVEL KU EVENTS IN OTHER RESEARCH

Table 5.1 reported the fifty-one different KU groups containing unscheduled events relevant for the stock market. Many of the groups have analogous scheduled data. For example, the KU group of "earnings/dividends," which involves unscheduled firm-level revisions to earnings projections, unscheduled announcements of forward dividend guidance, and so on, also has formal data releases running alongside it; in this case, quarterly earnings reports and scheduled dividend payments. For such corporate KU groups, one approach researchers may employ is to adjust the traditional scheduled data series with the data on novel KU events. One such application is provided here relating stock price behavior to information on dividends through the present value model.

### 12.2.1  The Present Value Model and KU Adjustment

The present value (PV) model is a workhorse in asset-pricing literature. For stock markets, the model states that the stock price today is equal to the present discounted value of the expected future dividend stream. The model takes the form:

$$P_t = \sum_{k=0}^{\infty} \gamma^{k+1} E_t[D_{t+k}|\Omega_t] \qquad (12.1)$$

where $P$ is the price of stock at the beginning of the period; $D$ denotes the end-of-period dividend; $\gamma = \frac{1}{1+r}$ is the discount factor assumed constant through fixed discount rate $r$; and $E_t[\cdot]$ is the mathematical expectation operator conditioned on the information set available at time $t$, $\Omega_t$. Early tests of the present value model for stock market prices based on variance bounds implied by Equation (12.1) (e.g. Shiller, 1981) produced results grossly inconsistent with the predictions of the model – actual stock market prices were excessively volatile compared to those predicted by the model based on *ex post* dividends. The variance of the RHS, once adding the variance of the forecast error, ought to exceed the variance of the LHS. Other studies corroborated Shiller's finding of excess volatility.

One explanation offered for the empirical struggles was that stock prices and dividends each exhibit nonstationary behavior (contain a unit root) that invalidates traditional statistical inference based on the assumption that a series' distribution is characterized by a constant mean and variance through time. The agreement that stock prices, dividends, and most financial and macroeconomic variables drift over time has led to a wave of cointegration tests between stock prices and dividends.

The idea behind cointegration tests of the PV model is that stock prices and dividends share a common trend by which linear combinations of the two variables are stationary over time. However, empirical cointegration studies have found rather weak results (e.g. Campbell and Shiller, 1987). For instance, Bohl and Siklos (2004), Engsted (2006) and others have found stock prices contain explosive unit roots, lending support to excess volatility and the bubble view of price fluctuations. But it has proven difficult to distinguish price bubbles from omitted fundamental variables (e.g. Flood and Garber, 1980). Mangee and Goldberg (2020), however, show that a cointegrating relationship exists when the PV model for stock prices is augmented to include fundamentals-based psychology, nonrepetitive KU events, and mean shifts in the cointegrating vector. Perhaps adjusting the dividend series for KU from novel events can shed light on the underlying dividend-based relationship driving stock market prices.

### 12.2.2 Adjusting Dividends for KU Effects

The idea of adjusting dividends, or other fundamental variables, to account for novel events and narrative dynamics under uncertainty can lead to many approaches for transforming the conventional data series. One approach is to first standardize the corporate KU "dividends/earnings" series $(D^{KU})$ by subtracting the mean $(\mu_D^{KU})$ from each observation and dividing by the standard deviation $(\sigma_D^{KU})$. This produces a new series with mean zero taking the form:

$$D_{standard}^{KU} = (D^{KU} - \mu_D^{KU})/\sigma_D^{KU} \qquad (12.2)$$

The new variable $D_{standard}^{KU}$ is then used to weight downward the scheduled dividend series, yielding an adjusted dividend series:

$$D^{adj} = D(1 - D_{standard}^{KU}) \qquad (12.3)$$

Multiplying the scheduled dividend series $D$ by $(1 - D_{standard}^{KU})$ reflects the idea that when unscheduled firm-level dividend events increase there is uncertainty about dividends that reduces the fundamental's value if the fundamental is predicted to share a positive relation with stock prices and vice versa. This adjustment is not dissimilar in spirit to including a risk premium in the denominator of the discount factor as many present value-based studies have done (e.g. Shiller, 1984). Therefore, uncertainty leads to a diminished dividend series while uncertainty associated with, say, interest rates would lead to an increased adjusted interest rate series. The adjusted dividend series is now tested for a cointegrating relation with stock market prices using the cointegrated VAR (CVAR) system framework. The graphical plots of $ln(D)$ and $ln(D^{adj})$, along with first-differences (below each series), are provided in Figures 12.1 and 12.2.

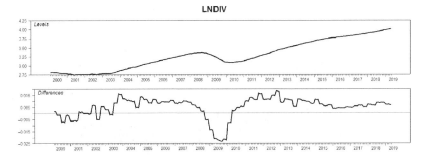

FIGURE 12.1 The figure plots $ln(D)$ for the SP500 Composite Index in levels (top panel) and in first-difference (bottom panel).

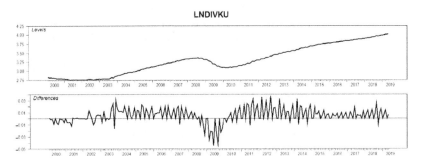

FIGURE 12.2 The figure plots $ln(D^{adj})$ in levels (top panel) and in first-difference (bottom panel).

Both $ln(D)$ and $ln(D^{adj})$ are nonstationary in levels, suggesting that tests for cointegration involving the two series is an appropriate econometric approach. However, the adjusted dividend series incorporating the unscheduled corporate dividends/earnings events, and their associated narratives, looks starkly dissimilar in first-difference. While the levels expression looks roughly similar across both series, the first-difference for $ln(D^{adj})$ is much less persistent and more volatile period-to-period than its first-differenced $ln(D)$ counterpart. The apparent oscillations result from the corporate KU dividends/earnings adjustment (plotted in Figure 7.4 and reproduced here in Figure 12.3).

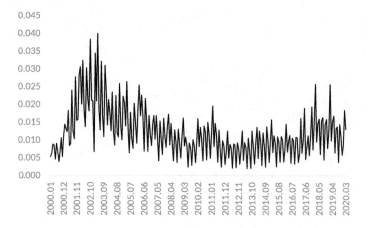

FIGURE 12.3 The figure plots the unscheduled corporate "dividends/earnings" occurrences as a proportion of total unscheduled firm events over the sample period January 2000 through March 2020.

The simple plots of $ln(D)$ against $ln(D^{adj})$ suggest that the KU adjustment for unscheduled firm dividend and earnings events may reduce the (double unit root) persistence in the underlying dividend series. The seminal study of Barsky and De Long (1993) was the first to formalize the idea that small movements in short-run dividends have large impacts on long-run stock price fluctuations because dividend growth rates contain a unit root. Could the KU dividends/earnings narratives transform SP500 dividends from I(2) through I(1)? One preliminary way to investigate this conjecture is to apply an ADF unit root test to $D$ and $D^{adj}$ in both levels and first-differences. The results are reported in Table 12.1.

The ADF test cannot reject the null hypothesis that the level specification contains a unit root for both $D$ and $D^{adj}$ with a $p$-value of 1.000 and 0.997, respectively. Although the ADF test statistically cannot reject a unit root in first-difference for both series, the $p$-value for the KU adjusted dividend series compared to the baseline dividends series is 0.213 and 0.791, respectively. The adjusted dividend series almost generates a weak rejection of the null that the first-difference contains a unit root. Results from other, more powerful, unit root

Table 12.1 *Unit root tests for dividends and KU adjustment*

| Dividends[a] | |
| --- | --- |
| Levels ($D$) | 1.883 (1.000) |
| First-difference ($\Delta D$) | −0.889 (0.791) |
| | |
| KU-adjusted Dividends | |
| Levels ($D^{adj}$) | 1.088 (0.997) |
| First-difference ($\Delta D^{adj}$) | −2.185 (0.213) |

[a] *Note:* The table reports ADF unit root test statistics for $D$ and $D^{adj}$ in both levels and first-difference. The $p$-values for the null hypothesis that the series contains a unit root are reported in parentheses. An intercept term is included in all tests. Lag-length was automatically selected based on minimizing SIC criterion.

tests were mixed, some finding dividends are I(1) for the sample while others found I(2)-ness. Dividends, for the present sample, appear to be fractionally integrated between single- and double-unit roots.

The results offer some support for the hypothesis that KU narrative effects may reduce the statistical presence of two unit roots in SP500 dividends down to one. Furthermore, the novel corporate dividends/earnings series allows for and reflects smaller-scale shifts in relationships driving stock prices. That the adjusted dividends series becomes less nonstationary may indicate that unit root persistence in many macroeconomic and financial variables may reflect their own novelty component and large- or small-scale shifts from corresponding unscheduled events. Next, the $D$ and $D^{adj}$ variables are separately tested for cointegrating relationships with SP500 prices.

## 12.2.3   CVAR Test for Cointegration

The CVAR is a multivariate approach that allows researchers to test whether stationary, or cointegrating, relationships exist from a linear expression of non-stationary variables (Johansen, 1995). Since the variables of interest (SP500 prices, SP500 dividends, and KU-adjusted SP500 dividends) are nonstationary this is a suitable approach.[1] Consider the $p \times 1$ dimensional data vector $x_t$ assumed to follow the VAR process:

$$\Pi(L)x_t = \Phi_t + \varepsilon_t \qquad (12.4)$$

where $\Pi(L)$ is a matrix polynomial of order $k$, and $L$ denotes the lag operator whereby $\Pi(0) = I$, $\Phi_t$ contains the deterministic terms $(DET)$ and $\varepsilon_t$ is a vector I.I.D. error term. Equation (12.4) can be transformed into:

$$\Delta x_t = \Pi x_{t-1} + \sum_{j=1}^{k-1} \Gamma_j \Delta x_{t-j} + \Phi DET_t + \varepsilon \qquad (12.5)$$

where

$$\Pi = \alpha \beta' \qquad (12.6)$$

The $\Pi$ term is the long-run matrix where $\alpha$ and $\beta$ are $p \times r$ matrices and $r$, the reduced rank of $\Pi$, denotes the number of stationary long-run relations present based on the unrestricted VAR model involving $p$ variables. In the presence of unit roots in $x_t$, the reduced-rank condition, $r \leq p$, can be imposed on the long-run matrix, $\Pi = \alpha \beta'$, testing for the existence of at least one cointegrating vector in $x_t$ such that $\beta' x_t \sim I(0)$. The idea is that cointegrated variables will share the same sources of nonstationarity, termed common stochastic trends, causing the variables to move together over time. Thus, linear relations of cointegrated I(1) variables will follow a stationary process. The $\beta$ matrix represents the longer-run cointegrating vectors given the system of equations in the unrestricted VAR while the $\alpha$ matrix represents the error-correction terms and their corresponding speed of adjustment toward equilibrium.

[1] For consistency with analysis of Chapters 5 through 10, SP500 prices in the present chapter are from www.yahoo.com/finance for ticker GSPC while dividend data is collected from Robert Shiller's website. The main results are unchanged if stock prices are collected from Shiller's data.

Table 12.2 *Trace tests for cointegration*

| | Cointegrating Rank $H_0$[a] | Eigenvalue | Trace Statistic | Critical Value (5%) | Probability |
|---|---|---|---|---|---|
| $x = [p\ d]$ | $r = 0$ | 0.044 | 16.005 | 20.164 | 0.177 |
| | $r \leq 1$ | 0.038 | 7.245 | 9.142 | 0.117 |
| $x = [p\ d^{adj}]$ | $r = 0$ | 0.110 | 30.775 | 20.164 | 0.001 |
| | $r \leq 1$ | 0.016 | 3.834 | 9.142 | 0.449 |

[a] *Note:* The table reports Trace test results under the null hypothesis of no cointegration within the data vector $x$. MacKinnon et al. (1999) $p$-values reported. For all tests a lag-length of $k = 2$ was used. Bartlett corrections made to the $p$-values.

The first CVAR data vector includes the log of SP500 prices $(p)$ and the log of dividends $(d)$.[2] The second data vector replaces the dividend series with the log of adjusted dividends $(d^{adj})$. The CVAR test results will focus on the test for reduced-rank $r \leq p$ across the two different data vectors. The CVAR analysis specifies a model with a constant restricted to the cointegrating space.[3] The cointegration results are reported in Table 12.2.

The number of cointegrating relations, conditioned on the assumptions of the deterministic trends, is determined sequentially from $r = 0$ through $r = p - 1$ until the test fails to reject the null hypothesis. The Trace test results suggest that the null hypothesis of no cointegration between $p$ and $d$, or $r = 0$, cannot be rejected with a $p$-value = 0.177. However, when the dividend series is adjusted to account for KU-narrative effects for dividends/earnings, the null hypothesis is rejected with a $p$-value = 0.001 and the analysis fails to reject one cointegrating relation, or $r = 1$, with $p$-value = 0.449.

[2] Both models are adjusted by including permanent and transitory intervention dummies to remove first- and second-order serial correlation in the residuals given a lag-length of $k = 2$ based on standard information criterion.

[3] See Juselius (2006) for a detailed discussion on the treatment of deterministic terms in the CVAR approach.

This brief CVAR analysis is meant to provide a possible application for researchers to pursue when using the narrative data on any KU
event category, group, or topic. A more comprehensive investigation
of the CVAR dynamics would consider the identification stage of the
$\beta$-vector and the adjustment parameters from the $\alpha$-vector. There is
also reason to consider the I(2) model since baseline dividends may
contain a double unit root. That the Trace test failed to reject the null
of no cointegration between stock market prices and dividends when
ignoring novelty and narrative effects, again, implies that unforeseeable structural change may be the reason for the tenuous connection
between stock market outcomes, in this case aggregate prices, and
fundamental factors such as dividends.

Though this analysis considered the PV model for aggregate
market data, the parsimonious results suggest that there may be
useful information in the narrative KU data that can be applied to
any model of stock market behavior at both the firm and aggregate
levels. Again, the KU-adjusted variables can be augmented further to
reflect sentiment, entity-event volume/inertia, and relevance reflecting enhanced narrative dynamics associated with unscheduled events
and temporal instability.

## 12.3  HOW INVESTORS MAY USE NOVELTY AND NARRATIVES

To assess the importance of novel events and associated narratives
in explaining stock returns following a more investment-minded
approach, the findings from a simple trading strategy are now presented. The trading strategy is intuitive and straightforward and
relies on the fifteen periods of (at least) moderate narrative intensity
connected to unscheduled corporate events. From Chapter 6,

> The moderate narrative intensity periods are identified by the top/bottom
> 25 percent of Event Sentiment Score (ESS), the top 25 percent of Event
> Novelty Score (ENS), and top 50 percent of Relevance month-value
> observations tracked within separate five-year sub-periods 2000–2004,
> 2005–2009, 2010–2014, and 2015–2019. The periods identified cluster at

the beginning of the sample (2000:03–04, 2000:10), at the financial crisis period (2008:02, 2008:05, 2008:08), and are scattered throughout the remainder of the sample (2013:05, 2013:11, 2014:08, 2014:11, 2015:08–09, 2016:08, 2017:01, 2017:03).

The trading strategy is as follows: If the period is identified as being of moderate narrative intensity, sell the SP500 and buy it one period later. If the period is not identified as moderate narrative intensity, buy the SP500 and sell it one period later. Although the strategy excludes transactions and borrowing costs, it still serves as a useful benchmark. For the period January 2000 through March 2020, this strategy involves taking 222 long positions and 15 short positions. The average monthly return from following this trading strategy is 0.005308 or 53.08 basis points. This monthly average return compounds to an economically meaningful annualized return of 6.56 percent. The actual average monthly return for the SP500 over the entire sample is 0.003285 or 3.285 percent, which generates an annual compound return of 4.01 percent.

It is worth noting two things about this simple trading exercise. First, the short/long trading strategy was also applied to highest values of the baseline corporate KU Index and the corporate KU Variation Index. Without incorporating novelty, sentiment, and relevance into these KU measures, as done with identification of all narrative intensity periods, none of the trading strategies could beat the market over the sample period. That is very interesting. Second, recall that the narrative intensity periods are based on four separate five-year windows for calculating time variant ESS, ENS, and Relevance thresholds. This stands as further evidence that accounting for temporal instability in the stock market offers additional explanatory power: Impacts on returns from novel events and associated narratives change over time in unforeseeable ways. The results presented here suggest that, although profitability would decline once accounting for transactions costs, the KU narrative intensity points, which involve time-varying effects, are potentially useful for investment strategies and a potential hedge under inherent instability and KU.

Chapter 13 takes a methodology of science approach to discuss how NNH implies a shift away from deterministic accounts of asset market behavior. The chapter will focus on the inability of traditional approaches to capture real-world rationality based on probabilistic representations of change under uncertainty. Recent approaches that stop short of fully prespecifying how and in which ways historically novel events may alter investor forecasting strategies are discussed.

# 13 The Future of Novelty, Narratives, and Uncertainty in Finance

## 13.1 INTRODUCTION

One may have heard that the ways in which financial markets manage and allocate risk is the *raison d'être* of modern-day capitalism.[1] Much less, however, has been claimed about the ability of markets to cope with and reveal Knightian uncertainty (KU). Is mismanaging risk more damaging for markets than ignoring uncertainty? Neoclassical finance tends to dismiss the nuanced indeterminacy of day-to-day events associated with uncertainty, not just because of the view that efficient markets will mechanically digest the minutia of information for prices in allocatively optimal ways or because of the still-employed Rational Expectations Hypothesis (REH). Rather, uncertainty associated with novelty and narratives is usually precluded from center stage because of researchers' treatment of *a priori* change within their models. Unforeseeable change in relationships driving asset market outcomes is simply not allowed. Even the behavioral approaches that are not REH-based, though many are, tend to assume that one particular heuristic dominates investor beliefs for extended periods of time. This is also a form of determinism.

To develop approaches which more openly allow for KU and narratives in financial markets researchers must jettison stochastic representations of change and divorce investor expectations from probabilistic rules. Then, and only then, will diversity of thought, novelty, narratives, and unforeseeable change be allowed to characterize real-world rationality driving stock market outcomes under true uncertainty. The historical uniqueness, and pervasiveness, of unscheduled events and their accompanying narratives discussed

---

[1] This chapter builds off of the arguments and content of Mangee (2015).

throughout this book present a challenge for the traditional approach's presupposition of determinate change based on an economist's probabilistic model, which, barring random shocks, is thought to be a fairly good approximation of reality. As Tversky and Kahneman (1986, p. 167) state, "deviations of actual behavior from the normative model are too widespread to be ignored, too systematic to be dismissed as random error, and too fundamental to be accommodated by relaxing the normative system." A scientific revolution is necessary and may well be underway.

This chapter suggests that the field of macro-finance is primed for a paradigm shift in Kuhnian terms (Kuhn, 1970) away from determinate modeling structures toward partially open ones that allow for KU events, narrative dynamics, and the unforeseeable structural change they engender. There will be a discussion on recent developments representing aggregate behavior and outcomes in financial markets based on model ambiguity and intervallic, as opposed to probabilistic, change over time. The necessary reenvisioning of rationality as it relates to narratives shaping the diversity of investor interpretations of news' impacts on returns as novelty and instability unfold in real time will be addressed. The main findings of the preceding analyses of Chapters 4 through 12 will be woven throughout.

## 13.2  WHAT TRADITIONAL APPROACHES MISS ABOUT KU EVENTS

Narrative dynamics are part and parcel with unforeseeable structural change in asset markets. That the future is objectively open is precisely the reason why narratives emerge to shape investor forecasting strategies in the face of novel events and imperfect knowledge. One can know little more *a priori* about how particular narratives unfold in the stock market than knowledge about tomorrow's human interest, social preoccupances, cultural trends, political institutions, and unscheduled events will allow. That said, researchers can develop models that allow for unforeseeable change in asset market relationships and diversity of news' interpretations for returns while still maintaining empirical relevance. One could argue that the most critical assumption for modeling capitalistic economies is the representation *ex ante* of how structural change in posited relationships is allowed to unfold over time.

Chapter 1 discussed the historical roots of unforeseeable change in capital market behavior through the lens of Frank Knight. Knight (1921) was astutely aware that "business decisions deal with situations which are far too unique" (p. 231) and that "profits are the result of dynamic change" (p. 35), but that if "changes ... could be foreseen ... in advance of their occurrence, profit or loss would not arise" (p. 198). Chapter 2 presented ample evidence supporting the view that not only does change characterize the relationships driving stock market outcomes over time, but also that change itself is more precarious and salient than is typically recognized. There is a diversity of change in stock price relations, and narratives naturally and necessarily become part of investors' forecasts as they cope with inherent ambiguity about the future. Investigating these pillars under the Novelty–Narrative Hypothesis (NNH) for stock market instability has been a core pursuit of this book.

Chapter 3 argued that disciplines outside economics and finance have taken a different path to understanding how and why people rely on stories to make sense of novel situations and real-world complexities. Psychologists, sociologists, anthropologists, and linguistitians have been dealing with nonroutine change in their respective research arenas for decades. Chapter 4 presented word clouds and histograms from *Bloomberg News* stock market wrap reports, which illustrated the relevance and time-varying composition of possible narrative topics and events likely connected to KU. Chapters 5 and 6 found that the majority of corporate events reported in *Dow Jones* equity news as influencing firm prospects and share prices were considered unscheduled. When such novel events were interacted with KU measures of extreme investor sentiment, enhanced novelty, and relevance, periods of the highest narrative intensity were able to be identified. Interacting KU events in such a way is a keen approach since narratives are made up of such considerations.

Chapter 7 showed that the composition of groups within the corporate KU Index exhibits dramatic variation over time: The number of most reported groups changed as did the group rankings over the last twenty years of data. The variation in uncertainty-laden firm events and narratives is undeniable in the data. Anticipating *ex ante* when "executive appointments," "corporate scandals," "labor strikes," "layoffs," "insider trading," "IPO considerations," "stock buybacks," "acquisition delays," or dramatic "credit rating revisions" will occur, let alone foreseeing how investors will interpret such news for returns, would be a challenge for any researcher, to say the least. Chapter 8 showed the close connection between micro and macro novel events and presented evidence that macro novelty, instability, and uncertainty feeds into future corporate novelty, instability, and uncertainty (but not the other way around). The relative promise of unscheduled corporate events for understanding stock market instability was discussed. The chapter also showed the remarkably high proportion of unscheduled macro events for the US.

Chapters 9 through 12 offered empirical analyses connecting unscheduled corporate events and their associated narrative characteristics to aggregate and firm-level stock market outcomes and formal tests of structural change. Knightian uncertainty events were shown to depress contemporaneous prices and valuation ratios, suggesting an uncertainty premium may be connected to corporate novelty. Moreover, the diversity of KU event groups mattered more for aggregate economic and financial outcomes and implied a gap-effect on valuations while the level count of such events mattered more for firm-level earnings per share (EPS) growth forecasts. Narrative intensity periods approximately aligned with statistical breakpoints in returns, volatility, and fund flow regressions with fundamentals. Scapegoat effects showed how combining narrative weights, historic events, and structural change can improve fundamentals' ability to explain and predict stock market returns. And, the narrative weights were connected to temporal movements in conventional fundamentals' autoregressive processes, further evidence that NNH is consistent with rationality in financial markets.

To be sure, extending models to capture asymmetric information and imperfectly competitive markets has greatly enhanced our knowledge of how markets function. However, great gaps between model prediction and the underlying data-generating process still puzzle economists, especially in subfields such as asset pricing. Investigating the role of narratives for asset markets adds a new layer of informational dynamics potentially useful in explaining prices and volatility while simultaneously requiring researchers to confront unforeseeable change and uncertainty in the processes driving outcomes. By recognizing the importance and interactions of both macro and micro novel events that produce higher orders of instability and uncertainty, models can better capture the dynamism of large- and small-scale shifts occurring through time.

Generally speaking, the economics profession tends to tweak additively its statistical toolkit and rigor by emphasizing that models are best thought of as "scaffolding."[2] For instance, applying time-varying parameter (TVP) analysis to financial market behavior is a way to allow the weights on informational factors to change over time. However, state-space TVP models presume the evolution of coefficients follows a determinate stochastic, or even constant, process over time, which precludes the possibility of any change that does not follow mechanically from the past.[3] But this is an empirical adjustment attempting to better reflect time-varying real-world relationships, not a theoretical shift in our understanding of how diversity of views and relationships driving outcomes unfold in unforeseeable ways. If differentiated theories are really just iterative models seeking to explain each subsequent wrinkle in market behavior, this implies

---

[2] For a comprehensive treatment of the practice of modern-day economics see Dani Rodrik's 2015 book *Economics Rules: The Rights and Wrongs of the Dismal Science*.

[3] Typically, every parameter at time $t$ only depends on values from period $t - 1$. For textbook treatment of state-space and time-varying parameter models see Hamilton (1994).

that the unbounded propagation of theories should be desirable. But what happens in the limit?

Is the field of macro-finance primed for a revolution toward incorporating novelty, unforeseeable change, and narrative dynamics in a serious way? Is the field ready to reallocate resources away from the traditional view that knowledge in the field "advances horizontally" through the multiplicative menu of models to explain circumstantial outcomes? To break free from the search for optimal solutions? To reframe contingency as not being solely an exercise in modeling market frictions, but rather a fluid scenario in which imperfect knowledge and uncertainty collide with the reflexivity of expectations?[4] To demote the methodology of additive models in favor of *a priori* pluralism and inherent model ambiguity? Recognizing the novelty of structural change and dealing with the role of narratives and uncertainty in financial markets requires researchers to set aside the model-first view of science and reconsider how nonmechanical markets work and which statistical toolkits are best suited. If a Kuhnian shift is not already underway, it should be.

## 13.3 KUHNIAN PARADIGM SHIFTS

In his path-breaking book, *The Structure of Scientific Revolutions*, Thomas Kuhn, the prominent twentieth-century philosopher and historian of science, argued that scientific progress over time is not a cumulative one honing in ever closer to a discipline's veracity through continuous "conjectures and refutations," – in the Popperian sense – but rather one defined by discontinuous leaps, in the form of scientific revolution, between "paradigms" in the pursuit of "normal science"

---

[4] It is commonplace for researchers responding to the empirical struggles of traditional asset-pricing theory in explaining stock return predictability and excess volatility by augmenting models to reflect market frictions and heterogeneous actors. Popular market frictions have included incomplete information, asymmetric information, short-sale constraints, liquidity constraints, so-called noise trader and sentiment risk, and poorly diversified portfolios. See Hou and Moskowitz (2005) for a survey and discussion for the stock market.

(Kuhn, 1970).[5] Unlike his contemporaries, such as Lakatos and Popper, in particular, who sought to define methodological rules against which science was measured, Kuhn emphasized that science is a social endeavor conducted and housed within a scientific community of practitioners that collectively defines the problems to be investigated, the questions to be posed, the analytic tools to be employed, and the standards against which its practice is assessed.[6] Accepted on a grand scale within the community, a paradigm is cultivated by problem-solving activity whereby the practitioners define, embrace, and propagate a particular view of nature.

Contemporary models of asset-price behavior have been predicated upon notions of informational efficiency, determinate change, and, thus, inherent market stability. Under this account, all change in the structure of an economic model – including the representation of individual expectations, preferences over choices, decision rules, constraints, and model predictions – is fully predetermined. Consequently, markets are presumed to allocate nearly perfectly a society's scarce capital; barring inefficiencies, prices fluctuate randomly around their so-called true intrinsic values, deviating from equilibrium only temporarily due to shocks that cancel out over time. The classical framework, therefore, dismisses the role of unforeseeable structural change (that which cannot be fully prespecified by an economist's model) due to the novelty of unscheduled events and the sentiment-infused narratives that emerge, become amplified, or even contorted as a result.

### 13.3.1 Conventional Models as Normal Science

For Kuhn, normal science is the "puzzle solving" that occurs within an established "paradigm." Under his view, the vast majority of

---

[5] See, for example, Hands (2001, chapter 3) for a textbook treatment of Thomas Kuhn.

[6] For Popper, this meant utilizing the tenets surrounding the scientific method and falsificationism to demarcate science from nonscience. Though closer to Kuhn's methodological perspectives than Popper, Lakatos also used progressive and degenerative strategies to constitute scientific research programs. See, for instance, Blaug (1975) for an excellent juxtaposition of Kuhnian and Lakatosian methodological perspectives.

practitioners within a discipline "inevitably spend almost all of their time [conducting] normal science ... predicated on the assumption that the scientific community knows what the world is like" (Kuhn, 1970, p. 5). For the field of asset pricing, mainstream researchers, when writing down equilibrium asset-pricing models, have adhered to the particular view that financial market relationships have a tendency toward stability. Divergence away from stasis, by way of "external shocks" to the system, is only a temporary state. Financial markets, left unfettered, will therefore "get prices right."

Normal science makes no room for the ubiquity of unscheduled events and associated cascades of unforeseen changes spilling over from the macro onto the micro level that jostle forecasting strategies and prices away from previous relationships. Nonroutine change spawns a great diversity of interpretations for news' impacts on returns. Consequently, narrative dynamics become part of forecasting strategies that, in turn, may serve as an additional source of instability and investor uncertainty. The price determination process is continuously being revised. When prices are "wrong" under the classical view, the menu of models is augmented horizontally to include frictions and systemic heuristics that prohibit stock prices from reaching so-called intrinsic values. This is what Kuhn referred to as the conceptual stage of problem-solving as a part of normal science.

Under Kuhn's view, a paradigm serves as the "vehicle" by which the scientific theory is delivered. To be considered a Kuhnian "paradigm," the theory must simultaneously meet the following criteria: "Their achievement was sufficiently unprecedented to attract an enduring group of adherents away from competing models of scientific activity," and that the theory "was sufficiently open-ended to leave ... problems for the redefined group of practitioners to solve" (Kuhn, 1970, p. 10). The incumbent paradigm in macrofinance models involves a class of determinate models that rely on REH to achieve internal coherence between market participants' understanding of outcomes and that based on the "relevant economic theory" as captured by the economist's model. Internal coherence is a desirable feature of empirically relevant models, but REH achieves it by assuming that probabilities describing outcomes can be known *ex ante*. The evidence presented in this book implies that such probabilistic rules governing change in the stock market cannot be known.

Muth (1961) proposed REH as a tool that individuals may use in forecasting the future and a tool that researchers may use to endow their knowledge of the economy's structure onto that of the individuals who populate it. However, Muth's seminal study was cautious of the mass employment of REH by mainstream economists as a description of how forecasting strategies and market relationships actually unfold over time.[7] For REH to capture real-world dynamics in asset markets, the economist must be able to simultaneously anticipate not only when a new CEO is appointed, a new production process is developed, a new government official or Fed chair is elected, or a new regulatory policy is adopted into law, but how these novel events will be interpreted by investors to impact future returns. No one, let alone a researcher, can foresee how the structure of the economy and the relationships driving asset returns will unfold over time. Applying REH to a determinate model of aggregate outcomes yields an adequate representation of reality only in a world in which knowledge and understanding does not grow (more on this fact within the context of the recent COVID-19 pandemic and Great Lockdown Recession in Section 13.3.2).

Internal consistency in describing aggregate outcomes within macro-finance models is important for many reasons. When applied to fully prespecified accounts of change, however, REH implies much more than internal consistency. First, individuals' expectations become an output of the economist's model reflecting over time only those features that the researcher presumed important based on *a priori* knowledge of the underlying relationships at hand. Second, there is one overarching conditional probability distribution (or

---

[7] Samuelson (1965, pp. 48–49) was also wary about how and from where such fully predetermined accounts may originate. See Frydman and Goldberg (2011, Chapter 3) for a detailed discussion on this.

quantitative rule) governing the causal processes, outcomes, and all change therein, at every point in time – past, present, and future. Consequently, the presumption of REH in determinate accounts prohibits all unforeseeable change stemming from novelty and ensuing narrative dynamics in asset markets that cannot be known *ex ante*.[8]

Assuming the model is an "approximate" description of the real world, REH is a means to calculate equilibrium outcomes by implying that *ex ante* forecasts of the future differ from *ex post* realizations by a white-noise mean-zero error term serially uncorrelated with all past and present information. These features enable the economist to make exact predictions today about outcomes tomorrow. However, as is often attributed to Keynes, it is better to be roughly right than precisely wrong.[9]

The previous nine chapters have presented extensive evidence on the presence and influence of both large- and small-scale events that are nonrepetitive and linked to unforeseeable change in the relationships driving stock market outcomes. The findings also highlighted the natural role of emotion in shaping the diversity of views about future returns as market instability unfolds. Under REH, such novelty, narratives, and innate sentiment – all considerations associated with temporal instability and uncertainty – are simply not allowed. Such a divisive stance on how outcomes unfold in financial markets is emblematic of how Kuhn viewed members of a scientific community dictating with authority that a particular science can be modeled with solutions. In his terms, "a scientific community

---

[8] Whenever these models recognize that the process underpinning outcomes undergoes change, they represent such change with a probabilistic rule, such as Markov-switching, determining completely how the model's specifications unfold over time *ex ante*. For an influential contribution to the development of models that represent change with probabilistic rules, see Hamilton (1988, 2008). For a seminal behavioral-finance model that formalizes with a stochastic process the role of market sentiment in how participants forecast returns, see Barberis et al. (1998).

[9] The original version, "It is better to be vaguely right than exactly wrong," is attributed to the nineteenth- and twentieth-century British philosopher Carveth Read from his 1898 book *Logic, Deductive and Inductive*.

acquires with a paradigm . . . a criterion for choosing problems that . . . can be assumed to have solutions . . . these are the only problems that the community will admit as scientific" (Kuhn, 1970, p. 3).

Alas, by subscribing to REH, the profession felt endowed with the tools necessary to describe how reasonable investors ought to behave, allowing "practitioners [to] concentrate on problems that only their lack of ingenuity should keep them from solving" (Kuhn, 1970, p. 37). However, foreseeing how particular narratives will behave in the future, let alone predict how investors will interpret their relevance, is beyond the reach of any researcher. No one knows when a particular narrative will emerge and grow or when it will abruptly change or die off. There are no universal laws or quantitative rules governing the processes driving novelty and narratives in asset markets.

In his doctrine, Kuhn takes very seriously the influence the structure of scientific communities has on the development of a discipline over time. Indeed, graduate programs in financial economics annually churn newly appointed Ph.D.s trained extensively, and often exclusively, in the REH-based framework of general equilibrium, such as the dynamic stochastic general equilibrium models (DSGE). The training of newly minted Ph.D.s in the conventional paradigm's approach serves as "membership in the particular scientific community with which [they] will later practice . . . The paradigm may endure as . . . this practice will seldom evoke . . . disagreement over fundamentals . . . committed to the same rules and standards" (Kuhn, 1970, p. 11). To some extent, this process of torch-passing within a paradigm is well understood. Needless to say, there are few dissertations written that collectively explore the ubiquity of nonrepetitive events, unforeseeable change, and narrative dynamics in financial markets. Are these the topics future dissertations will be written on?

One of Kuhn's principle explications lies with the treatment of "novelties of fact or theory" (i.e. continuous departures from model predictions) within an existing paradigm. Nowhere may this be more apparent and relevant than in the field of asset pricing.[10] Anomalous findings within a paradigm, according to Kuhn, are, "Produced inadvertently by a game played under one set of rules ... their assimilation requires the elaboration of another set" (Kuhn, 1970, p. 52). Puzzles in academic circles are, after all, a condition that exists whereby the predictions of conventional theory consistently fail to be reconciled with the observations of reality. Both researchers and practitioners in finance have acknowledged that mainstream REH models have encountered great empirical problems when confronted with the data. As Nicholas Barberis and Nobel Laureate Richard Thaler have noted, "after years of effort, it has become clear that basic facts about the aggregate stock market, the cross-section of average returns and individual trading behavior are not easily understood in this framework" (Barberis and Thaler, 2003, p. 1055).

One reason for the empirical difficulties of the determinate paradigm is that stock, and other asset, price behavior is simultaneously too persistent and too volatile to be explained by movements in fundamental factors. Prices tend to undergo wide swings of uneven duration and magnitude for extended periods of time. But swings are ultimately bounded: Eventually prices undergo sharp reversals in opposite directions, often shooting through estimates of historical benchmark levels all the while exhibiting a variance in short-run fluctuations that is not easily explained by the behavior of macro covariates. The corporate KU indices and event groups presented in Chapters 5 through 7 displayed both visible persistence and high volatility over the subperiods investigated. Moreover, KU adjustments to dividends in a present value model of Chapter 12 were able to match the "excess" volatility exhibited by aggregate stock market prices. Might these features of unscheduled events, and their emotion,

---

[10] A nonexhaustive list of puzzles and anomalous "effects" for the stock market includes the excess volatility puzzle, the predictability puzzle, the equity premium puzzle, the risk-free rate puzzle, the long swings or bubble puzzle, the closed-end fund puzzle, the Monday effect, the January effect, the end-of-the-year effect, the Friday effect, and the size effect. See Thaler (1987), Jeremy and Thaler (1997), Shleifer (2000), and Shefrin (2002).

relevance, and novelty underpinning narrative dynamics, be associated with the persistence and volatility observed in stock market prices over time? Future research may further support these findings.

Though numerous studies have been critical of REH in light of the empirical difficulties and unearthed puzzles in macro-finance, little has been questioned in terms of the core tenants of fully predetermined modeling structures. In a collection of research works, Imperfect Knowledge Economics (IKE) lays out a strong critique of the traditional REH-based framework by tracing its empirical and theoretical struggles to the inability of probabilistic modeling structures to allow for unforeseeable change in asset markets. The critique extends to behavioral models of price fluctuations, which base their notions of rationality on REH as well. Alas, though economists have shown "recognition that nature has somehow violated the paradigm-induced expectations that govern normal science" (Kuhn, 1970, pp. 52–53), they have primarily entertained only an "additive adjustment to the theory." Furthermore, most researchers have not "learned to see nature in a different way" and, as such, the numerous anomalies are viewed by many mainstream financial economists as "not quite a scientific fact at all" (Kuhn, 1970, p. 53).[11]

Kuhn understood that the extent to which anomalous findings exist within a particular science, "will not falsify that philosophical theory" (Kuhn, 1970, p. 78). Instead, "They will devise numerous articulations and *ad hoc* modifications of their theory in order to eliminate any apparent conflict" (Kuhn, 1970, p. 78). Through horizontal model development, this has largely been the response from many researchers to waves of empirical evidence against the theoretical predictions of efficient markets under determinate accounts. However, wrinkles of model articulation will not bring novelty and narrative dynamics into economics and finance; there must be a paradigm shift that offers a different lens through which to see the world and a

---

[11] For instance, Fama (1998, p. 304), in defending the view of market efficiency over that of behavioral accounts, argues that anomalous findings are "chance" results and that biases such as underreaction to information are "just as common" as that of overreaction.

different statistical toolkit with which to assess inherent instability under uncertainty.

Kuhn had tremendous foresight into the evolution of paradigms and the advent of increasingly sophisticated empirical tools to test their predictions. Early successes in the 1960s and 1970s in testing the implications of the Efficient Markets Hypothesis (EMH) and REH likely played a role in perpetuating a stubborn resistance to abandoning the paradigm's mechanical framework. As Kuhn (1970, p. 64) noted,

> In the development of ... science, the first paradigm is ... felt to account ... successfully for most of the observations and experiments ... accessible to ... practitioners. Further development ... ordinarily calls for the construction of elaborate equipment, the development of an esoteric vocabulary and skills ... That professionalization leads ... to an immense restriction of the scientist's vision and to ... resistance to paradigm change. The science has become increasingly rigid.

Accounts of asset-price behavior whereby market participants "learn" about the "true" parameters of the model have also become increasingly popular (Adam, and Marcet, 2011; Adam et al., 2015; Pastor and Veronesi, 2009b). In such learning-based models, a fixed information set of fundamentals are key factors in driving price-relations. Moreover, psychological considerations are typically treated as a symptom of irrationality that prohibit forecasting decisions from coinciding with the model's predictions. Under such accounts, individual beliefs concerning the causal process, or parameter weights, are updated over time usually following a Bayesian or algorithmic least-squares updating rule. That is, even though learning-based approaches allow for revisions in forecasting strategies over time, they too portray determinate accounts of such change in the processes underpinning asset price-relations.

Calibration techniques have also become popular as a way to "fit" a model to the data. Meant to provide more realistic assumptions about the micro-structure of individual behavior, this statistical toolkit relies on the estimation of so-called deep parameters from studies of utility functions, revealed preferences, and other micro-based research. Not only does such an approach disregard unforeseeable change, it is not clear which parameters are to be estimated and which are to be taken as given. What is more, adjusting parameters to match the statistical moments of the data may show promise in-sample but it is unclear what can be said about the out-of-sample performance of such a technique. Thus, calibration approaches appear unsuited for the unforeseeable change in stock market relationships uncovered throughout this book and elsewhere. Indeed, like the class of REH-based models, so-called rationality based on any determinate modeling approach is actually portraying *irrationality* since it presumes that investors adhere endlessly to the same forecasting strategy and that their understanding of the returns process never grows outside the structure of the researcher's model.

### 13.3.2    The Crisis and Revolution: Preparadigm Shift

The COVID-19 pandemic and ensuing Great Lockdown Recession have illuminated on a grand scale the limitations of contemporary macroeconomics and finance models to account for unforeseeable change. Asset-pricing models such as the intertemporal Capital Asset Pricing Model (CAPM), the consumption CAPM, or the present value model when based upon REH are unable to capture the large-scale shifts in returns processes from macro KU events that cascade into the underlying, and constantly flowing, stream of micro KU events occurring at the micro level. Roughly ten years ago, the global financial crisis exposed the importance of non-routine change in stock market relationships. Researchers and central bankers clamored to adapt models of asset-price fluctuations and risk, in a horizontal fashion, to reflect faulty credit ratings, overleveraging, subprime mortgage fraud, fire sales of toxic assets, and so on. Such incremental adjustments to capture financial market frictions sidestep the core issue with determinate models of asset-price behavior, namely that they are incapable of allowing for unforeseeable change in relationships driving outcomes. Yet, DSGE models based on REH and other quantitative rules governing change continue to be commonly relied upon by top regulatory officials and central bankers though they simply do not allow for departures from steady-state equilibria of the magnitude brought about by such a crisis.

Now, the COVID-19 crisis has researchers rushing to alter financial models in yet another round of additive, incremental tweaks. But there is a sense that this time really may be different in that new realities of the world around us now exist and may endure. As prominent businessman, Allianz's Mohamed El-Erian recently wrote, "Of particular concern now are the economics of viral contagion, of fear, and of circuit breakers. The more that economic thinking advances to meet changing realities, the better will be the analysis that informs the policy response."[12] El-Erian identifies the pandemic's impact on "changing realities" as he goes on to address the structural shifts that ought to keep policy-makers in the Western world up at night: the possibility that developed countries experience the type of abrupt economic and financial shuttering typically characteristic of the developing world. Consumers may wish to consume, sellers may wish to sell, savers may wish to lend, and debtors may wish to borrow. But a pandemic economy has changed the parameters connecting these activities to observed outcomes in financial markets. How can such change be assessed from a narratological standpoint?

Policy-makers would benefit from tracking the economic and financial novelty and associated narratives swirling throughout the world. It would be surprising to learn that central bankers and policy officials employ indicators that track the amount and associated dynamics of unscheduled events occurring at the corporate and macro level. Perhaps the indices presented throughout this book could become part of macro prudential and financial policies. Corporate disclosures could include a primer on the events and factors that were

---

[12] El-Erian discusses these issues in an article published with *Project Syndicate* on March 26, 2020 and can be found at www.project-syndicate.org/commentary/covid19-will-change-economics-three-ways-by-mohamed-a-el-erian-2020-03.

not closely tracked entering the quarterly reporting period but whose importance became critical over the course of time enough so that they have been discussed recently within executive-level boardrooms and communicated to stakeholders. Credit ratings of corporate debt could include the factors that were not part of their risk-profiles one year or six months prior but that underpinned a (dramatic) ratings change. If the abrupt stopping and starting of the economic engine becomes more commonplace for the US and Europe, then it would be imperative that researchers take much more seriously the need for models of aggregate market outcomes that allow for such indeterminate change.

Jettisoning the current orthodoxy, a few promising approaches to understanding nonroutine change in asset-price relations have been put forth. This promise is, however, quite common when entertaining alternatives to an existing paradigm in distress. As Kuhn (1970, p. 76) notes,

> invention of alternates is ... what scientists seldom undertake except during the preparadigm stage of their science's development ... So long as the tools a paradigm supplies ... prove capable of solving the problems it defines, science moves fastest ... retooling is an extravagance to be reserved for the occasion that demands it. The significance of crises is the indication ... that an occasion for retooling has arrived.

Substantial departure from the existing view, however, is often accompanied by long-winded and forceful resistance from the incumbent practitioners. This reflects Kuhn's theory-ladenness, or paradigm devotion, which makes a scientific transition a complicated process. Kuhn (1970, p. 68) writes,

> Because it demands large-scale paradigm destruction and major shifts in ... problems and techniques of normal science ... emergence of new theories is generally preceded by ... pronounced professional insecurity ... generated by ... persistent failure of the puzzles of normal science to come out as they should. Failure of existing rules is the prelude to a search for new ones.

Numerous epistemological and theoretical foundations have been laid in order to provide resolution to the puzzling behavior of financial market outcomes. Most aim to deliver and improve upon where the implications of stability and determinism using the toolkits of EMH and REH have gone astray. One area has focused on the interactions of market participants and corresponding coordination dynamics. Contrary to EMH and REH, network theory and agent-based computational economics are based on the premise that the expectations, strategies, and beliefs of heterogeneous individuals interacting in a marketplace may create, and endogenously respond to, persistent patterns of disequilibria in market outcomes (Tesfatsion, 2006). However, it is unclear which initial values to base the evolution of interactions upon in such closed systems.

Moreover, behavioral insights still provide a more pragmatic and realistic backdrop for describing reality-based individual behavior relative to traditional notions of rationality. In this light, neuroeconomics has begun to gain traction in describing cognitive processes of individuals when facing market-type decisions (Camerer et al., 2005). And, research organizations such as the Institute for New Economic Thinking are at the forefront of developing, promoting, and assessing the implications of alternative and creative approaches to understanding behavior of modern-day capitalistic markets.

### 13.3.3   Alternative Views and Knightian Uncertainty

A paradigm's rejection within a particular science depends on the existence of counter-theories. As Kuhn put it, "a scientific theory is declared invalid only if an alternate candidate is available to take its place" (Kuhn, 1970, p. 77). Kuhn was one of the first philosophers to contend that the views of paradigm adherents cannot be explicitly tested or justified. The decision of a scientific community to simultaneously denounce one paradigm and pursue with purpose an alternative, "involves the comparison of both paradigms with nature and with each other" (Kuhn, 1970, p. 77).

Scientific revolutions, and thus paradigm shifts, occur through the conduct of extraordinary science – the existence of an alternate scientific theory to provide resolution to the anomalous findings inconsistent with existing paradigms. To be sure, Kuhn recognized that the existing paradigm defined its own problems, methods, and rules to which the practitioners of the scientific community adhered; an alternate scientific school of thought will, in turn, develop its own apparatus of science exposing new problems and novelties of nature. As stated by Kuhn, "no paradigm that provides a basis for scientific research ever completely resolves all of its problems" (Kuhn, 1970, p. 79). New theories are, thus, incommensurate with old paradigms.

The widespread findings of unscheduled corporate and macro events connected to stock market fluctuations presented throughout this book point to the inherent instability in relationships driving outcomes. More importantly, however, the nature of the evidence implies that such change cannot be foreseen by researchers, investors, policy-makers, politicians, or the public at large. All observers of financial markets face model ambiguity. This evidence is consistent with KU-based accounts that imply that unforeseeable change in asset price-relations is an inherent feature of financial markets and cannot be captured with a stochastic rule *ex ante*. In Kuhnian terms, "scientists adopt new instruments and look in new places. Even more important, during revolutions scientists see new and different things when looking with familiar instruments in places they have looked before" (Kuhn, 1970, p. 111). When paradigm shifts have occurred, "the scientist's perception of his environment must be reeducated – in some familiar situations he must learn to see a new gestalt" (Kuhn, 1970, p. 112).

Many researchers have already found unique and creative ways to empirically assess the view of nonroutine change in asset markets.[13] Econometric techniques have focused on higher orders of persistence in prices and risk, recursive updates of structural change,

---

[13] For equity markets see, for example, Mangee (2011, 2014, 2016, 2017, 2018, 2019), Frydman et al. (2015), Baek (2016), Frydman and Stillwagon (2018), Mangee and Goldberg (2020), and Frydman et al. (forthcoming). For currency markets see, for instance, Goldberg and Frydman (1996a, 1996b), Frydman and Goldberg (2007), Johansen et al. (2010), Stillwagon (2018), and Stillwagon and Sullivan (2019).

piecewise linear approximations, and sentiment-based adjustment to fundamentals-based return relationships. Moreover, many of these studies incorporate textual data and survey forecasts into the structural change analysis. From a theoretical standpoint, allowing for unforeseeable change in asset markets also requires an alternative lens to that of the incumbent paradigm.

For example, Knightian Uncertainty Economics (KUE) offers a theoretical approach to allowing for "unforeseeable change in the process driving outcomes and the Knightian uncertainty faced by both market participants and economists" (Frydman et al., 2019). Knightian Uncertainty Economics relies on partially constrained intervals within which coefficients on forecasting variables and market outcomes lie at a point in time. Doing so, in part, allows KUE to maintain empirical relevance, model consistency, and investor rationality.[14] The authors develop the Knightian Uncertainty Hypothesis (KUH) that assumes that coefficients in asset-pricing models undergo unanticipated change over time. Thus, stochastic representations of instability are not applicable. This is accomplished through *ex ante* constraints on the coefficient values between upper and lower bounds, which are stochastically determined. Within such stochastic intervals, conventional fundamentals, broader information on novel events, and investor psychology are all allowed to interact in influencing investor expectations in unforeseeable ways determined by one of a family of unknown distributions. That is, change in the model's posited relationships, say between stock prices and earnings, is partially determined at a point in time and left to unfold in conditionally open ways over time, affording an autonomous role for investor expectations.

---

[14] In its critique of REH models' epistemological flaws, IKE has argued for change to be constrained by intervals of time wherein revisions to forecasting strategies may be more moderate. See, for example, Frydman and Goldberg (2007, 2013, 2015). The idea that partially determined representations of change may be necessary for empirical relevance in a world of KU can be linked to Hayek (1978) who states, "I prefer true but imperfect knowledge ... to a pretense of exact knowledge that is likely to be false." Of course, Knight, Popper, and others have commented extensively on the limits of knowability *ex ante*.

Unlike REH, KUH does not specify fully the precise values of informational factors and aggregate outcomes within the stochastically constrained coefficient intervals. Doing so allows for myriad diverse processes, and narrative dynamics, to influence future values of fundamental factors and outcome variables. Consistency between the economist's representations of the process driving aggregate outcomes and how forecasts thereof actually unfold over time is thus achieved within the intervals of the KUH model. Because there are no quantitative distributions or rules from which expectational parameters and possible future outcomes are derived, sentiment is allowed to assist investor forecasting strategies without presuming that market participants are irrational. One possible statistical toolkit for testing KUH models may include the impulse indicator saturation (IIS) models of Hendry et al. (2008) whose premise lies on the unknowability of where structural change has occurred, how often it may occur, and in which ways it may impact market outcomes. More will be said on econometric advances for future research in the concluding chapter.

By moving beyond stochastic representations of change and jettisoning determinate accounts of forecasting behavior, KUE provides a framework that allows for novel events, temporal instability, and narrative dynamics to unfold in partially open ways over time. This book provides KUE with an empirical foundation in support of unforeseeable change driving stock market outcomes and the normalcy of KU under NNH.

Kuhn noted that a paradigm internally determines the problems and potential solutions. For EMH and REH, the problems were defined in terms of allocative efficiency and "correct" prices. The solutions were well-defined sharp predictions of mechanical individual behavior and market outcomes. For KU-based models, the rules and standards are unequivocally different. There, the problems are inherent and unforeseeable change, KU, and forecasting diversity. The solutions are qualitative predictions and contingent interactions between historical events, market fundamentals, and psychology.

Such a view, therefore, recognizes that in real-world markets individuals cannot afford to adhere endlessly to determinate forecasting strategies. Rather, they are constantly seeking to interpret as best they can unscheduled news' impacts on future returns while novelty, narratives, and structural change are unfolding all around them in real time.

As Kuhn acknowledged, the transition from existing paradigm to general acceptance of a new paradigm through scientific revolution is a long and arduous and sometimes "invisible" one.

> The transition ... to a new tradition of normal science ... is not a cumulative process ... achieved by ... articulation ... of the old paradigm...[It] is a reconstruction of the field from new fundamentals ... that changes some of the field's most elementary theoretical generalizations as well as its paradigm methods and applications. [There] will ... be a decisive difference in the modes of solution. When ... transition is complete, the profession will have changed its view of the field, its methods, and its goals.
>
> *(Kuhn, 1970, pp. 84–85)*

From a Kuhnian vantage point, models based on unforeseeable change and KU meet the criterion for potential paradigm successor. First, the accounts have made unprecedented epistemological, theoretical, and empirical contributions to the field. Not only do the empirical studies, present evidence included, uncover the non-routine importance of fundamentals and novel events, they reveal the mediating role of psychological considerations. Further, they show that what once were thought of as anomalous findings were merely a consequence of constructing fully predetermined accounts of individual forecasting behavior and market outcomes. Second, the theories of KU and ambiguity leave enough flexibility for deeper application to the field of macro-finance and narratological research therein while encouraging extension into other areas of research.

For a paradigm to have successfully taken the place of its predecessor, the scientific field must be in a post-revolution period. The movement of a scientific community between paradigms is often blurred because the textbooks that serve as the "pedagogic vehicles for the perpetuation of normal science" must be "rewritten in the aftermath of each scientific revolution" (Kuhn, 1970, p. 137). Insofar as the textbook provides an historical mapping of the scientific field's progress, it will often date back only to the last revolution. As such, progression in the science appears to evolve in a linear lock-step fashion when really paradigm shifts "must occur all at once" (Kuhn, 1970, p. 150). The lagging nature of paradigm acceptance within academic circles compounds this: It may take a profession years to determine which research is important and worthy of mass incorporation into the field.

# 14 Concluding Thoughts and Future Research

Perhaps the biggest takeaway from the analyses presented in Chapters 4 through 12 is the sheer ubiquity of unscheduled, or novel, events that introduce unforeseeable change and, therefore, uncertainty into stock market relationships. The dynamic stream of continuously flowing novel corporate events, heightened by spillover of macro novelty, is just what Knight and Keynes predicted when discussing the uniqueness of business decisions and the indeterminacy of investment prospects under true uncertainty. The spectrum of both Black and Grey Swan events is undeniable. And, shaping the diverse interpretations of such events are the emotions and narrative dynamics needed to make sense of unforeseeable change as it unfolds in real time. Indeed, this book provides much support for the Novelty–Narrative Hypothesis (NNH). Based on the collective evidence presented here, it would seem that the scope of nonrepetitive events and their impacts on instability in the stock market have been overlooked.

Much of this book is dedicated to the textual analysis of unscheduled events identified in *Dow Jones* and *Bloomberg News* equity market reports. Researchers can utilize many textual sources that allow for Knightian uncertainty (KU) events to matter for stock prospects in open ways – a textual news analytics project involving such events and testimony excerpts from equity market professionals is provided in Appendix B – but one could imagine other creative mediums from which narrative dynamics could be tracked. Shiller (2019) discusses some alternatives to news for understanding the importance of stories for aggregate markets. He suggests analyzing dialogue and responses from "regular focus groups with members from different socioeconomic groups" and databases of "sermons," "personal letters," and "diaries." Shiller concludes that "as research methods advance ... textual analysis will become a stronger force in economics." (pp. 282–285). Indeed.

As mentioned in Chapter 13, studies could consider tracking the narrative attributes surrounding unscheduled events mentioned in 10-K and 8-K corporate statements, IPO prospecti, or in the SEC disclosures of venture capital firms' business expenditures. Researchers might consider the way CEOs and other executives discuss particular issues on their shareholder calls or through other investor relations. Which subsets of soft information are they emphasizing the most? How are they framing the soft information? How does the context shift beyond standard assessments of positive and negative tone? What do answers to these questions look like when documented over time?

Researchers could also explore the SEC "Comments" issued in response to corporate filings with the aim of offering clarifying information on the disclosures (Ryans, 2016). SEC Comments letters are between SEC staff and SEC filers.[1]

> The staff's comments are in response to a company's disclosure and other public information and are based on the staff's understanding of that company's facts and circumstances ... In issuing comments to a company, the staff may request that a company provide additional supplemental information so the staff can better understand the company's disclosure, revise disclosure in a document on file with the SEC, provide additional disclosure in a document on file with the SEC, or provide additional or different disclosure in a future filing with the SEC. There may be several rounds of letters from the SEC staff and responses from the filer until the issues identified in the review are resolved.

Which areas of information were reported as needing clarification? What, if anything, has been revised from the initial disclosure? Is the framing of soft information different this time around? Are there story threads that are being promoted or relegated through the successive exchanges of letters?

There are studies that have made such attempts, but researchers could go further by interacting the soft information with measures

[1] For more information see www.sec.gov/fast-answers/answerscommentlettershtm.html.

of sentiment, relevance, novelty, and event inertia as outlined in previous chapters, to gauge narrative dynamics. As Shiller and others have remarked, advances in artificial intelligence will likely intersect in a big way with narratological studies in economics and finance in the near future. Findings in this book may motivate research questions and analytical approaches at this juncture.

The second big takeaway from evidence presented here is the dramatic variation over time in novel events' importance for corporate prospects and stock market outcomes. Findings document great variation within and across KU event group diversity. The word clouds of Chapter 4, the KU indices of Chapters 5 and 6, and the individual micro and macro KU groups of Chapters 7 and 8, respectively, all tell a similar story: Unscheduled events' importance for the stock market changes at times and in ways that would be extremely difficult to foresee. Some of the corporate KU plots – Credit Ratings, Analyst Ratings, Assets, Stock Prices, Labor Issues, Legal, Products–Services, and Price Targets – display upward or downward persistence in the series for extended periods. Some KU groups' persistence was also marked by high volatility as with corporate Dividends/Earnings and Revenues. Other plots – Equity Actions, Regulatory, Industrial Accidents, and Indexes – are characterized by a seemingly stationary series marked by a number of abrupt outlier spikes. The dramatic variation in scapegoat narrative weights presented in Chapter 11 adds further evidence in support of the time-varying importance of novel events and the nonroutine change they engender in stock market relationships.

The third big takeaway from the preceding analysis is the close and dynamic connection between novel events, structural change, and associated narratives at the macro versus micro level. Chapter 3 discussed findings of narrative dynamics' higher-order effects on decision-making under uncertainty from other social and cognitive sciences. Empirical results in this book, particularly those from Chapter 8, provide support for these insights. Although corporate uncertainty events dwarf those at the macro level by count and group diversity, variation within the two realms of novel events closely tracks each other through time. This highly significant positive correlation is maintained when the KU indices of sentiment, relevance, novelty, and inertia are interacted to generate new micro and macro "narrative" variables. Interestingly, the macro KU event narratives are found to explain future micro KU event subnarratives, but not the other way around. This result suggests that there is a time-lag of amplifying novelty and instability that spills over from the macro level onto the corporate level. As further implied by NNH, Chapter 10 then connects the intensity of corporate narratives to formal breakpoints in regressions of returns, volatility, and equity fund flows.

There are also several epistemological ways in which this book's findings could influence the fields of economics and finance. First, ignoring the pervasiveness and diversity of such novel and destabilizing events in equity markets has far-reaching implications for what real-world rationality actually implies. This book makes a case for reenvisioning how researchers and regulatory officials think about rationality and the role of associated narrative dynamics as applied to investor behavior and the processes driving asset markets outcomes.

The volumes of nonrepetitive and somewhat unique events connected to unforeseeable change imply that it is not useful to view markets as either a mechanical environment sheathed in matchless efficiency or a hysteria-prone casino haphazardly allocating capital and setting prices. Rather, the prowess of asset markets is found in their ability to aggregate the wide range of interpretations of novel events' impacts on corporate prospects and future returns while different forms of structural change are unfolding in real time. This is the true beauty of financial markets. Consequently, it is not sensible to think about markets as being rational or irrational based on determinate accounts and stochastic representations of change. Rationality under KU implies that using different pockets of information, weighting them with sentiment and the narratives that necessarily emerge, and forming diverse interpretations of news' future impacts is completely logical.

For instance, stock price responses to novel events unfolding in the early months of the COVID-19 crisis in Q1 2020 were entirely in line with investor rationality. To think that there is such a thing as a so-called complete reaction to historical events that cause unforeseeable change and envelop forecasting strategies with uncertainty does not follow. *Ex post* accounts of irrational investor responses to novel events miss the fact that individuals facing uncertainty interpret news' impacts the best they can at a point in time, which naturally and necessarily involves considering, through narrative dynamics or other soft information, how other investors are interpreting the news. This higher order process, discussed in Chapter 3, is continuously unfolding in stock, and other asset, markets and is commensurate with rational decision-making in the real world, especially when the environments' parameters are shifting in unforeseen ways.

Second, the findings suggest that both unscheduled events and temporal instability are relevant informational factors useful for thinking about the future. Recognizing unforeseeable change and the KU it engenders under NNH does not imply that *ex ante* prediction is beyond reach or that researchers somehow "know less" if probabilistic models are jettisoned for partially predetermined accounts. Researchers, too, face uncertainty and ambiguity about the future returns process and how market participants will interpret unscheduled news events. Reflecting this fact of nature does not preclude an approach based on KU from being worthy of scientific status. Rather, this book suggests that KU-based models of price fluctuations are the best approximation of reality. As Figure 1.3 in Chapter 1 suggests, temporal instability in asset market relationships becomes part of the relevant information set under NNH. This view is consistent with evidence presented in Chapter 9 and elsewhere suggesting that there is an informational effect corporate KU events impart onto the market that reduces forecast variance and may contribute to an uncertainty premium, helping to bound long swings and excess in stock market prices and valuation ratios.

Knightian Uncertainty Economics, as discussed in Chapter 13, is consistent with these arguments and implications for asset market outcomes. It makes empirical relevance and prediction possible by allowing for one of myriad unknown distributions to describe coefficients and outcomes within interval constraints. Within these bounds novel events and narrative dynamics are allowed to unfold in open ways. Thus, diversity of news' interpretations of future outcomes is consistent with rationality under KUE and the Knightian Uncertainty Hypothesis introduced by Frydman et al. (2019).

How might other researchers incorporate the nuanced features of the KU data presented throughout the book into their own empirical research? When narratives (i.e. interactions between nonrepetitive events, sentiment, relevance, novelty, and inertia) about particular events become amplified or diminished, researchers would want information about those factors to enter investor forecasting strategies with increased or decreased weights, respectively. There are at least two empirical approaches to accomplish this and allow for structural change to unfold in open ways over time.

The first approach involves a piecewise linear approximation of subperiods demarcated by structural breakpoints that correspond to narrative intensity. Structural break tests which leave open the timing and magnitude of instability, such as the CUSUM, CUSUMSQ, and Bai and Perron unknown breakpoint tests, are great candidates for dealing with narrative dynamics. If breakpoints are detected and identified in a sequential way, as these tests allow for, then the linear relationships driving outcomes can be approximated within the subperiods of "statistical stability" and future pieces of the data sample are not biased by previous instances of instability. Asset-pricing models confronted with piecewise linear approximations informed by sequential break tests have been able to produce coefficients on fundamentals with correct sign and significance while improving overall model fit.[2]

The second econometric avenue for allowing novel events, structural change, and associated narratives to matter in open ways is

---

[2] For equity market studies using piecewise linear approximations after sequential, or recursive, structural change tests see, for instance, Mangee (2016). For currency markets see, for instance, Frydman and Goldberg (2007).

the Impulse Indicator Saturation (IIS) approach advanced by Hendry et al. (2008). Essentially, IIS begins with a candidate set of indicators that take on a value of unity at observation $t$ and 0 for every other observation. There is an indicator for each observation used to detect outlier events and points of structural change without predetermining the magnitude, location, type, or number of breaks. Castle and Hendry (2019) show that IIS allows for more variables than observations, wherein the former are eventually reduced for tractable estimation through the Autometrics block search algorithm.[3] Unlike the required data trimming of the Bai and Perron structural break procedure, the IIS approach is able to include all observations, and points of potential structural change, at the beginning and end of the sample. What is more, the IIS approach has the added benefit of jointly detecting different forms of structural change while simultaneously assessing model specification and functional form.

The IIS approach may be particularly well suited to deal with scapegoat effects and narrative dynamics through extensions involving Step Indicator Saturation (SIS) and Multiplicative Indicator Saturation (MIS). The former involves continuous blocks of indicators with the same sign for subperiods of time in the sample (Hendry et al., 2013). When step indicators are multiplied by variables in the model, MIS provides the ability to "turn on" or "turn off" the influence of, say, scapegoat, or narrative intensive, fundamentals. It has recently been applied by Castle et al. (2017) to economic policy shifts and the narratives associated with agency data releases underpinning the macro policy directive. There, the idea is that when direct economic forecasts and derived narratives from agency reports are very similar, which they often are, then "forecast failure entails forediction failure," a scenario whereby the forecast, the associated narrative, and ensuing policy changes fail. Connecting narratives to forecast failures in the stock market is a promising avenue of textual-

---

[3] See Doornik (2009) and Castle et al. (2012) for applications of IIS in Autometrics.

based research especially in light of the econometric advances in detecting structural change.

The future of financial market research is objectively open. Novel events and narratives do not replace hard data; they complement it, they interact with it, they give it context, they illuminate its meaning, and they augment investor information sets under uncertainty. The success in applying KUE-based models while fostering new avenues to emerge will depend on how seriously researchers take the role of unforeseeable change in driving asset market outcomes.

Will economics and finance research incorporate the nuances of novel events and narrative dynamics under KU on a larger scale? Only time will tell. McCloskey (2016) calls the economics profession, and even other disciplines, back to the study of "human meaning in speech" and "changes in rhetoric" to understand fluctuations in aggregate variables. "A new economic history uses all the evidence for the scientific task: books as much as bonds, entrepreneurial courage and hope as much as managerial prudence and temperance" (p. 503). In *Cents and Sensibility*, Morson and Schapiro (2017) argue that "good economics leads to bad policy." Why? Because researchers ignore the nonrepetitive nature of culture, business, and history. The solution? Literature. Books. Stories. Narratives.

# APPENDIX A  R Code for *Bloomberg News* Word Cloud and Histogram

You will need two files, and their location paths, for completing the R word cloud code. First you will need a source .txt file.[1] The .txt file used to generate each word cloud in this appendix was an annual set of *Bloomberg News* stock market wrap reports, but it could be any text file whose content you wish to analyze. Additionally, the file could be saved on your computer's directory or connected to a URL or website address. Second, you will need a lexicon dictionary of Knightian uncertainty (KU) terms. The KU dictionary used in Chapter 4 and in the appendix can be found on the author's website – you would want to download the Excel spreadsheet to your computer's directory as a CSV file.[2] In the following R code, the text file is denoted "file.txt" and the lexicon KU dictionary is denoted "KU_MasterDictionary.csv."

The R code requires five packages: "tm," "wordcloud," "RColorBrewer," "SnowballC," and "slam." The code converts the .txt file into a vector corpus that is then cleaned by removing punctuation, numbers, stopwords such as "a," "an," and "in," and stemming the document to identify root words. A document term matrix is then produced from the corpus. Identified terms from the KU lexicon dictionary are given columns in the output document term matrix. Finally, the word cloud plots the frequency of the column terms for each period of .txt files being investigated, in this case a year's worth. The code for generating a word cloud and associated frequency histogram is as follows:

```
library(tm)
library(wordcloud)
library(RColorBrewer)
library(SnowballC)
library(slam)

cname <- file.path("file.txt")
cname
```

---

[1] There are many open source and published resources for programming in R. For a treatment of textual mining using R, see, for example, Silge and Robinson (2017).

[2] The KU lexion dictionary is available at www.taskstream.com/ts/mangee/ NicholasMangee.

```r
dir(cname)
docs <- VCorpus(DirSource(cname))
summary(docs)
inspect(docs)
docs <- tm_map(docs, removePunctuation)
docs <- tm_map(docs, tolower)
docs <- tm_map(docs, removeNumbers)
docs <- tm_map(docs, removeWords, stopwords("english"))
docs <- tm_map(docs, stemDocument)
docs <- tm_map(docs, stripWhitespace)
docs <- tm_map(docs, PlainTextDocument)
dtm <- DocumentTermMatrix(docs)
dtm
tdm <- TermDocumentMatrix(docs)
tdm

lex =read.csv("KU_MasterDictionary.csv")
ku.lex = tolower(lex$Entry[lex$Uncertainty != ""])
terms = colnames(dtm)
ku.terms = terms[terms %in% ku.lex]
ku.scores = rowSums(as.matrix(dtm[ , ku.terms]))

freq <- col_sums(as.matrix(dtm[ , ku.terms]))
length(freq)
ord <- order(freq,decreasing=TRUE)
freq[head(ord,50)]

set.seed(1234)
wordcloud(words = ku.terms,freq,scale=c(4,1), min.freq = 1,
          max.words=200, random.order=FALSE, rot.per=0.35,
          colors=brewer.pal(8, ''Dark2''))

barplot(freq[head(ord,5)], las = 2, names.arg = ku.terms[head(ord, 5)],
        col ="lightblue", main ="Most frequent words",
        ylab = "Word frequencies")
```

# APPENDIX B    The *Bloomberg News* KU Stock Market Project

## B.I    INTRODUCTION

The preceding chapters advanced the argument that narrative dynamics are associated with novel events, sentiment, and temporal instability in the processes
driving stock market outcomes. The purpose of this project is to shed light on
the relationships driving daily stock market prices through the identification of
traditional fundamental, psychological, technical, and historically novel (Knightian uncertainty [KU]) events all while allowing for unforeseeable structural change
at every point in time. The focus is a rule-based approach in manual reading of
*Bloomberg News* market wraps dubbed the Mangee method. This approach has
been employed by Frydman and Goldberg (2011), Mangee (2014, 2017, 2018, 2019),
Frydman et al. (2015), and Mangee and Goldberg (2020).[1] Select findings from
these studies have been reported earlier in Chapters 4 and 11. Ultimately, you will
compile a unique time-series dataset of disaggregated factors' importance within
these groups that you can apply to any stock market narratological analysis you
wish. The possibilities of application are only bounded by your ideas and creativity.

More specifically, you will comb through *Bloomberg News* (or other financial news sources') stock market reports generated at the end of each trading day
to conduct some news analytics. You will score the factors reported by business
journalists, equity and hedge fund managers, and other market professionals as
driving investor trading decisions, and thus stock prices, on a given day. The
analysis is primarily concerned with two tasks: (i) identifying which factors are
mentioned in the reports as explicitly driving fluctuations in aggregate stock
market prices (i.e. SP500, DJIA, NASDAQ) and the prices of firms within each
index on a given day and (ii) determining the directional impacts the factor shares
with the stock price (positive, factors and prices move in the same direction;
negative, they move in opposite directions).

---

[1] This project is based on the publication, "Knightian Uncertainty and Stock Price
Movements: Why the REH Present-Value Model Failed Empirically," by Frydman et al.
(2015). The study, along with more information on the factor classification and scoring
approach, can be found at www.economics-ejournal.org/economics/journalarticles/2015-
24. You are encouraged to review the appendix of this published paper for more examples
from the *Bloomberg News* wraps using the Mangee-method textual analysis approach.

This project is essentially a recording in an Excel spreadsheet of a factor's reported importance for stock prices following the detailed classification rules and lexicon provided throughout this appendix. In your Excel spreadsheet (provided), you will input a "0" (or simply leave the cell blank) if there is no mention of the factor driving stock price behavior on the day in question or a "1" if the relevant factor is explicitly mentioned as driving the daily stock price. If different factors within the same category are mentioned on the same day you may record a "2," or "3," and so on. Moreover, if the factor has a clear quantitative data series, say quarterly GDP growth, one can input a "+1"(or "−1") if the relevant factor is reported to share a positive (or negative) relationship with the stock price. This delineation does not apply to psychological factors, technical trading factors, and some KU fundamental factors (i.e. Central Bank announcements). The scoring spreadsheet with disaggregated classifications, titled "Bloomberg_Classification," can be found at the author's website: www.taskstream.com/ts/mangee/NicholasMangee. A glossary of news excepts involving fundamental, KU, psychological, and technical factors is provided in Section B.8.

## B.2    SETTING UP YOUR SPREADSHEET

Completing task (i) takes some initial classification of the types of factors encountered in the wraps. The present value model implies that market fundamentals, such as earnings, dividends, and interest rates, matter for stock prices. However, Shiller (1981) famously found that theorized stock prices ($P^*$) based on *ex post* dividends cannot explain the "excess" volatility observed in actual stock price movements ($P$). Figure B.1 illustrates this stylized fact for the present value relation based on the SP500 Index from 1871 through 2015.

The persistent departures of stock market prices away from theorized values has led many economists and noneconomists alike to conclude that stock prices are driven primarily by purely extraneous psychological considerations (fear, optimism, confidence, etc.) and momentum-related factors (herding, chartism, trend chasing, etc.).

The broad categories involving market fundamentals, psychological, and technical considerations are discussed in detail in Sections B.4, B.5, and B.6. Importantly, the Excel worksheet with the classification structure is already set up for you, column by column. Note that the column headings within the three broad categories are not set in stone – they are a useful guide to the possible range of categories you may encounter when reading the stock market reports. However, if you find a factor (fundamental, psychological, or technical) you may wish to add a new column category to reflect it in your spreadsheet. That said, the spreadsheet is currently set up as follows: The fundamental categories correspond to columns

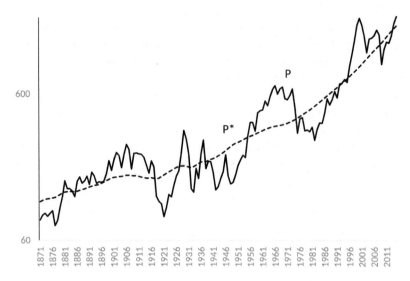

FIGURE B.1 $P$ (solid line) represents the real SP500 Composite Index price. $P_*$ (dashed line) represents the present value of future *ex post* real dividends accruing to ownership in a portfolio of 500 stocks from the SP500 discounted at a constant rate equal to the historical return of the index. Data is annual and adjusted for inflation based on the Consumer Price Index. Axes are expressed on a logarithmic scale with base 10. All data from Robert Shiller's webpage. Source: Mangee and Goldberg (2020)

under the YELLOW "Fundamental Factors" banner; the psychological categories correspond to columns under the ORANGE "Psychological Factors" banner; and the technical trading categories correspond to columns under the GREY "Technical Factors" banner. The columns in bright RED under fundamentals represent historical, somewhat novel, or KU factors. Download and familiarize yourself with this Excel spreadsheet as it is the baseline sheet you will use for coding, and preliminary analysis, of the textual data.

Once the scoring methodology and spreadsheet are understood and in place, you will need to access the *Bloomberg News* daily market wraps (or other textual financial news source). Go to your nearest *Bloomberg L.P.* terminal and in the input line on the top of any page type: "NI USS BN" and hit enter <GO>. The screen should populate rows of daily US stock market reports produced by *Bloomberg News*. You are looking for the "markets wrap" reports labeled after the headline for the report. Typically, the wraps are multiple pages long; so, do not forget to scroll down until you reach the end of the wrap! It is strongly encouraged that students read the entire wrap prior to any attempt at scoring the content. Note that you may download the wrap into a .txt file from the actions tab.

## B.3   EXPECTATIONS AND PRICES

Addressing whether or not to score a "+/−1" for task (ii) requires a measure of expectations to determine the directional relationship an identified fundamental (conventional or KU) shares with stock price fluctuations. Market participants' expectations of future outcomes (returns, cash flows, other fundamentals, etc.) determine the level of prices at each point in time. Consequently, revisions of these expectations drive movements in prices. The market reports contain information on whether these expectations tend to be revised upward or downward. For instance, stock prices can be expected to increase or decrease because either earnings go up or down (scenario "a" below) or because earnings increase or decrease relative to expectations (scenarios "b" and "c"). If the report stated earnings fell short of expectations investors may be disappointed, pushing prices downward even though earnings increased in absolute terms (scenario "d"). Even earnings that decrease, but by less than expectations, can imply higher stock prices (scenario "e"). For these cases, the relationship between stock prices and earnings is positive, and earnings would be recorded with a "+1." The opposite relationship involving earnings, or any fundamental, and stock prices would be recorded with a "−1." Rules for determining a factor's positive or negative directional relationship with stock prices are provided below in a–e and f–k, respectively.

Remember, you only need to accurately identify and score what the *Bloomberg* report says drove the firm's and/or market's price on a given day. Other text in the wrap may be superfluous for your project insofar as it provides information above that which informs your scoring based on tasks (i) and (ii).

A "+1" is recorded for a fundamental factor $(X)$ for any of the following five cases:

a. $X$ increases and $P$ increases or $X$ decreases and $P$ decreases;
b. $X$ increases by more than expected and $P$ increases;
c. $X$ decreases by more than expected and $P$ decreases;
d. $X$ increases but by less than expected and $P$ decreases;
e. $X$ decreases but by less than expected and $P$ increases.

A "−1" is recorded for a fundamental factor ($X$) for any of the following five cases:

> f. $X$ increases and $P$ decreases or $X$ decreases and $P$ increases;
> h. $X$ increases by more than expected and $P$ decreases;
> i. $X$ decreases by more than expected and $P$ increases;
> j. $X$ increases but by less than expected and $P$ increases;
> k. $X$ decreases but by less than expected and $P$ decreases.

## B.4   FUNDAMENTAL CONSIDERATIONS

A fundamental is any factor that affects the present value of cash flow prospects over short- or long-term horizons. There are two types of fundamentals: (i) repetitive, conventional, or routine such as GDP, earnings, employment or consumption data releases and (ii) nonrepetitive, novel KU factors such as management shake-ups, new production processes, a merger announcement, or bankruptcy. As shown throughout this book, stock markets receive news on both categories of factors every day. Consider the following excerpt from a *Bloomberg News* market wrap report illustrating the importance of both types of factors for stock prices:

> U.S. stocks rose as $35 billion in acquisitions and Merck & Co.'s better-than-forecast earnings carried the Standard & Poor's 500 Index and Dow Jones Industrial Average to the steepest gains in a week ... GlobalSantaFe Corp., the second biggest offshore oil and gas driller, climbed to a record after agreeing to be bought by larger rival Transocean Inc. Merck, the third-largest U.S. drugmaker, had its biggest advance since April and accounted for almost a third of the Dow average's rally.
>
> *(July 23, 2007)*

From this excerpt, you would score a "+1" for earnings announcements and a "+1" for mergers and acquisitions. But remember, for context and meaning, you need to read the whole market wrap, not just the first paragraph! The disaggregated conventional market fundamentals and KU fundamentals that you may encounter are listed in Sections B.4.1 and B.4.2, respectively.

## B.4.1   Repetitive

**Economy**: GDP, GDP Forecasts, Index of Leading Economic Indicators, Industrial Production, Productivity, Purchasing Managers Index, Personal Income, Service Sector Activity, Nonfarm Jobs, Unemployment Rate, Jobless Claims, Private Investment, Retail Sales National, Business Confidence, Manufacturing

Index/Activity, Factory Orders, Consumption, Private Credit, Household Credit, Durables Output, Nondurables Output, Construction Spending, Consumer Spending, Consumer Confidence

**Interest Rates**: Federal Funds, Discount, Treasury Bill, Treasury Note, Treasury Bond

**Inflation Rates**: Producer Price Index, Consumer Price Index, Manufacturing Price Index, Employment/Cost Index, Core Inflation, GDP Deflator

**Earnings**: Earnings Announcements, Earnings Forecast Announcements, Dividend Announcements, Dividend Forecast Announcements

**Sales**: Firm/Industry Revenue, Auto Sales

**Oil**: Crude Oil Price, OPEC Oil Supply

**International Trade/Flows**: Balance of Payments, Exports, Imports, Current Account, Capital Account

**Housing**: Housing Starts, Home Sales, New Home Sales, Mortgage Rates

**Government**: Federal Budget Surplus/Deficit, State/Local Budget Surplus/Deficit

**Central Bank**: Minutes

## B.4.2  Nonrepetitive KU

**KU**: Bankruptcy, Executive Turnover/Health, Legal/Accounting Issues, Firm Added to Index, Executive Salary Issues, Assets, Reorganization/Spinoffs/ Partnership, Liabilities/Debts, Share Issuances, IPOs, Business Spending, Mergers, Acquisitions, Accident/Recall, New Products/Production Processes, Insider Trad ing, Credit Ratings, Resource Discovery/Exploration, Labor Layoffs/Strike/Union, CEO/CFO Comments, Purchase/Sale of Large Stake, Stock Split, Share Buyback, Exchange Rates, FX Intervention, Gap from Benchmark, Overvalued, Undervalued, Trade Agreements/Negotiations, Tariffs, Quotas, Subsidies, Foreclosures, Home Prices, Real Estate Prices, Commercial Prices, Fiscal Policy, Comments by Officials, Stimulus Plan, Industry Regulation, Taxes/Rules on CEO Bonuses, Government Shutdown, Impeachment, Military Spending, Austerity

Measures, Credit Worthiness/Rating, Bailout/Nationalization of Private Firms, Healthcare Issues, Political Elections, Political Conflict/Instability/Corruption, Congressional Testimony, Financial Reform, Cabinet Changes, Financial Leverage/Credit Issues, Liquidity Issues, Credit Card Defaults, Firm Credit Ratings, Capital Funding, Monetary Policy, Macroprudential Policy, Commodity Prices, Armed Conflicts/Embargoes, Border Control/Immigration Policy, Travel Bans, Transportation, Nuclear Testing, Terrorism, Natural Disasters, Endemic/Pandemic, Climate Change/Pollution, Crime/Assassination/Shooting, Protests, Civil Unrest, Analyst Comments/Ratings.

An example excerpt is provided for most of the disaggregated fundamental factors in the glossary (Section B.8.1). If the *Bloomberg* wraps mention that a firm's or the market's stock price movement for a given day was driven by one or more of these disaggregated factors you will score a "+1" or "−1" (or "2"...) depending on the reported directional relationship with prices. Otherwise, you will record a "0" or simply leave the cell blank. Again, the *Bloomberg* Classification Excel spreadsheet may be expanded to include more factors than what are listed.

## B.5 PSYCHOLOGICAL CONSIDERATIONS

There are two classifications involving the ways in which psychology may matter for stock price fluctuations: (i) pure psychological considerations such as stand-alone fear, euphoria, or panic and (ii) psychological considerations mentioned in conjunction with fundamentals such as a better-than-expected economic report giving confidence to investors. Consider the following excerpt involving pure psychology, that is, without fundamentals:

> U.S. stocks slid . . . "This is what happens when the contagion of fear spreads," said Quincy Krosby, who helps manage about $380 billion as chief investment strategist at the Hartford in Hartford, Connecticut.
> *(October 9, 2008)*

For this excerpt, a "1" would be recorded for "fear." Or you may read, for instance,

> "I do think it's mania," said Ned Riley, chief investment officer at BankBoston Corp., which oversees $26 billion. "Anytime stocks appreciate 30 to 50 percent in a day, it's the greater fool theory. People think there will always be someone who will pay a higher price."
> *(April 21, 1998)*

Here, you would score "1" for "mania" and no mention of fundamentals. The psychological factors that you may encounter are listed here:

**Psychological Considerations**: Concern, Confidence, Crowd Psychology, Emotion, Euphoria, Exuberance, Fear, Greed, Mania, Optimism, Overreaction, Panic, Pessimism, Psychology, Sentiment, Underreaction, Worry.

Alternatively, you may encounter an excerpt involving psychological considerations connected to fundamentals such as,

> U.S. stocks rose for a second day, after Federal Reserve Chairman Alan Greenspan fueled optimism for a growing economy and higher company profits.
>
> *(July 23, 1997)*

Here one would record a "1" for "Central Bank Comments," a "1" for "psychology with Central Bank," a "1" for "psychology with economy," and a "1" for "psychology with earnings." There is also a column titled "psychology with fundamentals" for simplified scoring if you do not wish to track each detailed psychological consideration mentioned in conjunction with a particular fundamental. Other examples of pure psychological considerations and those in conjunction with fundamentals are provided in Section B.8.2.

## B.6 TECHNICAL CONSIDERATIONS

Technical factors are factors that involve past price movements or effects that may correspond to certain months or days of the week. Consider the following two excerpts:

> U.S. stocks rose as . . . some of the buying came from "momentum" traders, who buy stocks that are going up in order to realize a quick gain. "It's just money chasing stocks at this point, anticipating the market making a new high and then carrying forward on its own momentum," said Joseph De-Marco, head of trading at HSBC Asset Management Americas Inc.
>
> *(July 8, 1998)*

> U.S. stocks rose...[t]he so-called January effect was in evidence as communications equipment stocks, the worst-performing group in the major indexes last year, rose.
>
> *(January 3, 2002)*

The first excerpt would score a "1" for both "momentum traders" and "market momentum." The second excerpt would score a "1" for the January effect. Technical momentum and nonmomentum example news excerpts can be found in B.8.3 and B.8.4, respectively. The technical factors that you may encounter are listed here:

**Technical Considerations**: Firm/Industry/Index Stock Prices, Profit Taking, Market Rally, Market Momentum, Holiday Effect, Momentum Traders, January Effect, Bandwagon, End of Month Effect, Price-to-Price Loop, End of Quarter Effect, Moving Average, End of Year Effect, Chartism, RSI, Support Indicators, Advance–Decline Ratios, Monday Effect, Milestones, Market Highs, Friday Effect, Giving Back Effect, Triple/Quadruple Witching, Price Target Announcements.

## B.7    REMARKS ON EXCEL SCORING AND PRELIMINARY ANALYSIS

This section offers a few notes and tips for scoring and initially assessing the *Bloomberg News* KU Stock Market Project using the Mangee method in Excel. Of course, you can, and should, explore a wide range of ways to transform your raw data that coincide with your research hypotheses. First, it may be obvious but make sure that you input the date in column "A" for every wrap report that you score. Aside from dating when each factor mattered for driving stock prices, this will have the secondary advantage of providing a column for count data on the number of trading days each week, month, quarter, or year since many, in fact most, of the cells for each daily row will be empty (or set equal to zero, if you wish).

Second, it is useful to record the net movement in the broad market indices from market open to close. For instance, if the DJIA, SP500, and NASDAQ all increased in value from the day's opening to close, you would record a +1 for columns "B," "C," and "D," respectively. However, be careful as market indices do not always move in the same direction each day. Tracking the net movement in the broad index prices can be used to assess which sets of factors mattered on bullish versus bearish days over time. Moreover, it is much easier to score the price movement while you are collecting the data and the necessary information is likely included in the wrap report.

Third, you may wish to construct aggregated measures for the variables – aggregate fundamentals, aggregate psychology, aggregate technical, and aggregate KU. This is especially relevant for conventional fundamental and KU considerations that have numerous disaggregated factors within their categorical classification. One way to approach this is to generate new columns in your Excel spreadsheet reflecting count data of how many events occurred for a particular aggregate category. Alternatively, you could determine if at least one factor in an aggregate category mattered for stock prices on a given day. These columns will be based on "count" and "if-then" commands in Excel. Finally, it is suggested that KU events without quantitative scale be scored with a +1 or −1 if they are interpreted as "good" or "bad" for the market, respectively. Similarly, you may wish to apply this bullish versus bearish scoring to psychological and technical factors, it is up to you and depends on your hypotheses of interest.

## B.8   GLOSSARY OF NEWS FACTOR EXAMPLES

This section provides alphabetized classification of nearly all disaggregated factors – whether traditional or KU fundamental, psychological, or technical trading – that are mentioned by *Bloomberg News* journalists in driving stock market and firm prices into their broader categories. A specific example of each, along with scoring for the category in question, is provided. Note, novel events are occurring virtually every day in the stock market. Consequently, the following textual excerpt examples are not exhaustive of every subcategory that you may encounter in your own project incorporating the Mangee method into news analytics. Furthermore, there is often more than one consideration present in a single excerpt, but only single factors are being identified in the following glossary.

### B.8.1   *Fundamental Considerations*

**Benchmark Valuation**

*Gap from Benchmark Levels*

"U.S. stocks fell in a late-day slide amid concern that share prices may have overshot earnings prospects ... The Standard and Poors 500 index is trading at 19 times 1997 earnings, based on a Zacks Investment research survey, 25% higher than its average price-to-earnings ratio of 15.2 since 1980." (−1 for Gap from Benchmark Levels)

*Overvalued*

"Investors are looking for a reason to sell," said Gene Grandone, director of investment counseling at the Northern Trust Co., which oversees $130 billion. "With the market in the 7900 area, people see a market that is a little rich.". . . Many investors are uncomfortable with the markets price to earnings ratio which is near the high end of its historic range." (−1 for Overvalued)

*Undervalued*

"Bank of America, the largest U.S. bank by assets, jumped 9.3 percent to $12.99 after Whitney told CNBC it was the 'cheapest' U.S. bank. The shares are trading at less than 23 times profit over the past 12 months, compared with price-to-earnings valuation of 35 for JPMorgan Chase & Co. and 33 for Goldman Sachs." (−1 for Undervalued)

**Central Bank Communications**

*Comments by Officials*

"U.S. stocks had their biggest gain in two months after Federal Reserve policy makers said economic growth is poised to accelerate and reiterated a plan to raise borrowing costs at a 'measured' pace to contain inflation." (+1 for Comments by Officials)

*Macroprudential Policy*

"U.S. stocks fell for a fourth day amid concern economic growth is slowing and the Federal Reserve will boost capital requirements for the nation's largest banks." (−1 for Macroprudential Policy)

*Minutes*

"U.S. stocks erased an initial rally in the year's first day of trading after the Federal Reserve showed growing concern that the economy will slow and inflation will rise. Minutes from the Dec. 12 meeting of Fed policy makers said the central bank's 'predominant concern' is rising prices and the chance of an economic slowdown is increasing." (+1 for Central Bank Minutes)

**Company Variables**

*Bankruptcy*

"General Motors Corp. dropped 11 percent after saying bankruptcy is more probable than previously thought." (−1 for bankruptcy)

*Financial Ratio*

"Bear Stearns had its credit-rating outlook cut to negative by S&P on concern declining prices for mortgage-backed securities will decrease earnings ... Stocks fell to their lows of the day after the firm said its return on equity in July may be close to the lowest ever and borrowing costs may slow mergers and acquisitions." (+1 for Financial Ratios)

*Business Spending*

"Prices got a boost from optimism that an improving U.S. economy would spur business spending and corporate profits, which exceeded analysts' estimates on average for the second quarter." (+1 for Business Spending)

*CEO or CFE Comments*

"Benchmark indexes rebounded from losses after MBIA Inc. Chief Executive Officer Gary Dunton's comments sparked a rally in bank shares." (+1 for Company Variables)

*IPOs*
"Steelmakers jumped on speculation that U.S. Steel Corp., the country's largest producer, may be a takeover target. Nymex Holdings Inc., owner of the world's biggest energy market, had the largest gain for an initial public offering in 15 months." (+1 for IPOs)

*Labor Layoff or Strike*
"United Technologies Corp., a supplier of helicopters and jet engines to the military, retreated 1.2 percent after saying the shutdown would lead to as many as 5,000 temporary layoffs." (−1 for Labor Layoffs)

*Legal or Accounting Issues*
"U.S. stocks added to a weeklong rally, sending the Dow Jones Industrial Average to its longest winning streak in a year, after Altria Group Inc. and other tobacco companies won the right to head off a lawsuit seeking $200 billion." (+1 for Legal/Accounting Issues)

*Credit Issues/Ratings*
"Bear Stearns had its credit-rating outlook cut to negative by S&P on concern declining prices for mortgage-backed securities will decrease earnings. The perceived risk of owning the New York-based company's bonds rose to the highest in at least six years." (−1 for Credit Issues/Ratings)

*Mergers and Acquisitions*
"U.S. stocks rose, lifted by takeover proposals from Duke Energy Corp. and E*Trade Financial Corp." (+1 for Mergers and Acquisitions)

*Share Buyback*
"Coke gained 2.8 percent as profit benefited from cost-cutting efforts, while GM rose 4.2 percent on buyback speculation." (+1 for Share Buyback)

*Firm Added to Index*
"Google Inc. climbed after being picked to join the Standard & Poor's 500 Index." (+1 for Firm Added to Index)

*Stock Split/Stock Sale*
"Companies announcing share sales frequently decline because the additional stock dilutes the value of existing equity and reduce earnings per share. 'The market moving more towards concern about dilution may be a positive in terms of investors' outlook on the overall economy because they are less concerned

with balance-sheet issues and more concerned with earnings issues,' said Joseph Veranth, who oversees $2.2 billion as chief investment officer at Dana Investment Advisors in Brookfield, Wisconsin." (+1 for Stock Split)

### Currency Markets
*Exchange Rates*
"U.S. stocks rose, with the Dow Jones Industrial Average reversing a 184-point drop, as the euro's rebound from a four-year low bolstered optimism that the shared European currency will weather the region's debt crisis." (+1 for Exchange Rates)

### Earnings/Dividends
*Earnings*
"U.S. stocks suffered their biggest loss since the Oct. 27 market rout as Russia's debt defaults and weakening currency sent markets around the world tumbling, raising the prospect of a slump in corporate earnings." (+1 for Earnings)

*Earnings Announcement*
"U.S. stocks rose as $35 billion in acquisitions and Merck & Co.'s better-than-forecast earnings carried the Standard & Poor's 500 Index and Dow Jones Industrial Average to the steepest gains in a week." (+1 for Earnings Announcement)

*Earnings Forecast Announcement*
"U.S. stocks fell, after DuPont Co., the largest U.S. chemicals company, warned that second-quarter earnings will be below analyst forecasts." (+1 for Earnings Forecast Announcement)

*Dividend Announcements*
"Texas Instruments Inc. increased 2 percent on plans to boost its dividend. Texas Instruments gained 2 percent to $24.06. The second-largest U.S. chipmaker said it plans to raise its quarterly dividend 1 cent to 12 cents a share. The new dividend will be payable Nov. 16 to stockholders of record on Oct. 30." (+1 for Dividend Announcements)

### Financial Institutions
*Capital Funding*
"U.S. stocks rose, led by banks and energy shares, as forecasts that General Electric Co. has enough capital and oil's surge sent the Dow Jones Industrial Average up more than 150 points in the final 35 minutes of trading." (+1 for Capital Funding)

*Credit Card Defaults*

"U.S. stocks dropped, sending the Dow Jones Industrial Average to a six-year low, as Hewlett-Packard Co. cut its profit forecast and concern about rising credit-card defaults dragged financial shares to the lowest level since 1995." (−1 Credit Card Defaults)

*Credit Ratings*

"Ambac Financial Group Inc. and MBIA Inc., the two biggest U.S. bond insurers, retreated on concern their AAA credit ratings will be revoked." (−1 for Financial Credit Ratings)

*Leverage or Credit Issues*

"'This is a major credit crunch worldwide, and the banks are at the hub of it,' said Isabelle Merton, a European fund manager who helps look after $5 billion in assets for ABN Amro Asset Management in London." (−1 for Financial Leverage or Credit Issues)

*Liquidity Issues*

"U.S. stocks tumbled as subprime mortgage contagion and hedge fund losses halted a three-day rally and sent brokerage shares to their worst rout since 2002 . . . [There is] . . . 'Liquidity Panic' . . . 'What happened with Libor is clearly evidence of a liquidity panic in really what should be the most efficient part of the markets,' said John Lewis, who helps manage about $150 million at Sweetwater Asset Management LLC in Columbus, Ohio. 'That's going to be reason for concern for everybody in just about every asset class.'" (−1 for Liquidity Issues)

**Geopolitical Issues**

*Armed Conflicts*

"U.S. stocks erased losses as increasing violence in Ukraine sent oil prices to the biggest increase in a month and spurred a rally in energy producers." (+1 for Armed Conflict)

*Nuclear Testing/Deal*

"The Standard & Poor's 500 Index fell, after seven consecutive weekly gains that lifted the gauge to a record, as energy shares retreated following Iran's agreement to limit its nuclear program." (−1 for Nuclear Issues)

*Terrorism*

"Speculation that the U.S. will raise the terror alert level sent prices to the day's lows." (−1 for Terrorism)

### Government and Fiscal

*Bailout or Nationalization of Banks*

"The government-chartered companies, the largest sources of financing for U.S. home loans, still fell to 17-year lows on concern they will require a bailout that could wipe out shareholders." (−1 for Bailout/Nationalization of Firm)

*Budget Surplus or Deficit*

"U.S. stocks fell, halting a two-day gain in the Standard & Poor's 500 Index, as concern about the federal budget debate erased a rally led by Home Depot Inc." (−1 for Budget Surplus/Deficit)

*Comments by Official*

"Citigroup Inc. and JPMorgan Chase & Co. added at least 5.8 percent after Treasury Secretary Timothy Geithner said there are signs that financial markets are recovering." (+1 for Comments by Officials)

*Credit Worthiness*

"Moody's Investors Service, which placed a negative outlook on the U.S.'s Aaa grade in August, said in a statement today that the nation's rating would likely be cut to Aa1 if negotiations between lawmakers fail to produce policies that reduce the percentage of debt to gross domestic product." (−1 for Credit Worthiness)

*Financial Reform*

"Changes in financial regulation 'really could be good for the markets,' Peter Sorrentino, a senior portfolio manager at Huntington Asset Management, which oversees $15 billion in Cincinnati, said in an interview on Bloomberg Television. 'It could restore confidence and it could bring investors back into the marketplace.'" (+1 Industry Reform)

*Fiscal Policy or Stimulus Plan*

"U.S. stocks surged in the biggest two-day global rally in 38 years as the government announced plans to purge banks of bad assets and crack down on speculators who drove down shares of financial companies ... 'What the government and its regulatory agencies have tried to do here is restore some confidence and remove some fear,' Robert Doll, chief investment officer of global equities at New York-based BlackRock Inc., which manages $436 billion in stocks, told *Bloomberg* Television." (+1 for Stimulus)

*Healthcare Policy Issues*
"Humana Inc. jumped 5.5 percent as health-care providers rallied the most among 10 groups in the S&P 500, after medical insurers won an increase in a key Medicare payment rate." (+1 for Healthcare Issues)

*Political Elections*
"U.S. stocks advanced in the biggest presidential election day rally in 24 years ... 'The market has come to the conclusion that Armageddon is off the table,' said Philip Orlando, who helpds manage $330 billion as chief equity strategist at Federated Investors Inc. in New York. 'The elimination of the uncertainty of the campaign typically results in an end-of-the-year rally and you're starting to see that today.'" (+1 for Political Elections)

*Political Instability, Conflict, or Corruption*
"'When your government is in total (political) turmoil, your confidence goes down the chute,' said Cummins Catherwood, a managing director of Philadelphia-based Rutherford, Brown & Catherwood, which oversees $570 million. 'When your confidence goes down the chute, you're not going to pay 30 times earnings for GE.' (−1 for Political Instability)

*Taxes or Rules on CEO Bonuses*
"The early slide in banks came after Wall Street chief executives including Citigroup Inc.'s Vikram Pandit, JPMorgan's Jamie Dimon, and Bank of Bank of America's Ken Lewis were questioned by Congress yesterday about their lending under the Troubled Asset Relief Program. 'Seeing these CEOs being put through the ringer isn't confidence-inspiring to potential investors,' said Richard Sichel, who oversees $1.3 billion as chief investment officer at Philadelphia Trust Co. in Philadelphia. 'People are looking for earnings, but talking about bonuses and corporate jets isn't what future earnings is all about.'" (−1 for CEO Compensation)

**Housing**
*Commercial Real Estate/Prices*
"U.S. stocks rose, sending the Standard & Poor's 500 Index up for a fourth day, as easing concern over real-estate losses and gains in retail sales bolstered confidence the economic recovery will be sustained. Zions Bancorporation jumped 11 percent and financial shares in the S&P 500 extended their advance this week to 6.4 percent as Morgan Stanley analysts said commercial real-estate losses will not be a major drag on the economy." (+1 for Real Estate)

*Foreclosures*

"Pulte Group Inc. declined 3.9 percent as foreclosures reached a record." (−1 for Foreclosures)

*Home Prices*

"A measure of homebuilders in Standard & Poor's indexes jumped 3.8 percent as housing prices dropped at the slowest pace in more than a year." (+1 for Housing Prices)

*Home Sales*

"U.S. stocks rose for a fourth day as a bigger-than-estimated increase in pending sales of existing homes overshadowed concern that the market's recent rally has made American equities too expensive . . . 'The factors that have helped stocks over the past several months are still intact in terms of today's news,' said Dean Gulis, part of a group that manages $2.5 billion for Loomis Sayles & Co. in Bloomfield Hills, Michigan." (+1 for Home Sales)

*Housing Starts*

"PulteGroup Inc. and D.R. Horton Inc. fell at least 2.3 percent as housing starts slumped in April." (+1 for Housing Starts)

*Mortgage Rates*

"Homebuilders such as D.R. Horton Inc. gained as the jobs data suggested mortgage rates won't climb enough to choke off demand." (−1 for Mortgage Rates)

**Commodities Prices/Gold Prices**

*Commodity Prices*

"Alcoa Inc. and ConocoPhillips dropped at least 2.1 percent following a decline in commodities prices after the World Bank said China may raise interest rates further." (+1 for Inflation Rates)

**Inflation Rates**

*Consumer Prices*

"U.S. stocks tumbled the most since January after the latest government report on inflation shocked investors and increased speculation that the Federal Reserve may have to keep raising interest rates and restrain the economy . . . Exxon Mobil Corp. and Alcoa Inc. paced a selloff in commodity producers, the market's top performers this year, after government figures showed consumer prices rose more in April than economists forecast" (−1 for Consumer Prices)

*Employment Cost*

"U.S. stocks soared after a government report showed new jobs and wages grew less than expected in May." (−1 for Employment Cost)

*GDP Deflator*

"U.S. stocks surged for a second day after a government report showed the economy's growth hasn't sparked a higher inflation rate, buoying optimism that the Federal Reserve won't raise interest rates dramatically next month ... Stocks rallied after the Commerce Department estimated the economy expanded at a 3.4% annual rate in the third quarter, surpassing economists' expectations of 2.8% growth. More important, the report's implicit price deflator, a barometer of inflation rose at an annual rate of 1.6%, down from a 2.9% pace in the second quarter." (−1 for GDP Deflator)

*Manufacturing Prices*

"Stocks also declined as reports on wholesale prices and industrial production spurred concern the Federal Reserve will unwind stimulus measures. The government said producer prices climbed 1.8 percent in November, more than twice the median economist estimate in a survey." (−1 for Manufacturing Prices)

*Producer Prices*

"U.S. stocks rallied, sending the Standard & Poor's 500 Index to its biggest gain since April, after a government report showed producer prices rose less than expected in July, indicating inflation is in check even as the economy grows." (−1 for Producer Prices)

**Interest Rates**

*Discount*

"Nine of 10 industry groups in the Standard & Poor's 500 Index dropped after Fed Chairman Ben S. Bernanke said he may increase the discount rate on loans to banks." (−1 for Discount Rates)

*Federal Funds*

"U.S. stocks rallied the most in five years as ... the Federal Reserve cut its benchmark rate." (−1 for Federal Funds Rate)

*Treasury Bill*

"Goldman Sachs Group Inc. and Morgan Stanley ... plunged the most ever. Yields on three-month Treasury bills ... and a measure of corporate borrowing costs surged above the level seen during the crash of 1987." (−1 for Treasury Bill Yield)

*Treasury Bond*

"'The decline in interest rates ignited the stock market's rally and then computer buy orders kicked in,' said Jon Groveman, president of Ladenburg, Thalmann & Co. 'The market just took off when long-term interest rates fell below 7%,' he said." (−1 for Treasury Bond Yield)

*Treasury Note*

"U.S. stocks rallied, led by banking and energy shares, as a decline in 10-year Treasuries eased concern record government debt sales will trigger higher borrowing costs and oil climbed to a six-month high." (−1 for Treasury Bond Yield)

**International Trade**

*Tariffs*

"General Electric Co. and Boeing Co. fell after the government imposed new tariffs on Chinese imports, heightening concern trade tensions will strain U.S. exports." (−1 for Tariffs)

*Trade Agreements*

"U.S. stocks closed higher, as confidence in the economy was bolstered by expectations the North American Free Trade Agreement will pass and better-than-expected semiconductor sales for October." (+1 for Trade Agreement)

**Macroeconomic Activity**

*Construction Spending*

"U.S. stocks rose, sending the Dow Jones Industrial Average to a record, as biotechnology and energy companies rallied and data on construction spending boosted confidence in the economy." (+1 for Construction Spending)

*Consumer Confidence*

"U.S. stocks fell for a fourth day in five as disappointing manufacturing and consumer confidence reports stoked concern that economic and profit growth will slow." (+1 for Consumer Confidence)

*Consumer Spending*

"U.S. stocks rose for the first day in four as a report showing an increase in consumer spending bolstered confidence that the economy and earnings will grow fast enough to warrant further gains in benchmark indexes." (+1 for Consumer Spending)

*Durables Output*

"U.S. stocks gained after the government said orders for everything from computers to air conditioners rose in July, exceeding economists' forecasts." (+1 for Durables Output)

*Economy*

"There are competing forces at work out there, and the one that's winning today is that the economy is extraordinarily robust and that's a good environment for corporate earnings." (+1 for Economy)

*Employment*

"U.S. stocks soared after a government report showed new jobs and wages grew less than expected in May." (+1 for Employment)

*Factory Orders*

"U.S. stocks advanced, with the Standard & Poor's 500 Index rebounding from its biggest drop since June, as investors assessed corporate earnings and data showing factory orders fell less than estimated in December." (+1 for Factory Orders)

*GDP Growth*

"U.S. stocks fell, [after] the government reported first-quarter economic growth was slower than previous estimates." (+1 for GDP Growth)

*Index of Leading Economic Indicators*

"Stocks opened higher ... Gains accelerated after the Conference Board's index of leading economic indicators climbed 1.2 percent." (+1 for Index of Leading Economic Indicators)

*Industrial Production*

"Stocks also declined as reports on wholesale prices and industrial production spurred concern the Federal Reserve will unwind stimulus measures. U.S. industrial production increased 0.8 percent in November, more than estimated and the most in three months." (−1 for Industrial Production)

*Jobless Claims*

"U.S. stocks fell, trimming the market's biggest yearly gain since 2003, as a decrease in jobless claims added to evidence the economy is improving enough to allow the Federal Reserve to withdraw more stimulus." (+1 for Jobless Claims)

*Manufacturing Activity*
"U.S. stocks dropped, leaving the Dow Jones Industrial Average with its first weekly decline since June, as ... a gauge of manufacturing fell short of economists' forecasts." (+1 for Manufacturing Activity)

*Personal Income*
"Share prices were also hurt by a government report showing consumers' incomes increased less than forecast in July." (+1 for Personal Income)

*Productivity*
"U.S. stocks surged, sending the Dow Jones Industrial Average to its biggest gain since July, as jobless claims and worker productivity beat estimates." (+1 for Productivity)

*Retail Sales National Level*
"U.S. stocks fell, sending the Standard & Poor's 500 Index to a fourth straight loss, as a decline in American retail sales and slump in copper prices spurred concern that global growth is slowing." (+1 for Retail Sales National)

*Service Sector Activity*
"U.S. stocks fell, dragging the Standard & Poor's 500 Index down from a nine-month high, after reports on job losses and service industries were worse than economists estimated ... Equities extended losses as the Institute for Supply Management's index of non-manufacturing businesses, which make up almost 90 percent of the economy, fell to 46.4 from 47 in June. Fifty is the dividing line between growth and contraction." (+1 for Service Sector Activity)

*Unemployment Rate*
"Stocks retreated after the Labor Department said the economy lost 44,000 jobs last month, the sixth straight decline, and the unemployment rate fell to 6.2 percent from 6.4 percent in June. On average, economists predicted the creation of 10,000 jobs and a jobless rate of 6.3 percent, according to a Bloomberg poll." (+1 for Unemployment Rate)

**Oil Market**
*Crude Oil Prices*
"The U.S. stock market posted its first advance in four days after a rally in oil prices improved earnings prospects for fuel producers." (+1 for Crude Oil Prices)

*Oil Supply*

"Exxon Mobil Corp. and Schlumberger Ltd. led gains in all 39 Standard & Poor's 500 Index energy shares after oil topped $65 a barrel as OPEC left production quotas unchanged." (−1 for Oil Supply)

**Rest of World**

*All of the Disaggregated Fundamental Factors for Foreign*

"U.S. stocks suffered their biggest loss since the Oct. 27 market rout as Russia's debt defaults and weakening currency sent markets around the world tumbling." (−1 for Rest of World)

**Sales**

*Auto Sales*

"General Motors Co. jumped 3.6 percent after a surprise sales gain in the auto industry's best month since July 2006." (+1 for Auto Sales)

*Firm or Industry Revenues*

"U.S. stocks fell, finishing their fourth losing week in five, after Goldman, Sachs & Co. said demand for semiconductor equipment may weaken." (+1 for Firm Sales)

## B.8.2   Psychological Considerations – With and Without Fundamentals

*Concern*

"'People are nervous about Brazil, and when they have a serious concern they sell the biggest gainers,' said Anthony Conroy, director of equity trading at BT Global Asset Management." (+1 for Concern)

*Confidence*

"'When your government is in total turmoil, your confidence goes down the chute,' said Cummins Catherwood, a managing director of Philadelphia-based Rutherford, Brown & Catherwood, which oversees $570 million. 'When your confidence goes down the chute, you're not going to pay 30 times earnings for GE.'" (+1 for Confidence (and Government))

*Crowd Psychology*

"'Feels like we're on the edge of a panic to me,' said Jeffrey Saut, who oversees $33.7 billion as chief investment strategist at Raymond James & Associates in

St. Petersburg, Florida. 'In our business, psychology is everything and psychology has changed real quick on Wall Street.' " (+1 for Psychology)

### Fear/Pessimism

"And fear plays a role. 'The market goes through waves of euphoria and pessimism,' said Victor Niederhoffer, an independent trader in Weston, Connecticut. 'During pessimism, people refuse to take anything for granted, and they hurt companies with a speculative component to their values – like computer companies.' " (+1 for Fear/Pessimism)

### Exuberance

"U.S. stocks surged, pushing the Dow Jones Industrial Average through 8000 ... It's a time of great exuberance for investors. All mountains have peaks." (+1 for Exuberance)

### Fear

"'People have lost faith in everything,' said Philip Orlando, who helps manage $350 billion as chief equity market strategist at Federated Investors Inc. in New York. 'We're dealing with an investment community of atheists right now. Valuations no longer matter.' ... 'This is what happens when the contagion of fear spreads,' said Quincy Krosby, who helps manage about $380 billion as chief investment strategist at the Hartford in Hartford, Connecticut. 'No one is paying attention to fundamentals. People are very, very scared. Ultimately investors decide to sell.'" (+1 for Fear)

### Mania

"Internet mania carried Lycos Inc., Yahoo! Inc. and Egghead.com Inc. to all-time highs." (+1 for Mania)

### Optimism

"Prices got a boost from optimism that an improving U.S. economy would spur business spending and corporate profits, which exceeded analysts' estimates on average for the second quarter." (+1 for Psychology with Macroeconomic Activity and Dividends or Earnings)

### Overreaction

"Stocks tumbled for a second week as investors questioned whether the Federal Reserve will lift rates too far to curtail inflation. 'There's definitely an overreaction in the market,' said Ben Halliburton, who manages $430 million as chief investment officer of Tradition Capital Management in Summit, New Jersey. 'Inflation remains well under control.' " (+1 for Overreaction with Inflation Rates)

*Panic*
"Some people are starting to say, 'Get me out at any price.' We've started to see some panic, which feeds on itself. People who bought in the first two weeks of the year have sizable losses in these." (+1 for Panic)

*Sentiment*
"'The market is driven primarily by trader and investor emotion and sentiment,' Michael James, a Los Angeles-based managing director of equity trading at Wedbush Securities Inc., said in a phone interview. 'All that's going to remain consistent in the short term is that volatility is going to continue and that you're going to have significant swings just based on trader sentiment, without any specific data points.' " (+1 for Emotion/Sentiment)

*Underreaction*
"Today's decline 'is a delayed reaction to Greenspan's comments from yesterday,' said Peter Coolidge, head of equity trading at Brean Murray & Co. 'Investors are starting to take to heart that interest rates are going higher, and that's bad for stocks.' " (+1 for Underreaction)

*Worry*
"'The consumer prices report is scaring people up a bit,' said Tom Schrader, head of listed trading at Legg Mason Wood Walker Inc. in Baltimore. 'Sometimes you get the psychology during earnings season that this is as good as it's going to get. People are worrying that the Fed's moves are going to slow the economy.' " (+1 for Psychology with Interest Rates and Macroeconomic Activity)

## B.8.3   *Technical Trading Momentum Considerations*

*Bandwagon*
"The stock market also was buoyed by the surge of demand that often accompanies the end of a quarter, traders said. 'Institutions don't want to get caught with too much cash. They're paid to invest it. A lot of people are scrambling to mask some of that performance or just jump on the bandwagon,' he said. 'We all do it.' " (+1 for Bandwagon)

*Chartism*

"'We walked our way up to that level again and then when Bernanke got done talking, we didn't go through it,' Tapley said. 'Since we're not going up, we've got to go down. It seems to me like it's technical-driven.'" (+1 for Chartism)

*Market Momentum*

"It's just money chasing stocks at this point, anticipating the market making a new high and then carrying forward on its own momentum." (+1 for Momentum)

*Momentum Traders*

"The Nasdaq extended gains after 1 pm surging more than 2 percentage points in an hour, as 'momentum' investors, or those who make short term bets on a stock's direction, rushed to buy shares, traders said." (+1 for Momentum Traders)

*Moving Average*

"International Business machines Corp. led the Dow average's drop after falling below its 50-day moving average ... accounting for all of the Dow average's decline." (+1 for Moving Average)

## B.8.4   *Technical Trading Nonmomentum Considerations*

*End of Quarter Effect*

"The stock market also was buoyed by the surge of demand that often accompanies the end of a quarter, traders said. 'Institutions don't want to get caught with too much cash,' said Peter DaPuzzo, senior managing director at Cantor, Fitzgerald & Co. 'They're paid to invest it.'" (+1 for End of Quarter Effect)

*End of Year Effect*

"'We saw no fundamental reason for that drop,' said Michael Nasto, the senior trader at U.S. Global Investors Inc., which manages about $2.5 billion in San Antonio. 'We did see some large selling at the close. That could be for a variety of reasons as we approach the year-end.'" (+1 for End of Year Effect)

*Friday Effect*

"Analysts said today's rout was accentuated by the day of the week on which it occurred. Many U.S. investors cut their exposure to stocks ahead of the weekend rather than gamble that the status quo in Asia would be maintained. 'Here it is Friday afternoon; [investors] don't know what they might be looking at over the weekend, and they've decided to sell.'" (+1 for Friday Effect)

*Giving Back Effect*

"U.S. stocks declined today, breaking a string of record highs in 1994, as investors cashed in gains before tomorrow's crucial report on wholesale prices. 'It's a predictable backlash,' said Jim Benning, a trader at BT Brokerage. 'We were up so much in the past few days.' " (+1 for Giving Back Effect)

*Holiday Effect*

"Most of the losses occurred in the last hour of the session, as investors took advantage of the last full day of trading before the Christmas holiday to raise cash by locking in gains or selling stocks that have declined." (+1 for Holiday Effect)

*January Effect*

"Money typically flows into the market in early January from year-end bonuses and reinvestments by investors who sold stocks or mutual funds for tax purposes late the previous year ... Cash is coming in and we're putting the money right to work." (+1 for January Effect)

*Firm Added to Index*

"Today, everything was exaggerated by the volatility due to the Russell rebalance. It's a once-a-year event and we will probably erase it on Monday." (+1 for Firm Added to Index)

*Profit Taking*

"'You had two euphoric days on Thursday and Friday, so it's not surprising to see some profit-taking,' said Altabef of Matix Asset Advisors." (+1 for Profit Taking)

*Triple Witching*

"U.S. stocks closed broadly lower after a sell-off triggered by today's quarterly expiration of stock options and stock-index options and futures sent the market reeling in the final hour." (+1 for Triple Witching)

# APPENDIX C  *RavenPack* Terms for Event Output Record

(i) **TIMESTAMP_UTC**: The Date/Time (YYYY-MM-DD hh:mm:ss.sss) at which the news item was received by *RavenPack* servers in Coordinated Universal Time (UTC).

(ii) **ENTITY_NAME**: The official canonical name of the entity identified by the RP_ENTITY_ID.

(iii) **ENTITY_TYPE**: The type of entity associated with a particular RP_ENTITY_ID from five entity types:
1. COMP (Company): Business organization that may be traded directly on an exchange.
2. ORGA (Organization): Nonbusiness organization such as a government, central bank, not-for-profit, terrorist organization, etc.
3. CURR (Currency): Currencies of all financial and industrial countries.
4. CMDT (Commodity): Exchange traded commodities such as crude oil and soy.
5. PLCE (Place): Towns, cities, and countries.

(iv) **RP_ENTITY_ID**: A unique and permanent entity identifier assigned by *RavenPack* comprised of six alphanumeric characters.

(v) **POSITION_NAME**: The position held by an individual within the entity involved in a specific news event.

(vi) **RP_POSITION_ID**: A unique and permanent identifier for positions assigned by *RavenPack* comprised of six alphanumeric characters.

(vii) **COUNTRY_CODE**: The two-character ISO-3166 country code associated with an entity. Companies and organizations are associated with the country of incorporation, currencies are associated with the country where the central bank resides, and commodities are global and not associated with specific countries, so their COUNTRY_CODE label is "XX."

(viii) **RELEVANCE**: A score between 0 and 100 that indicates how strongly related the entity is to the underlying news story, with higher values indicating greater relevance.

(ix) **TOPIC**: A subject or theme of events detected by *RavenPack*. The highest level of the *RavenPack* Event Taxonomy.

(x) **GROUP**: A collection of related events. The second highest level of the *RavenPack* Event Taxonomy.

(xi) **TYPE**: A class of events, the constituents of which share similar characteristics.

(xii) **SUB_TYPE**: A subdivision of a particular class of events.

(xiii) **PROPERTY**: A named attribute of an event such as an entity, role, or string extracted from a matched event type. When applicable, the role played by the entity in the event is detected and tagged.

(xiv) **EVALUATION_METHOD**: A period of time used to measure changes from previous levels in an event from the following three evaluation methods:
1. YOY: year-over-year change
2. QOQ: quarter-over-quarter change
3. MOM: month-over-month change

(xv) **MATURITY**: For events related to debt, this named attribute indicates the period of time for which a financial instrument remains outstanding represented by the following formats:
1. (1–7)-DAY: Maturity in days. Prefix is a number from 1 to 7, e.g. 2-DAY.
2. (1–4)-WK: Maturity in weeks. Prefix is a number from 1 to 4, e.g. 4-WK.
3. (1–12)-MTH: Maturity in months. Prefix is a number from 1 to 12, e.g. 9-MTH.
4. (1–4)-Q: Maturity in quarters. Prefix is a number from 1 to 4, e.g. 1-Q.
5. (1–50)-YR: Maturity in years. Prefix is a number from 1 to 50, e.g. 40-YR.

(xvi) **CATEGORY**: A unique tag to label, identify, and recognize a particular type of an entity-specific news event.

(xvii) **ESS – EVENT SENTIMENT SCORE**: A granular score between 0 and 100 that represents the news sentiment for a given entity by measuring various proxies sampled from the news. The score is determined by systematically matching stories typically categorized by financial experts as having short-term positive or negative financial or economic impact. The strength of the score is derived from a collection of surveys where industry experts with extensive backgrounds in finance and economics rated entity-specific events as conveying positive or negative sentiment and to what degree. Their ratings are encapsulated in an algorithm that generates a score ranging from 0 to 100 where 50 indicates neutral sentiment, values above 50 indicate positive sentiment, and values below 50 show negative sentiment.

(xviii) **AES – AGGREGATE EVENT SENTIMENT**: A granular score between 0 and 100 that represents the ratio of positive events reported on an entity compared to the total count of events (excluding neutral ones) measured over a rolling ninety-one-day window in a particular package (Dow Jones, Web, or PR Editions). Only news items that match a *RavenPack* event category receiving an ESS score are included in the computation of AES. An event with ESS > 50 is counted as a positive entry whereas one with ESS < 50 is counted as a negative entry. Events with ESS = 50 are considered neutral and excluded from the computation. Events matching "Order Imbalance" and "Insider Trading" categories are filtered out as these tend to add noise given their lack of sentiment, high volume, and frequency. Changes in the AES score, however, are observed only when an event category is matched or when one drops out of the ninety-one-day window calculation. AES leverages the *RavenPack* Taxonomy and is based on *RavenPack*'s Expert Consensus methodology.

(xix) **AEV – AGGREGATE EVENT VOLUME**: A value that represents the count of events for an entity (excluding neutral ones) measured over a rolling ninety-one-day window in a particular package (Dow Jones, Web, or PR Editions). Only news items that match a *RavenPack* event category receiving an ESS score are included in the computation of AEV. Both events with an ESS score above and below 50 are counted by AEV, effectively signaling the volume of highly relevant news on the entity over the past ninety-one days. Events with ESS = 50 are considered neutral and excluded from the computation. Events matching "Order Imbalance" and "Insider Trading" categories are filtered out as these tend to add noise given their lack of sentiment, high volume, and frequency. Changes in the AEV value, however, are observed only when a new event category is matched or when it drops out of the ninety-one-day window calculation. AEV leverages the *RavenPack* Taxonomy and is based on *RavenPack*'s Expert Consensus methodology.

(xx) **ENS – EVENT NOVELTY SCORE**: A score between 0 and 100 that represents how "new" or novel a news event is within a twenty-four-hour time window across all news stories with news events in a particular package (Dow Jones, Web, or PR Editions). Any two stories that match the same event for the same entities will be considered similar according to ENS. The first story reporting a categorized event about one or more entities is considered to be the most novel and receives a score of 100. Subsequent stories from the same package about the same event for the same entities receive scores following a decay function whose values are (100 75 56 42 32 24 18 13 10 8 6 4 3 2 2 1 1 1 1 0 ...) based on the number of stories in the past twenty-four-hour window. If a news event is published more than twenty-four hours after any other similar news event, it will again be considered novel and will start a separate chain with a score of 100.

(xxi) **ENS_SIMILARITY_GAP**: The number of days since a similar event was detected in this RavenPack News Analytics (RPNA) edition (Dow Jones, Web, or PR Editions). Values range between 0.00000 and 100.00000 inclusive. The value 100.00000 means that the most recent similar event occurred 100 or more days in the past. The value 0.00000 means a similar event exists with the exact same timestamp.

(xxii) **ENS_KEY – EVENT NOVELTY KEY**: An alphanumeric identifier that provides a way to chain or relate stories about the same categorized event for the same entities. The ENS_KEY corresponds to the RP_STORY_ID of the first news event in the sequence of similar events. The identifier allows a user to track similar stories reporting on the same event about the same entities. As with ENS, for two events to receive the same ENS_KEY they must be published within twenty-four hours of one another. However, the overall time range of a chain may extend beyond twenty-four hours.

(xxiii) **ENS_ELAPSED – EVENT NOVELTY ELAPSED TIME**: The number of milliseconds between the first event and the current event in an event novelty chain. The first event in a chain will always be given a value of zero milliseconds (ENS_ELAPSED = 0). Subsequent events in the same event novelty chain will receive higher values indicating the number of milliseconds elapsed since the first news story reporting the event. ENS_ELAPSED is only based on news stories from a particular package (Dow Jones, Web, or PR Editions).

(xxiv) **G_ENS – GLOBAL EVENT NOVELTY SCORE**: A score between 0 and 100 that represents how "new" or novel a news event is within a twenty-four-hour time window across all news providers covered by *RavenPack*. Any two stories that match the same event for the same entities will be considered similar according to G_ENS. The first story reporting a categorized event about one or more entities is considered to be the most novel and receives a score of 100. Subsequent stories from any news provider covered by *RavenPack* about the same event for the same entities receive scores following a decay function whose values are (100 75 56 42 32 24 18 13 10 8 6 4 3 2 2 1 1 1 1 0 ...) based on the number of stories in the past twenty-four-hour window.

(xxv) **G_ENS_SIMILARITY_GAP**: The number of days since a similar event was detected across all product editions (Dow Jones, Web, or PR Editions). Values range between 0.00000 and 100.00000 inclusive. The value 100.00000 means that the most recent similar event occurred 100 or more days in the past. The value 0.00000 means a similar event exists with the exact same timestamp.

(xxvi) **G_ENS_KEY – GLOBAL EVENT NOVELTY KEY**: An alphanumeric identifier that provides a way to chain or relate stories about the same categorized event for the same entities across all news providers covered by *RavenPack*. The G_ENS_KEY corresponds to the RP_STORY_ID of the first news story in the sequence of similar events, across all news providers covered by *RavenPack*. The identifier allows a user to track similar stories reporting on the same event about the same entities across all news providers covered by *RavenPack*. As with G_ENS, for two events to receive the same G_ENS_KEY they must be published within twenty-four hours of one another. However, the overall time range of a chain may extend beyond twenty-four hours.

(xxvii) **G_ENS_ELAPSED – GLOBAL EVENT NOVELTY ELAPSED TIME**: The number of milliseconds between the first event and the current event in an event novelty chain across all news providers covered by *RavenPack*. The first event in a chain will always be given a value of zero milliseconds (G_ENS_ELAPSED = 0). Subsequent events in the same event novelty chain will receive higher values indicating the number of milliseconds elapsed since the first event. G_ENS_ELAPSED is based on news stories from all providers covered by *RavenPack*.

(xxviii) **EVENT_SIMILARITY_KEY**: A unique thirty-two-character key that identifies similar stories in the RPNA data. All similar stories across the entire archive and those arriving on the real-time feed share the same EVENT_SIMILARITY_KEY.

(xxix) **NEWS_TYPE – TYPE OF NEWS STORY**: Classifies the type of news story into one of five categories:

1. HOT-NEWS-FLASH: A news article composed of a headline and no body text marked as breaking news during the editorial process.

2. NEWS-FLASH: A news article composed of a headline and no body text.

3. FULL-ARTICLE: A news article composed of both a headline and one or more paragraphs of mostly textual material.

4. PRESS-RELEASE: A corporate announcement originated by an entity and distributed via a news provider.

5. TABULAR-MATERIAL: A news article composed of both a headline and one or more segments of mostly tabular data.

(xxx) **SOURCE**: A unique and permanent news source identifier assigned by *RavenPack*. Every news provider tracked is assigned a unique identifier comprised of six alphanumeric characters. This field can be linked to the "Source Mapping" file for additional details about the publication name and type, coverage dates, and trustworthiness of each provider.

(xxxi) **RP_STORY_ID – RAVENPACK UNIQUE STORY IDENTIFIER**: An alphanumeric character identifier to uniquely identify each news story analyzed. This value is unique across all records. Example: 1FB2B3F5E99C4D3BCF59FDB3E8 C8C9BD

(xxxii) **PRODUCT_KEY**: Identifies which subscription package contains the record. Its value can be one of the following:

DJ-EQ: Dow Jones Edition – Equities

DJ-GM: Dow Jones Edition – Global Macro

WE-EQ: - Web Edition – Equities

WE-GM: Web Edition – Global Macro

PR-EQ: Press Release Edition – Equities

PR-GM: Press Release Edition – Global Macro

# APPENDIX D   Unscheduled Events from *RavenPack*

**BUSINESS**

**Acquisitions–Mergers**

acquisition-acquiree; acquisition-acquirer; acquisition-bid-rejected-acquiree; acquisition-bid-rejected-acquirer; acquisition-blocked-acquiree; acquisition-blocked-acquirer; acquisition-delayed-acquiree; acquisition-delayed-acquirer; acquisition-failed-acquiree; acquisition-failed-acquirer; acquisition-interest-acquiree; acquisition-interest-acquirer; acquisition-merger-termination-fee; acquisition-opposition-acquiree; acquisition-opposition-acquirer; acquisition-regulatory-scrutiny-acquiree; acquisition-regulatory-scrutiny-acquirer; acquisition-regulatory-scrutiny-authority; acquisition-rumor-acquiree; acquisition-rumor-acquirer; acquisition-rumor-denied-acquiree; acquisition-rumor-denied-acquirer; merger; merger-blocked; merger-delayed; merger-failed; merger-opposition; merger-regulatory-scrutiny; merger-regulatory-scrutiny-authority; merger-rumor; merger-rumor-denied; stake-acquiree; stake-acquirer; unit-acquisition-acquiree; unit-acquisition-acquirer; unit-acquisition-bid-rejected-acquiree; unit-acquisition-bid-rejected-acquirer; unit-acquisition-blocked-acquiree; unit-acquisition-blocked-acquirer; unit-acquisition-delayed-acquiree; unit-acquisition-delayed-acquirer; unit-acquisition-failed-acquiree; unit-acquisition-failed-acquirer; unit-acquisition-interest-acquiree; unit-acquisition-interest-acquirer; unit-acquisition-opposition-acquiree; unit-acquisition-opposition-acquirer; unit-acquisition-regulatory-scrutiny-acquiree; unit-acquisition-regulatory-scrutiny-acquirer; unit-acquisition-regulatory-scrutiny-authority; unit-acquisition-rumor-acquiree; unit-acquisition-rumor-acquirer; unit-acquisition-rumor-denied-acquiree; unit-acquisition-rumor-denied-acquirer; unit-acquisition-termination-fee

**Analyst Ratings**

analyst-ratings-change-negative; analyst-ratings-change-negative-rater; analyst-ratings-change-neutral; analyst-ratings-change-neutral-rater;

analyst-ratings-change-positive; analyst-ratings-change-positive-rater;
analyst-ratings-history-negative; analyst-ratings-history-negative-rater;
analyst-ratings-history-neutral; analyst-ratings-history-neutral-rater;
analyst-ratings-history-positive; analyst-ratings-history-positive-rater;
analyst-ratings-set-negative; analyst-ratings-set-negative-rater;
analyst-ratings-set-neutral; analyst-ratings-set-neutral-rater;
analyst-ratings-set-positive; analyst-ratings-set-positive-rater

**Assets**
asset-down; asset-sale; asset-up; assets; commodity-buy; commodity-buy-target;
commodity-offer; commodity-offer-target; commodity-sell;
commodity-sell-target; company-for-sale; facility-close; facility-close-location;
facility-close-output; facility-fire-disaster; facility-open; facility-open-location;
facility-open-output; facility-sale; facility-sale-location; facility-sale-output;
facility-upgrade; facility- upgrade-location; facility-upgrade-output; fire-sales;
headquarters-change; headquarters-change-location; patent-filing;
patent-filing-authority; patent-filing-rejected; patent-filing-rejected-authority;
patent-revoked; patent-revoked-authority; theft; vandalism

**Bankruptcy**
bankruptcy; bankruptcy-exit; bankruptcy-fears; bankruptcy-unit

**Commodity-Prices**
commodity-futures-gain; commodity-futures-loss; commodity-price-gain;
commodity-price-loss

**Credit**
credit-extension-provider; credit-extension-recipient; debt;
debt-extension-provider; debt-extension-recipient; debt-increase; debt-reduction;
debt- renegotiation; debt-restructuring; debt-restructuring-approval;
debt-restructuring-considered; debt-restructuring-failed;
debt-restructuring-rejection; debt-shelf-registration;
deposit-facility-use-down-depositor; deposit-facility-use-down-facilitator;
deposit-facility-use-up-depositor; deposit-facility-use-up-facilitator;
government-bailout; government-bailout-authority; government-bailout-denied;
government-bailout-denied-authority; government-bailout-request;
government-bailout-request-authority; loan-provider; loan-recipient; mixed-shelf
registration; note-acquisition; note-sale

## Credit Ratings

credit-rating-action; credit-rating-action-rater; credit-rating-affirmation; credit-rating-affirmation-rater; credit-rating-confirmation; credit-rating-confirmation-rater; credit-rating-corrected; credit-rating-corrected-rater; credit-rating-downgrade; credit-rating-downgrade-rater; credit-rating-expected; credit-rating-expected-rater; credit-rating-matured; credit-rating-matured-rater; credit-rating-no-rating; credit-rating-no-rating-rater; credit-rating-outlook-developing; credit-rating-outlook-developing-rater; credit-rating-outlook-negative; credit-rating-outlook-negative-rater; credit-rating-outlook-positive; credit-rating-outlook-positive-rater; credit-rating-outlook-revision; credit-rating-outlook-revision-rater; credit-rating-outlook-stable; credit-rating-outlook-stable-rater; credit-rating-outlook-unchanged; credit-rating-outlook-unchanged-rater; credit-rating-paid-in-full; credit-rating-paid-in-full-rater; credit-rating-provisional-rating; credit-rating-provisional-rating-rater; credit-rating-publish; credit-rating-publish-rater; credit-rating-reinstated; credit-rating-reinstated-rater; credit-rating-revision-enhancement; credit-rating-revision-enhancement-rater; credit-rating-set; credit-rating-set-rater; credit-rating-unchanged; credit-rating-unchanged-rater; credit-rating-upgrade; credit-rating-upgrade-rater; credit-rating-watch; credit-rating-watch-developing; credit-rating-watch-developing-rater; credit-rating-watch-negative; credit-rating-watch-negative-rater; credit-rating-watch-positive; credit-rating-watch-positive-rater; credit-rating-watch-rater; credit-rating-watch-removed; credit-rating-watch-removed-rater; credit-rating-watch-unchanged; credit-rating-watch-unchanged-rater; credit-rating-withdrawn-rating; credit-rating-withdrawn-rating-rater

## Dividends

dividend-guidance; dividend-guidance-down; dividend-guidance-up; dividend-suspended

## Earnings

earnings-early-release; earnings-guidance-suspended; earnings-misstatement; earnings-misstatement-rater; earnings-per-share-guidance; earnings-revision; earnings-revision-down; earnings-revision-down-rater; earnings-revision-rater; earnings-revision-up; earnings-revision-up-rater

**Equity Actions**

bought-deal; buyback-suspended; buybacks; capex-guidance;
capex-guidance-down; capex-guidance-up; capital-increase;
capital-increase-approved; equity-shelf-registration; expenses-charge; fundraising;
going-private; investment-investor; investment-location; investment-recipient;
ipo; ipo-considered; ipo-delayed; ipo-extended; ipo-failed; ipo-issuance-decrease;
ipo-issuance-increase; ipo-opposed; ipo-price-decrease; ipo-price-increase;
ipo-pricing; ipo-regulatory-approval; ipo-regulatory-approval-authority;
ipo-regulatory-scrutiny; ipo-regulatory-scrutiny-authority; ipo-rumor;
ipo-rumor-denied; ipo-unit; ipo-unit-considered; ipo-unit-delayed;
ipo-unit-extended; ipo-unit-failed; ipo-unit-rumor; ipo-unit-rumor-denied;
name-change; ownership-decrease-held; ownership-decrease-owner;
ownership-increase-held; ownership-increase-owner; private-placement;
private-placement-suspended; public-offering; public-offering-delayed;
public-offering-suspended; reorganization; reorganization-approval;
reorganization-considered; reorganization-costs; reorganization-delayed;
reorganization-denied; reorganization-failed; reorganization-rejection;
reorganization-savings; reorganization-unit; reorganization-unit-approval;
reorganization-unit-rejection; reverse-stock-splits; rights-issue;
rights-issue-suspended; savings; savings-guidance; shareholder-rights-plan;
shareholder-rights-plan-suspended; spin-off; spin-off-suspended; stock-splits;
trading-delisting; trading-delisting-review; trading-halt; trading-resumed

**Exploration**

drilling; drilling-authority; drilling-commodity; drilling-location;
drilling-suspended; drilling-suspended-authority; drilling-suspended-commodity;
drilling-suspended-location; resource-discovery; resource-discovery-authority;
resource-discovery-commodity; resource-discovery-location

**Indexes**

index-delisting; index-delisting-issuer; index-listing; index-listing-issuer;
index-rebalance; index-rebalance-decrease; index-rebalance-decrease-issuer;
index-rebalance-increase; index-rebalance-increase-issuer; index-rebalance-issuer

**Industrial Accidents**

aircraft-accident; aircraft-accident-commodity; automobile-accident;
automobile-accident-commodity; dam-accident; dam-accident-commodity;
facility-accident; facility-accident-commodity; facility-accident-contained;

facility-accident-contained-commodity; facility-accident-contained-location;
facility-accident-location; factory-accident; factory-accident-commodity;
force-majeure; force-majeure-commodity; force-majeure-lifted;
force-majeure-lifted-commodity; force-majeure-lifted-location;
force-majeure-location; mine-accident; mine-accident-commodity;
pipeline-accident; pipeline-accident-commodity; platform-accident;
platform-accident-commodity; power-outage; power-outage-commodity;
power-plant-accident; power-plant-accident-commodity;
public-transport-accident; public-transport-accident-commodity;
refinery-accident; refinery-accident-commodity; spill; spill-commodity;
tanker-accident; tanker-accident-commodity

**Insider Trading**
insider-buy; insider-gift; insider-sell; insider-sell-registration; insider-surrender;
insider-trading-lawsuit-defendant; insider-trading-lawsuit-plaintiff
**Investor Relations** major-shareholders-disclosure

**Labor Issues**
executive-appointment; executive-compensation; executive-death;
executive-firing; executive-health; executive-resignation; executive-salary;
executive-salary-cut; executive-salary-increase; executive-scandal;
executive-shares-options; hirings; hirings-location; layoffs; strike; strike-ended;
strike-ended-location; strike-location; union-pact; union-pact-rejected;
workforce-salary-decrease; workforce-salary-increase

**Marketing**
campaign-ad-release; campaign-ad-retired

**Order Imbalances**
buy-imbalance; delay-imbalance; mkt-close-buy-imbalance;
mkt-close-sell-imbalance; mkt-open-buy-imbalance; mkt-open-sell-imbalance;
no-imbalance; no-mkt-close-imbalance; sell-imbalance

**Partnerships** joint-venture; joint-venture-terminated; partnership;
partnership-terminated

**Price Targets**
price-target-downgrade; price-target-downgrade-rater; price-target-set;
price-target-set-rater; price-target-upgrade; price-target-upgrade-rater

**Products–Services**

award; business-combination; business-contract; business-contract-terminated; clinical-trials; clinical-trials-filed; clinical-trials-negative; clinical-trials-positive; clinical-trials-start; clinical-trials-suspended; demand-decrease; demand-decrease-commodity; demand-decrease-rater; demand-guidance-decrease; demand-guidance-decrease-commodity; demand-guidance-decrease-rater; demand-guidance-increase; demand-guidance-increase-commodity; demand-guidance-increase-rater; demand-guidance-unchanged; demand-guidance-unchanged-commodity; demand-guidance-unchanged-rater; demand-increase; demand-increase-commodity; demand-increase-rater; demand-unchanged; demand-unchanged-commodity; demand-unchanged-rater; fast-track-designation; government-contract; government contract-terminated; grant-provider; grant-recipient; market-entry; market-entry-location; market-guidance; market-guidance-commodity; market-guidance-down; market-guidance-down-commodity; market-guidance-up; market-guidance-up-commodity; market-share; market-share-gain; market-share-loss; orphan-drug-designation; orphan-drug-designation-authority; patient-enrollment-start; patient-enrollment-suspended; product-catastrophe; product-delayed; product-discontinued; product-outage; product-price-cut; product-price-raise; product-recall; product-resumed; product-side-effects; production-outlook; production-outlook-negative; production-outlook-positive; project-abandoned; regulatory-product-application; regulatory-product-application-authority; regulatory-product-application; regulatory-product-application-authority; regulatory-product-application-withdrawn; regulatory-product-application-withdrawn-authority; regulatory-product-approval-conditional; regulatory-product-approval-conditional-authority; regulatory-product-approval-denied; regulatory-product-approval-denied-authority; regulatory-product-approval-granted; regulatory-product-approval-granted-authority; regulatory-product-review-negative; regulatory-product-review-negative-authority; regulatory-product-review-positive; regulatory-product-review-positive-authority; regulatory-product-warning; regulatory-product-warning-authority; supply-decrease; supply-decrease-commodity; supply-decrease-rater; supply-guidance-decrease; supply-guidance-decrease-commodity; supply-guidance-decrease-rater; supply-guidance-increase;

supply-guidance-increase-commodity; supply-guidance-increase-rater; supply-guidance-unchanged; supply-guidance-unchanged-commodity; supply-guidance-unchanged-rater; supply-increase; supply-increase-commodity; supply-increase-rater; supply-unchanged; supply-unchanged-commodity; supply-unchanged-rater

### Regulatory
auditor-appointment; auditor-appointment-auditor; auditor-resignation; auditor-resignation-auditor; exchange-compliance; exchange-compliance-authority; exchange-noncompliance; exchange-noncompliance-authority; regulatory-investigation; regulatory-investigation-authority; regulatory-investigation-completed; regulatory-investigation-completed-authority; regulatory-investigation-completed-no-sanction; regulatory-investigation-completed-no-sanction-authority; regulatory-investigation-completed-sanction; regulatory-investigation-completed-sanction-authority; short-selling-ban; short-selling-ban-authority; short-selling-ban-lifted; short-selling-ban-lifted-authority

### Revenues
revenue-guidance; revenue-guidance-above-expectations; revenue-guidance-below-expectations; revenue-guidance-down; revenue-guidance-meet-expectations; revenue-guidance-up; same-store-sales-guidance; same-store-sales-guidance-down; same-store-sales-guidance-up

### Stock Prices
stock-gain; stock-loss

### Technical Analysis
relative-strength-index; relative-strength-index-overbought; relative-strength-index-oversold; relative-strength-index-rater; technical-price-level-resistance-bearish; technical-price-level-resistance-bullish; technical-price-level-resistance-rater; technical-price-level-support-bearish; technical-price-level-support-bullish; technical-price-level-support-rater; technical-view; technical-view-bearish; technical-view-bullish; technical-view-overbought; technical-view-oversold; technical-view-rater

## ECONOMY

### Balance of Payments

bop-guidance; bop-guidance-deficit; bop-guidance-deficit-rater;
bop-guidance-rater; bop-guidance-surplus; bop-guidance-surplus-rater;
current-account-guidance; current-account-guidance-deficit;
current-account-guidance-deficit-down;
current-account-guidance-deficit-down-rater;
current-account-guidance-deficit-rater; current-account-guidance-deficit-up;
current-account-guidance-deficit-up-rater; current-account-guidance-rater;
current-account-guidance-surplus; current-account-guidance-surplus-down;
current-account-guidance-surplus-down-rater;
current-account-guidance-surplus-rater; current-account-guidance-surplus-up;
current-account-guidance-surplus-up-rater; exports-guidance;
exports-guidance-down; exports-guidance-down-exporter;
exports-guidance-down-rater; exports-guidance-exporter; exports-guidance-rater;
exports-guidance-unchanged; exports-guidance-unchanged-exporter;
exports-guidance-unchanged-rater; exports-guidance-up;
exports-guidance-up-exporter; exports guidance-up-rater; imports-guidance;
imports-guidance-down; imports-guidance-down-importer;
imports-guidance-down-rater; imports-guidance-importer;
imports-guidance-rater; imports-guidance-unchanged;
imports-guidance-unchanged-importer; imports-guidance-unchanged-rater;
imports-guidance-up; imports-guidance-up-importer; imports-guidance-up-rater;
trade-balance-guidance; trade-balance-guidance-deficit;
trade-balance-guidance-deficit-down; trade-balance-guidance-deficit-down-rater;
trade-balance-guidance-deficit-rater; trade-balance-guidance-deficit-up;
trade-balance-guidance-deficit-up-rater; trade-balance-guidance-rater;
trade-balance-guidance-surplus; trade-balance-guidance-surplus-down;
trade-balance-guidance-surplus-down-rater; trade-balance-guidance-surplus-rater;
trade-balance-guidance-surplus-up; trade-balance-guidance-surplus-up-rater

### Business Activity

business-confidence-guidance; business-confidence-guidance-down;
business-confidence-guidance-down-rater; business-confidence-guidance-rater;
business-confidence-guidance-unchanged;
business-confidence-guidance-unchanged-rater; business-confidence-guidance-up;
business-confidence-guidance-up-rater

### Consumption

consumer-confidence-guidance; consumer-confidence-guidance-down; consumer-confidence-guidance-down-rater; consumer-confidence-guidance-rater; consumer-confidence-guidance-unchanged; consumer-confidence-guidance-unchanged-rater; consumer-confidence-guidance-up; consumer-confidence-guidance-up-rater; consumer-spending-guidance; consumer-spending-guidance-down; consumer-spending-guidance-down-rater; consumer-spending-guidance-rater; consumer-spending-guidance-unchanged; consumer-spending-guidance-unchanged-rater; consumer-spending-guidance-up; consumer-spending-guidance-up-rater; cpi-guidance; cpi-guidance-down; cpi-guidance-down-rater; cpi-guidance-rater; cpi-guidance-unchanged; cpi-guidance-unchanged-rater; cpi-guidance-up; cpi-guidance-up-rater; deflation-guidance; deflation-guidance-down; deflation-guidance-down-rater; deflation-guidance-rater; deflation-guidance-up; deflation-guidance-up-rater; durable-goods-guidance; durable-goods-guidance-down; durable-goods-guidance-down-rater; durable-goods-guidance-rater; durable-goods-guidance-unchanged; durable-goods-guidance-unchanged-rater; durable-good-guidance-up; durable-goods-guidance-up-rater; inflation-guidance; inflation-guidance-down; inflation-guidance-down-rater; inflation-guidance-rater; inflation-guidance-unchanged; inflation-guidance-unchanged-rater; inflation-guidance-up; inflation-guidance-up-rater; retail-sales-guidance; retail-sales-guidance-down; retail-sales-guidance-down-rater; retail-sales-guidance-rater; retail-sales-guidance-unchanged; retail-sales-guidance-unchanged-rater; retail-sales-guidance-up; retail-sales-guidance-up-rater

### Credit

sovereign-debt-guidance; sovereign-debt-guidance-down; sovereign-debt-guidance-down-rater; sovereign-debt-guidance-rater; sovereign-debt-guidance-unchanged; sovereign-debt-guidance-unchanged-rater; sovereign-debt-guidance-up; sovereign-debt-guidance-up-rater; sovereign-debt-purchases-guidance; sovereign-debt-purchases-guidance-buyer; sovereign-debt-purchases-guidance-decrease; sovereign-debt-purchases-guidance-decrease-buyer; sovereign-debt-purchases-guidance-decrease-rater; sovereign-debt-purchases-guidance-increase; sovereign-debt-purchases-guidance-increase-buyer; sovereign-debt-purchases-guidance-increase-rater;

sovereign-debt-purchases-guidance-rater;
sovereign-debt-purchases-guidance-unchanged;
sovereign-debt-purchases-guidance-unchanged-buyer;
sovereign-debt-purchases-guidance-unchanged-rater; treasury-bill-yield;
treasury-bill-yield-down; treasury-bill-yield-down-issuer;
treasury-bill-yield-issuer; treasury-bill-yield-unchanged;
treasury-bill-yield-unchanged-issuer; treasury-bill-yield-up;
treasury-bill-yield-up-issuer; treasury-bond-yield; treasury-bond-yield-down;
treasury-bond-yield-down-issuer; treasury-bond-yield-issuer;
treasury-bond-yield-unchanged; treasury-bond-yield-unchanged-issuer;
treasury-bond-yield-up; treasury-bond-yield-up-issuer; treasury-note-yield;
treasury-note-yield-down; treasury-note-yield-down-issuer;
treasury-note-yield-issuer; treasury-note-yield-unchanged;
treasury-note-yield-unchanged-issuer; treasury-note-yield-up;
treasury-note-yield-up-issuer

**Domestic Product**
economic-growth; economic-growth-down; economic-growth-down-rater;
economic-growth-guidance; economic-growth-guidance-down;
economic-growth-guidance-down-rater; economic-growth-guidance-rater;
economic-growth-guidance-unchanged;
economic-growth-guidance-unchanged-rater; economic-growth-guidance-up;
economic-growth-guidance-up-rater; economic-growth-rater;
economic-growth-unchanged; economic-growth-unchanged-rater;
economic-growth-up; economic-growth-up-rater; gdp-guidance;
gdp-guidance-down; gdp-guidance-down-rater; gdp-guidance-rater;
gdp-guidance-unchanged; gdp-guidance-unchanged-rater; gdp-guidance-up;
gdp-guidance-up-rater; real-gdp-guidance; real-gdp-guidance-down;
real-gdp-guidance-down-rater; real-gdp-guidance-rater;
real-gdp-guidance-unchanged; real-gdp-guidance-unchanged-rater;
real-gdp-guidance-up; real-gdp-guidance-up-rater; recession; recession-guidance;
recession-guidance-rater; recession-rater; stagflation; stagflation-guidance;
stagflation-guidance-rater; stagflation-rater; stagnation; stagnation-guidance;
stagnation-guidance-rater; stagnation-rater

**Employment**
employment-guidance; employment-guidance-down;
employment-guidance-down-rater; employment-guidance-rater;
employment-guidance-unchanged; employment-guidance-unchanged-rater;

employment-guidance-up; employment-guidance-up-rater;
jobless-claims-guidance; jobless-claims-guidance-down;
jobless-claims-guidance-down-rater; jobless-claims-guidance-rater;
jobless-claims-guidance-unchanged; jobless-claims-guidance-unchanged-rater;
jobless-claims-guidance-up; jobless-claims-guidance-up-rater;
nonfarm-payrolls-guidance; nonfarm-payrolls-guidance-down;
nonfarm-payrolls-guidance-down-rater; nonfarm-payrolls-guidance-rater;
nonfarm-payrolls-guidance-unchanged;
nonfarm-payrolls-guidance-unchanged-rater; nonfarm-payrolls-guidance-up;
nonfarm-payrolls-guidance-up-rater; unemployment-guidance;
unemployment-guidance-down; unemployment-guidance-down-rater;
unemployment-guidance-rater; unemployment-guidance-unchanged;
unemployment-guidance-unchanged-rater; unemployment-guidance-up;
unemployment-guidance-up-rater

### Foreign Exchange

currency-adoption-guidance; currency-adoption-guidance-adopter;
currency-adoption-guidance-currency; currency-adoption-guidance-rater;
currency-guidance; currency-guidance-appreciate; currency-guidance-depreciate;
currency-guidance-rater; currency-rate; currency-rate-appreciate;
currency-rate-depreciate; currency-rate-rater; currency-valuation;
currency-valuation-devalue; currency-valuation-issuer;
currency-valuation-revalue

### Housing

home-sales-existing-guidance; home-sales-existing-guidance-down;
home-sales-existing-guidance-down-rater; home-sales-existing-guidance-rater;
home-sales-existing-guidance-unchanged;
home-sales-existing-guidance-unchanged-rater; home-sales-existing-guidance-up;
home-sales-existing-guidance-up-rater; home-sales-new-guidance;
home-sales-new-guidance-down; home-sales-new-guidance-down-rater;
home-sales-new-guidance-rater; home-sales-new-guidance-unchanged;
home-sales-new-guidance-unchanged-rater; home-sales-new-guidance-up;
home-sales-new-guidance-up-rater; house-prices-guidance;
house-prices-guidance-down; house-prices-guidance-down-rater;
house-prices-guidance-rater; house-prices-guidance-unchanged;
house-prices-guidance-unchanged-rater; house-prices-guidance-up;
house-prices-guidance-up-rater

**Interest Rates**

interest-rate-guidance; interest-rate-guidance-down;
interest-rate-guidance-down-rater; interest-rate-guidance-rater;
interest-rate-guidance-unchanged; interest-rate-guidance-unchanged-rater;
interest-rate-guidance-up; interest-rate-guidance-up-rater

**Production**

composite-pmi-guidance; composite-pmi-guidance-down;
composite-pmi-guidance-down-rater; composite-pmi-guidance-rater;
composite-pmi-guidance-unchanged; composite-pmi-guidance-unchanged-rater;
composite-pmi-guidance-up; composite-pmi-guidance-up-rater;
construction-pmi-guidance; construction-pmi-guidance-down;
construction-pmi-guidance-down-rater; construction-pmi-guidance-rater;
construction-pmi-guidance-unchanged;
construction-pmi-guidance-unchanged-rater; construction-pmi-guidance-up;
construction-pmi-guidance-up-rater; industrial-production-guidance;
industrial-production-guidance-down;
industrial-production-guidance-down-rater; industrial-production-guidance-rater;
industrial-production-guidance-unchanged;
industrial-production-guidance-unchanged-rater;
industrial-production-guidance-up; industrial-production-guidance-up-rater;
manufacturing-index-guidance; manufacturing-index-guidance-down;
manufacturing-index-guidance-down-rater; manufacturing-index-guidance-rater;
manufacturing-index-guidance-unchanged;
manufacturing-index-guidance-unchanged-rater;
manufacturing-index-guidance-up; manufacturing-index-guidance-up-rater;
manufacturing-pmi-guidance; manufacturing-pmi-guidance-down;
manufacturing-pmi-guidance-down-rater; manufacturing-pmi-guidance-rater;
manufacturing-pmi-guidance-unchanged;
manufacturing-pmi-guidance-unchanged-rater; manufacturing-pmi-guidance-up;
manufacturing-pmi-guidance-up-rater; nonmanufacturing-pmi-guidance;
nonmanufacturing-pmi-guidance-down;
nonmanufacturing-pmi-guidance-down-rater;
nonmanufacturing-pmi-guidance-rater;
nonmanufacturing-pmi-guidance-unchanged;
nonmanufacturing-pmi-guidance-unchanged-rater;
nonmanufacturing-pmi-guidance-up; nonmanufacturing-pmi-guidance-up-rater;
ppi-guidance; ppi-guidance-down; ppi-guidance-down-rater; ppi-guidance-rater;
ppi-guidance-unchanged; ppi-guidance-unchanged-rater; ppi-guidance-up;

ppi-guidance-up-rater; services-pmi-guidance; services-pmi-guidance-down;
services-pmi-guidance-down-rater; services-pmi-guidance-rater;
services-pmi-guidance-unchanged; services-pmi-guidance-unchanged-rater;
services-pmi-guidance-up; services-pmi-guidance-up-rater

**Public Finance**

austerity-measures; austerity-measures-rater; defense-budget-guidance;
defense-budget-guidance-down; defense-budget-guidance-down-rater;
defense-budget-guidance-rater; defense-budget-guidance-unchanged;
defense-budget-guidance-unchanged-rater; defense-budget-guidance-up;
defense-budget-guidance-up-rater; government-budget-guidance;
government-budget-guidance-deficit; government-budget-guidance-deficit-down;
government-budget-guidance-deficit-down-rater;
government-budget-guidance-deficit-rater;
government-budget-guidance-deficit-up;
government-budget-guidance-deficit-up-rater; government-budget-guidance-rater;
government-budget-guidance-surplus;
government-budget-guidance-surplus-down;
government-budget-guidance-surplus-down-rater;
government-budget-guidance-surplus-rater;
government-budget-guidance-surplus-up;
government-budget-guidance-surplus-up-rater

**Taxes**

corporation-tax; corporation-tax-authority; corporation-tax-decrease;
corporation-tax-decrease-authority; corporation-tax-guidance;
corporation-tax-guidance-authority; corporation-tax-guidance-decrease;
corporation-tax-guidance-decrease-authority;
corporation-tax-guidance-decrease-rater; corporation-tax-guidance-increase;
corporation-tax-guidance-increase-authority;
corporation-tax-guidance-increase-rater; corporation-tax-guidance-rater;
corporation-tax-guidance-unchanged;
corporation-tax-guidance-unchanged-authority;
corporation-tax-guidance-unchanged-rater; corporation-tax-increase;
corporation-tax-increase-authority; corporation-tax-unchanged;
corporation-tax-unchanged-authority; export-tax; export-tax-decrease;
export-tax-decrease-issuer; export-tax-guidance; export-tax-guidance-decrease;
export-tax-guidance-decrease-issuer; export-tax-guidance-decrease-rater;
export-tax-guidance-increase; export-tax-guidance-increase-issuer;

export-tax-guidance-increase-rater; export-tax-guidance-issuer;
export-tax-guidance-rater; export-tax-guidance-unchanged;
export-tax-guidance-unchanged-issuer; export-tax-guidance-unchanged-rater;
export-tax-increase; export-tax-increase-issuer; export-tax-issuer;
export-tax-unchanged; export-tax-unchanged-issuer; import-tax;
import-tax-decrease; import-tax-decrease-issuer; import-tax-guidance;
import-tax-guidance-decrease; import-tax-guidance-decrease-issuer;
import-tax-guidance-decrease-rater; import-tax-guidance-increase;
import-tax-guidance-increase-issuer; import-tax-guidance-increase-rater;
import-tax-guidance-issuer; import-tax-guidance-rater;
import-tax-guidance-unchanged; import-tax-guidance-unchanged-issuer;
import-tax-guidance-unchanged-rater; import-tax-increase;
import-tax-increase-issuer; import-tax-issuer; import-tax-unchanged;
import-tax-unchanged-issuer; tax-break; tax-break-authority; tax-break-ended;
tax-break-ended-authority; tax-break-guidance; tax-break-guidance-authority

## ENVIRONMENT
### Natural Disasters
animal-infestation; animal-infestation-warning;
animal-infestation-warning-lifted; avalanche; avalanche-warning;
avalanche-warning-lifted; blizzard; blizzard-warning; blizzard-warning-lifted;
cold-wave; cold-wave-warning; cold-wave-warning-lifted; cyclone;
cyclone-warning; cyclone-warning-lifted; drought; drought-warning;
drought-warning-lifted; earthquake; earthquake-warning;
earthquake-warning-lifted; flood; flood-warning; flood-warning-lifted; hail-storm;
hail-storm-warning; hail-storm-warning-lifted; heat-wave; heat-wave-warning;
heat-wave-warning-lifted; hurricane; hurricane-warning;
hurricane-warning-lifted; ice-storm; ice-storm-warning; ice-storm-warning-lifted;
landslide; landslide-warning; landslide-warning-lifted; monsoon;
monsoon-warning; monsoon-warning-lifted; sand-storm; sand-storm-warning;
sand-storm-warning-lifted; sink-hole; sink-hole-warning;
sink-hole-warning-lifted; snow-storm; snow-storm-warning;
snow-storm-warning-lifted; solar-flare; solar-flare-warning;
solar-flare-warning-lifted; storm; storm-warning; storm-warning-lifted;
thunder-storm; thunder-storm-warning; thunder-storm-warning-lifted; tornado;
tornado-warning; tornado-warning-lifted; tropical-storm; tropical-storm-warning;
tropical-storm-warning-lifted; tsunami; tsunami-warning;
tsunami-warning-lifted; typhoon; typhoon-warning; typhoon-warning-lifted;
volcanic-ash-cloud; volcanic-ash-cloud-warning;

volcanic-ash-cloud-warning-lifted; volcanic-eruption; volcanic-eruption-warning; volcanic-eruption-warning-lifted; water-shortage; water-shortage-warning; water-shortage-warning-lifted; wild-fire; wild-fire-warning; wild-fire-warning-lifted

## Pollution

air-pollution; air-pollution-down; air-pollution-down-polluter; air-pollution-down-rater; air-pollution-polluter; air-pollution-rater; air-pollution-up; air-pollution-up-polluter; air-pollution-up-rater; air-pollution-warning; air-pollution-warning-issuer; air-pollution-warning-lifted; air-pollution-warning-lifted-issuer; air-pollution-warning-lifted-polluter; air-pollution-warning-polluter; water-contamination; water-contamination-down; water-contamination-down-polluter; water-contamination-down-rater; water-contamination-polluter; water-contamination-rater; water-contamination-up; water-contamination-up-polluter; water-contamination-up-rater; water-contamination-warning; water-contamination-warning-issuer; water-contamination-warning-lifted; water-contamination-warning-lifted-issuer; water-contamination-warning-lifted-polluter; water-contamination-warning-polluter

## POLITICS
### Elections

candidacy-authority; candidacy-location; candidacy-withdrawn-authority; candidacy-withdrawn-location; early-election; early-election-authority; early-election-location; elections-postponed; elections-postponed-authority; elections-postponed-location; poll-survey-advancer; poll-survey-decliner; poll-survey-location

### Foreign Relations

diplomatic-recall-host; diplomatic-recall-location; diplomatic-recall-requester; diplomatic-visit-suspended-host; diplomatic-visit-suspended-location; diplomatic-visit-suspended-visitor; state-visit-suspended-host; state-visit-suspended-location; state-visit-suspended-visitor

### Government

cabinet-appointment; cabinet-appointment-authority; cabinet-resignation; cabinet-resignation-authority; congressional-testimony; congressional-testimony-authority; congressional-testimony-summoned;

coup-d-etat; coup-d-etat-authority; coup-d-etat-overthrower;
government-administration-appointment;
government-administration-appointment-authority;
government-administration-resignation;
government-administration-resignation-authority; government-power-deadlock;
government-power-deadlock-adversary; government-power-deadlock-ended;
government-power-deadlock-ended-adversary; government-treaty;
government-treaty-rater; government-treaty-terminated;
government-treaty-terminated-rater; impeachment-authority;
impeachment-plaintiff; judicial-appointment; judicial-appointment-authority;
judicial-resignation; judicial-resignation-authority;
law-enforcement-appointment-authority;
law-enforcement-appointment-location; law-enforcement-resignation-authority;
law-enforcement-resignation-location; legislative-appointment;
legislative-appointment-authority; legislative-expulsion;
legislative-expulsion-authority; legislative-resignation;
legislative-resignation-authority; monarchy-abdication;
monarchy-abdication-authority; monarchy-enthronement;
monarchy-enthronement-authority; official-visit-suspended-host;
official-visit-suspended-location; official-visit-suspended-visitor;
presidential-resignation; presidential-resignation-authority; referendum;
referendum-terminated

## SOCIETY
### Aid
international-aid-provider; international-aid-rater; international-aid-recipient;
international-aid-suspended-provider; international-aid-suspended-rater;
international-aid-suspended-recipient

### Civil Unrest
civil-unrest; civil-unrest-accuser; civil-unrest-instigator; civil-unrest-threat;
civil-unrest-threat-accuser; civil-unrest-threat-instigator; evacuation;
evacuation-authority; evacuation-warning; evacuation-warning-authority;
protest; protest-ended; protest-ended-protestee; protest-ended-protester;
protest-protestee; protest-protester

### Corporate Responsibility
donation; sponsorship

## Crime

assassination; assassination-attacker; assassination-location; hijacking-attacker; hijacking-released-attacker; hijacking-released-commodity; hijacking-released-target; hijacking-target; hijacking-target commodity; hostage-situation; hostage-situation-captor; hostage-situation-released; hostage-situation-released-captor; kidnapping; kidnapping-captor; kidnapping-released; kidnapping-released-captor; murder-murderer; murder-victim; piracy; piracy-attacker; piracy-location; robbery-burglar; robbery-location; robbery-victim; shooting; shooting-shooter

## Health

epidemic; epidemic-authority; epidemic-warning; epidemic-warning-authority; pandemic; pandemic-authority; pandemic-warning; pandemic-warning-authority

## Legal

antitrust-investigation; antitrust-investigation-authority; antitrust-settlement; antitrust-settlement-authority; antitrust-suit-authority; antitrust-suit-defendant; antitrust-suit-plaintiff; appeal-authority; appeal-defendant; appeal-plaintiff; blackmail; blackmail-authority; blackmail-defendant; blackmail-plaintiff; confidentiality-pact; confidentiality-pact-authority; copyright-infringement-authority; copyright-infringement-defendant; copyright-infringement-plaintiff; corruption; corruption-authority; corruption-defendant; corruption-plaintiff; death-penalty; death-penalty-authority; defamation; defamation-authority; defamation-defendant; defamation-plaintiff; discrimination; discrimination-authority; discrimination-defendant; discrimination-plaintiff; embezzlement; embezzlement-authority; embezzlement-defendant; embezzlement-plaintiff; fraud; fraud-authority; fraud-defendant; fraud-plaintiff; legal-issues-authority; legal-issues-defendant; legal-issues-dismissed-authority; legal-issues-dismissed-defendant; legal-issues-dismissed-plaintiff; legal-issues-plaintiff; patent-infringement-authority; patent-infringement-defendant; patent-infringement-plaintiff; sanctions-guidance-issuer; sanctions-guidance-lifted-issuer; sanctions-guidance-lifted-rater; sanctions-guidance-lifted-target; sanctions-guidance-rater; sanctions-guidance-target; sanctions-issuer; sanctions-lifted-issuer; sanctions-lifted-rater; sanctions-lifted-target; sanctions-rater; sanctions-target; settlement; settlement-authority; tax-evasion; tax-evasion-authority

## Security

border-control-enforcee; border-control-enforcer; border-control-location; corporate-espionage-defendant; corporate-espionage-plaintiff; cyber-attacks; cyber-attacks-hacker; cyber-attacks-threat; cyber-attacks-threat-hacker; explosion; explosion-commodity; explosion-provoker; state-of-emergency; state-of-emergency-issuer; state-of-emergency-lifted; state-of-emergency-lifted-issuer; travel-warning; travel-warning-issuer; travel-warning-lifted; travel-warning-lifted-issuer; weapons-testing; weapons-testing-location

## Transportation

airspace-closure; airspace-closure-location; airspace-closure-warning; airspace-closure-warning-location; airspace-open; airspace-open-location; airspace-violation; airspace-violation-intrude; airspace-violation-location; transportation-disruption; transportation-disruption-location; transportation-disruption-warning; transportation-disruption-warning-location

## War–Conflict

bombing-attack-attacker; bombing-attack-target; bombing-threat-attacker; bombing-threat-target embargo; embargo-issuer; embargo-lifted; embargo-lifted-issuer; embargo-lifted-target; embargo-target; military-action-attacker; military-action-defender; military-action-exercise-suspended-attacker; military-action-exercise-suspended-defender; military-action-exercise-suspended-location; military-action-location; military-action-occupation-invader; military-action-occupation-location; military-action-occupation-occupant; military-action-threat-attacker; military-action-threat-defender; military-action-threat-location; military-action-withdrawal-attacker; military-action-withdrawal-defender; military-action-withdrawal-location; peace-process-failed-location; peace-process-failed-opposer; peace-process-failed-supporter; peace-process-location; peace-process-opposer; peace-process-rejected-location; peace-process-rejected-opposer; peace-process-rejected-supporter; peace-process-supporter; pipeline-bombing-attack; pipeline-bombing-attack-attacker; pipeline-bombing-attack-target; pipeline-bombing-threat; pipeline-bombing-threat-attacker; pipeline-bombing-threat-target; suicide-bombing-attacker; suicide-bombing-target; suicide-bombing-threat-attacker; suicide-bombing-threat-target; terrorist-attack-attacker;

terrorist-attack-foiled-attacker; terrorist-attack-foiled-target;
terrorist-attack-target; terrorist-threat-attacker; terrorist-threat-target;
violent-attack-attacker; violent-attack-false-alarm-attacker;
violent-attack-false-alarm-target; violent-attack-target;
violent-attack-threat-attacker; violent-attack-threat-target;
war-declaration-issuer; war-declaration-location; war-declaration-target;
war-demonstration-location; war-demonstration-opposer

# Bibliography

Abolafia, M. 1996. *Making Markets: Opportunism and Restraint on Wall Street.* Harvard University Press.

Adam, K. and Marcet, A. 2011. Internal Rationality, Imperfect Market Knowledge and Asset Prices. *Journal of Economic Theory*, **146**(3), 1224–1252.

Adam, K., Marcet, A., and Nicolini, J. P. 2015. Stock Market Volatility and Learning. *Journal of Finance*, **71**(1), 33–82.

Akerlof, G. A. and Shiller, R. J. 2009. *Animal Spirits*. Princeton University Press.

Akerlof, G. A. and Snower, D. J. 2016. Bread and Bullets. *Journal of Economic Behavior & Organization*, **126**(B), 58–71.

Albrecht, K., Volz, K. G., Sutter, M., Laibson, D. I., and von Cramon, D. Y. 2010. What Is for Me Is Not for You: Brain Correlates of Intertemporal Choice for Self and Other. *Social Cognitive and Affective Neuroscience*, **6**(2), 218–225.

Aliber, R. Z. and Kindleberger, C. P. 2015. *Manias, Panics and Crashes: A History of Financial Crises.* Palgrave Macmillan.

Allen, F., Morris, S., and Shin, H. S. 2006. Beauty Contests and Iterated Expectations in Asset Markets. *Review of Financial Studies*, **19**(3), 719–752.

Andersen, T., Bollerslev, T., Diebold, F., and Vega, C. 2007. Real-Time Price Discovery in Global Stock, Bond and Foreign Exchange Markets. *CREATES Research Paper*, No. 2007–20.

Anderson, C. A. 2004. An Update on the Effects of Playing Violent Video Games. *Journal of Adolescence*, **27**(1), 113–122.

Andreassen, P. B. 1987. On the Social Psychology of the Stock Market: Aggregate Attributional Effects and the Regressiveness of Prediction. *Journal of Personality and Social Psychology*, **53**(3), 490–496.

Ang, A. and Bekaert, G. 2007. Stock Return Predictability: Is It There? *Review of Financial Studies*, **20**(3), 651–707.

Ang, A. and Timmermann, A. 2012. Regime Changes and Financial Markets. *Annual Review of Financial Economics*, **4**(1), 313–327.

Antweiler, W. and Frank, M. Z. 2005. Is All That Talk Just Noise? The Information Content of Internet Stock Message Boards. *Journal of Finance*, **59**(3), 1259–1294.

Aspinwall, L. G. 1998. Rethinking the Role of Positive Affect in Self-Regulation. *Motivation and Emotion*, **22**(1), 1–32.

Avramov, D. and Chordia, T. 2006. Asset Pricing Models and Financial Market Anamolies. *Review of Financial Studies*, **19**(3), 1001–1040.

Bacchetta, P. and van Wincoop, E. 2004. A Scapegoat Model of Exchange Rate Determination. *American Economic Review, Papers and Proceedings*, **94**(2), 114–118.

Bacchetta, P. and van Wincoop, E. 2006. Can Information Heterogeneity Explain the Exchange Rate Determination Puzzle? *American Economic Review*, **96**(3), 552–576.

Bacchetta, P. and van Wincoop, E. 2009. On the Unstable Relationship between Exchange Rates and Macroeconomic Fundamentals. *NBER Working Paper*, No. 15008.

Bacchetta, P. and van Wincoop, E. 2013. On the Unstable Relationship between Exchange Rates and Macroeconomic Fundamentals. *Journal of International Economics*, **91**(1), 18–26.

Baek, C. 2016. Stock Prices, Dividends, Earnings, and Investor Sentiment. *Review of Quantitative Finance and Accounting*, **47**, 1043–1061.

Bai, J. and Perron, P. 1998. Estimating and Testing Linear Models with Multiple Structural Changes. *Econometrica*, **66**(1), 47–78.

Bai, J. and Perron, P. 2003. Computation and Analysis of Multiple Structural Change Models. *Journal of Applied Econometrics*, **18**(1), 1–22.

Baker, M. and Wurgler, J. 2006. Investor Sentiment and the Cross-Section of Stock Returns. *Journal of Finance*, **61**(4), 1645–1680.

Baker, M. and Wurgler, J. 2007. Investor Sentiment in the Stock Market. *Journal of Economic Perspectives*, **21**(2), 129–151.

Baker, S. R., Bloom, N., and Davis, S. J. 2016. Measuring Economic Policy Uncertainty. *Quarterly Journal of Economics*, **131**(4), 1593–1636.

Baker, S. R., Bloom, N., Davis, S., and Sammon, N. 2019. What Triggers Stock Market Jumps? University of Chicago, Becker Friedman Institute for Economics Working Paper No. 2021–42.

Bal, M. 1997. *Narratology: Introduction to the Theory of Narrative*, 3rd ed. University of Toronto Press.

Bandelj, N. 2009. Emotions in Economic Action and Interaction. *Theory and Society*, **38**(4), 347–366.

Bao, Y. and Datta, A. 2014. Simultaneously Discovering and Quantifying Risk Types from Textual Risk Disclosures. *Management Science*, **60**(6), 1351–1616.

Bar-On, R. and Parker, J. D. A. 2000. *Handbook of Emotional Intelligence*. Jossey-Bass.

Barberis, N., Shleifer, A., and Vishny, R. 1998. A Model of Investor Sentiment. *Journal of Financial Economics*, **49**(3), 307–343.

Barberis, N. and Thaler, R. 2003. A Survey of Behavioral Finance. In G. M. Constantinides, M. Harris, and R. Stulz (eds.), *Handbook of the Economics of Finance*. Elsevier, 1051–1121.

Barro, R. J. 2006. Rare Disasters and Asset Markets in the Twentieth Century. *Quarterly Journal of Economics*, **121**(3), 823–866.

Barsky, R. B. and de Long, J. B. 1993. Why Does the Stock Market Fluctuate? *Quarterly Journal of Economics*, **108**(2), 291–311.

Bekaert, G., Hoerova, M., and Lo Duca, M. 2013. Risk, Uncertainty and Monetary Policy. *Journal of Monetary Economics*, **60**(7), 771–788.

Berezin, M. 2005. Emotions and the Economy. In N. J. Smelser and R. Swedberg (eds.), *The Handbook of Economic Sociology*. Princeton University Press, 109–130.

Bewley, T. F. 1986. Knightian Decision Theory: Part I. *Cowles Foundation Discussion Paper*, No. 807.

Bewley, T. F. 1987. Knightian Decision Theory: Part II: Intertemporal Problems. *Cowles Foundation Discussion Paper*, No. 835.

Birz, G. 2017. Stale Economic News, Media and the Stock Market. *Journal of Economic Psychology*, **61**, 87–102.

Bittlingmayer, G. 1998. Output, Stock Volatility, and Political Uncertainty in a Natural Experiment: Germany, 1880–1940. *Journal of Finance*, **53**(6), 2243–2257.

Blaug, M. 1975. Kuhn versus Lakatos, or Paradigms versus Research Programmes in the History of Economics. *History of Political Economy*, **7**(4), 399–433.

Bloom, N. 2014. Fluctuations in Uncertainty. *Journal of Economic Perspectives*, **28**(2), 153–176.

Bodnaruk, A., Loughran, T., and McDonald, B. 2015. Using 10-K Text to Gauge Financial Constraints. *Journal of Financial and Quantitative Analysis*, **50**(4), 623–646.

Bohl, M. T. and Siklos, P. 2004. The Present Value Model of U.S. Stock Prices Redux: A New Testing Strategy and Some Evidence. *Quarterly Review of Economics and Finance*, **44**(2), 208–223.

Bordalo, P., Gennaioli, N., and Shleifer, A. 2013. Salience and Asset Prices. *American Economic Review: Papers and Proceedings*, **103**(3), 623–628.

Boudoukh, J., Feldman, R., Kogan, S., and Richardson, M. 2013. Which News Moves Stock Prices? A Textual Analysis. *NBER Working Paper*, No. 18725.

Bourdieu, P. 1980. *The Logic of Practice*. Stanford University Press.

Boyd, J., Hu, J., and Jagannathan, R. 2005. The Stock Market's Reaction to Unemployment News: Why Bad News Is Usually Good for Stocks. *Journal of Finance*, **60**(2), 649–672.

Brennan, M. J. 1998. The Role of Learning in Dynamic Portfolio Decisions. *Review of Finance*, **1**(3), 295–306.

Brooks, P. 2006. Narrative Transactions – Does the Law Need a Narratology? *Yale Journal of Law & Humanities*, **18**(1), 1–28.

Brown, K. C., Lockwood, L. J. and Lummer, S. L. 1985. An Examination of Event Dependency and Structural Change in Security Pricing Models. *Journal of Financial and Quantitative Analysis*, **20**(3), 315–334.

Brown, R. L., Durbin J., and Evans, J. M. 1975. Techniques for Testing the Constancy of Regression Relationships over Time. *Journal of the Royal Statistical Society*, **37**(2), 149–192.

Bruner, J. 1986. *Actual Minds, Possible Worlds*. Harvard University Press.

Bruner, J. 2004. Life as Narrative. *Social Research*, **71**(3), 691–710.

Caggiano, G., Castelnuovo, E., and Groshenny, N. 2014. Uncertainty Shocks and Unemployment Dynamics in U.S. Recessions. *Journal of Monetary Economics*, **67**(C), 78–92.

Calvet, L. E., and Fisher, A. J. 2007. Multifrequency News and Stock Returns. *Journal of Financial Economics*, **86**(1), 178–212.

Camerer, C., Loewenstein, G., and Prelec, D. 2005. Neuroeconomics: How Neuroscience Can Inform Economics. *Journal of Economic Literature*, **43**(1), 9–64.

Campbell, J. L., Chen, H., Dhaliwal, D. S., Lu, H., and Steele, L. B. 2014. The Information Content of Mandatory Risk Factor Disclosures in Corporate Filings. *Review of Accounting Studies*, **19**(1), 396–455.

Campbell, J. Y. and Hentschel, L. 1992. No News Is Good News: An Asymmetric Model of Changing Volatility in Stock Returns. *Journal of Financial Economics*, **31**(3), 281–318.

Campbell, J. Y. and Shiller, R. J. 1987. Cointegration and Tests of Present Value Models. *Journal of Political Economy*, **95**(5), 1062–1087.

Campbell, J. Y. and Thompson, S. 2008. Predicting the Equity Premium Out of Sample: Can Anything Beat the Historical Average? *Review of Financial Studies*, **21**(4), 1509–1531.

Carr, D. 1986. *Time, Narrative, and History*. Indiana University Press.

Castle, J. L., Doornik, J. A. and Hendry, D. F. 2012. Model Selection When There Are Multiple Breaks. *Journal of Econometrics*, **169**(2), 239–246.

Castle, J. L. and Hendry, D. F. 2019. *Detectives of Change: Indicator Saturation*. In *Modeling our Changing World*. Palgrave Texts in Econometrics. Palgrave Pivot, 67–84.

Castle, J. L., Hendry, D. F. and Martinez, A. B. 2017. Evaluating Forecasts, Narratives and Policy Using a Test of Invariance. *Economterics*, **5**(39), 1–27.

Chae, J. 2005. Trading Volume, Information Asymmetry, and Timing Information. *Journal of Finance*, **60**(1), 413–442.

Chan, W. S. 2003. Stock Price Reaction to News and No-News: Drift and Reversal after Headlines. *Journal of Financial Economics*, **70**(2), 223–260.

Cherniss, C., Goleman, D., Emmerling, R., Cowan, K., and Adler, M. 1998. Bringing Emotional Intelligence to the Workplace. *The Consortium for Research on Emotional Intelligence in Organization*, Technical Report, 1–34.

Chib, S. 1998. Estimation and Comparison of Multiple Change Point Models. *Journal of Econometrics*, **86**(2), 221–241.

Chow, G. C. 1960. Tests of Equality between Sets of Coefficients in Two Linear Regressions. *Econometrica*, **28**(3), 591–605.

Chung, K. H. and Chuwonganant, C. 2014. Uncertainty, Market Structure, and Liquidity. *Journal of Financial Economics*, **113**(3), 476–499.

Claessens, S., Kose, M. A., Laeven, L., and Valencia, F. (eds.) 2013. *Financial Crises: Causes, Consequences, and Policy Responses*. International Monetary Fund.

Cobley, P. 2001. *Narrative: The New Critical Idiom*. Routledge.

Cochrane, J. H. 2011. Presidential Address: Discount Rates. *Journal of Finance*, **46**(4), 1047–1108.

Colander, D., Follmer, H., Haas, A., et al. 2009. The Financial Crisis and the Systemic Failure of Academic Economics. *Kiel Institute for the World Economy Working Paper*, No. 1489.

Collins, R. 2005. *Interaction Ritual Chains*. Princeton University Press.

Crowder, W. J. and Wohar, M. E 1998. Stock Price Effects of Permanent and Transitory Shocks. *Economic Inquiry*, **36**(4), 540–552.

Damasio, A. 1994. *Descartes' Error: Emotion, Reason and the Human Brain*. The Hearst Corporation.

Das, S. R. 2014. Text and Context: Language Analytics in Finance. *Foundations and Trends in Finance*, **8**(3), 145–260.

Das, S. R. and Chen, M. 2007. Yahoo for Amazon: Opinion Extraction from Small Talk on the Web. *Management Science*, **53**(9), 1375–1388.

David, A. and Veronesi, P. 2009. What Ties Return Volatilities to Price Valuations and Fundamentals? *University of Chicago Working Paper*.

Davis, A. K., Piger, J. M. and Sedor, L. M. 2006. Beyond the Numbers: An Analysis of Optimistic and Pessimistic Language in Earnings Press Releases. *Federal Reserve Bank of St. Louis Working Paper*.

De Fina, A. and Georgakopoulou, A. 2012. *Analyzing Narrative: Discourse and Sociolinguistic Perspectives*. Cambridge University Press.

De Long, J. B., Shleifer, A., Summers, L. H. and Waldmann, R. J. 1990. Noise Trader Risk in Financial Markets. *Journal of Political Economy*, **98**(4), 703–738.

Demers, E. and Vega, C. 2008. Soft Information in Earnings Announcements: News or Noise? *International Finance Discussion Papers, Board of Governors of the Federal Reserve System*, No. 951.

Deng A. and Perron, P. 2008. A Non-local Perspective on the Power Properties of the CUSUM and CUSUM of Squares Tests for Structural Change. *Journal of Econometrics*, **142**(1), 212–240.

Diebold, F. X., Lee, J. H., and Weinbach, G. C. 1994. Regime Switching with Time-Varying Transition Probabilities. In Hargreaves, C. (ed.), *Time Series Analysis and Cointegration*. Oxford University Press, 283–302.

DiMaggio, P. 2002. Endogenizing "Animal Spirits": Toward a Sociology of Collective Response to Uncertainty and Risk. In M. F. Guillen, R. Collins, P. England, and M. Meyer (eds.), *The New Economic Sociology: Developments in an Emerging Field*. Russell Sage Foundation, 79–100.

Doornik, J. A. 2009. Autometrics. In J. Castle and N. Shephard (eds.), *The Methodology and Practice of Econometrics*. Oxford University Press, 88–121.

Dow, S. 2011. Cognition, Market Sentiment and Financial Instability. *Cambridge Journal of Economics*, **35**(2), 233–249.

Driffill, J. and Sola, M. 1998. Intrinsic Bubbles and Regime-Switching. *Journal of Monetary Economics*, **42**(2), 357–373.

Duranti, A. 1992. *Rethinking Context: Language as an Interactive Phenomenon*. Cambridge University Press.

Durland, J. M., and McCurdy, T. H. 1994. Duration-Dependent Transitions in a Markov Model of U.S. GNP Growth. *Journal of Business and Economic Statistics*, **12**(3), 279–288.

Durre, A. and Giot, P. 2005. An International Analysis of Earnings, Stock Prices, and Bond Yields. *European Central Bank Working Paper Series*, No. 515.

Ellsberg, D. 1961. Risk, Ambiguity, and the Savage Axioms. *Quarterly Journal of Economics*, **75**(4), 643–669.

Engel, R. F. and Granger, C. W. J. 1987. Cointegration and Error Correction: Representation, Estimation and Testing. *Econometrica*, **55**(2), 251–276.

Engelberg, J. 2008. Costly Information Processing: Evidence from Earnings Announcements. *AFA Meetings Paper*.

Engsted, T. 2006. Explosive Bubbles in the Cointegrated VAR Model. *Finance Research Letters*, **3**(2), 154–162.

Eroglu, C. and Hofer, C. 2011. Lean, Leaner, Too Lean? The Inventory-Performance Link Revisited. *Journal of Operations Management*, **29**(4), 356–369.

Evans, M. D. D. 1996. Peso Problems: Their Theoretical and Empirical Implications. In G. S. Maddal and C. R. Rao (eds.), *Handbook of Statistics*, **14**. Elsevier, 613–646.

Fama, E. F. 1998. Market Efficiency, Long-Term Returns, and Behavioral Finance. *Journal of Financial Economics*, **49**(3), 283–306.

Fama, E. F. and French, K. R. 1996. Multifactor Explanations of Asset Pricing Anomalies. *Journal of Finance*, **51**(1), 55–84.

Fama, E. F. and French, K. R. 2015. A Five-Factor Asset Pricing Model. *Journal of Financial Economics*, **116**(1), 1–22.

Fama, E. F. and French, K. R. 2019. Comparing Cross-Section and Time-Series Factor Models. *Chicago Booth Research Paper*, No. 18–08.

Fang, L. and Peress, J. 2009. Media Coverage and the Cross-Section of Expected Returns. *Journal of Finance*, **64**, 2023–2052.

Fedyk, A. and Hodson, J. 2019. When Can the Market Identify Old News? *Working Paper*.

Feldman, R., Rosenfeld, B., Bar-Haim, R., and Moshe F. 2011. The Stock Sonar Sentiment Analysis of Stocks Based on a Hybrid Approach. In *Proceedings of 23rd IAAI Conference on Artificial Intelligence*, 1642–1647.

Fiedler, K. 1988. The Dependence of the Conjunction Fallacy on Subtle Linguistic Factors. *Psychological Research*, **50**(2), 123–129.

Filardo, A. J. 1994. Business-Cycle Phases and Their Transitional Dynamics. *Journal of Business and Economic Statistics*, **12**(3), 299–308.

Flood, R. and Garber, P. 1980. Market Fundamentals versus Price-Level Bubbles: The First Tests. *Journal of Political Economy*, **88**(4), 745–770.

Fratzscher, M., Rime, D., Sarno, L., and Zinna, G. 2015. The Scapegoat Theory of Exchange Rates: The First Tests. *Journal of Monetary Economics*, **70**, 1–21.

Friberg, R. 2015. *Managing Risk and Uncertainty: A Strategic Approach*. MIT Press.

Friberg, R. and Seiler, T. 2017. Risk and Ambiguity in 10'Ks: An Examination of Cash Holding and Derivatives Use. *Journal of Corporate Finance*, **45**(C), 608–631.

Frydman, R. and Goldberg, M. D. 2007. *Imperfect Knowledge Economics: Exchange Rates and Risk*. Princeton University Press.

Frydman, R. and Goldberg, M. D. 2011. *Beyond Mechanical Markets: Asset Price Swings, Risk and the Role of the State*. Princeton University Press.

Frydman, R. and Goldberg, M. D. 2013. Opening Models of Asset Prices and Risk to Non-routine Change. In R. Frydman and E. S. Phelps (eds.), *Rethinking Expectations: The Way Forward for Macroeconomics*. Princeton University Press, 207–250.

Frydman, R. and Goldberg, M. D. 2015. Change and Rationality in Macroeconomics and Finance Theory: A New Rational Expectations Hypothesis. *Institute of New Economic Thinking Working Paper*, No. 8.

Frydman, R., Goldberg, M. D. and Mangee, N. 2015. Knightian Uncertainty and Stock-Price Movements: Why the REH Present-Value Model Failed Empirically. *Economics: The Open-Access, Open-Assessment E-Journal*, **9**, 1–50.

Frydman, R., Johansen, S., Rahbek, A., and Tabor, M. N. 2017. The Qualitative Expectations Hypothesis: Model Ambiguity, Consistent Representations of Market Forecasts, and Sentiment. *Institute of New Economic Thinking Working Paper*, No. 59.

Frydman, R., Johansen, S., Rahbek, A., and Tabor, M. N. 2019. The Knightian Uncertainty Hypothesis: Unforeseeable Change and Muth's Consistency Constraint in Modeling Aggregate Outcomes. *Institute of New Economic Thinking Working Paper*, No. 92.

Frydman, R., Mangee, N., and Stillwagon, J. R. Forthcoming. How Market Sentiment Drives Forecasts of Stock Returns. *Journal of Behavioral Finance*.

Frydman, R. and Phelps, E. S. 2013. Which Way Forward for Macroeconomics and Policy Analysis? In R. Frydman and E. S. Phelps (eds.), *Rethinking Expectations: The Way Forward for Macroeconomics*. Princeton University Press, 1–48.

Frydman, R. and Stillwagon, J. R. 2018. Fundamental Factors and Extrapolation in Stock-Market Expectations: The Central Role of Structural Change. *Journal of Economic Behavior & Organization*, **148**(12), 189–198.

Gabriel, V. J. and Martins, L. F. 2011. Cointegration Tests under Multiple Regime Shifts: An Application to the Stock Price-Dividend Relationship. *Journal of Empirical Economics*, **41**(3), 639–662.

Ganguly, A. 2018. Textual Disclosure in SEC Filings and Litigation Risk. *PhD Dissertation*, University of Pittsburgh.

Garcia, D. 2013. Sentiment during Recessions. *Journal of Finance*, **68**(3), 1267–1300.

Gennaioli, N. and Shleifer, A. 2018. *A Crisis of Beliefs: Investor Psychology and Financial Fragility*. Princeton University Press.

Gennotte, G. 1986. Optimal Portfolio Choice under Incomplete Information. *Journal of Finance*, **61**(3), 733–749.

Goetzmann, W. N., Kim, D., and Shiller, R. J. 2016. Crash Beliefs from Investor Surveys. *National Bureau of Economic Research Working Paper*, No. 22143.

Goldberg, M. D. and Frydman, R. 1996a. Imperfect Knowledge and Behaviour in the Foreign Exchange Market. *Economic Journal*, **106**(437), 869–893.

Goldberg, M. D. and Frydman, R. 1996b. Empirical Exchange Rate Models and Shifts in the Cointegrating Vector. *Structural Change and Economic Dynamics*, **7**(1), 55–78.

Goldberg, M. D. and Frydman, R. 2001. Macroeconomic Fundamentals and the DM/$ Exchange Rate: Temporal Instability and the Monetary Model. *International Journal of Finance & Economics*, **6**(4), 421–435.

Goodell, J. W. and Vahamaa, S. 2013. US Presidential Elections and Implied Volatility: The Role of Political Uncertainty. *Journal of Banking and Finance*, **37**(3), 1108–1117.

Goyal, A. and Welch, I. 2008. A Comprehensive Look at the Empirical Performance of Equity Premium Prediction. *Review of Financial Studies*, **21**(4), 1455–1508.

Granovetter, M. 1985. Economic Action and Social Structure: The Problem of Embeddedness. *American Journal of Sociology*, **91**(3), 481–510.

Guo, L., Shi, F., and Tu, J. 2016. Textual Analysis and Machine Learning: Crack Unstructured Data in Finance and Accounting. *Journal of Finance and Data Science*, **2**(3), 153–170.

Gutierrez, M. J. and Vazquez, J. 2004. Switching Equilibria: The Present Value Model for Stock Prices Revisited. *Journal of Economic Dynamics and Control*, **28**(11), 2297–2325.

Hamilton, J. D. 1988. Rational-Expectations Econometric Analysis of Changes in Regime: An Investigation of the Term Structure of Interest Rates. *Journal of Economics Dynamics and Control*, **12**(2–3), 385–423.

Hamilton, J. D. 1989. A New Approach to the Economic Analysis of Nonstationary Time Series and the Business Cycle. *Econometrica*, **57**(2), 357–384.

Hamilton, J. D. 1994. State-Space Models. In R. F. Engle and D. L. McFadden (eds.), *Handbook of Econometrics*, **4**. Elsevier, 3039–3080.

Hamilton, J. D. 2008. Regime-Switching Models. In S. Durlauf and L. Blume (eds.), *New Palgrave Dictionary of Economics*, 2nd ed. Palgrave McMillan, 120–155.

Hands, D. W. 2001. *Reflection without Rules: Economic Methodology and Contemporary Science Theory*. Cambridge University Press.

Hansen, L. P. 2013. Uncertainty Outside and Inside Economic Models. *The Nobel Prize Lecture, The Nobel Foundation*.

Hayek, Friedrich A. 1945. The Use of Knowledge in Society. *American Economic Review*, **35**(4), 519–530.

Hayek, Friedrich A. 1978. The Pretense of Knowledge. *Nobel Lecture, 1974*, in *New Studies in Philosophy, Politics, Economics and History of Ideas*. University of Chicago Press, 23–34.

Healy, A. D. and Lo, A. 2011. Managing Real-Time Risks and Returns: The Thomson Reuters NewsScope Event Indices. In G. Mitra and L. Mitr (eds.), *The Handbook of News Analytics in Finance*. Wiley, 73–108.

Hendry, D. F., Doornik, J. A. and Pretis, F. 2013. Step-Indicator Saturation. *Economics Series Working Papers*, No. 658. University of Oxford, Department of Economics.

Hendry, D. F., Johansen, S., and Santos, C. 2008. Automatic Selection of Indicators in a Fully Saturated Regression. *Computational Statistics*, **33**, 317–335.

Henkel, S. J., Martin, J. S. and Nardari, F. 2011. Time-Varying Short-Horizon Predictability. *Journal of Financial Economics*, **99**(3), 560–580.

Herman, D. 2002. *Story Logic: Problems and Possibilities of Narrative*. University of Nebraska Press.

Hetwig, R., Benz, B., and Krauss, S. 2008. The Conjunction Fallacy and the Many Meanings of and. *Cognition*, **108**(3), 740–753.

Hoffman, J. C. 1986. *Law, Freedom and Story: The Role of Narrative in Therapy, Society, and Faith*. Wilfrid Laurier University Press.

Hosseini, H. 1997. Cognitive Dissonance as a Means of Explaining Economics of Irrationality and Uncertainty. *Journal of Socio-economics*, **26**(2), 181–189.

Hou, K. and Moskowitz, T. J. 2005. Market Frictions, Price Delay, and the Cross-Section of Expected Returns. *Review of Financial Studies*, **18**(3), 981–1020.

Howitt, P. and McAfee, R. P. 1992. Animal Spirits. *American Economic Review*, **82**(3), 493–507.

Huang, K. and Li, Z. 2008. A Multilabel Text Classification Algorithm for Labeling Risk Factors in SEC for 10-K. *ACM Transactions on Management Information Systems*, **2**, 1–19.

Jeremy, J. S. and Thaler, R. H. 1997. Anomalies: The Equity Premium Puzzle. *Journal of Economic Perspectives*, **11**(1), 191–200.

Joas, H. 1996. *The Creativity of Action*. Polity Press.

Johansen, S. 1995. *Likelihood-Based Inference in Cointegrated Vector Autoregressive Models*. Oxford University Press.

Johansen, S., Juselius, K., Frydman, R., and Goldberg, M. D. 2010. Testing Hypotheses in a Model with Piecewise Linear Trends: An Analysis of the Persistent Long Swings in the Dmk/$ Rate. *Journal of Econometrics*, **158**(1), 117–129.

Joyce, P. G. 2012. The Costs of Budget Uncertainty: Analyzing the Impact of Late Appropriations. *IBM Center for the Business of Government*, 1–42.

Jung, J. and Shiller, R. J. 2005. Samuelson's Dictum and the Stock Market. *Economic Inquiry*, **43**(2), 221–228.

Juselius, K. 2006. *The Cointegrated VAR Model: Methodology and Applications*. Oxford University Press.

Kaminsky, G. L. 1993. Is There a Peso Problem?: Evidence From the Dollar/Pound Exchange Rate 1976–1987. *American Economic Review*, **83**(3), 450–472.

Kanas, A. 2005. Nonlinearity in the Stock Price-Dividend Relation. *Journal of International Money and Finance*, **24**(4), 583–606.

Kermack, W. O. and McKendrick, A. G. 1927. A Contribution to the Mathematical Theory of Epidemics. *Proceedings of the Royal Society of London. Series A, Containing Papers of a Mathematical and Physical Character*, **115**(772), 701–721.

Keynes, J. M. 1936. *The General Theory of Employment, Interest and Money*. Harcourt, Brace and World.

Kim, M. S. 2018. The Effect of Uncertain and Weak Modal Words in 10-K Filings on Analyst Forecast Attributes. *FIU Electronic Theses and Dissertations*, No. 3786.

Kim, S. B., Han, K. S., Rim, H. C. and Myaeng, S. H. 2006. Some Effective Techniques for Naive Bayes Text Classification. *IEEE Transactions on Knowledge and Data Engineering*, **18**(11), 1457–1466.

Knight, F. H. 1921. *Risk, Uncertainty and Profit*. Houghton Mifflin.

Koenigs, M., Young, L., Adolphs, R., et al. 2007. Damage to the Prefrontal Cortex Increases Utilitarian Moral Judgments. *Nature*, **446**(7138), 908–911.

Krajbich, I., Adolphs, R., D. Tranel Denburg, N. L., and Camerer, C. F. 2009. Economic Games Quantify Diminished Sense of Guilt in Patients with Damage to Prefrontal Cortex. *Journal of Neuroscience*, **29**(7), 2188–2192.

Kravet, T. and Muslu, V. 2013. Textual Risk Disclosures and Investors' Risk Perceptions. *Review of Account Studies*, **18**, 1088–1122.

Kuhn, T. 1970. *The Structure of Scientific Revolutions*, 2nd ed. University of Chicago Press.

Labov, W. and Waletzky, J. 1967. Narrative Analysis. In J. Helm (ed.), *Essays on the Verbal and Visual Arts*. University of Washington Press, 12–44.

Leinweber, D. and Sisk, J. 2011. Event Driven Trading and the New News. *Journal of Portfolio Management*, **38**(1), 110–124.

Lewis, M. 2009. *Panic: The Story of Modern Financial Insanity*. W.W. Norton and Company.

Li, F. 2006. Do Stock Market Investors Understand the Risk Sentiment of Corporate Annual Reports? *SSRN Working Paper*.

Li, F. 2008. Annual Report Readability, Current Earnings, and Earnings Persistence. *Journal of Accounting and Economics*, **45**(2–3), 221–247.

Li, F. 2010a. Textual Analysis of Corporate Disclosures: A Survey of the Literature. *Journal of Accounting Literature*, **29**, 143–165.

Li, F. 2010b. The Information Content of Forward-Looking Statements in Corporate Filings: A Naive Bayesian Machine Learning Approach. *Journal of Accounting Research*, **48**(5), 1049–1102.

Liberti, J. M. and Mitchell, P. A. 2018. Information: Hard and Soft. *NBER Working Paper*, No. w25075.

Liu, X., Margaritis, D., and Wang, P. 2012. Stock Market Volatility and Equity Returns: Evidence from a Two-State Markov-Switching Model with Regressors. *Journal of Empirical Finance*, **19**(4), 483–496.

Lo, A. W. and Mueller, M. T. 2010. Warning: Physics Envy May Be Hazardous to Your Wealth. *Journal of Investment Management*, **8**(2), 13–63.

Lo, A. W. and Repin, D. V. 2002. The Psychophysiology of Real-Time Financial Risk Processing. *Journal of Cognitive Neuroscience*, **14**(3), 323–339.

Lo, A. W. and Zhang, R. (eds.) 2018. Biological Economics: Volume I. *The International Library of Critical Writings in Economics*. Edward Elgar.

Lobell, D. B., Bonfils, C., and Duffy, P. B. 2007. Climate Change Uncertainty for Daily Minimum and Maximum Temperatures: A Model Inter-comparison. *Geophysical Research Letters*, **34**(5), 1–5.

Lott, J. R. 2010. *More Guns, Less Crime*. University of Chicago Press.

Loughran, T. and McDonald, B. 2011. When Is a Liability Not a Liability? Textual Analysis, Dictionaries, and 10-Ks. *Journal of Finance*, **66**(1), 35–65.

Loughran, T. and McDonald, B. 2015. The Use of Word Lists in Textual Analysis. *Journal of Behavioral Finance*, **16**(1), 1–11.

Loughran, T. and McDonald, B. 2016. Textual Analysis in Accounting and Finance: A Survey. *Journal of Accounting Research*, **54**(4), 1187–1230.

Machina, M. J. and Siniscalchi, M. 2013. Ambiguity and Ambiguity Aversion. In M. Machina and K. Viscusi (eds.), *The Handbook of the Economics of Risk and Uncertainty*, **1**. Elsevier, 720–807.

MacKinnon, J. G., Haug, A. A., and Michelis, L. 1999. Numerical Distribution Functions of Likelihood Ratio Tests for Cointegration. *Journal of Applied Econometrics*, **14**(5), 563–577.

Maggio, R. 2014. The Anthropology of Storytelling and the Storytelling of Anthropology. *Journal of Comparative Research in Anthropology and Sociology*, **5**(2), 89–106.

Malmendier, U. and Nagel, S. 2011. Depression Babies: Do Macroeconomic Experiences Influence Risk-Taking? *Quarterly Journal of Economics*, **126**(1), 373–416.

Malmendier, U. and Nagel, S. 2014. Learning from Inflation Experiences. *UC Berkeley and University of Michigan. Working Paper*.

Manela, A. and Moreira, A. 2017. News Implied Volatility and Disaster Concerns. *Journal of Financial Economics*, **123**(1), 137–162.

Mangee, N. 2011. *The Long-Swings Puzzle in Equity Markets: Which Way Forward?* PhD Dissertation, University of New Hampshire.

Mangee, N. 2014. Stock Prices, the Business Cycle and Contingent Change: Evidence from *Bloomberg News* Market Wraps. *Economics Bulletin*, **34**(4), 2165–2178.

Mangee, N. 2015. A Kuhnian Perspective on Asset Pricing Theory. *Journal of Economic Methodology*, **22**(1), 28–45.

Mangee, N. 2016. Can Structural Change Explain the Meese-Rogoff Puzzle?: An Application to the Stock Market. *Journal of Economics and Finance*, **40**(2), 211–234.

Mangee, N. 2017. New Evidence on Psychology and Stock Returns. *Journal of Behavioral Finance*, **18**(4), 417–426.

Mangee, N. 2018. Stock Returns and the Tone of Marketplace Information: Does Context Matter? *Journal of Behavioral Finance*, **19**(4), 396–406.

Mangee, N. 2019. Empirical Evidence on the Scapegoat Model of Stock Prices. *Working Paper*.

Mangee, N. and Goldberg, M. D. 2020. A Cointegrated VAR Analysis of Stock Price Models: Fundamentals, Psychology and Structural Change. *Journal of Behavioral Finance*, **21**(4), 352–368.

McCloskey, D. 2016. Adam Smith Did Humanomics: So Should We? *Eastern Economic Journal*, **42**(4), 503–13.

McClure, S. M., Ericson, K. M., Laibson, D. I., Lowenstein, G., and Cohen, J. D. 2007. Time Discounting for Primary Rewards. *Journal of Neuroscience*, **21**, 5796–5804.

McKee, R. 1997. *Story: Substance, Structure, Style, and the Principles of Screenwriting*. Harper Collins.

McLay, J. G., Reynolds, C. A., Satterfield, E., and Hodyss, D. 2016. Changes to Intrinsic Weather Forecast Uncertainty in One Scenario of Extreme Future Climate. *Quarterly Journal of the Royal Meteorological Society*, **142**(698), 2102–2118.

McQueen, G. and Roley, V. 1993. Stock Prices, News and Business Conditions. *Review of Financial Studies*, **6**(3), 683–707.

Mehra, R. and Prescott, E. C. 1985. The Equity Premium: A Puzzle. *Journal of Monetary Economics*, **15**(2), 145–161.

Mian, G. M. and Sankaraguruswamy, S. 2012. Investor Sentiment and Stock Market Response to Earnings News. *The Accounting Review*, **87**(4), 1357–1384.

Michel, J. B., Shen, Y. K., Aiden, A. P., et al. 2011. Quantitative Analysis of Culture Using Millions of Digitized Books. *Science*, **331**(6014), 176–182.

Minsky, H. P. 1982. *Can "IT" Happen Again: Essays on Instability and Finance*. M.E. Sharpe.

Minsky, H. P. 1986. *Stabilizing an Unstable Economy*. Yale University Press.

Mitra, G. and Mitra, L. (eds.) 2011. *The Handbook of News Analytics in Finance*. John Wiley and Sons.

Morson, G. S. and Schapiro, M. 2017. *Cents and Sensibility: What Economics Can Learn from the Humanities*. Princeton University Press.

Muth, J. H. 1961. Rational Expectations and the Theory of Price Movements. *Econometrica*, **29**(3), 315–335.

Nasseh, A. and Strauss, J. 2004. Stock Prices and the Dividend Discount Model: Did Their Relation Break Down in the 1990's? *Quarterly Review of Economics and Finance*, **44**(2), 191–207.

Nelson, P. 1987. *Narrative and Morality: A Theological Inquiry*. Pennsylvania State University Press.

Niederhoffer, V. 1971. The Analysis of World Events and Stock Prices. *Journal of Business*, **44**(2), 193–219.

Onega, S. and Landa, J. A. G. 1996. *Narratology: An Introduction*. Routledge.

Pagan, A. R. and Sossounov, K. R. 2003. A Simple Framework for Analyzing Bull and Bear Markets. *Journal of Applied Econometrics*, **18**(1), 23–46.

Page, R., Busse, B., and Norgaard, N. (eds.) 2019. *Rethinking Language, Text and Context: Interdisciplinary Research in Stylistics in Honour of Michael Toolan*. Routledge Studies in Rhetoric and Stylistics.

Pastor, L. and Stambaugh, R. F. 2001. The Equity Premium and Structural Breaks. *Journal of Finance*, **56**(4), 1207–1239.

Pastor, L. and Veronesi, P. 2009a. Technological Revolutions and Stock Prices. *American Economic Review*, **99**(4), 1451–1483.

Pastor, L. and Veronesi, P. 2009b. Learning in Financial Markets. *Annual Review of Financial Economics*, **1**(1), 361–381.

Paye, B. S. and Timmermann, A. 2006. Instability of Return Prediction Models. *Journal of Empirical Finance*, **13**(3), 274–315.

Pearce, D. and Roley, V. 1985. Stock Prices and Economic News. *Journal of Business*, **58**(1), 49–67.

Pesaran, M. H. and Timmermann, A. 2002. Market Timing and Return Prediction under Model Instability. *Journal of Empirical Finance*, **9**(5), 495–510.

Pettenuzzo, D. and Timmermann, A. 2011. Predictability of Stock Returns and Asset Allocations under Structural Breaks. *Journal of Econometrics*, **164**(1), 60–78.

Pixley, J. 2004. *Emotions in Finance: Distrust and Uncertainty in Global Markets*. Cambridge University Press.

Pixley, J. 2012. *Emotions in Finance: Booms, Busts and Uncertainty*. Cambridge University Press.

Politzer, G. and Noveck, I. A. 1991. Are Conjunction Rule Violations the Result of Conversational Rule Violations? *Journal of Psycholinguistic Research*, **20**(2), 83–103.

Polletta, F., Chen, Ching, P., Chen, B., Gardner, B. G., and Motes, A. 2011. The Sociology of Storytelling. *Annual Review of Sociology*, **37**(1), 109–130.

Polletta, F. and Jasper, J. M. 2001. Collective Identity and Social Movements. *Annual Review of Sociology*, **27**(1), 283–305.

Popper, Karl R. 1946. *The Open Society and Its Enemies*. Princeton University Press.

Popper, Karl R. 1957. *The Poverty of Historicism* Routledge.

Przybylski, A. K. and Weinstein, N. 2019. Violent Video Game Engagement Is Not Associated with Adolescents' Aggressive Behavior: Evidence from a Registered Report. *Royal Society Open Science*, **6**(2), 171474.

Rapach, D. E. and Wohar, M. E. 2006. Structural Breaks and Predictive Regression Models of Aggregate U.S. Stock Returns. *Journal of Financial Econometrics*, **4**(2), 238–274.

RavenPack News Analytics 2018. Version 4, www.ravenpack.com/page/ravenpack-news-analytics/.

Read, C. 1898. *Logic, Deductive and Inductive*. Simkin, Marshall.

Ricoeur, P. 1986. *Time and Narrative*. University of Chicago Press.

Rodrik, D. 2015. *Economics Rules: The Rights and Wrongs of the Dismal Science*. W.W. Norton and Company.

Rosen, R. J. 2006. Merger Momentum and Investor Sentiment: The Stock Market Reaction to Merger Announcements. *Journal of Business*, **79**(2), 987–1017.

Ryan, M. L. 2004. *Narrative across Media: The Languages of Storytelling*. University of Nebraska Press.

Ryans, J. P. 2016. *Textual Classification of SEC Comment Letters. PhD Dissertation*, University of California, Berkeley.

Sadka, R. 2006. Momentum and Post-Earnings Announcement Drift Anomalies: The Role of Liquidity Risk. *Journal of Financial Economics*, **80**(2), 309–349.

Sakai, Y. 2018. Daniel Ellsberg on J.M. Keynes and F.H. Knight: Risk, Ambiguity and Uncertainty. *CRR Discussion Paper Series*, No. 31. Shiga University, Center for Risk Research.

Samuelson, P. A. 1965. Proof That Properly Anticipated Prices Fluctuate Randomly. *Industrial Management Review*, **6**(2), 41–49.

Savage, L. 1954. *The Foundations of Statistics*. John Wiley and Sons.

Schaller, H. and van Norden, S. 1997. Regime Switching in Stock Market Returns. *Applied Financial Economics*, **7**(2), 177–191.

Schlicht, E. 1983. Cognitive Dissonance in Economics. *Darmstadt Discussion Papers in Economics*, No. 26. Darmstadt University of Technology, Department of Law and Economics.

Shefrin, H. 2002. *Beyond Greed and Fear: Understanding Behavioral Finance and the Psychology of Investing*. Harvard Business School Press.

Sheng, J. 2019. Macro News, Micro News, and Stock Prices. *Working Paper presented at the 2017 European Finance Association Conference*.

Shiller, R. J. 1981. Do Stock Prices Move Too Much to Be Justified by Subsequent Changes in Dividends? *American Economic Review*, **71**(3), 421–436.

Shiller, R. J. 1984. Stock Prices and Social Dynamics. *Brookings Papers on Economic Activity*, **2**, 457–510.

Shiller, R. J. 2000. *Irrational Exuberance*. Princeton University Press.

Shiller, R. J. 2017. Narrative Economics. *American Economic Review*, **107**(4), 967–1004.

Shiller, R. J. 2019. *Narrative Economics: How Stories Go Viral and Drive Major Economic Events*. Princeton University Press.

Shiller, R. J. 2020. Popular Economic Narratives Advancing the Longest U.S. Expansion 2009–2019. *Journal of Policy Modeling*, **42**(4), 1–8.

Shiller, R. J. and Pound, J. 1989. Survey Evidence on the Diffusion of Interest and Information among Investors. *Journal of Economic Behavior and Organization*, **12**(1), 47–66.

Shleifer, A. 2000. *Inefficient Markets*. Oxford University Press.

Silge, J. and Robinson, D. 2017. *Text Mining with R: A Tidy Approach*. O'Reilly.

Simon, H. A. 1959. Theories of Decision-Making in Economics and Behavioral Science. *American Economic Review*, **49**(3), 252–283.

Snow, D. A., Rochford, E. B., Worden, S. K., and Benford, R. D. 1986. Frame Alignment Processes, Micromobilization, and Movement Participation. *American Sociological Review*, **51**(4), 464–481.

Soros, G. 1987. *The Alchemy of Finance*. John Wiley and Sons.

Soros, G. 2008. *The New Paradigm for Financial Markets*. Public Affairs, USA.

Stanzel, F. K. 1984. *A Theory of Narrative*. Cambridge University Press.

Stillwagon, J. R. 2018. Are Risk Premia Related to Real Exchange Rate Swings? Evidence from I(2) CVARs with Survey Expectations. *Macroeconomic Dynamics*, **22**(2), 255–278.

Stillwagon, J. R. and Sullivan, P. 2019. Markov Switching in Exchange Rate Models: Will More Regimes Help? *Empirical Economics*, **59**(2).

Stock, J. H. and Watson, M. W. 1996. Evidence on Structural Instability in Macroeconomic Time Series Relations. *Journal of Business and Economic Statistics*, **14**(1), 11–30.

Sutton-Smith, B. 2001. *The Ambiguity of Play*. Harvard University Press.

Taleb, N. N. 2007. *The Black Swan: The Impact of the Highly Improbable*. Random House.

Tesfatsion, L. 2006. Agent-Based Computational Economics: A Constructive Approach to Economic Theory. In L. Judd and K. L. Tesfatsion (eds.), *Handbook of Computational Economics*, **2**. Elsevier, 831–880.

Tetlock, P. C. 2007. Giving Content to Investor Sentiment: The Role of Media in the Stock Market. *Journal of Finance*, **62**(3), 1139–1168.

Tetlock, P. C. 2011. All The News That's Fit to Reprint: Do Investors React to Stale Information? *Review of Financial Studies*, **24**(5), 1481–1512.

Tetlock, P. C., Saar-Tsechansky, M., and Macskassy, S. 2008. More Than Words: Quantifying Language to Measure Firms' Fundamentals. *Journal of Finance*, **63**(3), 1437–1467.

Thaler, R. H. 1987. Anomalies: The January Effect. *Journal of Economic Perspectives*, **1**(1), 197–201.

Timmermann, A. 1996. Excess Volatility and Predictability of Stock Prices in Autoregressive Dividend Models with Learning. *Review of Economic Studies*, **63**(4), 523–557.

Timmermann, A. 2001. Structural Breaks, Incomplete Information, and Stock Prices. *Journal of Business and Economic Statistics*, **19**(3), 299–315.

Toolan, M. 1988. *Narrative: A Critical Linguistic Introduction*. Routledge.

Toolan, M. 1992. *Language, Text and Context*. Routledge.

Tuckett, D. 2009. Addressing the Psychology of Financial Markets. *Economics: The Open-Access, Open-Assessment E-Journal*, **3**, 1–24.

Tversky, A. and Kahneman, D. 1983. Extensional versus Intuitive Reasoning: The Conjunction Fallacy in Probability Judgment. *Psychological Review*, **90**(4), 293–315.

Tversky, A. and Kahneman, D. 1986. Rational Choice and the Framing of Decisions. *Journal of Business*, **59**(4), 251–278.

Uhl, M. W., Pedersen, M., and Malitius, O. 2015. What's in the News? Using News Sentiment Momentum for Tactical Asset Allocation. *Journal of Portfolio Management*, **41**(2), 100–112.

Veblen, T. 1923. *Absentee Ownership and Business Enterprise in Recent Times: The Case of America*. B. W. Huebsch.

Veronesi, P. 1999. Stock Market Overreaction to Bad News in Good Times: A Rational Expectations Equilibrium Model. *Review of Financial Studies*, **12**(5), 975–1007.

Verweij, M., Senior, T. J. Dominguez, J. F. and Turner, R. 2015. Emotion, Rationality and Decision-Making: How to Link Affective and Social Neuroscience with Social Theory. *Frontiers of Neuroscience*, **9**(332), 3–32.

Viceira, L. M. 1997. Testing for Structural Change in the Predictability of Asset Returns. *Manuscript*, Harvard University.

Vuolteenaho, T. 2002. What Drives Firm-Level Stock Returns. *Journal of Finance*, **57**(1), 233–264.

Wachter, J. A. 2013. Can Time-Varying Risk of Rare Disasters Explain Aggregate Stock Market Volatility? *Journal of Finance*, **68**(3), 987–1035.

Whitford, J. 2002. Pragmatism and the Untenable Dualism of Means and Ends: Why Rational Choice Theory Does Not Deserve Paradigmatic Privilege. *Theory and Society*, **31**(3), 325–363.

Zweig, J. 2007. *Your Money and Your Brain: How the New Science of Neuroeconomics Can Help Make You Rich.* Simon & Schuster.

# Index